The Paradox of Freedom

The Paradox of Freedom

A study of
Nicholas Mosley's
intellectual development
in his novels and
other writings

Shiva Rahbaran

Dalkey Archive Press
Champaign · London

Copyright © 2006 by Shiva Rahbaran
First edition, 2006
First paperback edition, 2007
All rights reserved

Library of Congress Cataloging-in-Publication Data available.
ISBN-13: 978-1-56478-488-9

Partially funded by a grant from the Illinois Arts Council, a state agency,
and the University of Illinois, Urbana-Champaign.

Dalkey Archive Press is a nonprofit organization whose mission is
to promote international cultural understanding and
provide a forum for dialogue for the literary arts.

www.dalkeyarchive.com

Printed on permanent/durable acid-free paper, bound in the United States of America,
and distributed throughout North America and Europe.

Acknowledgements

I would like to thank everybody who accompanied me through my five-year journey through Nicholas Mosley's maze of observations and self-observations. I am particularly indebted to my two guides, Christopher Butler and Nicholas Mosley, without whom it would have been impossible to come out from the other side. At crossroads, the green light of one would be accompanied by the other's warning sign. In this way they taught me how to take the right path, by making me do the impossible and take both ways; in other words, they taught me how to make a conjunction out of a disjunction.

I would also like to thank John Banks for his stimulating correspondence, which helped me outline a map for my journey.

My special thanks go to Verity Mosley, who provided a framework where I could embark on my journey.

TABLE OF CONTENTS

Foreword   xi

Introduction   xiii

Chapter I   1
Conceiving the paradox of freedom and the
birth of Mosley's artistic career (1940s-1950s):
Spaces of the Dark, Rainbearers, Corruption

Chapter II   31
The paradox of freedom and aesthetic vision (1960s):
Meeting Place, Accident, Assassins, Impossible Object, Natalie Natalia

Chapter III   115
The paradox of freedom and the science of
the mind (1970s-1980s): *Catastrophe Practice Series*

Chapter IV   197
The paradox of freedom and mysticism (1990s to the present):
*Children of Darkness and Light, Journey into the Dark,
Hesperides Tree, Inventing God*

Notes   253

Bibliography   293

Foreword

In 1965, with the publication of the novel *Accident*, Nicholas Mosley attracted the attention of reviewers and scholars of English literature on the contemporary literary scene. Almost immediately after its publication, *Accident* was filmed under the collaboration of Harold Pinter and Joseph Losey, two prominent figures of the 'avant-garde' British theatre and cinema. From this point on, Nicholas Mosley has been seen as an 'avant-garde,' or 'experimentalist' novelist. Henceforth, he has attracted a wide range of—more often than not controversial—reviews over the course of the past four decades. He has been admired by scholars such as George Steiner, Allan Massie and Malcolm Bradbury[1] and criticised by those such as Valentine Cunningham, John Naughton and Auberon Waugh.[2] In his review of *Accident* (1965) and *Impossible Object* (1968), Steiner attributed the legacy of Virginia Woolf to Mosley by comparing him to a successful contemporary novelist, C. P. Snow.

> What Virginia Woolf's pointillist fables were to Bennett's solid carpenting, the art of Mosley is to Snow's workmanship. *Impossible Object* is all witchfire and mercury.[3]

Robert Scholes found Mosley's perspectives far from ordinary and his insight 'visionary'[4] and Richard Lister appreciated his efforts to 'push the language a stage further' with 'each new novel' as a means to 'quarry out deeper and deeper layers of meaning from experience.'[5] Malcolm Bradbury admired Mosley as 'one of the most significant instances' the British have that experimental writing 'can still be brilliantly done,' without having 'anything small about the experimental that [the author] has engaged upon.'[6] One of his latest published novels, *The Hesperides Tree*, has been reviewed as 'fascinating in its form and peerless in its intellectual ambition' written by a 'master author at the height of his powers.'[7] At their most unsympathetic, critics have accused Mosley of a pretentious 'inarticulateness.'[8] His novels have been attacked by some on grounds of his style, which has been said to be in accordance with the 'anti-novel' fashions of the Continent.[9] Consequently, his novels have been seen as 'un-English' by these critics.[10] These felt that Mosley, following the example of his French contemporaries, has sacrificed plot and characterisation in favour of an experimentalist style.[11]

In spite of the continuing controversy regarding his novels, Mosley's work has not become an area of academic research like those of his contemporaneous novelists of ideas and 'experimentalists' such as Lessing, Murdoch or Spark.[12] One reason could be his 'difficult' style and his 'un-Englishness.' The main reason, however, seems to be the role of his father, Oswald Mosley, in the history of Britain in the past century. His father being the founder of the Fascist Party and later on the British National Party, the academic and public attention veers towards him at the mention of Mosley's name. In a way, the reception of Nicholas Mosley's work suffers from the long shadow of his father. Nicholas Mosley himself, however, seems extraordinarily free from such a formidable figure. He thinks the reason for this freedom to lie in Oswald's being 'such an obvious bogey-figure.'[13] Apart from that, it must also be remembered that Nicholas—despite all the disagreements, disputes and conflicts—liked his father and felt that he had learnt a lot from him.[14] In this sense, the novels are not a son's psychological or political grappling with an overpowering father.

The following study will examine the emergence and development of Nicholas Mosley's works in the hope of contributing to fill what the present author conceives to be a gap in the study of contemporary British fiction.

Introduction

> The individual, and groupings of people, have to learn that they cannot reform society in reality, nor deal with others as reasonable people, unless the individual has learned to locate and allow for the various patterns of coercive institutions, formal and also informal, which rule him. No matter what his reason says, he will always relapse into obedience to this coercive agency while its pattern is with him.[15]

> Poets are shameless with their experiences: they exploit them.[16]

The novels of Nicholas Mosley could be seen as chapters of a single novel in which a single theme evolves: the possibility of man's freedom through overcoming the paradox of freedom. The paradox—or, as Mosley often calls it, the 'impossibility'—of freedom arises due to man's awareness of the *necessity* of limiting structures for freedom. Hence the question is: how could man fulfil the paradoxical task of overcoming these structures in order to attain freedom?

For the purpose of showing the development of this theme, Mosley's writing career is divided into four different phases, in which a series of novels dramatise one aspect of this endeavour and consequently lead onto the next phase, which supersedes the previous one by addressing the possibility of overcoming the paradox of freedom on a higher level and in a more complex context.

I. Conceiving the paradox of freedom and the birth of Mosley's artistic career (1940s-1950s): *Spaces of the Dark, The Rainbearers, Corruption*

In the first phase of his writing career, Mosley introduces the overall theme of his oeuvre—is overcoming the paradox of freedom possible?—in the shape of moral dilemmas: the 'absolute moment of choice' when a choice with possibly damaging consequences must be made. That is, when man's *responsibility* compels him to exploit his freedom of choice in order to decide *between* given mutually exclusive options (i.e., *either* this *or* that) where the only not morally evil choice would be *none* of the mutually exclusive options, i.e., *neither* this, *nor* that or *both* this *and* that. In such a situation man is trapped, as he cannot but choose evil. It must be noted that it is not the circumstances themselves that are 'evil,' and which man must make the best out of, but his decision itself, which will also inevitably make him 'evil.'

Mosley's protagonists, being faced with the choice between their beloved wives/families and their beloved mistresses, can only make an evil choice and consequently become evil. It is not morally possible for them to make the best out of their situation, because their choice is either to hurt the wives/families or the mistresses (and in both cases also themselves). Mosley conceives of this paradox as an 'impossible situation' and often refers to it as an 'impossibility.' As each choice logically excludes the other, the only way to resolve this impossibility within logic's 'either-or' system (i.e., *Tertia non datur*) is through renunciation of the choice altogether.

In the early novels of Mosley this renunciation was portrayed either in tragic death or in (existentialist) despair. In these novels the struggles of the protagonists in face of their moral dilemmas ended in helplessness. Except for *Corruption*, where Robert has an ecstatic glimpse (albeit a short one) of hope in face of his moral dilemma, the heroic efforts of the early protagonists against their situation shows the extent to which they are trapped. Mosley himself sees his early protagonists as descendants of the larger part of European literature, where the heroes could not find any better way of resolving the paradox that they were facing than 'by some sort of "negative" way—if not martyrdom, then slightly nostalgic resignation.'[17]

II. Experiments in the art of overcoming the paradox (1960s): *Meeting Place, Accident, Assassins, Impossible Object, Natalie Natalia*

In this phase of his writing Mosley's characters can overcome the paradox of freedom, which again is introduced in the shape of moral dilemmas. They can achieve this by observing their moral dilemmas in the framework of aesthetics.

Contrary to his early heroes, the protagonists of Mosley's experimental novels can deal with their moral dilemmas in a positive way by choosing *the only* morally not evil choice and thus influencing the outcome of events in a morally 'good' way: namely, by doing the 'impossible' and choosing both of the *given mutually* exclusive alternatives. However, since this cannot be done in a logical framework, Mosley's protagonists have to do this within a different framework, where the co-existence of mutually exclusive alternatives is possible.

Mosley's idea that this can only be done in an aesthetic framework brings to mind Kierkegaard's differentiation between the aesthetic and the ethical. For Kierkegaard the aesthetic is establishing a *conjunction* of the either-or. From the aesthetic point of view one doesn't *choose* between the *either* and the *or*, but rather tries to understand how to experience them simultaneously. The ethical, on the other hand, is establishing a *disjunction* of the either-or conjunction and thus the compulsion to choose between the *either* and the *or*. However, whereas from Kierkegaard's point of view the move should essentially be from the aesthetic to the ethical, Mosley finds it to be in the exact opposite direction: namely, from the ethical to the aesthetic. Within a moral dilemma the ethical on its own always brings the individual to a dead-end because it primarily compels the individual to choose 'good' in a situation where he is prevented from doing so due to the paradoxical nature of the moral dilemma. The aesthetic, on the other hand, enables the individual to step outside the moral dilemma (and thus free himself from its paradoxicality), and ironically do what the ethical obliges him to do, which is choosing 'good.'

This phase of Mosley's writing marks the classification of his works as 'experimental novels.' From this point on, one can see a clear shift in the content and form of his novels after *Corruption*, beginning with *Meeting Place* (1962) and fully realised in *Accident* (1965), *Impossible Object* (1968) and *Natalie Natalia* (1971). As mentioned earlier, these novels explore the possibilities of overcoming moral dilemmas by breaking out of the pattern of renunciation. In this sense Mosley's experiments with form can be clearly linked to the shift in his ideas and outlooks. The idea behind the novel provided him with new technical and formal challenges, which he tried to tackle in his experimental novels. Mosley, like his experimental precursors and contemporaries became acutely aware of the importance of the novel's form for its content: the idea that the content *adapts* to the form and structure.

III. Mind, Science and Freedom: *The Catastrophe Practice Series: Catastrophe Practice, Imago Bird, Serpent, Judith, Hopeful Monsters* (1970s-1980s).

In his *Catastrophe Practice Series* (1979-1990) the focus of Mosley's explorations into the possibilities of achieving freedom by overcoming its paradoxicality shifts from the outer world to the inner world. That is to say, whereas in the previous novels the protagonists tried to liberate themselves from the moral dilemmas that the conventions and dictates of the outer world—such as family, society, duties etc.—provided them with, here they set to free themselves from the restricting structures (patterns) of the mind. Consequently, Mosley is not concerned with moral dilemmas—these being primarily due to social conventions—anymore, but concentrates on philosophical and scientific concepts of the mind. Mosley is investigating the dilemma that the freedom of the mind is restricted by its own structures. Analogous to his previous novels in which the protagonists freed themselves from the patterns of their moral dilemmas by way of observing them in an aesthetic framework, here Mosley suggests a way of freeing oneself from the restricting structures of the mind by means of observing them. He is well aware that this sort of self-reflexive observation could, as many of his contemporary fellow-novelists have shown, lead to solipsism and *regressus ad infinitum* and instead of liberating the individual, plunge him into an even more self-destructive entrapment.

Mosley, however, maintains that 'valid freedom and healing and choice'[18] only have a chance to prevail through the consciousness' observation of the *split* between the conscious self and the self it is conscious of as that which *unites* the two halves—or as the *unity of* the division. To show this Mosley appropriates Bateson's three levels of Learning, where each level is a standing back from and an observation of the former pattern of learning and thus a liberation from it. These levels culminate onto the third level of Learning, where the individual can free himself from the patterns of his consciousness by being aware of and thus being in contact with a greater whole—a 'circuit of circuits.'[19] It is from the locale of his connection with this greater whole that he has the chance to see the patterns of his observational faculty and by this not just be free of it but perhaps even influence and change it. In this sense, his self-reflection will not fall into the trap of solipsism and tautology.

IV. The paradox of Freedom and Mysticism (1990s to the present): *Children of Darkness and Light* (1996), *Journey into the Dark* (1997, excerpted in *The Uses of Slime Mold*, 2004), *Hesperides Tree* (2001), *Inventing God* (2003)

This phase of Mosley's writing sums up his aesthetic examination of the paradox of freedom on a mystical level. That is to say, whereas in his previous novels Mosley saw man's freedom in his ability to choose a possibility rather than another by way of observation, in his present novels he sees man's freedom in choosing a *reality* rather than another. And whereas this choice was possible by man's awareness of the connection of these possibilities in a greater network—a greater whole—now his choice is possible by his awareness of a greater network of realities; an Ultimate Reality—i.e., that of God. In this sense, the present novels examine man's freedom on a spiritual and mystical level. Considering the preoccupation with modern scientific theories in the previous phase of his writing, the concern with universality and mysticism in the present phase seems only to be a small step: just as quantum physics operates on a level beyond rationality/irrationality, man's liberation could only be achieved beyond the scientific chance/determinism plane.

The new novels of Mosley, as their titles so often indicate, respond to the present millennial feeling of confusion and chaos: the sense of an ending and standing at the threshold of an utterly unknown future. Looking into the uncertain future of mankind and mapping the unknown have always belonged to the realm of mystical activities. Mosley's novels now are trying to find out how man with the 'help of God' can liberate himself from the chaos that he has created—especially in recent history—and sustain the continuation of Life and the human race.

* * *

In order to gain access to his novels, I will, to a large extent, use a biographical approach; that is to say, I will consider Mosley's own interpretation of his biographical and historical background. His aesthetic and intellectual development will also be examined in the context of history of ideas and the literary developments of the time.

A biographical approach seems particularly suitable, since Mosley's novels are explicitly based on his 'real life' experience. Mosley himself makes a point about drawing from his 'real life' experiences for the purpose of his novel-writing. He mainly writes about his 'real world' in retrospect. In remembering and interpreting the events then, he interprets what meaning his experiences had or could have had for his works. He also believes that by making aesthetic patterns—works of art—out of his observations of real life, he influences the pattern and, thus, the outcome of what the future brings with it. This is what Timothy Wilson believes to be essential for understanding Mosley's works: 'What is most important about understanding Mosley . . . is that he lives totally from his imagination, so that rather than withdrawing from experience to write, in the process of writing he creates his own future. One could call it remembering the future or *forward memory*.'[20] Mosley is preoccupied with his 'real life' to a great extent. He has written extensive biographies and an autobiography and is rarely seen by scholars—and himself—as wholly separate from his extraordinary background. In numerous essays and interviews quoted throughout this study he draws the attention of the reader to the fact that his novel-writing stands in direct relation to his experiences of the 'real world.' In his autobiography he writes about the different phases of his life in relation to the phases of his writing (or one could say, he writes about the phases of his writing in relation to the different phases of his life). He even goes as far as using the fictional names that he gave his mistresses when writing about them in his autobiography.[21] However, this study is not interested in a Freudian or Jungian interpretation of the author's mind, but only uses his *explicit* accounts of his 'real life,' as a secondary literature (like any other critical source) to help interpret the primary literature: his novels.

Apart from the novels themselves, the material that I use mainly comprises Mosley's novels, his non-fictional writings—essays, reviews, articles and biographies—and other writers' essays on and reviews of his works. Furthermore, I will draw extensively from personal interviews and correspondence with him and also material from his archives.

Chapter I

Conceiving the paradox of freedom and
the birth of Mosley's artistic career (1940s-1950s):
Spaces of the Dark, The Rainbearers, Corruption

Introduction: the impossibility of freedom

In the following chapter, I will look at the first phase of Mosley's artistic activity (1940s-1950s), i.e., the first stage in the evolution of his theme of the possibility of freedom. These books can be seen as the question for which Mosley finds an answer in his later novels: namely, is real freedom possible? In this stage his characters realise that what they take to be reality is only an illusory state of being in which the concept of freedom also becomes an illusion. However, they also realise that they have no way of escaping from this situation and either shatter when trying to break out or they fall back. They are taken to the point of (existentialist) despair, beyond which the protagonists of Mosley's later novels seek to move.

There are three elements of Mosley's life which are particularly interesting for an interpretation of his novels, especially in the first stage of his artistic activity. These consist of his aristocratic background, his acquaintance with Existentialism and his discovery of Faulkner. These experiences especially shed light on the first stage of his treatment of freedom, in which he depicts the experience of freedom as an illusion.

Biographical background

I. Aristocracy: rules of the game and the illusion of freedom

English aristocracy and class-consciousness are much debated and controversial issues. The opinions vary from the well-known view of holding aristocracy responsible for backwardness, inequality and injustice in English society[22] to seeing aristocracy in a special allegiance with the working class: Oswald Mosley believed that 'there had always been an instinctive and emotional sympathy between the aristocracy and the working class' and Lord Randolph Churchill thought the two classes to be 'united in the indissoluble bonds of common immorality' against the puritanism of left-wing intellectuals and the bourgeoisie.[23] Some scholars, such as Sampson and Hennessy, diagnose it as irreparably damaged, whereas others, such as Martin Jacques, Stuart Hall and Christopher Lasch, believe it to have confirmed itself over the past few decades.[24] Christopher Lasch goes even as far as seeing it as a danger to democracy and the consistency of society, whereas others see the phenomenon of aristocracy and class-consciousness in England as a myth: a 'delusion,' as Stein Ringen puts it, under which the 'British suffer real pain.'[25] A detailed analysis of aristocracy and its effects on the English society does not contribute to the objective of this study. What the following aims to do is to explore Mosley's own experiences and perception of his aristocratic background and Etonian education, which can then be used as a means to interpret—i.e., make sense of—Mosley's novels.

Aristocracy had a considerable influence on Mosley's conception of freedom. By origins he is firmly anchored in this class. He is the son of the notorious British Fascist leader, and the grandson of Lord Curzon.[26] Although the two are the antipodes of each other in political terms, they are closely related to one another in social terms. They have their roots in the same social institution: the British aristocracy. The enclosure of this class of society is best conceived of by the term that Nicholas's father used to refer to them: 'the circle of six-hundred.'[27] The restriction of this circle, however, was not meant to imprison its members, but to endow them with freedom.

There was of course the 'guarded and pampered' lifestyle, which freed them from even the most basic responsibilities such as bringing up one's own children.[28] The more subtle mechanism, however, with which they ensured both the integrity of their group and evasion from responsibility was by games-playing: that is, by obeying certain rules and codes of behaviour and at the same time regarding these as arbitrary; in other words, as rules of a game. The inner integrity of the circle was taken care of by strict rules. These rules were strictly observed.[29] The members of the group did not take anything as seriously as the rules—both in the private and public sphere. These served as a means for creating an artificial—a virtual—reality. In this way they could protect themselves from being confronted with the reality outside their own constructions. For example, it was an accepted convention that a husband commits infidelities; however these infidelities strictly took place within the rules:

> Virtue was held to depend on the *style* in which this was done. . . . (one did not go to bed with unmarried women nor to those of a different social background: one did not try to separate wives from husbands).[30]

Mosley himself refers to his father's infidelities as games: as something whose rules are *arbitrary*—in other words, only taken seriously if one *chose* to pursue the game. By doing this they somehow stood above the rules and showed their awareness that a disobedience of these rules did not matter really. However, at the same time, one stuck to the rules when playing the game. They felt that they had a freedom of choice. Even in the private spheres of their lives one can see how the pursuit of these games is both aimed at a prevention from getting involved in anything beyond one's virtual reality and endowing one with a feeling of freedom. In regards to their love-relationships, for example, Mosley's father could both swear eternal love to his wife and pursue other women by sending her childish love letters.[31] In this way he felt free in several respects: by looking at the affairs as games, he showed his disrespect for the rules, and thus stood above them. On the other hand, by writing a childish letter to his wife, he showed that since the affairs were only meaningless games, they need not be taken seriously as a breach of their marriage. In this way he could evade the consequences of his adultery and thus feel free. Furthermore, the childish love letters were meant to show the receiver, Cynthia Mosley, that the sender should anyway be excused for his misdemeanours, as children (naughty boys) cannot be punished or held responsible for these. Oswald, of course, could only be regarded as a free-of-fault naughty boy, due to Cynthia's mixture of mocked vexation and forgiveness. In other words, to show the triviality of the affair-games, Oswald and Cynthia played yet another game.[32] Hence, they could free themselves from the consequences of facing the reality of their marriage. In this way they could uphold their marriage and, yet, feel free from the restraints that a relationship entails.

Nicholas Mosley came to perceive of this idea of 'freedom' based on game-playing and the evasion of contact with the outside world as an illusion—as sheer dependence and self-deception.

He saw the evasion of responsibility by giving over the daily tasks and duties to servants and nannies as non-freedom. The more they tried to evade the pressure of outside influences and responsibility by putting these onto their servants, the more imprisoned and dependent they became. 'Vicious circle' is an appropriate phrase to define this mechanism.[33] He himself experienced the fallacy of this sort of freedom when he married the granddaughter of Lady Desborough. He and his wife had to make a conscious effort to break away from this tradition of 'handing over children to nannies' and take responsibility for their children in order to achieve some freedom. In his autobiography, Mosley conveys the dependence which the aristocratic notion of freedom leads to. Those who have been brought up to believe that affording to give up responsibility implies power and freedom, actually sense powerlessness and helplessness. He recalls: 'confidence had to be learned, inch by inch; both in the time we spent with the children, and through what we could gather about why this seemed so difficult.'[34]

Regarding the mechanism of games-playing, Mosley conceives of it as one which can only function if the players avoid fully admitting either to themselves or to others that they are playing a game. If one saw through the games, then they ceased to be such and the freedom that the participants achieved through their playing could be nullified. In this case one would either have to carry the consequences for one's action or be accused of being a hypocrite:

> One of the rules of the game was that you could not exactly explain what was and what was not a game: if you did, then someone who did not accept that there was a game could simply make you seem a hypocrite.[35]

It seemed to Nicholas Mosley as if the participants almost evolved a 'schizophrenic' state of mind, where one half refused quite to see what the other half was doing. Mosley realised that the only way in which his parents achieved the freedom and power over their virtual reality was by not facing any reality beyond the rules of the game. They were in fact powerless. At Eton he had a first-hand experience of this mixture of self-preservation and self-destruction:

> Eton is unlike other English public schools in that it inculcates the patterns of a ruling class not only by making boys undergo the mixture of brutality and reassurance by which tribal loyalties are fashioned, but it provides a level of confidence and sophistication from which some boys can look down on these loyalties with charm.[36]

The charm of Etonians provided the best vantage point and defence mechanism. Mosley himself profited from these mechanisms. Even when his father was imprisoned and humiliated as the arch betrayer of England, it simply did not matter at Eton.[37] This is what Nicholas Mosley has been grateful for:

> I felt that Eton had been good to me because it had taught me to be both part of and yet not part of its odd, self-confident world: some such balancing act seemed to be necessary if life was not to become too savage or too blind....[38]

During the war, he was thankful for the practical and nihilistic 'nonchalance' with which the Etonians treated practical matters, such as the war itself.[39] Although the teachers taught the students 'to accept the War in the same unquestioning style as they teach them the history of the Trojan or the Peloponnesian Wars, or indeed the story of Medea so beautifully murdering her children,'[40] the students did not go to the war with bright eyes, slogans and hymns. They saw it as a game in which one has to try to survive in order to have the maximum pleasure, but in which one will most probably end up dead. This attitude seems to have conveyed for him a means of detaching himself from the madness of war in order to see its absurdity.

This charm, though, carried with it the seed of destruction. Charm was in effect utter attachment and dependence. At Eton 'criticism' or even 'rebellion' was a way of charming others, rather than an effort at striving for understanding or freedom. In other words, rebelliousness and charm fed off each other.[41] What was 'inculcated is charm, and charm is a way of manipulating society,'[42] and, therefore, inevitably, the way to a stronger dependence on society. 'Charm lacks substance; so it is to society that a charming person is tethered, however much he dislikes society. He is beholden to society because there is not much inside himself.'[43] The charming Etonian protests actually perpetuated the system by simultaneously upholding the tradition and laughing at it. The Etonian's confidence lay in his standing back from, while feeling part of, the society in which he found himself.[44]

'Freedom' was thus only achieved if these rules, and consequently their effect, were *simultaneously* upheld *and* looked down upon as meaningless. Here, more poignantly than with the aristocratic adults, Mosley became aware of the nihilism, which he both profited from (as in the case of his father's imprisonment) and was repelled by. He came to believe that a notion of freedom based on nihilism was illusory, since in a meaningless state of being it did not make any sense.[45] From his point of view, one could only claim freedom to exist, if one had faith in existence. For Mosley the lack of such an attitude ultimately and plausibly would lead to self-destruction:

> As I walked round the playing fields I swore that I would never send any of my own children to Eton . . . Eton had been good to me because it had oiled wheels with regard to my father; but perhaps the same oil might be making smooth the slope down which people seemed to be sliding to perdition. [. . .] What had happened, what would happen, to the things that my friends and I tried to talk about as we hid away in our by-ways and hedgerows—God, truth, love?[46]

During his last year at Eton he viewed it as such:

> I had written to my sister about my last year at Eton—'Vice, sordidity and sloth have come into their proper place at the head of things': this was a joke, of course, but then—what was not a joke?[47]

II. Father and son's joint search for freedom; the discovery of philosophy and literature

Mosley's lineage did not only serve as a 'bad example' to be avoided, but also contributed positively towards the intellectual development of the artist as a young man. His father especially proved a teacher and a patient listener at least while he was in the Holloway Prison. During this time Oswald became some sort of a 'mentor' for Nicholas's 'intellectual affairs'—the latter having joined the army and preparing to go to war.[48] Their correspondence during this time—January to June 1943—between Holloway Prison,[49] London and Ranby Camp, Nottinghamshire, gives a good picture of Nicholas's fascination with ideas which shape the grounds upon which Mosley writes his novels.[50] In this correspondence their admiration for and contemplation on Teutonic literature, music and philosophy and their pondering on the Christian faith is striking.[51] Wagner's music is what young Nicholas listens to on his visits to Holloway.[52] The fascination with Nietzsche's philosophy is especially noteworthy. Nietzsche came to accompany Mosley throughout his career up to the present day. In a Nietzschean spirit Mosley's appreciation of the philosopher underwent numerous metamorphoses: Oswald's 'anti-Christian,' fascist interpretation of him gave way to an 'anti-Christian' existentialist understanding only to become one of the cornerstones of Mosley spiritual worldview in the later phases of his writing.[53] Bearing in mind the fascist tailoring of Nietzsche, Mosley remarks:

I came across Nietzsche for all the wrong reasons, really! My father told me all about Nietzsche. My father didn't understand Nietzsche . . . And so I thought of reading him for all the wrong reasons and [saw] that people have misunderstood him.[54]

In his correspondence, however, the critical view of the novelist as a young man towards Nietzschean philosophy—or rather his father's interpretation of it—is clearly stated. His apprehension clearly conveys his fascination with this philosophy and thus foreshadows the never-ending grappling of Mosley with this philosopher to this day. In most of his letters Nicholas seems to be both fascinated by and distrustful of the two opposing 'God-centred' Christianity and 'anthropocentric' Nietzschean philosophy in regards to their effectiveness for the deliverance of the human race. On his visits to Holloway prison he discussed with his father the problems and merits of pity (Christian doctrine) and arrogance (Nietzschean philosophy) for the evolution of human race into a higher state.[55] He seems to have seen the point of these doctrines, but at the same time found them inconsistent and impractical. Nicholas questioned the Christian doctrine of Faith and Humility:

Can one be actively, vitally, and effectively humble? Humble towards God, yes: . . . if you recognise yourself to be one of God's elect your gratitude and devotion to him will take the form of humility; but surely the doctrine of Humility implies as a general form of behaviour toward one's fellow men; and as one's fellow men are 90% . . . dull, indifferent baboons . . . what place has Humility in [one's] relations with them?[56]

and at the same time he seems not to have been convinced by its antipode—the Nietzschean contention that Christian humility should be substituted by 'Härte'—

With Nietzsche's values I have very little sympathy: 'Heiterkeit' . . .— yes, that is perhaps the most desirable quality that any mortal can possess. But 'Härte' . . . why always the emphasis on domination and power through 'Härte'? With the principles of Herrenmoral . . . I agree entirely—duties towards one's equals; a belief that 'what is harmful to me is harmful in itself etc'—but is it necessary for the Herrenmoral to take Härte as its primary value? There is no beauty, and I would say very little nobility, in Härte.[57]

The possibility of solving the dilemma of these opposing doctrines is yet again sought in the Germanic philosophy: Hegelian synthesis is suggested by the father to his son as a possible way of reconciling Nietzsche with Christianity. In a letter to Nicholas he writes:

> In Christianity you have the thesis: in Nietzsche the antithesis. There remains synthesis, eternal synthesis, which is the task and hallmark of all supreme minds. I mean not merely the narrower terms of the Hegelian dialectic which you should one day study . . . but the wide clashes of the great spiritual movements whose fiery collisions can fuse into a higher unity. You might attempt the Christian-Nietzsche synthesis one day . . .[58]

In the later phases of his writing career (1960s onwards), the period starting with his 'experimentalist' novels, Mosley is mainly concerned with a synthesis of the two, however, not as his father suggest from a rational, Hegelian point of view. Nicholas suggests the (Nietzschean) aesthetic observation as a way of connecting contradictions. Up to this very day he is concerned with this undertaking and would like to see Nietzsche not as an opponent towards the heart of Christianity, but an enemy of the Church, as an institution, which tries to 'keep people down' in order to facilitate their exploitation.

The fascination with existentialism was a matter of course considering his grappling with Nietzsche. After the war, he read Sartre's novels 'with intensity.'[59] However, he neither could 'tackle' *Being and Nothingness*, nor does he remember 'thinking much of *La Nausée*.'[60] What came to intrigue him most was Sartre's failure to complete *Les Chemins de la Liberté*, for which 'he had in mind a fourth volume with some sort of 'answer' to existentialist negativity.'[61] Existentialism's failure to answer the task that it had set for itself—the possibility of freedom in a world where there is no meaning other than that created by man—became of interest to Mosley especially in his later experimentalist novels.

III. The discovery of Faulkner

The literary style with which Mosley started to express what these philosophies had taught him were strongly shaped by the modernist writers and their conception of 'good' literature. To him it seems that in the 1940s 'anyone interested in literature was aware of what was called "the great tradition" of English novel writing.'[62] Mosley remarks that he, without having read Leavis, was aware that 'a main stream ran through Jane Austen, George Eliot, Henry James, D. H. Lawrence.'[63] He was also interested in the other stream of English novel, which 'swirled and eddied around James Joyce and Virginia Woolf.'[64] E. M. Forster was his 'early love.'[65] He was also acquainted with and influenced by those non-English writers that had a great impact on modern British fiction. During the war, he read Tolstoy, Dostoyevsky and Turgenev, Stendhal and Flaubert.[66] He was aware and in awe of Henry James and Proust, who seemed to 'spin magnificent filigree-screens with words so that through these, by such filtering and focusing processes, there might break through—aesthetically, morally[67]—some profound illumination.'[68] However, his eye-opener was William Faulkner. He came across Faulkner's *Sound and the Fury* in a Red Cross library in Italy during the war.[69] For Mosley this novel was a 'knock-out.'[70] His first impression of this novel foreshadows the grounds upon which Mosley based his conception of a 'good novel': the idea that true art is directly connected to life and must thus try to reflect it as truly as possible.

It was the first time where he read a novel that was a 'true' portrayal of life[71]—a chaos which all of a sudden illuminates into a pattern where everything becomes clear because the reader keeps observing it (reading it) and trying to make sense of it:

> I'd never heard of anyone writing like this. Not only the style, but the way in which you don't exactly know what on earth has happened or is happening till about page two hundred—then it all becomes apparent in a blinding flash. The whole book. This seems not only intensely exciting (the wondering for two-hundred pages was exciting) *but to be exactly like life*. What in God's name, after all, was I doing aged twenty in Italy in a war?[72]

His discovery of Faulkner led to his acquaintance with two other American novelists: Hemingway (*The Sun also Rises*) and Scott Fitzgerald (*The Great Gatsby*). He was attracted to these writers' 'sense of the tragic,' which emerged when the respective hero honestly faced his predicament and 'out of it—out of the facing it—comes some sort of an understanding.'[73] In his first novels, Mosley tended to combine the 'turgid' prose of Faulkner and James with the 'heroic' poise of Hemingway's and Fitzgerald's protagonists.[74]

With all these philosophies, ideas and novels roaring in his head, he at the end of the war wrote to his father about his urge to go to university for reorganising his thoughts after the chaos that the War has produced in his mind.[75] The intellectual atmosphere that awaited him became one of the major disappointments with lasting consequences for his artistic career. The fundamental questions of existence which had preoccupied and frustrated him during the war were not of interest for his fellow-students and tutors. He was now faced with an intellectual ground, which was predominated with 'common-sense views, [which constituted] anachronism and obscurantism at their most unimaginative.'[76]

Literary and intellectual background

I. Common-sense and the war against ideas

From the beginning of his artistic career Mosley stood at odds with his surroundings. His preoccupation with freedom, his 'love of ideas,' did not become the British intelligentsia. Love of ideas is generally considered to be 'un-English.' As John Naughton, in a review of Mosley, put it the British tend to be 'inclined to regard abstract theorising on the human condition as a kind of disease . . . which is tolerated in foreigners but abhorred in natives.'[77] Mosley himself points out the 'suspicion of ideas, of intellectuality' amongst the English intelligentsia.[78] In his biography of Julian Grenfell,[79] for example, he traces the tradition of this hostility back to the nineteenth-century England. He mentions the intellectual circle, 'the Souls,' whose members were prominent aristocrats such as Lady Desborough, George Curzon, Arthur Balfour and George Wyndham. Mosley sees the name of this circle as a misleading one, since 'it suggested seriousness and intensity, whereas what "the Souls" wanted to be above everything was "witty." '[80] In an article on Virginia Woolf he does not see any major changes in the habits of the English Intelligentsia some four decades later: he believes the same mechanism of words, wit and gossip kept the highly intellectual Bloomsbury circle together instead of a passion for ideas.[81]

For a picture of the philosophical and intellectual insularity that he personally felt in the immediate years after the War, Mosley finds Bryan Magee's *Confessions of a Philosopher* a good guide—particularly due to its treatment of philosophy in light of the modern history of ideas in England.

[82] Magee was a contemporary of Nicholas Mosley, who entered Oxford only two years after Mosley in 1947-48. According to Magee, the period from 1945 to 1960 is the era of 'Oxford Philosophy': i.e., the time where the two philosophies of logical positivism and linguistic analysis predominated the English philosophical landscape.[83] Logical positivism claimed to be devoted to finding 'truth'—which meant separating sense from nonsense—by means of scientific and empirical observations. The main principle of positivism derived from the so-called Vienna Circle's 'Verification Principle.' This principle said that only 'assertions that were in principle verifiable by observation or experience could convey factual information. Assertions that there could be no imaginable way of verifying must either be analytic or meaningless . . . either something is scientific, or capable of becoming a science, or it is merely an expression of opinion or feeling, in which case it is subjective, not factual.'[84] The positivists of the Vienna Circle, thus, set upon revealing German metaphysics as 'high-flown nonsense'[85] and their English colleagues followed suit. English Neo-Hegelian metaphysicians—Bradley and McTaggart—were convicted of talking nonsense.[86] Magee, however, is aware that the hostility of the English intellectuals towards German Metaphysics has deeper roots in England itself. The two leading English philosophers, who broke away from German idealism before logical positivism was widely introduced to the English through Ayer's *Language, Truth and Logic*, were Moore and Russell.[87] They embraced, 'with the enthusiasm of converts,'[88] the British empiricist tradition represented by Locke, Berkeley, Hume and Mill.[89] Russell and Moore, according to Magee, had enormous influence on the intellectual and philosophical life of the English-speaking world; Russell even came to be seen as some sort of a Godfather for the logical positivists, including those in the Vienna Circle.[90] This shows that the hostility towards the metaphysicians had already a firm tradition in England itself.

The other school, that of linguistic analysis, was dominated by Austin and Ryle, who, under the influence of Wittgenstein's philosophy, set to dismiss logical positivism by declaring that our knowledge about the world is not the domain of science, but of language. Science itself was declared a domain of language. According to Magee, Linguist analysts insisted that 'in any philosophical enquiry we must start not from theoretical considerations but from reality, from what actually happens, which includes what people do in fact say.'[91] If an utterance has no imaginable or possible use, then it has no meaning. For the linguist analysts the task of philosophy was to dissolve rather than solve philosophical problems, by way of analysing 'conceptual tangles' and showing that the philosophical problems did not properly arise.[92]

These two dominant philosophies functioned as opposing schools, but were essentially similar. They both dismissed the problems of existence and human condition to be the main domain of philosophy and instead claimed to solve and do away with all philosophical problems by means of empirical and analytical thinking. Philosophy in this period was defined as nothing but, according to Ryle, 'talk about talk.'[93]

II. The British post-war novel of the fifties

The 'back-to-the-roots' and 'common-sense' philosophy of the time both supported and was in turn perpetuated in a majority of novels, which constituted the dominant trait in the literary background against which Mosley wrote his early novels. The novel in post-war Britain was mainly concerned with the disillusionment that the war had caused. Pre-war, modernist utopian ideologies, philosophies and intellectualities had exposed themselves not only as dreams and fantasies but also as highly destructive devices. For the British a most tangible dilemma was the weakening of their national morale, despite the victory of the allies over the axis.[94] The sense of 'British identity' and consensus, which had strongly relied on British political and economic hegemony, was now suffering strong blows. This is not to say that the self-confidence of the British was waning, as was that of the Germans, for example. Doris Lessing believes that the British in the Fifties still saw Britain as the best, but in need of social and economical improvement which they optimistically endeavoured to achieve.[95] One could, thus, observe that the Fifties were very much concerned with *social* criticism and improvement; they were the years of the National Health Service and the Welfare State.

The criticisms and reforms of the Fifties affected the cultural and political landscape, as well. Those who had long dominated it were now being criticised for their snobbery, hypocrisy and alienation from reality and society, and were even blamed for the present critical situation of Britain. In the eyes of many novelists the project of modernism which had prevailed in British culture in the '20s and '30s had now failed: not only had it greatly damaged the British culture, but nearly killed the novel. A great majority of writers believed that the revival of the novel could take place if the 'self-indulgent' modernist novel was substituted by a novel which criticised society and offered a moral solution to its ills. What marks the cultural mood of this era is 'the arrival of *working-class* or at least not middle-class talent into the arts, and, above all, the *political optimism*, which has so completely evaporated.'[96] It is not surprising that a considerable number of novelists at this time had strong Marxist inclinations—to put it in Lessing's words, in the post-war era 'everyone' in Europe had been a communist or been in a communist 'ambience.'[97] What is more noteworthy about Britain as opposed to Europe at this time, however, is the overwhelmingly 'anti-communist' reaction of many writers to the situation by calling for a restoration of British society and common-good based on contemporary and ordinary English reality, sense of community and morality.[98] In their 'Condition of England' novels these writers saw the redemption of English literature and culture not in the embracing of the international workers' community, but in a return to the tradition strongly rooted in the English culture; in other words, a return to liberal realism. Thus, the Fifties saw, in both the liberal-realist and the socialist camps, the emergence of 'social novels,' which through both subject matter and form reject the moral relativism and experimental aestheticism of modernism.[99]

Anthony Powell noted that these novelists constituted the chief movement in the Fifties. Powell sees them as an 'Anti-Romantic' movement 'of which Mr. Kingsley Amis is the uncrowned King, with its headquarters at the provincial universities.'[100] Amis, Wilson, Larkin, to name a few, were the representatives of the so called 'Movement,' which also came to be known as the 'Angry Young Men.'[101] As is the case with most classifications, the label 'Angry Young Men' suffers from being an inadequate overgeneralisation. Doris Lessing, who for a while was considered an 'angry young man,' believes this term to be a manifestation of the media's lack of originality.[102] In order to give a picture of the literary mood of the Fifties, Lessing refers to the importance and popularity of the Royal Court Theatre. This theatre was full of 'young, talented, clever young men, mostly form the North, mostly working class, and intending to make their mark.'[103] It was here where men full of 'irreverence for the established order'[104] such as Tony Richardson and John Osborne flourished and came to dominate the literary scene. It was here where *Look Back in Anger*—a play which Miles Malleson, while being distressed by, conceived of as 'the equivalent of a fart let off in the face of respectability, and as useful'[105]—largely set the trend for and became the epitome of the mood of the Fifties. Jimmy Porter's anger about the political and social failings of the 'established order' was one with which many, including Lessing, despite her dislike for the protagonist,[106] identified.[107] The epithet 'Angry Young Men' might very well be an awkward and narrow phrase produced by the newspapers, but it can still be used to describe the cultural and literary mood of this era.

Instead of an appreciation for the modern novelists' experiments—their 'stream-of-consciousness' and their scepticism toward the notion of reality—British novelists, for the moment, seemed to be determined to seek the 'real': the novel was to be a 'plain social chronicle.'[108] They attacked the modern novelists for their snobbish, naive and obscurely unrealistic style.[109] Their aim was to communicate directly to their audience. Amis declared that he and his fellow-poets and fellow-novelists were for a 'new sincerity,' moving away from the allusive and obscure style of the pre-war period towards a more precise and lucid one.[110] He commented on the style of the 'Movement' as follows: 'From my point of view, all we really have in common is a desire to write *sensibly*, with out emotional hoo-ha; this boils down to saying that we all try to write poems that are intelligible in the sense that they can be paraphrased; there may be obscurities but no answerless riddles.'[111]

The hallmark of the fiction of this group was straightforward plot and characterisation: in short, telling a good story. Bradbury, leaning on Trilling, defines the 'Fifties Novel' as a 'repository of social reality in literature' being consequently 'anti-experimental and anti-Romantic, anti-ideological and eminently realistic.'[112] The main concern of these novels seems to have been the individual's manners and moral values, which inevitably have to take into account the society. Angus Wilson, one of the more dominant novelists of this era, dismissed the representation of the individual as a being that is closed and separated from society: 'No sharpening of the visual image, no increased sensibility, no deeper penetration of individual consciousness . . . could fully atone for the frivolity of ignoring man as a social being.'[113] This is obviously an attack on the novels of the modernist, pre-war era, where the concerns of the novels were more descriptive and observational than moral. In modernist novels much attention is given to the inner-world of the individual and his preoccupation with his existence in a mysterious world, rather than to his relation towards and his function in society. This is what was being satirised and criticised by the young novelist in post-war Britain of the Fifties. The enemies of justifiably the most famous protagonist of the British fiction in this era: namely, Amis's Dixon, are (bad) imitations of Gide and Strachey, whom he triumphs over in a feat of bad manners.[114] To make things worse, his comrade-in-arms,

Bowen in *I Like It Here*, is overcome with 'uncontrollable laughter' at the sight of one of the monuments of modern British fiction; namely, *Portrait of a Lady*.[115]

This is not to say that the literary landscape of the Fifties consisted entirely of 'anti-modernist' fiction. It is impossible to overlook gigantic figures such as Beckett, Graham Greene, Evelyn Waugh, Durrell and Powell himself, who wrote some of their most important works in these years. These writers, however, seem to have been in exile in this reactionary era. They were, for the moment, the 'hangovers' of a decade which ideologically, artistically and materially ended in dismay, despair and death. As Bradbury notices, the damage this did to the novel was so severe that it had to be almost re-invented.[116] The young novelists of the Fifties even declared the necessity of 'eliminating' their modernist predecessors from the scene for the resurgence of the novel to take place.[117] And as observed earlier, this novel was to investigate and confirm a certainty and identity embedded in ordinary, common-sense, English social reality. The exceptional language, social settings and psychological-fantastical landscapes of Greene, Powell, Durell and Beckett actually serve to magnify the anti-intellectual, anti-experimental literary mood of the time. The writings of Durrell and Beckett were even more 'foreign' to the present mood than their other fellow-modernists, as writing in Paris made them also spatially removed from the landscape of English novel. In Beckett's case, especially, the question of the identity of English novel became even further complex in regards to his nationality and bilinguality. The thematic, linguistic and stylistic experiments of these novelists remained more or less dormant only to be picked up and allowed to thrive in the openly liberationist and experimentalist Sixties.[118]

The young writers who were to pick up the thread of modernism—and in the eyes of many, to embark on the project of 'postmodernism'—and experiment with the form of the novel were already emerging in the Fifties, but their writings attract the attention rather as 'stages to something else'[119] than contributions to the general mood of time. William Golding, Anthony Burgess, Muriel Spark and Iris Murdoch were amongst those who were showing signs of deviation from the realist, anti-experimentalist movement and preparing the ground for the 'Sixties' innovations and experimentations with the form. However, Murdoch along with Lessing—both of whom came to be important figures of the experimentalist novel of ideas—were initially seen as 'Angry Young Men,' before their style came to be considered as 'experimental.'[120] Angus Wilson who was an important founder of the realist, anti-modernist movement in the Fifties, only proved doubtful of realism at the end of the decade and writers of Catholic background such as Burgess, Spark and Golding were just beginning to undermine the certainties of liberal realism by exploiting allegorical, metaphysical and surreal dimensions of the narrative. These writers paved the way for the experiments of the forthcoming two decades. One can, thus, conclude that the literary scene of the Fifties was dominated by the realistic, moral and social novel.

Whereas the majority of post-war novels dealt with disillusionment and uncertainty mainly in form of protest against pre-war modernism and longed-for a return to ordinary English sense of reality, morality and common sense, Nicholas Mosley's novels dealt with the post-war dilemma by diverging from this movement and in a way by positioning themselves against it.[121] His novels dealt with the very concepts and questions that the majority of his contemporaries found nonsensical. Mosley was not so much interested in the consequences of the war for the 'Condition of England,' but rather for the sense of human existence and activity. His own experience of the absurdities and atrocities of war universalised and actualised the questions that had preoccupied him throughout his youth and his years at Eton: is freedom possible in a state of being where human activity seems to make no sense? This question seems almost to beg a style of writing contrary to that of the 'no-nonsense' Angry Young Men. This is the question which the modernist English and European writers, especially those under whose influence the literary taste of Mosley had developed, treated as a mystery—or, to put it in Amis's words, as the 'answerless riddle'—and seemed not to offer a clear-cut answer to; hence the complex and obscure style of writing.[122] Mosley's modernist style was noticed by most of his reviewers at the time and does not escape his own eye when he judges his novels retrospectively.[123] Critics rightly detected the influence of James, Eliot, Hemingway and others in his early novels.[124]

Mosley's novels dealt with his experience of war in the context of a contemporary doctrine which went against the grain of the social-realism and satires of the Fifties: i.e., existentialism. The sense of existentialist emptiness and despair, as we shall see, is evident in his novels. In the British literary setting of the Fifties, Mosley was increasingly being seen by many critics not so much as a contemporary novelist anymore, but rather as an old-fashioned one.[125]

Mosley's novels of the fifties:
an enquiry into the possibility of freedom

The features of Mosley's early novels are conventional; that is to say, they have a more or less a straightforward notion of plot, setting, characterisation, and narrative devices. It is not until his novel *Accident* (1965) that Mosley greatly explored and exploited the potentials of the form of the novel. Yet, the features of his early novels show how much he diverged from the dominant style of novel-writing in the Fifties. His settings are just what Amis's characters would avoid: in *Spaces of the Dark* it is mainly fashionable Chelsea and the smoky bars of Kensington, in *The Rainbearers* it is the Riviera and Paris, and in *Corruption* the protagonists frequent amongst the rich Venetian aristocrats.

The voice of the characters is by no means vernacular. The reader has access to the inner thoughts and feelings of the protagonists, which are shown in often long, lyrical, stream-of-consciousness passages. The inner world of the protagonists and its incompatibility with the outside world is shown often by juxtaposing the stream-of-consciousness with what the protagonists say or do in the outside world. The extent of Faulkner's and James's influence on his style is evident. As Peter Lewis in a retrospective glance notices—

> His [Mosley's] novels of the 1950s are long, doom-laden books characterised by a fashionable pessimism, and by a stylistic and syntactical complexity owing much to Faulkner and James. Implicit in *Corruption* (1957) is, for example, a belief that experience can be pinned down exactly by words—if enough are used, and in sufficiently torturous manner . . .[126]

This opposes the narration of Amis, who would have declared such a style of narration as obscure, emotional and unintelligible. This style conveys the conception of Mosley's characters of their outside world and shows their uncertainty about dream and reality. In this way Mosley succeeds in creating a somewhat surrealistic atmosphere. Amis's characters, on the other hand, never doubt that they are living in a tangible, real, social world.

Mosley's characters are introverted, life-weary and despairing. They tend to be very self-conscious and self-seeking and possess none of the partly naive, partly tongue-in-cheek witticism of Amis's protagonists.

They are, contrary to 'Angry Young Men' protagonists, artistic and rich individuals, whose struggles do not result from social and moral unfairness and inequality, but from preoccupation with the self. The following analysis of his novels of this period is an attempt to show how these features are realised in his fiction.

I. *Spaces of the Dark*: despair and the inevitability of death

In his first novel, *Spaces of the Dark* (1951),[127] Mosley negates the possibility of freedom both in a tragic and an existentialist context. The fusion of tragedy and existentialist despair is most evidently conceivable in this novel. From both viewpoints the hero cannot free himself from the inner and outer forces by any means other than death. From the tragic point of view, the hero, Paul, is helpless before his guilt and the force of a higher moral law which he unintentionally but inevitably has violated. From the existential point of view he is helpless before the realisation that the bourgeois reality around him is only an illusion which he cannot fully denounce. On the other hand, he is powerless before his (existential) sincerity and cannot pretend to conform to the 'bourgeois' reality. He is thus put into a situation in which death seems to be the most plausible consequence and choice.

In the tragic context he must die, since he carries the immense guilt of having killed his best friend, John, to save the lives of the other soldiers, who would have perished at obeying the orders of John. This is a classical case of *hamartia*, where the tragic hero, on grounds of an inevitable judgement, violates a moral law, which will irreversibly bring upon him a misfortune greater than he deserves. Coming back home he becomes emotionally involved with both Paul's lover, Sarah, and Paul's sister, Margaret. He confesses his secret to Sarah, who loves him and with whom he is in love. However, despite the latter's attempts to forgive and redeem him, Paul cannot find fulfilment with her, since this would mean sacrificing the beloved and loving Margaret, to whom he also feels he owes a fulfilled life as some sort of a compensation for his deed. In the end, he is put into a situation where he can save Margaret only by getting himself killed. He does this almost readily: by embracing his death he saves Margaret. Both women are left hopelessly devastated and helpless against such cruelty. In terms of tragedy, the tone of this novel is traditional.[128] The hero is offered opportunities to get out of his situation and fulfil his love, but he cannot take them as they are constantly blocked by fate, i.e., hazard and accidents, which rationally are not conceivable, but are inevitable as the hero, no matter how benevolently, has violated a moral law which can only be put to right through his death. The most obvious one being Margaret's accident, where Paul can stop the cars from running over her only by heroically sacrificing himself. Being a tragic hero, he readily accepts his fate and in an emotionally moving scene embraces his death.

The sense of contemporary existentialist despair and emptiness is evident in *Spaces of the Dark* and Mosley's two following novels. *Spaces of the Dark* ends with Sarah completely giving up on everything: 'So she closed her eyes. There was nothing else to do.'[129] The novel was praised for the honest and sincere picture that it gave of the disillusioned youth, who had experienced the absurdity and horrors of war.[130] Paul has experienced the irrational and total destruction of Europe. He is not only the victim of Fate and his *hamartia*, but also the victim of the contemporary ungraspable irrationality. Like other existential heroes, the war is for him the 'denuding experience of radical reflexion,'[131] where he sees that he stands alone and naked in a world where no God, Reason, Society, Government or Soul are there to offer him hold.[132] Paul, being an existentialist anti-hero, possesses the virtue of sincerity, which is necessary for this 'denuding experience.'[133] For those who do not have this virtue he has only contempt:

> It was the weakness of all talented optimists, the weakness of ease, the failure to face up to the horror of the world, the failure to accept the facts of life's *insoluble contradictions*, the failure of the tragic spirit. This was the weakness that Paul had faced in the war and had conquered in hospital. He now knew it when he saw it in others. . . . He was lonely. He was twenty-two . . .[134]

In this world Paul is a young man 'despairing the necessity to scream' against 'the deadland, the carpet world; knives clicking, napkins spread, remarks passing flatly like the patterned plates of food' of bourgeoisie.[135] Paul's disgust is a very Eliotic one—the 'deadland' could almost be substituted by the 'wasteland.' He also seems to have borrowed the voice of surrealist poets through which he sees the illusions and fears of the bourgeoisie, yet cannot bring himself to scream in their face. His guilt and sense of responsibility for Margaret make him conform and be polite—in contrast to Sarah and Adam who have taken the consequences and show their contempt openly for the bourgeois world and live the lives they have chosen. He is faced with what he calls 'insoluble contradictions.' He sees his inevitable downfall nearing. He sees himself as if in an nightmarish illusion. He is faced with that famous existentialist state of being, which according to this doctrine must be gone through before real freedom and life can begin: the state of despair. In a dreamlike, nightmarish prose, reminiscent of Faulkner and Joyce, he portrays this state, which is nothing but a divorce between inner and outer realities:

> He ate little, spoke automatically, watched the encroachment of time creep in on him with the indeterminate yet disastrous speed of the fall of darkness. . . . And yet at tea he was static again, the movement running past him, the minutes flowing into his cup like the liquid from the teapot which Mrs. Longmore tilted so expertly above the china. . . . And the drops that spilled were like the impressions of the evening that came through to him—a chauffeur in the mews outside embarking upon a piercingly laborious whistling of the current popular song, Mrs. Longmore rising to shut the window, Margaret standing by the piano pressing the pedals up and down. . . .[136]

Paul, similar to other existentialist heroes, such as the ones in *Les Chemins de la Liberté*,[137] is taken to this point of insight—i.e., the realisation of reality being only an illusion—and left there.[138] He is not offered a way through to the 'other side of despair.' His only choices are either death or a relapsing into his former situation out of which he wanted to break out initially. Paul's death confirms the existentialist nothingness for the remaining protagonists.

II. *The Rainbearers*: learning to live with despair

Whereas the critics classified *Spaces of the Dark* as a contemporary novel, *The Rainbearers*, published only four years later, was already seen as one that does not comply with the *Zeitgeist*. Peter Green foresaw that the 'New Realists' would hate Mosley's protagonist and his tortured soul as much as his 'enormous serpentine paragraphs, punctuated by sharp hiccups of dialogues,'[139] and Anthony Powell's observation of Mosley's opposition to the dominant 'anti-Romanticism' was contemporary with the publication of this novel.[140]

This novel's treatment and negation of the possibility of freedom goes a step further than that of *Spaces of the Dark* in that the protagonists do not choose self-annihilation as the only alternative to their disillusionment, but learn to accept this state and live with it. Richard, like Paul, is brought to the point of insight and despair, and does not know where to go on from there. However, the existentialist 'denuding experience of radical reflexion,' which makes Richard face the illusion of his reality, but also his inadequacy to deal with this, does not compel him to embrace death, but instead to relapse into a disillusioned state of being. The component of tragedy and sacrifice is also strongly present in this novel, but the characters, similar to Hemingway's or Fitzgerald's heroes, whom Mosley admired so much at the time, learn to face and survive the tragic situation in which they find themselves.

The question and treatment of the possibility of freedom is closely biographical in this novel. The endeavour of the hero, Richard, and his wife Elizabeth, to free themselves from the dishonesty and self-deceptive virtual reality of their parents and background, is very similar to that of Mosley and his wife.[141] Both the real and fictional couples try to get away from their pasts by deceiving themselves into yet another artificial reality. Instead of freeing themselves from the aristocratic charming games and virtual realities, they now find themselves in the restrictions of a seeming bourgeois, idyllic marriage.[142] The marriage and idyllic farmhouse in which Richard and Elizabeth reside resembles the farmhouse that Mosley and his wife inhabited in North Wales and to which Mosley often refers as their would-be Garden of Eden.[143] The collapse of Richard's illusory idyll runs parallel to that of Mosley's. The encounter and brief affair with a woman, whom Mosley in his autobiography calls by her fictional name in *The Rainbearers* (i.e., 'Mary'),[144] is the existentialist 'denuding experience of radical reflexion' for both the author and his protagonist. They are both taken to a point of despair and do not know how to go on from there. This time instead of death, a relapse into the former state, but void of its idyllic element is chosen: the protagonist, like the author, goes back to his former life, but with a world-weary knowledge.

The setting of the novel—a decadent, sleepy hotel in the contemporary French Riviera in high summer, on a smart social holiday—enhances the feeling of a rundown idyll threatening to collapse at any moment. Richard's confrontation with Mary, his love from his days at an art academy, is the moment where the fall of this virtual reality realises itself. Richard meets Mary first in memory (here we have the Proustian element, which Mosley tried to appropriate in his early novels: Richard remembers Mary accidentally, by the tone of one of the guest's voice, which leads to a long flash-back) and then in person on his way back from South of France. The fictional Mary, similar to the real-life Mary, is also the embodiment of the horrors of war (in the novel the scene of Mary's tortures is removed from Japan to France); the horrors upon which Paul's disillusionment and helplessness were based in *Spaces of the Dark*. The hero in this novel supersedes Paul, since he not only honestly faces the horrors of war, but also learns to survive this insight, even if in a state of disillusionment.

It is indeed difficult to overlook the 'old-fashionedness' of *Rainbearers*. The scene where Richard is leaving Mary, for example, has the atmosphere of a pre-Raphaelite painting showing the beloved virgin dying. Mary looks 'as light as a leaf with the body quite drained of all the pain that had bled out of it.'[145] Richard, her lover, puts her head on the pillow, smoothes her hair and covers her with a sheet, which reminds him of a shroud.[146] The remorse, peace and passivity that he feels is very much a feeling of other-worldliness: it has a religious and metaphysical touch about it.

> He saw her breathing then, . . . a faint and almost imperceptible peace like the leaf-like lightness that had also escaped him, the face once more beautiful and composed. . . . and he [Richard] stood quite quiet and peaceful too with his arms by his sides and he did not mind if he was hit, he even wanted it, he wanted the blood to run down his chin like the faint signs of bruising that had been on Mary's . . . he waited with no defiance and no defence.[147]

However, this religious feeling only lasts for that moment and gives way to the existentialist emptiness and loneliness for the protagonists. The voice of existentialist despair is obvious in this novel, too. 'Jazz' is the voice of the characters' nihilism. They are seen to be 'walking in a trance, at once fevered and sluggish'; as if they had been 'listening to a piece of music scored solely for French horns.'[148] After all their almost religious suffering, for these protagonists nothing really life-affirming emerges. Life beyond despair cannot fulfil itself.

III. *Corruption*: a glimpse beyond despair

His third novel, *Corruption*, is stylistically quite in line with the preceding novels. Here again we have self-indulged characters trying to come to grips with their tormented souls in a decadent surrounding. Peter Green, who also reviewed the previous novel as being against the mood of contemporary novel, sees similar problems with this novel: obsoleteness. Green believes that Mosley has all the virtues of a good novelist, except interesting themes: 'the hedonist rich are not interesting.'[149] The tragic narration is also present in this novel. The torturously romantic voice of *Corruption* is seen as a 'foggy language,' more suitable for poetry than novel-writing.[150]

However, *Corruption* supersedes the two previous novels as it tries to break both with tragic narrative and existentialism. It is an attempt to seek for the possibility of life beyond despair by turning the self-lacerating tragic voice of the narrator, Robert, against him. The hero is a step further than those in Mosley's previous novels, since in the end he sees that his *predicament* rather than his *heaven* was an illusion; in other words, he realises that he was not a prisoner and victim as he thought. The novel 'shows the steady involvement with the self as corruption: as a proud and terrible loneliness pretending to be enlightened sensuality.'[151] This time the tragic style turns against the protagonist and reveals his insistence on being a tragic victim. It is not, as was the case in Mosley's former novels, showing an alienated, tragic hero helpless before external forces (i.e., history, society, relationships) and internal forces (i.e., sincerity, consciousness of being an alienated, lonely individual) only. The reader and the hero both have a glimpse—a moment of illumination—where the despairing situation of the protagonist reveals itself rather as a state that he has decided to deceive himself into, than one imposed on him.

Corruption is the story of an impoverished aristocrat, Robert, who has been abandoned by his beloved older and richer cousin Kate in his youth and for whom he still harbours a hopeless love. He comes across his cousin some years later in Venice and it now seems as if she wants to leave her husband for him, but once again he is used by her and abandoned for another multi-millionaire. Years later, Robert comes across Kate yet again in Venice. She is now living in a Venetian palace with her lover and her child. The party attends a political demonstration in Trieste, at which Kate's child is in danger of getting hurt. Kate must now tell Robert the truth about the child in order to break through his bitterness and stir him to action. She tells him that the child is his, and was conceived on their only sexual encounter while they were school children and that she could not tell him then, for she loved him and did not want to ruin his future. Here there is a moment of illumination where Robert simultaneously glimpses his illusory despair and the possibility to go beyond this.

There is a feeling that he realises, that he has not really been a hopeless victim of Kate (and Fate), as he had believed all along, and that he could go on beyond his despairing situation:

> There was a blindness, then. I remember her eyes like the edge of a moon and a wave obscuring it. Then the wave withdrew and with my mind I saw the whole of it and it was clear and exact like the bed of a blue sea and I understood it. . . . There was the whole of my life there and everything I had done and it was as if I were a child that only waited to be reborn and there were the waves and the dead membranes to prevent me. I saw it in coral and crystal on the bed of the blue sea and I had to fight to give it life and to be forgiven it. I began to go back to where it should have been born before and her eye stretched again like the opening at the end of a cave and I let my arms trail away down the length of her. And as I moved away from this eye into which the light had suddenly come there was a pain and a desolation such as there always are in births when things are born into the necessity for forgiveness . . .[152]

At this point he experiences a moment of illumination where he sees the pattern of his ignorance, which has spread itself throughout the whole of his life. Simultaneously, by understanding this, he seems to gain a new hopeful outlook and perceive a chance to free himself from this pattern. He sees the possibility of a re-birth and a new start, but chooses to renounce it and fall back into his former situation:

> but I left her, and I went back to where there was a tunnel of tall trees and somewhere, like a bird, the sound of crying.[153]

His awareness of the possibility to break away from the 'dead membranes' of his past and start a new life reveals his rejection as a deliberate act of self-renunciation. It seems as if the imprisonment of the protagonist is rather a state welcomed by him, rather than one imposed on him. This makes him—as Richard Sullivan notices—a corrupted person. This whole tortured self-conscious self-observation, narrated in a most elaborate style, only leads the narrator back to the illusion of being a lonely, hopeless individual that he was in the beginning. Whereas Mosley's preceding heroes end up in states of hopelessness on grounds of seeing the necessity of leaving their states of illusion (i.e., prospects of happy bourgeois marriage, fulfilled passionate love or a realised happy bourgeois marriage), Robert ends up in a hopeless situation because he goes *back* into what reveals itself as an illusion. He not only has been taken to the point of insight, but—as opposed to Sartrean characters—has a glimpse of what might be beyond despair. However, he, too, does not know how to go on from this point and the only choice that he has is falling back into his former disillusioned state.

Corruption was an attempt to break out of this cross between tragedy and existentialism. In his autobiography Mosley writes: 'I was beginning to feel a compulsion to . . . face what did seem to be a rottenness in the old style of Romantic dalliance or agony . . . at the same time there seemed to be creeping in on me some dissatisfaction with novels: or at least with the way in which I had been following tradition in writing novels.'[154] However, he does not succeed in breaking away from this tradition, since—as Virgilia Peterson writes in *Sunday Herald Tribune* (26.1.58)—'the equivocal psychological facts of his story are drowned in the baroque flourish of his embellishments.' As a critic of the early stage of his writing, Mosley believes that it was due to this dramatic language—this convoluted voice— that Robert could not take the chance of going beyond despair. Robert could in a sudden, sensational and romantic style have a momentarily grasp of a state of freedom, but could not know how to go on into such a state.[155] In his tragic style Mosley's protagonists seem to be only able to weave themselves more and more into an unfree state, or put themselves deliberately in a position to be tortured as this is the nature of tragic heroes. This is the time when Mosley himself realised that if he wanted to explore the possibilities of real freedom in a state 'beyond despair,' then he must look for a new *style* to write this.[156]

Conclusion

In the early phase of his novel writing, *Spaces of the Dark*, *The Rainbearers*, and *Corruption*, Nicholas Mosley developed the first part of the theme that evolves throughout his artistic career: is real freedom possible for the individual in spite of the internal and external forces that rule and determine his life? In this phase of his writing, Mosley showed that freedom is often an illusion.

Mosley's obsession with enquiry into illusory freedom is foremost related to his experience of aristocracy during his childhood and youth.

He realised that in this class the only way to acquire freedom was to construct a virtual reality by obeying a set of self-made rules, which were then looked down upon as rules of a game, in order to make their restricting potentials impotent. However, this game could only go on as long as one did not openly admit to regarding every important matter of life as a game. In other words, hypocrisy and self-deception were necessary components. Furthermore, Mosley observed, in a state of being where all human activity is regarded as a meaningless game, the concept of freedom cannot make sense either. He saw the vicious circle which aristocrats had brought themselves into: the more they tried to preserve their games in pursuit of freedom, the less free they became. On the other hand, if the players did honestly face their hypocrisy and confessed that they regarded every matter of life as a game (except for the game itself!), then their virtual reality would have shattered and they would have been brought to the point of despair.

The disillusionment that Mosley experienced became a symptom of post-war years in Europe and Britain. In the West the enquiry into the possibility of freedom for the individual and life's sense-making have always been the cornerstones of metaphysical doctrines such as existentialism and Christianity. However, in Britain of the Fifties, a strong strand of writers tried to deal with disillusionment and feeling of uncertainty by way of radically ignoring and even criticising the enquiry into the possibility of freedom and the meaning of life. These writers asked for a return to English practicality, sense of social reality, and morality. Their language was respectively anti-romantic, realistic, vernacular and lacked the modernist complexity and ambiguity. These writers tended to write in the form of comedy and satire in order to criticise the modernist residues in the contemporary English society. The English academic and intelligentsia of this time were also highly suspicious of metaphysical doctrines. Language and logic were now seen as the main domains for philosophical enquiries. The concern of these philosophers was not understanding and putting forward solutions to the problems—mysteries—of existence and human condition anymore, but ascertaining truth by way of verifying statements empirically, logically and scientifically. There was a belief that philosophical problems could be tackled or put out of the way if they were formulated precisely or logically enough. These common-sense and no-nonsense attitudes backed the dominant strand of novels in Britain intellectually and stylistically.

It is not surprising that Nicholas Mosley was soon considered old-fashioned and out of date in such a literary and intellectual setting. This claim is at least partly unjustified as Mosley was concerned with a contemporary, albeit foreign doctrine: that is, existentialism. As Murdoch notices, the existentialists never showed in their works of art how life and consequently freedom beyond despair was possible. Beyond despair was death: an escape out of the nauseating lie of our reality. The only alternative to death was relapsing into the former state of disillusionment. Life beyond existentialist despair could not go on.

In his third novel Mosley tried to show that there is the possibility of freedom and life beyond despair, but succeeded at showing a glimpse of this possibility only. His hero, yet again, fell back into his state of world-weary disillusionment. At this point Mosley realised that as long as he enquired into the possibility of real freedom within the fusion of tragic and existentialist styles, he would not be able to depict it. The nature of the tragic hero necessitated the turgid and emotional self-lacerations which only lead to dramatic glimpses of metaphysical possibilities. The existential anti-hero, on the other hand, could neither have a glimpse of freedom in this world nor in a metaphysical reality, as for him both of them were states of illusions; man-made construction. Mosley saw that he must break out of these frameworks, if he wanted to seek the possibility of real freedom in life.

One cannot, however, dismiss his early novels as futile attempts. He himself realises that the involvement with these doctrines and styles of enquiry was necessary for a move towards a more alert state of understanding.[157] In order to break into new structures of thinking, he had to be acquainted with old ones. At such a stage the paradox of the so-called 'paradigm break' makes itself apparent: if one were to express a new concept, it must be done so in the old, familiar structures in order for it to be communicated intelligibly. However, if a new idea is expressed in the old structures, it is not new. This was Mosley's problem when he was trying to convey the possibility of freedom in his third novel *Corruption*. The idea expressed in the tragic style inevitably adapted to that style and lost its identity. On the other hand, if Mosley were to express his idea in a fully new language and style, it would not be communicated intelligibly. He therefore had to integrate his awareness of this paradox in his style of writing. Experimenting with the form of the novel where such a project could be realised became inevitable.

CHAPTER II

The paradox of freedom and aesthetic vision (1960s):
Meeting Place, Accident, Assassins, Impossible Object, Natalie Natalia

Introduction:
aesthetic observation and the possibility of freedom

> 'Liveliness is in the effort, even hopelessly, to get the best of both worlds . . .'[158]

In the second stage of his writing Mosley's investigations into the possibility of freedom rejected the findings of the previous stage. He came to see that the search for freedom did not have to end in death or existentialist despair—in other words, overcoming the paradox of freedom was possible.

In both his tragic novels and the following 'experimental' novels, Mosley examined the possibility of man's freedom of choice in face of moral dilemmas: the moment when a choice with possibly damaging consequences must be made. That is, when man's *responsibility* compels him to exploit his freedom of choice in order to decide *between* given mutually exclusive options—i.e., *either* this *or* that—where the only not morally evil choice would be *none* of the mutually exclusive options—i.e., *neither* this, *nor* that or *both* this *and* that. In such a situation man is trapped, as he cannot but choose evil. It must be noted that it is not the circumstances themselves that are 'evil' (and which man would have to make the best of), but his decision itself, which will also inevitably make him 'evil.' A surgeon, for example, faced with the decision between exposing a terminally ill patient to the ordeal of a risky operation, in order to possibly prolong his life and not undertaking the operation in order to spare the patient does not have to make an 'evil' choice and consequently become evil himself. Although both options have negative consequences, the decision itself is not morally bad. In this case the surgeon must make the best out of the situation. However, a man—as is the case with all the protagonists in Mosley's early novels (1950s) and experimental novels in the second phase of his writing (1960s)—who is faced with the choice between his beloved wife/family and his beloved mistress can only make an evil choice and consequently become evil. It is not morally possible for him to make the best out of his situation, because his choice is either to hurt his wife/family or his mistress (and in both cases also himself).

Mosley conceives of this paradox as an 'impossible situation' and often refers to it as an 'impossibility.'[159] As each choice logically excludes the other, the only way to resolve this impossibility within logic's 'either-or' system (i.e., *Tertia non datur*) is through renouncing the choice altogether.

In the early novels of Mosley this renunciation was portrayed either in tragic death or in (existentialist) despair. In these novels the struggles of the protagonists in face of their moral dilemmas ended in helplessness. Except for *Corruption*, where Robert has an ecstatic glimpse (albeit a short one) of hope in face of his moral dilemma, the heroic efforts of the early protagonists against their situation shows the extent to which they are trapped. Mosley himself sees his early protagonists as descendants of the larger part of European literature, where the heroes could not find any better way of resolving the paradox that they were facing than 'by some sort of "negative" way—if not martyrdom, then slightly nostalgic resignation.'[160]

> I think this sort of idea had been with me from the very beginning of my writing novels: my first three novels had fairly conventional tragic/romantic stories: the first about the impossibilities attendant on war, the second about those attendant on romantic love; in both the protagonists were doomed to tragedy, whatever their good intentions. In the third novel, *Corruption*, there was an effort to break out of this conventional pattern: but still, life could only 'work' through renunciation.[161]

One can see a clear shift in the content and form of Mosley's novels after *Corruption*, beginning with *Meeting Place* (1962) and fully realised in *Accident* (1965), *Impossible Object* (1968) and *Natalie Natalia* (1971). In these novels he set to explore the possibilities of overcoming moral dilemmas by breaking out of the pattern of renunciation. Contrary to his early heroes, the protagonists of Mosley's experimental novels can deal with their moral dilemmas in a positive way by choosing *the only* morally not evil choice. In other words, by doing the 'impossible' and choosing both of the *given mutually* exclusive alternatives they can meet the right choice and consequently influence the outcome of events in a morally 'good' way. However, since this cannot be done in a logical framework, Mosley's protagonists have to do this within a different framework, where the co-existence of mutually exclusive alternatives is possible.

> One cannot alter the impossibilities or tragedies of life; but by 'standing back' from them—in art? in a state of mind within oneself of which

art is a model?—one can make them possible; and thus life can be glimpsed for what it often is—a going concern.[162]

Mosley's idea that this could only be done in an aesthetic framework brings to mind Kierkegaard's differentiation between the aesthetic and the ethical.[163] For Kierkegaard the aesthetic is establishing a *conjunction* of the either-or. From the aesthetic point of view one doesn't *choose* between the either and the or, but rather tries to understand how to experience them simultaneously. The ethical, on the other hand, is establishing a *disjunction* of the either-or conjunction and thus the compulsion to choose between the either and the or. However, whereas from Kierkegaard's point of view the move should essentially be from the aesthetic to the ethical, Mosley finds it to be in the exact opposite direction: namely, from the ethical to the aesthetic.[164]

> To take life simply as a moral business doesn't work, because choices in fact are often choices between evils: . . . but still, morally, one cannot choose bad. This is the sort of 'impossible' predicament that one can stand back from, however, . . . and perhaps get some working view of it aesthetically: to do this is like learning a *style* rather than a code of morals.[165]

Within a moral dilemma the ethical on its own always brings the individual to a dead-end because it primarily compels the individual to choose 'good' in a situation where he is prevented from doing so due to the paradoxical nature of the moral dilemma. The aesthetic, on the other hand, enables the individual to step outside the moral dilemma (and thus free himself from its paradoxicality), and ironically do what the ethical obliges him to do, which is choosing 'good.'

> The moral and imaginative faculty are very closely related: . . . For the exercise of one's imaginative faculty becomes a moral imperative: the writing of a serious novel becomes an aid-to-life.[166]

In this sense Mosley's experiments with form can be clearly linked to the shift in his ideas and outlooks. The idea behind the novel provided him with new technical and formal challenges, which he tried to tackle in his experimental novels. Mosley, like his experimental precursor and contemporaries became acutely aware of the importance of novel's form for its content: the idea that the content *adapts* to the form and structure. In his case, the old tragic style was appropriate for conveying the trap of ethical dilemmas, but not the way out of it. In his experimental novels he was able to go beyond his old novels and show an aesthetic way out of the trap. The following will look at the development of Mosley's ideas and their impact on his new conception of the novel.

Mosley's conversion to Christianity

I.   Mosley's dismay with Rationality and his conversion to Christianity

The shift in the content and form of Mosley's novels runs parallel to the shift in his personal life. In an interview with John O'Brien he said: 'basically, I think, the change [in my style of writing] was due to my own desire, determination, to feel less trapped.'[167] In the early phase of his artistic career, Mosley had examined the situation of people trapped by their moral dilemmas and their conditioning. Now he started to examine the possibility of freeing oneself from these by making choices where good could prevail. Mosley's conversion to Anglo-Catholicism is central to his seeing the possibility of freedom of choice and thus 'feeling less trapped.' Whereas in the earlier phase of his career, he had been preoccupied with the feeling of existentialist imprisonment, in this phase of his life Christianity granted him with a more sovereign and liberated outlook in important areas of his life, such as his relationship to his father and the tension between his artistic career and his personal relationships. It is important to point out that Mosley's understanding of Christianity is controversial and not at all shared by all believers of the Catholic faith. For the purpose of this thesis, however, it is not useful to discuss this controversy, as such a discussion will not contribute to our examination of Mosley's understanding of Christianity and its influence on his works.

Nicholas Mosley's conversion to Anglo-Catholicism took place at a time when he was increasingly becoming aware of the need to get away from the cynicism and nihilism that he had acquired both by his background and during the years of fighting in Italy.[168] At the time of war and right after it nihilism and cynicism seemed to be the only possibilities known to Mosley for handling his dismay with rationality and reason.[169] In the following it will be shown how Mosley's dismay—on both the personal and socio-political levels—developed into a nihilism, only to become an existentialist despair which gave way to a conversion to Anglo-Catholicism.

Through Paul, the hero of his first novel *Spaces of the Dark*, Mosley expressed how he had come to see the world as 'inevitably a place of killing one's friends, of worshipping a god that sanctifies such murder, of defiling and destroying the beauty that might be loved.'[170] In this world sanity could only be maintained by the 'avoidance of all loyalties, the denial of ideals, the rejection of all dogma, the development and initiation of the individual soul in defiance of the communal madness.'[171] Mosley's pessimism was typical of post-war Europe, where, if not a lack of belief in, at least a suspicion towards rational doctrines and their capacity for sense-making was on the agenda. Mosley believes that this senselessness was, however, not so much felt throughout the war, as during the peace that followed it:[172] 'I was very cynical about the war, yet I thought one had to fight in the war. I don't think that I thought that it would be wrong to fight. After the war one did think what had been the point of it all? A lot of one's friends had been killed. But the feeling was not really so much what was the point of the war, because there was some point to the war, but what was the point of peace? Where was it going?'[173] The horrors of the war and the systematic mass murders were not alone responsible for the post-war disillusion with the redeeming powers of rationalism. The disillusionment of these years was mainly due to the advent of the Cold War—or the 'Phoney Peace.'[174] Mosley remembers that as early as 1948 the threat of a Third World War and, thanks to the Bomb, total annihilation loomed over the world. Simultaneously, however, there was also the belief that the Bomb was an indispensable guarantor against total annihilation and the Third World War. This paradoxicality restored the feeling of entrapment: 'the world,' according to Mosley, 'seemed to be absolutely mad'[175] and rationality seemed to be incapable of making an order out of this chaos and offer a way out of the madness.

Mosley's suspicion towards rationalism was not only the result of historical changes, but had its roots in his attitude towards his father's politics.[176] Oswald Mosley's reappearance on the political scene as the leader of the Union Movement—a continuation of the pre-war fascist union—further persuaded Nicholas about the inadequacy of rationalism for dealing with important issues. Its simplifications inevitably coupled with hypocrisy made it an inadequate tool for dealing with complicated issues. This was revealed to him foremost by Oswald's 'solutions' for the problems raised by the chaos after the war. One instance, which illustrates this tension between father and son is the scheme of the Union Movement for dealing with the social problems, which had arisen in post-war England with the immigration of vast numbers of people from the former and also the existing British colonies in the 1950s.[177] In 1958 Oswald Mosley stood for Parliament at the forthcoming election in the North Kensington constituency, which included the black immigrant community in Notting Hill and was now the site of street fights between groups of white and black youths. Oswald's aim was to bring order to the area through a scheme in which immigrants were to be repatriated—as a last resource by force—'with fares paid . . . and to good jobs with good wages.'[178] For Nicholas the trouble with this seemingly 'reasonable' and 'rational' plan—besides its latent appeal to racism and isolationism—was its disregard for complexities, its reductionism and simplifications. When he argued with his father about the wrongs of applying force, his father would argue that no one in their *right* mind would have to be forced back to their native land, where they could earn a good living.[179] The impracticality of such a scheme—'my father imagined that humans could be arranged and rearranged'[180]—made Nicholas wonder not only about the applicability of rational, blueprint solutions to real life problems, but also about his father's political credibility. Nicholas Mosley could not see how people could vote for Oswald according to the 'rationale' in his arguments, when 'humans,' as it seemed, 'were not so much interested in rationality as *dependent* on often unconscious needs and passions.'[181] This is what showed Mosley the indispensability of hypocrisy and self-deception for faith in rationality. Oswald Mosley would, on one hand, offer these reasonable and fair schemes, but while looking for voters he would not try to win them over via their rational faculties and reason, but by indeed trying to appeal to their 'unconscious needs and passions.' At his Notting Hill campaign in 1958, Oswald would suddenly switch from promoting his reasonable case 'about the need to create jobs in the West Indies,' to 'some uproar about black men keeping teenage white girls in attics.'[182] When Nicholas tried to show his father the rational and moral discrepancies of the latter's political behaviour, he was faced with his father's fierce denials, verbal attacks and rationalisations.[183] The only sincere way to treat this disillusionment with rationality seemed to be either a cynical acceptance—facing—of the prevailing madness or death. Any other way would be hypocrisy.

II. The appeal of existentialism to Mosley

Paul, the hero of *Spaces of the Dark*, is a typical existentialist (anti-)hero. Existentialism was naturally attractive for Mosley and many of his contemporaries, as it justified and indoctrinated what they felt: it neatly conveyed the inadequacy of rational systems and doctrines and revealed all of the taken-for-granted values as social constructions, which limited man's freedom. It heralded the possibility of true freedom. However, its promise of empowerment quickly gave way to helplessness. Mosley, too, reached this despair shortly after his preoccupation with existentialism. It ultimately failed in his eyes because of the impracticality of its notion of freewill. This philosophy could not deal with the claim at its heart: namely, the claim that the individual was fully *responsible* for his actions (i.e., possessed freewill) in an intrinsically meaningless world.[184]

Existentialism showed that the notion of life having an intrinsic meaning or purpose was an artificial, social construction which restricted man's freewill. Within this philosophy the realisation of this freewill was man's only *raison d'être*. The first step towards this realisation would thus be facing the artificiality of these constructions. Consequently, the primary and only virtue for this stage was sincerity, necessary for 'the demanding experience of a radical reflexion,' which would take the individual 'up to the point of insight, realisation and despair.'[185] Having gone through these stages, the individual was then supposed to achieve his full freedom.

Initially Mosley was especially impressed by the two prominent exponents of this doctrine, Camus and Sartre, who had 'the idea that, really, you made your decision. You made your life, but there was no reason why you should make your life one way rather than any other way.'[186] This seemed to be a liberating message at first sight, since it empowered man with the capability of acting without relying on any outside elements. At the same time, however, existentialism insisted on the imperative of *facing* one's helplessness in a world discarded of all meaning or purpose.[187] Although self-contradictory, this was a very liberating view for Mosley and his post-war generation, who were 'young and on the loose'[188]—on one hand it told them to do as they willed, and on the other, it commanded them to face their helplessness and purposelessness. Thus it empowered them to live for the moment, where one could be negligent of the consequences of one's actions. But the feeling of empowerment quickly gave way to that of helplessness as '[one] had no idea what to do with [one's] freedom of will'[189] in a *meaningless and arbitrary world*. What

Existentialism succeeded in was showing the *illusory* quality of life, but what it failed in was to show what was to be done—how life was to go on—*after* having been confronted with illusions.

Mosley himself felt this despair of living by illusions very early in the Fifties. His marriage and attempts at settling down in 'would-be Gardens of Eden,'[190] only temporarily helped him by sorting out some of his personal feelings and giving him an aim in life.[191] Only a few years after his marriage he started to have 'waves of, what . . . would be called, [a] clinical feeling of helplessness. . . . But it wasn't an intellectual feeling. It was a physical feeling. . . . It was certainly a feeling of what was the point of getting out of bed?'[192] Like Sartre's heroes of *Les Chemins de la Liberté*, Mosley was 'taken up to the point of insight, realisation, despair'[193] and knew that all the *reasons* that he had for *not* feeling despair were inadequate. Like Sartre's heroes he encountered 'the fear of the senseless':[194]

> I had got what I wanted: I was lucky and in love; I loved the farm with its mountain stream that glistened in sun or rain. And yet . . . I would sit up suddenly in bed at night with the impression of the blade of a guillotine coming swinging in a horizontal arc to cut off my head.[195]

And again like Sartre's heroes he did not have the means to get over this despair. Within the existentialist realm of thinking his choices were those of the hero of his favourite novel at the time, Faulkner's *Wild Palms*: namely; grief and nothing.[196] Through his encounter with Fr. Raynes, however, Mosley was able to escape both of these choices altogether and find a way of life 'beyond despair.'

III. The necessity of existentialist despair for conversion to Christianity

> On Sunday morning, in some outrage at all this, I said I preferred a universe that admitted that it was crazy. Father Raynes said, 'You'd better get out of it quick.'[197]

It is important to note that the existentialist despair of Mosley was an integral part of his conversion. Without this despair he wouldn't have felt the urgency to save himself by putting his life into a different context. Mosley's conversion to Christianity is perhaps the most important turning point in his life and artistic career. It would not be too farfetched to divide Mosley's novels into two main periods of B. C. and A. D.! His novels before his conversion were beset with a turgid 'baroque'[198] prose, which was used to depict a feeling of helplessness and despair. In contrast, his novels after his conversion to Anglo-Catholicism—up to his latest published un-novel *Inventing God* (2001)—have a much more transparent prose through which the possibilities of freedom and optimism can be glimpsed.

Mosley's conversion to Christianity was triggered by his encounter with an Anglo-Catholic Monk of the Community of the Resurrection called Father Raynes. Mosley sees his conversion neither as an intellectual nor an emotional event, but rather an experiential one; that is an event which cannot fully be explained in rational terms: 'It was this strange experience. It sort of happened. And for the next forty-five years I have gone on trying to learn what this means?'[199] In his biography of Fr. Raynes Mosley gives a detailed account of his first meeting with him,[200] during which Fr. Raynes was neither trying to reason with his audience, nor to emotionally arouse them. Mosley remembers that Fr. Raynes did not even seem keen on winning his audience over: 'He spoke with extraordinary hesitancy as though he was quite shy of putting this over. . . . It was a great struggle for him to have the brashness to say the things he was saying. And I found that very appealing. He wasn't using words to go at you.'[201] This, especially when one considers Mosley's disapproval of his father's rhetoric and manipulative way with words, attracted him:

> [Conversion] is a very strange experience.[202] I suddenly thought—Look, everything I am thinking is absolute rubbish. It simply doesn't matter what I feel. This man knows something; 'something came through him' (I don't know what this phrase means, but I think it is the religious way of putting it). I thought—I am now at a moment of my life, where I either accept that there is something here and start the process of finding out more about it or I say, I am going to turn my back on what I *know*. That is the sort of key moment in life: one can so easily, in a moment of weakness, turn one's back . . . So for a long time I found out more about it and the way one found out about it was by becoming a practising Christian.[203]

The conscious observation of Christianity, however, did not come easily to Mosley. It took him almost seven years—from 1951, where he made his first confession, to 1958 where he took over the editorship of the Anglo-Catholic magazine *Prism*—before he started to lead a committed

'Christian life' in the conventional sense of the word, which was to last for another seven years. It is also important to note that the first step of Mosley's conscious conversion—his first confession—took place when he was experiencing a moral dilemma or a practically impossible situation in his life: a situation where he both wanted to be a good and honest husband and at the same time the lover of a woman other than his wife without causing anybody any pain. The authority and knowledge of Fr. Raynes initiated an opening in Mosley's attitude towards Christianity, but it was foremost the ethical and practical side of Christianity—its treatment of the question 'how should I act?'—that triggered Mosley's active conversion. In due course, though, he became aware of the limitations of Christian ethics and moved towards an aesthetic perception of Christianity, which made him leave organised religion altogether. Hence in Christianity Mosley found the possibility of dealing with moral dilemmas firstly on a conventional ethical level, and gradually on an aesthetic level. An examination of his most crucial moral dilemmas—or as he puts it, 'moments of absolute choice'[204]—in relation to his writing shows how his two respective understandings of Christianity—i.e., the ethical and the aesthetic—led to the experimental period of his writing.

Shortly before and during the course of his conversion Mosley was confronted with two moral dilemmas: firstly, his extra-marital affair with a woman to whom in his autobiography he refers by her fictional name in *The Rainbearers* (i.e., 'Mary'),[205] and secondly his relationship with his father. Existentialism failed to help him out of these dilemmas because of its insistence that the individual was completely on his own in the world. In this doctrine all human relations to and feeling of *responsibility* for things or persons 'other' than oneself were social constructions. The only true imperative was to face and dismantle these artifices and achieve one's full freedom. For Mosley this seemed to be a simplification of the complexities of real life.[206] As Iris Murdoch puts it, Sartrean Existentialism 'by-passes the complexity of the world of ordinary human *relations*'[207] on all levels of life. The inadequacy of this simplicism is at its most obvious in a moral dilemma, which is a moment when the complexity of human relations becomes especially acute. In this moment one is responsible for one's actions and choices foremost because of its effect on the 'other.' Without the reality of such relations a moral dilemma would of course not arise. From the existentialist point of view, then, Mosley's problems were non-problems. One could say that Existentialism's disregard for human relations to the world outside them had something in common with what Mosley reproached his father's views for: their disregard for the complexities of human realities, which could not be only rationally observed and defined.

The treatment of moral dilemmas is crucial for Mosley both in fictitious and real-life terms. The movement from the ethical treatment to the aesthetic treatment of these dilemmas is the turning point in his writing. In his first novel, *Spaces of the Dark*,[208] his hero Paul had to face two moral dilemmas simultaneously: firstly, that of having killed his best friend accidentally in a battle and secondly that of getting emotionally involved with both the sister and the lover of the deceased. His second novel, *The Rainbearers* reflected Mosley's preoccupation with a 'real life' dilemma, where Mosley himself became emotionally involved with another woman soon after his marriage. His dilemma was how could he have a good marriage and a relationship with this woman without causing anybody any pain?[209] In fictitious terms, Mosley's hero could only deal with his moral dilemma by getting himself killed in the end (or by having the author kill him.) In real life Mosley could not deal with his dilemma by rationally dismissing it as a social artifice. He only came to terms with it by discarding the existentialist simplifications and converting to Anglo-Catholicism, which offered him a framework for a serious preoccupation with moral dilemmas.[210]

IV. Conventional Christianity and the practicality of ethics: the ethical treatment of his relationship with 'Mary/Kate' and with his father

Christianity in conventional terms gave Mosley a framework—a set of rules—within which to act. [211] What Existentialism had taken away was returned by Christianity: the sense of morality and redemption. Primarily it was Christianity's dealing with moral dilemmas that triggered Mosley's first step towards showing commitment to Christianity by the act of confession.[212] In his autobiography Mosley recalls how he had then thought of this act 'as a jump in the dark,' by way of which the impossibility of life might be handled.[213] However, Mosley eventually understood the ethical as a *stage* necessary for conceiving the aesthetic vision of Christianity. He, as was mentioned earlier and will be discussed in detail later, came to claim that Christianity was ultimately leading man towards an aesthetic rather than an ethical vision.

The stages of conversion which Mosley went through have been often dramatised in the tradition of English literature—John Bunyan's *The*

Pilgrim's Progress springs readily to mind. In the previous chapter it was shown how Mosley's early novels dramatise his acceptance, struggle and rejection of Existentialism as a context for dealing with the madness that he felt surrounded by. In this chapter, his early novels will briefly be seen from the viewpoint of his conversion. From this viewpoint they dramatise the stages that he went through in order to come to accept Christianity: sin, the encounter and struggle with 'Truth,' doubt, despair, self-laceration, confession, repentance and finally acceptance.

Mosley's fictional treatment of his unhappy affair with 'Mary' illustrates the stages of his conversion well. The affair took place when he was half way through his novel *The Rainbearers* and in a way resulted in his conversion to Anglo-Catholicism. It lasted a short time only and, as a result of Mosley's decision to repent and end it, had almost near fatal consequences for 'Mary.'[214] The years in which Mosley tried to write this novel and also get 'Mary's' consent to publish it (1951-55) were the years where he was caught in a Sisyphus-like struggle with his conscience and the Christian calling, which, being in a Christian context, did not continue in the never-ending ancient Greek cycle, but got him to a destination. In his novel *The Rainbearers* Mosley's hero—reflecting Mosley's mood of this time—sins, hates himself for this, repents and feels damned. The more he tries not to choose evil and cause pain, the more he is caught up in it. Richard, who is modelled according to how Mosley saw himself in relation to his wife and 'Mary' at the time, is depicted as follows by one of the characters, Mr. Gabriel, who ends up marrying the misused and wounded Mary:

> He has been rotten from the start—a man with no hope of anything but rottenness, someone who preys upon what is given him and then smashes it and runs in fear. . . . He will go back to his wife's bed and he will beg her cold forgiveness and then he'll be off again for another bed to make filthy. . . .
>
> . . . He's finished, empty, someone with too many curses from the beginning, a wastrel rich and impotent on the edge of the world's decadence like a plant that goes to seed without ever flowering.[215]

The novel becomes a sort of self-flagellation and self-deprecation. The hero, however, seems not to find comfort or a sense of freedom through this act of penance, but rather perpetual suffering and helplessness. In face of his moral dilemma he realises that a 'good' choice is not possible.

However, the recognition of this helpless and, to use an existentialist term, nausea is necessary for a further evolution. In *Corruption*, the following novel, the hero Robert goes a step further by repenting of his sins and accepting his moral responsibility for the heroine's (in this novel 'Mary' is called 'Kate') fate without delving into nausea and self-pity. He does not try to justify himself or even put things to right, but solemnly accepts his loss and glimpses that by accepting it he is freeing himself from it.

> There was a blindness, then. I remember her eyes like the edge of a moon and a wave obscuring it. Then the wave withdrew and with my mind I saw the whole of it and it was clear and exact like the bed of a blue sea and I understood it. . . . There was the whole of my life there and everything I had done and it was as if I were a child that only waited to be reborn and there were the waves and the dead membranes to prevent me. . . . And as I moved away from this eye into which the light had suddenly come there was a pain and a desolation such as there always are in births when things are born into the necessity for forgiveness. . . . but I left her, and I went back to where there was a tunnel of tall trees and somewhere, like a bird, the sound of crying.[216]

The scales have fallen from Robert's eyes and now he can see the absurdity of his illusion: what he has done cannot be undone by a 'selfless' act of taking Kate and her child away from her present husband and life. He must leave her. In the previous chapter it was shown how Robert has only a glimpse of life beyond despair without really being able to realise the possibilities of such a life. In the 'tunnel of trees' we could only see the existentialist fear of the unknown. However, in the Christian context, the simile of a 'tunnel' promises that the hero after having recognised his mistake and responsibility (i.e., confession) and gone through an ordeal (i.e., penance) will come out into the light on the other side (i.e., redemption). Robert's feeling of entrapment is in this sense different from that of Paul's in *Spaces of the Dark* and Richard's in *The Rainbearers* because Robert is voluntarily, as opposed to helplessly, going through an ordeal, after which things sort themselves out and 'the light at the end of the tunnel' will be perceived.

In real life, after finishing *Corruption* (1956) Mosley himself went into some sort of an ordeal and, again to use a Christian term, put on his 'hair-shirt' and abided by the Anglo-Christian disciplines and values.[217] His affair with 'Mary/Kate' had come to a close and now he felt that the only way that he could go on was to admit his wrong-doing and humble himself by going into a sort of asceticism.[218] Mosley believes that while the existentialists could not properly define and deal with moral and ascetic values, Nietzsche, the most eminent destroyer of ascetic values, could. Mosley thus explains his ethical and ascetic period in Nietzschean terms:

> One of the things that Nietzsche went on about was the idea that old moralities don't work anymore and that there has to be a transformation. [But] Nietzsche also said that these old, ascetic moral values were absolutely crucial to humans at a certain stage of development. [Humans] needed [these values] in order to face themselves. . . . But moral values had gone wrong in modern world: they had lost their force. We were now in a worse position than ever because we had no values to look at ourselves by; to transform ourselves by. That was the truth that people had to face now. So, everyone must now find new values by which to see and transform themselves.[219]

After writing *Corruption* this became an imperative for Mosley:

> It was absolutely necessary to get out of existentialist despair. And get into ascetic values, disciplines, rules of life. For me that was the only way to get a mirror and look at myself.[220]

In 1958 he accepted the editorship of the Anglo-Catholic magazine *Prism* for two years and moved out of London to the country with his family where he tried to lead a good Christian life. He became the churchwarden of their local Church, worked with a group of Christian youths, prayed, gave to charity and, as he puts it, did a lot of 'either-or.'[221] Mosley believes that this 'torturous stuff'[222] was crucial for learning the most important Christian creed that one's beliefs were not only demonstrated by one's words, but also by one's activity and one's style of activity.[223] This creed gave rise to the turning point in his relationship with his father and his treatment of this change within the Christian context.

Mosley's relationship with his father culminated in a second 'moment of absolute choice.' In this relationship he did not carry the same sort of responsibility as he did in regards to his affair with 'Mary' and his marriage and fatherhood. While he directly felt responsible for the damages caused through his affair, he was not an accomplice of his father's misdeeds and criticised them severely. However, as Oswald's son he felt an indirect responsibility for putting the wrongs of his father right not only by means of criticism, but also by engaging in political activities. Mosley's relationship to his father is not artistically treated in his novels, except marginally in the transitional novel *Meeting Place*, which marks the beginnings of his experimental style. However, his confrontation with his father and the resulting years of his engagement in anti-Apartheid politics were of utmost importance for his ethical and aesthetic conception of Christianity.

Nicholas Mosley's 'idyllic wartime and just post-war relationship' with his father, during the time which 'he had been imprisoned and then had led the life of a retired country gentleman, had come to an end in 1947 when [Oswald] had gone back into politics as the leader of Union Movement.'[224] As was mentioned before, Mosley felt despair at his father's rationalisations, rhetoric and his refusal to see the discrepancy between his own schemes and his political campaigns.[225] Oswald Mosley claimed, on one hand, that he wanted to gain his votes by drawing reasonable and 'fair' schemes, but, on the other, when it came to winning votes he relied on tapping the weaknesses, the fears and prejudices of his audience by racist comments, manipulative words and his famous aptitude for debates.[226] Nicholas now felt that a confrontation with his father was absolutely necessary.[227] This confrontation, which broke up their relationship for many years, is similar to Mosley's confrontation with 'Mary/Kate.' The similarity lies in his feeling responsibility within his relations (as a lover; as a son). In contrast to the existentialists, Mosley could not, to put it in Murdoch's words, 'by-pass . . . the complexity of the world of ordinary human *relations*.'[228] It is a matter of course, then, that in both cases his confrontations took place within the context of Christian ethics.

In his autobiography Mosley mentions how it strikes him today that his socio-political stance within the Anglo-Catholic context was partly a reaction to his father's 'knock-down' attitude and his policies.[229] Christianity demanded that he criticise his father 'by activity and style of his activity and not just by words.'[230] Bearing in mind that Oswald Mosley and his Party followers were justifiers of Apartheid, Nicholas Mosley's involvement with the anti-Apartheid activities of the Community of the Resurrection in South Africa and in England in the early Sixties could be seen as a way of coming to terms with his father. In the following years Nicholas Mosley tried to expose the English public to the evils of Apartheid by writing many articles analysing the nature of Apartheid and pointing out its dangers. He witnessed the increasing waves of arrests of

African and white anti-Apartheid activists in South Africa and contributed to the campaign against the arrest of the anti-Apartheid fighter Hannah Stanton both in Johannesburg and in England in a time, where the English public was not only hardly susceptible for any such campaigns, but also mainly suspicious of any activity against racism in Africa as being hostile propaganda.[231] Via the Community of the Resurrection he became involved in looking after some of the South Africans who came to England as political refugees. In this way he met Desmond Tutu, who was on his way to study at King's College, London; and Thabo Mbeki, whom Mosley helped to get into Sussex University.[232]

The Christian doctrine of ethics thus helped Mosley resolve his two major moral dilemmas by way of submitting to the rules and trying to bring words and deeds in concord with each other. On a practical level, then, Christian ethics helped him put right what he believed had gone wrong. The cost of this involved a *retreat* into a narrower life where he was able to concentrate on what the rules demanded, but due to its objective— i.e., undoing what *had been*—this retreat was mainly directed towards the *past*. It was noted earlier how Mosley could see the benefits of this life in Nietzschean terms. Nevertheless, he also agrees with Nietzsche's appeal for a life beyond ascetic ideals based on his own experiential conception of asceticism: 'But [asceticism] was also an illusion. As Nietzsche would say, [in asceticism] one is *willing* something negative. Having been through it myself I could see what Nietzsche meant. That was a *retreat* from life.'[233] Mosley's understanding of the ethical and practical gradually gave way to a spiritual—or aesthetic—understanding of Christianity which demanded yet another radical change in his life. In the following we will look at the development of Mosley's liberation, which eventually led to the experimental phase of his writing.

V. Liberation from the ethical: aesthetic vision and the incompleteness of rules

> [I felt] responsible for illusions; mistakes. [I felt] I must purify myself in some sort of asceticism. . . . Having gone through that (there is no way to skip that stage) at some further stage when one has done one's penance, there is, according to the Christian attitude, eventually a liberation of the spirit.[234]

> After these three novels I gave up writing novels for a time; I was dissatisfied with romantic doom, yet didn't see much way

> around it. I became something of a Christian, specifically in an effort to find something of all this. But *it was in my process of getting out of conventional Christianity rather than getting in*, that I got hold of the idea that all right, life is impossible, but once you know it's impossible, all right, it mysteriously isn't.[235]

The 'truth' that became apparent to Mosley, after having undergone the trial of ethical behaviour, was the incompleteness of ethics as a means for meeting the right choice in face of moral dilemmas where one's choices are between two evils, neither of which one can choose from a *moral point of view*.[236] In such a situation moral rules inevitably reach a paradox and thus their own limits. The individual is thus paralysed, as he now cannot make a choice by applying the either-or of ethics. Consequently, he must find a way of choosing (i.e., taking the necessary action for solving the moral dilemma) outside the logical, either-or system of ethics. He therefore, needs a realm, within which he can deal with this paradox.

After having read the Bible through[237] Mosley felt that this was precisely what the Bible was teaching. The Bible's paradoxical message seemed to be that by committing oneself to the rules of Christianity on a simple level, one learnt to liberate oneself from them and consequently from conventional religion.[238] One might argue that through the practice of Christian ethics Mosley experienced what Existentialist philosophy advocated, but could not successfully realise: namely, that all values and regulations were man-made. However, whereas Christianity would not regard these manmade constructs as *illusions*, but structures necessary for the operation of freedom of choice,[239] Existentialism saw these constructs as illusions only. In this way, the Existentialist doctrine called for the individual to choose and at the same time declared ethics—those constructs through which choice-making was made possible—as illusions which *had to be completely discarded*. The application of these constructs—or ethics—by an existentialist individual would thus go against the sincerity principle of this philosophy and would be called hypocritical. This is a contradictory statement as making a choice is ultimately a moral matter: one chooses *either* this *or* that in order for something *rather than* other to result. Having destroyed all either-or rules necessary for choice-making, the existentialist individual became paralysed. Existentialism, Mosley believes, offered the individual on a theoretical basis a freedom of movement, which in end effect was redundant.

> I think the trouble with Existentialism is that they talk about freedom, but freedom in a vacuum. Freedom in a vacuum isn't anything. It is being like an astronaut, who has broken away from his spaceship and is free . . . Existentialists were rather like astronauts, . . . floating in space. So what if they [were] free?[240]

This feeling of paralysis and helplessness could only be overcome if the individual would set an end to it through physical self-annihilation—as was the case with many fictional and non-fictional existentialists—or if he returned to what he had discarded as an illusion formerly: namely, rules according to which choices could be made. Mosley believes that the serious existentialists felt this:

> The only way that Sartre—with all his existentialist freedom—could feel something was happening was by calling himself a Marxist. A lot of Existentialists in the Fifties or Sixties either called themselves a Marxist or a Maoist. There was no point in just being free. You had to be in relation to some order.[241]

The paradox of the necessity of restricting structures (i.e., order) for freedom crushed the existentialist doctrine: by going back to what they had denounced as illusions they now had to live a lie, for Marxism, according to the existentialist doctrine, would be just as much a system of artificial rules (and thus illusory structures) of conduct as Conventional Christian ethics. Marxism assigns the individual a purpose in life which it believes would be reached if the individual acted according to a particular code of behaviour. The Existentialists thus sawed the branch that they were sitting on and collapsed by their own rationale.

In Christianity, however, Mosley felt that he could get through ethics without falling into existentialist despair because Christianity, as Mosley puts it, provided a 'built-in safety net.'[242] It simultaneously showed the necessity of ethical rules and the contingency of any particular form of ethics. For Mosley the Christian *Weltanschauung*, allowed for a distance to the rules—an awareness that all perceivable rules were manmade, as God's rule was ultimately incomprehensible by man—while demanding their application according to the needs of the situation. One could thus conclude that the 'safety-net' which Mosley mentions is Christianity's awareness of paradoxicality at its own heart and at heart of all human matters. Christianity not only did not try to avoid or rationally resolve the paradox but took sustenance from it. In his *Experience and Religion* (1965) Mosley elaborates on this by examining the Church on one hand—

> The rules give order, reference, but also make death and petrifaction. In Christian terms the rule-giving institution is the Church. By perpetuating the rules [it is] both the life-giver and the destroyer. It stands opposed to everything that a free man stands for. . . . [Simultaneously] preserved in the framework of the Church is the truth of the Story, the history, the art, the secret. Within it the possibilities of freedom are held, through which freedom could be experienced. (How else could it be preserved except in something so paradoxical?)[243]

And freedom on the other—

> Spontaneity, the other extreme, has its own paradoxes; the tragedies of which are also obvious. Spontaneity is healing, life giving. [It is] Also pain, impossibility, only finding itself in death. People who live for the moment [seem to be] liberated, joyous, but also [have] a will to extinction, in which nothing becomes real except themselves—and finally they find themselves in a vacuum.[244]

In Existentialism the individual's freedom of movement is only this spontaneity, which eventually ends in a nothingness on grounds of the inability of the existentialist rationale to deal with the paradox. On the opposite pole, Conventional ethical Christianity seemed to dwell only in the realm of rule and also ended in 'petrifaction,' again due to its inability to deal with the paradox. In neither of the situations did man have a freedom of choice; in both cases he was 'taken over by necessity.'[245] The aesthetic or spiritual (mystical) viewpoint of Christianity made Mosley see that man's only freedom of choice lay 'within the area between law, the recognition of the way things work (ought to work), and spontaneity, the altering (or creation) of the way things can work.'[246] What was required, thus, was a state of mind where a person could hold himself between opposites and by this influence the outcome of his choice, instead of directly aiming at it.[247] This is vital especially when one is caught in a moral dilemma. As was discussed previously, in 'an absolute moment of choice' the individual is compelled to choose evil due to the mutually exclusive options. The dilemma compels the individual to move in one direction only and inevitably *choose* the wrong option (or evil): to put it in Christian terms, the dilemma sets out to blind him. But by holding all the choices in his mind he can distance himself from the dilemma and look at what the situation truly is; what his responsibilities for and his possibilities in the situation are. The moral rules thus lose their absolute value and become relative: they are only important as means for making the right choice *according to the situation*: in a different situation one set of moral behaviour might be wrong or even immoral.

This understanding is precisely the point where Mosley's movement in the opposite direction to that of Kierkegaard crystallised itself. While the latter argued for a universality of morals from the Christian point of view, Mosley came to see the relativity of morals from within the Christian context: or better still, he came to see that *one could only be moral if one saw the relativity of ethics*. And the relativity of ethics could only be conceived if one appropriated an aesthetic point of view from which one could see the situation as a *whole*: that is, with all the responsibilities and possibilities involved. This is what, according to Mosley, is called 'informing the conscience' in terms of Christian moral philosophy and what Mosley himself means by the 'aesthetic':

> I use the word 'aesthetic.' The word 'aesthetic,' however, has such overtones. What I mean by it is some sort of *informed* style of life. Christians used to talk about this. When one talked to Christians about moral philosophy, then they said, . . . yes, you act according to your conscience, but you have to go through enormous trouble to inform your conscience properly. Your active effort goes into keeping your conscience properly informed. That is your duty. That is what you have to do. And then your conscience tells you—you get a feeling, a sort of knowledge, that is—[what is not right to do].[248]

This idea of the relativity and relevance of rules according to each unique situation is dangerously close to the game-playing mentality of his aristocratic background and also to the literary mood of the Sixties and Seventies, where the preoccupation with the paradox was rapidly yielding attention to the importance of games. It is important to note that Mosley did *not* come to see subjective aestheticism or aesthetic subjectivity as a way of getting away from religion, but actually as a possibility for staying 'at the centre of religion.'[249] As was mentioned earlier, one detects a move away from 'conventional Christianity' in the course of Mosley's conversion. This, however, does not mean that Mosley left religious faith behind as a way to perceive of an aesthetic vision. The contrary is the case.

> How can there be any aesthetics (as opposed to 'taste') without a belief in, [without] the experience and validation of, something *objective* that might as well be called 'God'? I think the experience of 'pattern' is a reason to believe in—to trust—well, whatever you like to call it.[250]

For Mosley what differentiated the Christian conception of the relativity of rules from the other notions of game-playing was the belief in a greater pattern—a Godly design—where all events are interconnected and have a proper place. The notion of such a pattern prevents the subjective experience from falling into a solipsistic meaninglessness. It is the process of *enquiry* into and discovery of this pattern that Mosley understands as 'aesthetic vision':

> The dangers of aestheticism, *as those of an unenquiring trust in God*, are that they can just be a grandiose justification of subjective tastes. It's the existence—or the enquiry into the existence—of some sort of objectivity to test them against that may ([but] does not always) give them some validity.[251]

As was discussed in the previous chapter the notion of the relativity of rules amongst the members of aristocracy was only to serve to uphold the game itself.[252] The same thing could be said about many writers of the Sixties and Seventies—such as Barthes and Barth—who advocated that the role of aesthetics should be the pursuit of the pleasures of the game.[253] In other words, whereas the game played for its own sake takes sustenance from the idea that any application of the rules, or, in other words, any *choice* has meaning within the game only, for a Christian the notion of choice-making only makes sense in a greater pattern which it is part of and is surrounded by. And which, consequently, effects and is affected by the choice.[254] In an 'absolute moment of choice' man has a chance to become aware of his freedom of choice because the paradoxicality or impossibility of the moment demands a detachment from the situation for the sake of a 'good' choice to prevail. From Christianity Mosley learnt that man could only detach himself from the paradox by evolving a multiple vision—or an 'aesthetic' view—which could 'dissolve' the paradox by seeing the place of excluding and contradictory options in the greater Godly Design: 'What mattered about human tragedy or comedy was the chance to see the place of these in some cosmic pattern that was being worked out (that had been worked out?) as it were round some corner.'[255] Through the aesthetic view the paradox, raised in the moral dilemma, is caught, dissolved and, consequently, is *made sense of.* In other words, aesthetic vision *empowers* man to liberate himself from outer and inner coercive factors, which determine his life. He becomes the master of his own life as his life is not determined for him, but by seeing the sense of his life (its place in a greater pattern) he is also involved in determining and making his life. The classical example of the sculptor who creates an art-work by discovering what has been there in the stone clarifies this idea. For Mosley it is therefore not farfetched to say that the Christian aesthetic conception of man's freewill has an affinity with Nietzsche's conception of man's freewill:

> The philosopher Nietzsche suggested that a person might see his or her life as an art-work—in the looking back on it and the discovering of what has been there; and by this affecting the future. For it is in the nature of pattern, shape, that the observance of a past forms a future. You watch, you listen; if you do this 'truly' a future unfolds in a manner in which it is seen that you are a *partner*. . . .
>
> . . . Nietzsche announced that God was dead—'God' having been a word for the experience of what is other than oneself or one's assessments. Nietzsche seemed to mean— Now humans can know themselves to be in the business of discovery and creation.[256]

If man was involved in the process of creation, then he was not anymore a subordinate to the power of God or of Fate, but a partner of that power. In this context tragedy (or, its inversion, farce) would not make sense: man could not be a tragic figure, as none of his efforts would go into the so-called ancient Greek or Byronic rebellions against an oppressive and tyrannical higher figure. A partner of God could neither be a Prometheus or a Satan but would, to use a phrase of Mosley's, 'walk hand in hand with Fate' and, thus, see life as a 'successfully going concern.'[257] This understanding of man's freewill helped Mosley to part from his old tragic voice. The old tragic voice was the response of an individual caught inevitably at the limits of rules: he should *not* in the first place have tried to break or trespass them. The voice of these novels was the voice of what Mosley (referring to Nietzsche) refers to as ascetic values; of limits:

one can formulate the ascetic values: thou shalt not murder, shalt not commit adultery. But if one were to formulate *thou shalt* one couldn't.[258]

The new voice of Mosley investigated the possibilities of trespassing borders into a territory, where the individual has a real chance of surviving. Mosley came to see that for doing this another style was needed: one which could go beyond the realm of general 'prescriptions' and still be able to deal with the inevitable paradoxes that inevitably emerged as a result of this trespassing. For Mosley this voice could only be an aesthetic one in contrast to an ethical one—one which could show his protagonists' process of 'discovery and creation'[259] and by this make the reader see his or her own possibilities of discovery and creation: 'You have to find your own "thou shalt" like a work of art.'[260] One could thus say that Mosley's experimental novels are neither a mirror of the world outside or the world inside, nor are they to be seen as didactic tales. They try to fulfil what C. S. Lewis thought to be the task of literature: the discovery and creation of new possibilities and perceptions in the human mind.[261]

Literary and intellectual background: the age of the paradox

If one were to find one theme, which would signify the most common feature in Mosley's philosophical and literary concerns and those of his contemporaries it would be the preoccupation with the paradox. The treatment of paradox in the area of fiction gave rise to many experiments with the form of the novel on grounds of which the Sixties came to be seen as the highpoint of experimentalism in post-war English fiction. Therefore, in this chapter Mosley's literary background will be examined in a direction opposite to the examination in the previous chapter. In the first chapter the discussion of the literary background was undertaken in order to show the contrast between Mosley's art and his artistic-intellectual milieu. He seemed not to be too open to the 'en-vogue' literary developments of the Fifties and his novels manifest this. In the Sixties, however, Mosley was much more 'at home' in his contemporary literary and intellectual setting because the ideas and themes that interested him on grounds of his personal experiences and studies were also widely discussed amongst the writers, artists and scholars of the time. His novels testify this openness. However, this is not to say that he was in an easy relationship with his contemporaries. He seemed to reject just as much as he accepted from the different literary streams of the time, with which he shared common features and grounds. It is the aim of the following to show this relationship in the hope of placing Mosley's artistic career in a historical context. We will first look at the rise of the centrality of the paradox and then try to distinguish the different modes of writing that it gave rise to.

I. The arbitrary and the fragmented: liberation or entrapment?

The closeness of the 'Sixties' to our own time seems to make it difficult to evaluate this era by seeing a definite pattern in it. This difficulty is further enhanced, since the feeling of living in the aftermath of what has happened in the past forty years still persists. We seem not to be able to begin and realise a new era—our own era—yet. In his *Language and Silence* George Steiner famously defined the generation(s) of this period as the generation that comes *after*.[262] As Bradbury has put it, the 'Sixties and after'[263] come after the ruins of Modern Man, Modern Cities, Modern ideologies and most importantly the ruins of Modern literature, in the shape of that monumentally unreadable 'text' *Wake*.[264] What could be said about this age is that it is the age of the fragmentation of all truths and verities—indeed 'the era of doubt.'[265]

In the West the growing distrust of the people and intellectuals towards their post-war governments—or the so-called liberators—prepared the grounds for what came to be known as the 'Sixties.' The Suez Canal crisis of 1956 and the 1963 murder of Kennedy, followed by political scandals, hypocrisies, and the increasing production and application of mass-destruction weapons in the names of humanity, peace and democracy, are often seen as the beginnings of distrust in the ideologies and values upon which the Western democratic civilisations had been based for over two hundred years. This loss of trust between the 'people' and the 'state' is not similar to the mistrust between a totalitarian regime and its subjects. That the manipulation of reality in totalitarian regimes was possible had already been apparent. But in the West for the last two centuries there had always been the notion that real reality was conceivable through Hegelian dialectics. This gave rise to the notion of a *true*, transparent and democratic discourse. In 'real life,' however, all devices, that communicated the democratic discourse—spoken, written, transmitted and televised—

seemed to prove an anti-Hegelian conjecture. They were shown to be manipulated by mass media. Consequently, the outlook emerged, that: 'if the content of history can be manipulated by mass-media, or by literature, if television and the press can falsify historical facts, then the unequivocal *relation* between the real and the imaginary becomes blurred.'[266] When Facts—historical facts—become imaginary (i.e., fiction), they also become revisable: *arbitrary* narratives to be told and re-told. History and all reality, become mere *processes*, rather than absolute and rationally interpretable and meaningful entities. What was evident for the physicists of the pre-war years, was now realised culturally: there were no absolutes, no way of justifying one theory over the other, or arguing for one worldview as opposed to another. This was the age of complete pluralism, where, terms such as depth and hierarchy suffered fatal blows. All theories and worldviews coexisted and could not refute each other, as none could serve as a more valid point of *reference* than the other. Being built on arbitrary structures and replaceable values, there could be no valid hierarchy which justifiably preferred one to the other. *Evident* reality—scientifically *provable* reality—was becoming increasingly ephemeral, instantaneous and dissolvable.[267] Thus, the concepts of history, scientific progress and, most importantly, the individual around which the Western humanism and its idea of democratic civilisation had been constituted seemed to be coming to an end.

Now one was confronted with the historical realisation of the Structuralist and Post-Structuralist conjectures based on Wittgenstein's and Saussure's linguistic theories: that is, the loss of the intrinsic 'truth' of the linguistic element.[268] Wittgenstein had introduced the idea of *Sprachspiel*: he showed that all communications were incommensurate language-games, governed by their own rules of the game. The only meaning and value that was there resided, therefore, in these rules necessary for the continuation of the game. As a result the notion of a meaning beyond these rules—of a pointing towards or a connecting to something outside the game—did not hold anymore. Furthermore, the notion of a *Sprachspiel* robbed the signifier of its intrinsic value. The Structuralist, Post-Structuralist, and Deconstructivist theories[269] (which drew strongly from Saussure's linguistics) conveyed that the meaning of a linguistic element did not reside in the element, but in the relation between the signifier and the signified which constitutes the sign. This relation, however, was one that was socially *agreed upon* and consequently contingent. Its contingency was further enhanced by its fragmentation within the social system: in every section of society the meaning of the sign changed according to the relevant agreements. The relation between the signifier and the signified (Derrida coined the term *différance* for this) and thus that of the sign and its meaning was conceived to be perpetually shifting. In this way, the sign and its meaning also became arbitrary or as the Deconstructivists put it 'undecideable.' Hence, the Hegelian dialectics as a way of getting closer to reality was rapidly losing its credibility and was increasingly seen either as way of getting *away* from reality or as *the only* reality out of which no reality as such existed; in other words, 'reality' became an illusion.

The ontological gap between the real and what man knew about the real was not to be overcome. It was further argued by the Structuralists and Deconstructivists that not only could language not convey a reality outside itself, but it was the only conceivable reality itself. Symbolisation did not represent the world, but rather reified and *created* it. Consequently, the conception of language and symbolisation as being the creator of reality did not leave man's individuality and identity intact. The postmodern language philosophies did not see man as a being outside reality, who created it by speaking it (in the same vein as the Old Testament God), but saw man himself to be created or spoken by language. In other words, it was language which existed prior to reality and human consciousness and not the other way around.[270] Hence, the difference between the modern and the postmodern outlook lay in the latter's subversion or reversal of the former's 'foundations' in the Platonic philosophy, where language is rooted in the 'essence of being.'[271] Language was now granted liberation from any extratextual framework: in other words, all existence was seen as a text. This phenomenon was seen by the new language philosophers as the only possibility for the liberation of man. In contrast to the modern ideals, the demand was no more for wholeness and unification, but for an increase in fragmentation and alienation: man was now free from being a conceivable entity that had to be unified with or reach the true reality. He was only a process which at the same time was free to alter and make up himself and his reality by way of narration. Indeed, he was now being seen as a narrative. The paradoxes of this *Weltanschauung* are obvious: 'if individuals don't have any status for the theory, what sense does it make to speak of them as "dominated" by social structures or of "liberating" them from them?'[272] The question was now how could fiction—the 'Mirror of Reality' or, the novel—'that bright book of life'—deal with the paradox of the absence of the individual or that of reality? How could fiction deal with the paradox of a liberation for whose realisation the annihilation of the subject of liberation was necessary?

II. The paradox of literature: The postmodern deconstruction of modern literature

> God, King, Father, Reason, History, Humanism have all come and gone their way, though their power may still flare up in some circles of faith. . . . And now we have nothing—nothing that is not partial, provisional, self-created—upon which to found our own discourse.[273]

With the death of God and religion in the Modern era, literature had been endowed with a divine role in the Western culture. The modern prophets were authors, who like their predecessors were seen as saviours and liberators of humanity because of their capability to show the 'Truth of Reality': that is, the 'whole' of life or that which is greater than the sum of its fragments. Their aim was accordingly to create a form—*an order*—which could be used by the individual as a map or tool for exploring and coming closer to the uncharted reality. And accordingly each generation was in search of a better map or tool than the traditional one: the manifestos and pamphlets of the *avant-garde* artists and writers of the first half of this century testify this. At the same time, the difficulty of this task was especially felt by the modernist artists and writers: the more they tried to make the appropriate order, the more they failed. The project of modernism steadily gave way to the heretical literature of the late Joyce, Beckett, Borges and Kafka: 'modernist art had proposed its own coherences as a defence against anarchy—not confidently, it must be said, but with a desperate, stubborn conviction concerning the need for consonance. For the postmodernist, it seems, even this desperation has been surrendered. The imagination, it is implied, no longer presses back against the real, since reality has been exposed as no more than a series of competing fictions, experiences shaped by language and perceived through prismatic roles.'[274]

The Postmodern art and literature, emerged out of the failure of modern art to fulfil what it had taken to be its task. According to Eco it was 'the moment . . . when the avant-garde (the modern) [could] go no further.'[275] With the fall of that immanent 'whole' and the predominance of the fragmented, everything that justified the centrality of literature—reality, truth, the liberation of the individual—was invalidated. Nathalie Sarraute and her fellow writers of *nouveau roman* declared the age of suspicion.[276] Everything that until now was taken for granted was now doubted. William H. Gass contended that 'reality is not a matter of fact, it is an achievement'[277] and Sukenick declared that 'the contemporary writer. . . . is forced to start from scratch: Reality doesn't exist, time doesn't exist, personality doesn't exist.'[278] Roland Barthes and his fellow Structuralists, whose works inspired the Deconstructivists, declared the meaninglessness and un-interpretability of reality, by claiming it to be only an assemblage of signs which could only be read and decoded as a text. Consequently, the author—the source and the creator of the work of art—lost his centrality as well and became a mere text to be only decoded by the reader. The death of the author was declared.[279]

The text was now devoid of any inherent meaning, or message or mystery behind or beyond it, that was to be unravelled and *understood*. In other words, both reality and fiction became arbitrary and interchangeable texts only to be decoded. The interpretation of reality and fiction as mere texts inevitably gave all the powder to the reader, who read the texts and decoded them. Every reader could thus decode the text according to his subjective taste or understanding, knowing that there is no objectivity that he must abide to. Theodore Roszak put it as such: 'objective consciousness . . . like mythology . . . is an arbitrary construct in which a given society in a given historical situation has invested its sense of meaningfulness and value.'[280] The novel, or the text, could henceforth not have any *relation* to a reality outside itself. It was not transcendent anymore and could consequently not be interpreted. In other words, fiction did not owe its existence to or justify itself by referring to a reality outside itself, but was a reality itself, as arbitrary or as meaningful as any reality.[281] The realist (mimetic representation of reality and life through fiction) and romantic (expressive mirroring of the soul and the inward world of the individual), literature were severely attacked.[282] These two seemingly opposing modes of narrative were believed to be the two sides of the same coin, as they both claim to represent and have special access to an irrefutable reality: either an outward (as in the case of Realism) or an inward one (as in the case of Romanticism). With the death of reality and that of the novel's transcendence and coherence the notion of originality did not make sense anymore.[283] As Baudrillard suggested it was now the map that preceded the territory and not the other way around. All art was thus a copy of an infinite number of copies.[284] If the novel could not mirror reality, then its features which were to serve this purpose could also not be justified. Hence the features of the novel—plot, setting, characterisation, theme—were declared as the 'true enemies' of the novel.[285]

The more the postmodern writers deconstructed the modernist art and literature by pointing out its paradoxes, the more they seemed to be sinking into the paradox themselves, or in other words, 'digging out their own graves.' For the postmodern novelist, however, this suicide became the saving grace. In the following it will be shown how the de-constructors of literature survived the paradox of killing literature and themselves by 'living' their deaths. It will also be shown that this literature did not, as the post-structuralists had advocated, lead to the real liberation of the individual, but actually perpetuate his entrapment.

III. The literature of paradox or metafiction

The involvement in this paradoxical process—the Cretan saying that 'all Cretans are liars'—left the postmodern novelists only with the option of the integration of their awareness of their dilemma into their works. In this way they (and their novels) could avoid self-destruction by infinitely reflecting upon their death. The emergence and development of literature of paradox has been observed by many novelists and scholars under different headings: 'metafiction,'[286] 'surfiction,'[287] 'problematic novel' or 'novel-about-itself,'[288] 'self-begetting novel'[289] or 'experimental novel'[290] were some of the more popular terms concerning this sort of fiction. Such a novel is constantly doubting itself and trying to overcome its dilemma by building its hesitation into itself.[291] These novels are preoccupied with the paradoxical task of declaring their own deaths by being—living—their own death.[292] Indeed in the Sixties the authors and their novels were erasing themselves: the hand not only drew itself—as the self-creating, omniscient author used to—but it also erased itself.[293] As was mentioned earlier this development was already happening during the late Modern literature:[294] the works of Kafka, (late) Joyce, Beckett and Borges contributed largely to the failure of the modernist notion of coherence by undermining the notion of mimesis and the interpretability of literature. Having lost the capacity to mirror reality—or to 'say the world'[295]—the options of the postmodern fiction were only a 'silence of vacancy'[296] or the indulgence into an endless language-game, which was a 'rewriting of literary tradition by embedding it in contemporary tradition.'[297] In both cases the novel could only be an enquiry into its own narrative—its own becoming. This is of course not to say that the literature of this era was completely governed by the postmodern silence and self-indulgent games. As David Lodge observes in his 'The Novelist at the Crossroads'[298] many novelists were still writing novels in the modernist spirit, in which fiction was seen as a tool for gaining access to an extratextual reality. Lodge consents, however, that these novels were highly conscious of the problematic and paradoxical relation of fiction to reality and accordingly tried to 'straddle the conventional boundary'[299] between fiction and fact. The novels of Murdoch, Fowles, Lessing and Spark amongst others belong to this group of fiction. For the study of Mosley's novels it is important to look at both these modernist-transcendentalist and the 'postmodern,' poststructuralist, as his works integrate the former's extratextual assumptions, but also the latter's aesthetic and technical treatment of the paradox.

1. *Meaningless literature and neo-aestheticism:*[300] *literature of silence and literature of exhaustion*

> All is ready. Except me. I am being given, if I may venture the expression, birth to into death, such is my impression. The feet are clear already, of the great cunt of existence. Favourable presentation I trust. My head will be last to die. Haul in your hands. I can't. The render rent. My story ended, I'll be living yet. Promising lag. That is the end of me. I shall say I no more.[301]

Literature of silence and literature of exhaustion are largely considered to be the two main groups of which metafiction consists.[302] Ihab Hassan saw that the French *nouveau roman* carried Beckett's legacy and represented the silence: the 'disruption of all connection between language and reality'[303] gave rise to a literature that tried to show that the real cannot be ultimately shown. Literature was thus *nothing*. Introducing the English to the *nouveau roman* Christine Brooke-Rose (herself an exponent of French literary theories, translator of Robbe-Grillet's *In the Labyrinth*, and writer of highly experimentalist fiction) compared the venture of this sort of writing to that of science after Heisenberg's 'Uncertainty Principle': *nouveau roman* was aware that literature—like science—only constructed models of the world based on an *absence* of empirically verifiable reality.[304] These novelists set out to reveal the Aristotelian concept of reality as an inadequate *model* of reality[305] by trying to problematise the traditional elements of fiction such as character, plot, theme, metaphor, which are supposed to help the author represent a meaningful reality: that is historicity, linearity, causality and three-dimensional or round characters. Their novels were supposed to show that we live alone with a flat and meaningless world. It must, however, be noted that the philosophy of the *nouveau roman* had a major contradiction at heart: the call for anti-mimetic, non-representational fiction was simultaneously accompanied by the claim about a new and true search for reality: Butor criticised the assumptions of 'short sighted critics' about the objectives of the *nouveau roman* and declared 'formal invention in the novel' as 'the *sine qua non* of a greater realism.'[306] Robbe-Grillet called the style of the *nouveaux romanciers* 'nouveau réalisme' and Sarraute famously declared that 'formalism is realism.'[307] These claims contradicted the initial notion of the *nouveaux romanciers* about the impenetrability of reality through fictional models and thus made the new novel a direct inheritor of the Modern tradition, in which literature tried to come as close as possible to a reality outside itself.[308]

The paradoxical task that the New Novelists set for themselves led to many vital innovations in the form of the novel, which had been declared dead in its history many times over.[309] The development of the Beckettian two dimensional character—based on the idea that a person cannot be known—the absent first-person narrator and the unfulfilled plot especially are hallmarks of the *nouveau roman*.[310] These fictions are told by first-person-absent narrators with detailed, camera-like observation, which gives no access to the minds of their protagonists: the protagonists are flat, depth-less and psyche-less. The reader has no idea of what they think or feel. They are merely observed. Nothing is interpreted by an omniscient author. The meticulously objective description of the protagonist in his surroundings is to bar any possibility of the reader interpreting his character. The emphasis is given to the *visual*: the eye—the objective physical eye and not the soul's eye—sees dispassionately. In Claude Simon's *The Palace* we encounter a good example of this technique: a detailed description of a post-card image of Christ from an absent first person narrator with a camera-like eye and immediately after that a very similar description of two sombre Mediterranean men.[311] The absent omniscient camera-eye conceives of a photographic image in the same way as of two human beings. The human beings become just as flat as the post-card. The plot of the novel never resolves and seems to be eternally frozen in its process of becoming. The 'story' is without a beginning: the opening 'And' gives the impression of the story starting somewhere in the middle. The sense of coherence is further subverted by the fragmentation of the 'plot' into five chapters which seem both to be related to each other—regarding the recurring setting (a Spanish-speaking country) and protagonist (i.e., the American)—and isolated from each other. None of the chapters seems to start where the previous one had ended. Each seems to start in the middle of a different story (Chapter II, for example, starts thus: '. . . of a ceremony that itself was like a masquerade.'[312]). The actions are isolated and arbitrarily connected. The detailed sequential descriptions of the actions give the impression of a slow motion film, where every little movement is frozen in an isolated moment. In this way the unity of the action is broken into a series of movements, which consequently make the action seem eternally unfinished.[313]

The other extreme of postmodern literature,[314] (or what increasingly came to be seen as literature of exhaustion) differed from the literature of silence, in that it tried to show that all reality including the self was fiction.[315] For the writers of this fiction meaning was not something that could not be reached by literature (as the *nouveaux romanciers* proclaimed), but something artificial.[316] Fiction mirrored only fictions: in the beginning was the myth and not 'reality.'[317] Literature was thus *everything*. Borges is often seen as the founder of the narrative techniques, which depict this conception. Using intertexual games and self-reflexivity, the reader cannot distinguish between fact and fiction, dream, game and waking reality any more. [318] The plot and story-line are broken through non-linear and non-causal narration. In his fable 'Tlön, Uqbar, Orbis Tertius,' for example, he uses the 'Chinese box system,'[319] in which the real and the imaginary are infinitely woven into each other: the structure is a visual puzzle, revealing that everything is a story reflecting a story. Tlön is an imaginary land that exists in the literature of another imaginary land Uqbar, which in turn seems to exist in a dubious encyclopaedia in possession of a dubious secret society.[320] Furthermore, the labyrinthine structure of Borges's fables, in which all times run parallel and at times overlap or fork-out depicts that all possibilities exist simultaneously. In his 'the Garden of Forking Paths,' for instance, the choice of one path does not lead to the elimination of the others:[321] in other words, the labyrinth is not resolved by the actions and the choices of the protagonists. The multiple answers to the puzzle actually mean no answer. The novels of John Barth and Thomas Pynchon also employ similar narrative techniques. Pynchon's *The Crying of Lot 49*[322] achieves a puzzling ambiguity built upon the game between reality and counter-reality, until the reader is inclined to ask what is real and what is imagined? The answer is obviously withheld.[323] Bath's *Lost in the Funhouse*[324] is another work in which the notion of fiction mirroring reality is completely subverted. He exploits the intertextual and self-reflexive game to an extent where the narrator Ambrose regresses (or progresses?) from a historical time into a mythical time—or as Ziegler puts it, from historical identity to mythical anonymity—and metamorphoses from the author/narrator into the voice of the 'anonymous mythical minstrel, mentioned in passing by Homer in the Odyssey.'[325] The barriers between reality and fiction are blurred and dissolved: history—'fact'—equals myth—'fiction'; imagination *is* reality.

Despite the distinction between the literature of silence and literature of exhaustion, both of these modes of narration gave rise to novels which shared very similar features. Just as Federman saw realism and romanticism as the two faces of the same coin—i.e., mimesis—Hassan himself came to see that the literature of silence and the literature of exhaustion had a similar relation and became almost indistinguishable. Whether the author's point of departure was the notion that literature was nothing or that literature was everything, the outcome of both endeavours gave rise to similar narrative techniques and forms because both groups sought to 'de-realise' (i.e., alienate or *Entfremden*) the world by subverting the traditional literary forms.[326] Most obviously the Borgesian method for dissolving the plot was not only exploited by the writers of literature of exhaustion such as Barth, but especially by the *nouveaux romanciers*.[327] The structures of the labyrinthine and the detective novel were very useful as a way of subverting the traditional mimetic forms: this form could be used to lure the reader into getting engaged in seeking out the withheld information only in order to make him realise the futility of this venture.[328] The infinite and often paradoxical possibilities of this narrative technique generated an 'arbitrary causality' or a 'causal arbitrariness' (these being paradoxical terms themselves) in the plot, which made a resolution of the story impossible. The *nouveaux romanciers* used this structure to bring home the idea that literature is not, as the modernists believed, a (Jamesian) window to the world. Robbe-Grillet's *In the Labyrinth*,[329] is a lucid example to show this: the soldier, waiting simultaneously in rain, snow and sun, occasionally asks for the direction, but is never able to arrive at a destination. He is not given any answers or clues to his enquiries: both ends of the street on which we repeatedly and infinitely catch him waiting leads not to his destination, the 'boulevard.'[330] Another example is his detective novel *Les Gommes* (*The Erasers*),[331] in which the story is never resolved and disappears in the labyrinth of its own signs and structure.

Other novelists such as B. S. Johnson or William Burroughs also stepped in the path set by Borges. Their *mise-en-abyme* was achieved through assembling arbitrary pieces without any continuity or coherence. The techniques that they evolved differed from those of the other novelists mentioned above, in that they discouraged the reader at the outset to look for coherence and meaning. Whereas the *nouveau roman* or the literature of exhaustion revealed in the course of the novel that there was no resolution or causality, the physical aspects of the writings of Burroughs and Johnson made this claim at first glance. Burroughs' 'cut-up, fold-in,' technique in novels such as *The Naked Lunch*[332] and *Nova Express*[333] was supposed to break the linearity and causality of plot through the juxtaposition of randomly picked fragments and pieces and thereby 'extend to writing the flash back used in films, enabling the writer to move backwards and forwards on his time track.'[334] The topography of the novel already disclosed the objective of the novel: numbing the mind of the reader—often in form of a pornographic chaos—and thus preventing him from seeking meaning or truth.[335] In England Alan Burns and B. S. Johnson tried to depict chaos and randomness also in the same way as William Burroughs. Johnson, for example, created the 'shuffle novel.' *The Unfortunates* (1969)[336] came in unbound sheets a box, to be shuffled and put into any order by the reader as he pleased. In this way the novel became a mere collection of fragments of interchangeable fictions which could be arranged and rearranged infinitely.

One could therefore conclude that after the death of 'reality' and 'meaning' the self-conscious fiction was left with its own structure, form and language only,[337] with which it seemed not to be able to do anything other than to play. What remained for the postmodern novel/author to do was playing with itself by constructing itself for the sake of deconstructing itself eternally:

> This time I know where I am going, it is no longer the ancient night, the recent night. Now it is a game I am going to play. I never knew how to play, till now. . . . I shall never do anything anymore from now on, the greater part, if I can. . . . Perhaps as hitherto I shall find myself abandoned in the dark, without anything to play with. Then I shall play with myself.[338]

Parody and tongue-in-cheek irony—mainly a legacy of Joyce's late works, *Ulysses* and *Wake*, and of Beckett's novels[339]—were widely used by the novelists of this time to perpetually pull the ground not only from under the reader's feet but also from under their own feet and yet to pull themselves up in a Münchhausenesque fashion by the hair.[340] In John Barth's *Lost in the Funhouse*, for example, self-reflexive parody is used as a device by the narrator to make and then unmake himself eternally. Ambrose parodises the modernists through out the chapters of his tale—'clearing away the rubble of the immediate past to make space for rebuilding the present'[341]—by self-consciously imitating their various styles from realism to the fragmentary and subjective mode of writing only to arrive at the subversion of the old myths by retelling them in a 'slangy' narrative.[342] In this way he goes through the process of un-making (deconstructing) himself as a modernist narrator to re-making himself as mythical personalities, which in turn are unmade (made?) into an anonymous, bodiless, timeless voice of a minstrel.[343]

The game of regression into the infinite could only continue if meaninglessness was ensured. If the process of the game would accidentally hit upon a meaning,[344] then the interpretation of the text—i.e., the discovery of the meaning hidden behind the text—would become an imperative. In such a context the game would be a teleological process, which could only be justified in view of the message or meaning that it would eventually lead to. The text would hence become transcendental. In order to avoid this the form had constantly to be emptied of any meaning that the intertextual game might accidentally lead to. The detective form, without a solution, or the labyrinthine form, without a centre were, yet again, especially suitable for this venture.[345] The labyrinth, the puzzle, endowed the writer and reader with an appropriate playground for playing an endless game. Reader and writer or writer/reader could indulge into the pleasure of endlessly searching without finding, since every combination that could lead to a solution of the puzzle was destroyed and the 'rubble' was yet again used to build another possibility *ad infinitum*.[346] Thus, through playing the game the players both re-enforced and dissolved the game.

The primacy of the game in metafiction led to a strong return of aestheticism.[347] In its preoccupation with its own form the novel increasingly became narcissistic. Its players were not only aware of the arbitrariness of its rules and coherence but also of each other's awareness of this. In this sort of game, nobody could lose or win, and the only aim of the game became the continuation of the game for the sake of pleasure. Playing the game increasingly gained attention, as it was beginning to be seen as the liberator of the individual. For Barthes, playing the aesthetic game for its own sake was the only genuine way in which liberation could be achieved.[348] Reading the experimental novel became a pleasure not because it finally fulfilled the reader's 'wishful thinking,' but because it constantly 'contest[ed] the coherence-conferring interpretation, and thus liberate[ed] the reader from attempts to control the text in terms of . . . belief and ideology, and [drew him] into the game of [its] own disruptive procedures.'[349] This is how the novel, as Barthes puts it, became a text of 'Bliss':[350] the pleasure of the game, never coming to a fulfilling peak (and thus an end), eventually would reach the extreme of boredom,[351] where the reader could literally toss the novel aside and free himself from it. By resisting to be interpreted the text resisted any relation to the reader. Meaninglessness, arbitrariness and the endless game were thus believed to free the reader from the responsibility of making any choices in regards to the text and its meaning.

Apart from the fact that the post-structuralist theories and literature, could not solve the contradiction of having to found their assumptions on a given reality outside themselves for the sake of showing the non-existence of a reality outside themselves, they were unable to meet their objective either. That is to say, they did not succeed in freeing the individual (whom they assumed to be non-existent, anyway). Not surprisingly, this notion undermined itself as soon as it was conceived. The *regressus ad infinitum* also meant the imprisonment of the reader in incomprehension and anxiety. The re-vision of all language and reality was liberating only as long as a system of meaning was upheld. In a meaningless context, however, the game soon became stifling as the reader lost all points of reference. The reader and the writer were muzzled, like Kafka's K., in the labyrinth of arbitrariness and meaninglessness. The reader was indeed entrapped in the Funhouse.

2. *Meaningful literature: the transcendental novel*

As was mentioned earlier, the novel of this era was not wholly governed by the exhaustive postmodern games, where man, despite the theoretical promises of the post-structuralists, seemed ultimately to be entrapped. In England the traditional/modernist idea that the novel was a tool of liberation by being a window to real possibilities, truths or ideas outside itself still prevailed strongly—in fact, more than in the rest of the Western world, such as the USA and France.[352]

The novels of Golding, Spark, Fowles, Lessing and Murdoch amongst others showed that transcendentalism could be a fertile ground for experimentation with the form of the novel. Contrary to expectation, the experiments of the postmodern writers and their declarations about the death of a meaningful reality and the death of the meaningful novel did not disenchant the transcendentalist writers with the form of the novel, but invigorated their quest for new forms of the novel as *tools* for coming as close as possible to the truth of life. However, the novels of these writers, like those of their postmodern contemporaries, also reflect their concern with the dilemma of their era: i.e., the concern with the irreversibly damaged mimetic literature. In view of their awareness of the problematic and often paradoxical relation of literature and reality, their novels are highly self-conscious and consequently reflect on the novel's process of becoming. In *The Fabulators*[353] Scholes defined this sort of literature as one that insisted on its own unreality and artificiality. But this was not done as a means for conveying the gap between literature and reality (as in the case of the *nouveau roman*), but as a means for conveying moral, social or metaphysical truths, through the realisation of which the individual could free himself from the stifling illusions of life. That is why, these novels are primarily concerned with showing the reader his illusions in order to prepare him for the possibilities of coming closer to reality. John Fowles' memorandum about *The French Lieutenant's Woman*, summarises this conjecture: 'If you want to be true to life, start lying about the reality of it.'[354] The lie only brings the reader closer to reality, if the liar, i.e., the author, can simultaneously convince the reader of its integrity and warn him not to be fooled by it. In Murdoch's words, art should 'invigorate . . . without consoling, and defeat . . . our attempts, in W. H. Auden's words, to use it as magic.'[355] Iris Murdoch, Muriel Spark, Anthony Burgess, William Golding, Doris Lessing and John Fowles, among others, were writing this sort of literature by freely drawing from different literary traditions and forms—the Gothic, the Jamesian novel of manners, the biblical parables, the historical tales, the Woolfian stream of consciousness, the Joycean language-games etc.—including the contemporary ones.[356] This, however, was done in a necessarily self-conscious manner, in which the novelist could assume the role of the didactic 'daemon,' who by telling lies aims at teaching the reader the difference between falsehood and truth. The tongue-in-cheek irony of Fowles's narrator in *The French Lieutenant's Woman*

(1969), by which the reader is constantly forced to reflect upon the novel's convention reminds one to a great extent of the ironic narrator of *Lost in the Funhouse*. Illusions are constantly built only to show their 'intrinsically fictional' quality by use of self-parody, and, thus throws the reader into a Deconstructivist undecideability.[357] As the novel proceeds the boundaries between the real and the imaginary levels become increasingly blurred: all conventions concerning the concept of the novel are put to question by showing the reader that a novel is a 'provisional frame, created by the combined work of the author and "the willing suspension of disbelief" of the reader.'[358] But Fowles does not intend to reach the same end as a post-structuralist novelist and by leaving the reader in a state of meaninglessness. The novel's three different endings are to convey Fowles' belief that man's future is not predetermined, but is largely influenced by his choices. The reader is being made aware of his freewill in designing not only the lives of the protagonists, but also his own life. This view of the possibility of freedom, however, seems not to be very convincing. Fowles shows that there are choices, but does not show *how* the best possible choice could be met. The fact that there are choices is not enough for investigating the mechanisms of choice-making. This is the paradox and dilemma of postmodernism: the more freedom of choice; the more 'everything-goes,' the less the individual is free.

Iris Murdoch—a philosopher and also the most eloquent amongst her contemporaries in the exposition of her conception of true literature—is another transcendental novelist, whose works in the Sixties revealed the importance and dangers of form (i.e., fabrication) concerning the liberation of the individual from his illusions. An exponent of Existentialism in England, she soon became critical of their 'facile idea of sincerity'[359] and illusory absolutist notion of freedom, where man stood 'as a brave naked will surrounded by an easily comprehended empirical world.'[360] She called for a return to the 'hard idea of truth'[361] in which the 'simple-minded faith in science, together with the assumption that we are all rational and totally free' would be exchanged for a return to picturing 'the transcendence of reality.'[362] This transcendence, however, could only be liberating if it did not mean a return to the totalitarian and reductionist myths of religion or metaphysics, where a higher order—or master planner—watched and controlled the activities of the individual. The transcendence that Murdoch was talking about was seeing 'ourselves against a background of values' and renewing the 'sense of the difficulty and complexity of the moral life and the opacity of persons.'[363] Murdoch insisted that reality—including individuals—was not a given whole, but an often unpredictable and chaotic contingency.[364] Building on this notion she meticulously differentiated between 'fantasy'—the imposition of our facile orders on reality, which we eventually come to accept as reality—and 'imagination'—the recognition and understanding of the contingent reality.[365] In her view, literature must move away from the realm of fantasy[366] and come back to the realm of imagination, where it could remind the reader of the sense of the density of his life and his real potentials and possibilities.[367] Real freedom is thus not the fantastic, absolute romantic/existentialist freedom, but what *is available* in the unique situation of each unique individual. Murdoch's was a 'relativist' as opposed to an 'absolutist' view of freedom: she asked for 'degrees of freedom.'[368]

Her insistence on the form of the novel gave her a paradoxical status: a formalist severely critical of the neo-aestheticism on the march; a novelist acutely aware of the evil-potentiality of her métier, yet, determined to restore the moral and restorative powers of fiction. Consequently, her fictions set themselves the paradoxical task of showing how the sense of aesthetic order could dangerously be imposed on reality's contingency, how 'myth-making' could fatally reduce the individuals' complexity and how form could deform human's sense of morality.[369] She shows the dangers of fantasy—'unreality'—by juxtaposing the ordinary with the extraordinary. In this way she foretells the reader about the illusory quality of the lives and hopes of her protagonists. In order to liberate them, she must first shatter their/our illusions. She alienates reality by having everyday-life actions take place in Gothic or Underworld settings or supernatural actions taking place in everyday-life settings. In *The Bell*, for example, the emergence of a huge bell from an ordinary, moonlit lake gives the ordinary setting an eerie, dangerous feeling;[370] on the other hand ordinary activities and communications in Mischa Fox's Gothic villa in *The Flight from the Enchanter* foreshadow the diabolical revelations towards the end of the novel: that is, the suicide and the sensational photos of the protagonist and the Polish brothers.[371] Such revelations shatter the illusions of Murdoch's protagonists, but the question is what degree of freedom does this bring to the protagonists? The freedom of her protagonists seems to be what A. S. Byatt calls, 'the tragic freedom'; or the 'acceptance of the incomplete.'[372] Any sense of fulfilment is either postponed to an indefinite future, as in *The Bell*, where the true 'fulfilment,' according to the closing lines of the book, looks very much like the repetition of the 'tragic freedom,'[373] or where fulfilment can only be depicted in a jokingly picaresque form, as in *Bruno's Dream*.[374] In this novel, the only couple that seems to have achieved a non-tragic freedom are Adelaide and Will, whose future life is conveyed in a sudden, extraordinarily short and jolly passage, completely distinct from the sombre and dark mood of the novel—like a flicker of light in darkness. The transient quality of this short passage does not convince the reader of this couple's achievement, as for example, the tragic, incomplete freedom of Michael at the end of *The Bell*.

Bearing in mind Mosley's conversion to Catholicism, a third group of his contemporary fellow-transcendentalist novelists also come to mind: novelists such as Muriel Spark, Anthony Burgess and William Golding. These novelists were concerned with the traditional Catholic theme: that is, showing the evil at heart of human vanity and godlessness, which inevitably is turned against humans themselves. The apocalyptic and anti-utopian novels of Burgess and Golding of this era vividly depict the Catholic belief in the fall of man in a world of moral absence. And they also show the dangers of self-appointed saviours—be it in form of a leader (as in Golding's *Lord of the Flies*),[375] or an uprising of the masses (as in Burgess's *Wanting Seed*)[376]—who inevitably bring catastrophe upon humans. Their novels are the tale of 'human disaster' and satires of 'human absurdity.'[377] It is true that these novels were preoccupied with the traditional themes of Catholic literature, but their preoccupation with form puts them in the category of the contemporary self-conscious novels. The fantastic and fabulative novels of these writers (in Burgess's case, one could even speak of science-fiction)[378] are obvious examples.

Considering the experiments of these Catholic writers, Muriel Spark's novels make her placing amongst her contemporaries quite difficult. Her formal experiments show an affinity with the experiments of the *nouveaux romanciers*[379] and bear little resemblance to the fabulations of her above mentioned fellow-Catholic writers. Except for *The Mandelbaum Gate*,[380] her novels of this era, such as her best known work *The Prime of Miss Jean Brodie*[381] are presented to the reader from an objective, almost camera-like eye, which is not interested in a psychological view of the characters and thus prevents the reader from succumbing to any form of (bourgeois/ humanist) sympathy and emotional identification with them. On the other hand, her severe criticism of the present immoral world expressed in her unique didactic black humour and her Catholic obsession with 'plots and plotters' put her novels on the opposite pole to the *nouveau roman* and in the same league as her above mentioned Catholic writers. Being a Catholic she was aware that man (knowingly or unknowingly) is participating in and is predestined by a higher Godly Plot which, due to the imperfect human nature and life's limitations, he will only—except perhaps at the end of his life, where he is about to transcend those limitations—understand imperfectly.[382] Accordingly, Spark (like Mosley) believed in the Christian paradox, whose realisations causes suffering for the believers, but ultimately leads them to redemption: namely, the paradox that one was free only if one accepted the pain of being 'inextricably bound.'[383] In her novels, Spark conveyed this by exploiting her omniscience as the writer to the full: in *The Prime of Miss Jean Brodie*, for example, her use of flash-forward device conveys to the reader that all is pre-determined and that those who see themselves as plotters completely in control of themselves and others, are destined to fail, die and suffer endless despair due to their ignorance of The Master Plotter.[384] Not accepting the Christian paradox of freedom, they are doomed to be defeated. One could of course accuse Spark of assuming the role of the master planner herself. However, her self-conscious use of the *double-entendres* (e.g. in *The Comforters*, where Helena says of Georgina: 'I am beginning to think that Georgina is not all there'[385]) on one hand, and her exaggeratedly obvious and overtly brisk omniscient narration (as in *The Girls of Slender Means*, for example, where she broke the story line 'from above' and consequently provided a distance between the reader and the story by saying 'So much for the portrait of the martyr as young man . . .' or 'We are in the summer of 1945 . . .'[386]) on the other, constantly 'sabotage' the reader's belief in Spark's plots 'because [he is] made highly aware that they are stories being told to [him].'[387] The reader thus understands that Spark's are didactic satirical tales, by which a message similar to that of Murdoch's is being given: the paradox of man's entrapment, where freewill is wrongly understood as imposing one's fantasies on reality.

Looking at Mosley's novels against the literary background sketched above, one could observe that he both was and was not part of the literary activities taking place at the time. In regard to the growing concern with the paradox and the rising self-consciousness of the novel he fit well into his literary framework and like both the postmodern post-Structuralists[388] and the transcendentalists he was interested in the role of the novel as a means for the liberation of the individual. His belief in the meaningfulness of the novel would rather put him in the same league as the transcendental novelists. However, he set himself apart from them, in that he was not only interested in showing the dilemma of man's entrapment in his illusions and the idea of his freedom of choice, but also the *real* possibilities of choice-making in face of dilemmas. Consequently, Mosley was not, in contrast to Murdoch and Spark, primarily interested in showing the fragility of human fictions and thus his tragic freedom. Neither was he, in contrast to Fowles, only interested in showing that there are alternative choices, which in the end seemed to hinder the protagonists' choice-making. What his above-mentioned fellow-novelists ended up showing was man's failure in face of the quest for freedom.

He being a transcendentalist, Mosley's experiments were tools to an end, rather than an end in themselves. His novels of this era are highly self-conscious and show an acute awareness of the paradoxical and problematic relation between reality and life. Amongst the experimentalist literatures of this era, Mosley's novels have a close affinity to the *nouveau roman*. For Mosley the experiments of the *nouveaux romanciers* were interesting in so far that they took a stand against 'imposing' one's fantasy as facts over reality and realised life's irreducability:[389] 'I was fascinated at the time by Robbe-Grillet, I was fascinated by the [*nouveaux romanciers'*] techniques. At the time I welcomed them [because] their characters didn't think that they could manipulate.'[390] However, by not showing what man could do and choose—what were his freedoms; what were his possibilities—in face of the impenetrable reality, they moved very close to the borders of existentialist despair. This is why, in Mosley's eyes, they soon lost their relevance:

> II. I think they did one thing in the Fifties and Sixties: they thought that the old idea [about] people [being] masters of their fate was rubbish—one was helpless. But in their novels one just goes on with the feeling of helplessness. They didn't go through the conversion experience to learn how not to be helpless: [namely], the Christian experience. One becomes a Christian because one feels helpless and so one feels like someone in a Robbe-Grillet novel and then one spends the rest of one's life finding out how one isn't helpless.[391]

The Christian experience of freedom (as Mosley experienced it) was what Mosley set out to express in his novels. It was ironically because of this purpose that Mosley radically set himself apart from writers with whom he shared the same faith, such as Muriel Spark. The fact that Mosley started to write his highly original novels *after* leaving organised religion, and not like Spark after conversion, already indicates the rift between Mosley's and Spark's perception of Christian notion of freedom:

Spark's was confined to the ethical (the moral laws), whereas Mosley's went beyond into the aesthetic vision of Christianity. Furthermore, Mosley did not share Spark's and other Catholic writers' belief in the complete predestination of man through God's design, but came to believe in man's ability to take part in shaping his life through his commitment to Christianity. His notion of a 'partnership' between God and man, implies that both man and God are dependent on each other in shaping the pattern of man's life. This notion was a rejection of Spark's and other Catholic writers' belief in an Almighty God. Mosley, in other words, came to see man and God as equal partners in matters of creation. Consequently, his novels are not satirical moral tales about the evil and absurdity of human endeavour, but are rather in awe of human endeavour[392] and investigate man's real possibilities for exploiting his freedom of choice and participation in making his life.[393] Therefore, one could say that, whereas the novels of Spark (and other Catholic writers, such as Golding and Burgess) are pessimistic and with little hope for humanity due to Catholic faith, Mosley's novels become optimistic and hopeful after his commitment to this faith.

Mosley's novels

I. *Meeting Place*: breaking away from conventional writing

Meeting Place (1962) was Mosley's first novel written after the long pause that followed his dissatisfaction with the tragic style of his earlier novels *Spaces of the Dark*, *The Rainbearers* and *Corruption*. It seemed to Mosley that his old, tragic style of writing could not convey his new sense of freedom. The wordiness, the long sentences and the tragic voice of the novel only conveyed the entrapment of the individual in impossible situations without making the reader see the possibility of getting out of them. Mosley now realised that he needed a 'terser style . . . which offered gaps, openings which a character, or reader, could leap over, free himself by. It was a style evolved to try to deal with the possibilities of choice—this way or that.'[394] The journalistic activity that he undertook in the gap between *Corruption* and *Meeting Place* seems to have influenced the 'terser style' of his later novels.[395] Through journalism Mosley learned to look out of rather than inside of himself only: there is a greater degree of 'objectivity' and less of an emotional subjectivity in this novel. Mosley's first contact with journalism came during a trip to West Africa (1957). The trip and the travel book, *African Switchback*,[396] that came out of it had a vital and everlasting impact on Mosley's style:

> My journey through West Africa with Hugo [Charteris] was of importance to me because [Hugo] did indeed teach me something about objectivity: I learned to look, to listen—to people, at a landscape . . .
>
> . . . I tried to keep [*African Switchback*] to descriptions of events, shapes, colours, sounds; to keep away from sentences weaving in and out like fog.[397]

The objectivity of *African Switchback* appears in the first novel of Mosley after a five-year gap and indicates the turn in the style of Mosley's future novels. It only indicates this turn because *Meeting Place* is definitely a transitional novel in more than one sense. It is an attempt to get out of the old and 'baroque' romantic voice of the previous novels, yet it manifests that Mosley had not yet arrived at the voice, which was to become characteristic of all his later novels. Furthermore, the novel was not written after Mosley clearly signed off from organised religion in 1965.[398] The novel depicts Mosley's contemplations about and preparations for leaving his ethical understanding of Christianity behind. In many ways, this novel is an introduction to Mosley's new investigation into man's freewill in face of moral dilemma. Whereas in the earlier novels, the protagonists shattered at facing a morally impossible or paradoxical situation, in *Meeting Place* we see the beginning of Mosley's endeavour for showing man's ability to 'see oneself in partnership with life; not imposing a pattern on experience (and thus experiencing failure) but trying to look for, and proceed in a pattern that might be there.'[399] The novel's open-ending, where the protagonists Harry and Melissa seem to depart from their past endeavours (Harry, who is very much Mosley's fictional alter-ego, bids farewell to his charity work in a Christian institution in London and Melissa finishes her work for an agency working with nuclear disaster victims somewhere in America)[400] and walk forth towards an unknown future,[401] could be seen as a sign for Mosley's future conduct, where he closed his, as he calls it, 'churchy period,' and embarked on a new period of artistic activity.[402]

The 'objective' and visual narrative of *Meeting Place* told from the perspective of an impassive and meticulous observer was the beginning of Mosley's departure from the 'subjective' tragic voice of his earlier novels.[403]

The narrative's 'objectivity' was not only due to Mosley's journalistic activities at the time, but also owed much to the style of the French *nouveau roman*.[404] The descriptions of actions, scenes and dialogues are recorded from the camera-eye point of view.

> He tipped his chair back. He stared at the ceiling and screwed up his face in a theatrical gesture. He said 'I do hate the night!' He put his feet on the table and folded his hands in his lap. After a time he sat forward again and tore the top sheet off a writing pad . . . .[405]

The detailed descriptions and the refusal to interpret the actions and show their relevance for the plot remind the reader of the narrative techniques of Claude Simon or Robbe-Grillet. The events are presented as loosely connected scenes[406] and are constantly disjointed by the introduction of cuts. The cuts render the novel with a cinematic quality—recalling the 'nouvelle vague'[407]—which increases the impenetrability of the characters and events. As an interruption of the linearity of the plot, however, this technique does not work. In contrast to the following novels such as *Impossible Object* and *Natalie Natalia*, where the juxtapositions make it almost impossible for the reader to see what is exactly happening in the story, the plot of *Meeting Place* is coherent, in spite the cinematic cuts between the events, and the story-line can be followed fairly easily. The last section of the novel, is an exception to this which, when read in the light of the following novels, can be seen as an introduction to or a first draft of the opaque, contingent and labyrinthine plots that came to be characteristic of Mosley's later works.[408] In this section of the novel, where the narrator goes to America to pick up his wife and take her home, the objective narrative is abandoned and instead the protagonist and the reader plunge into a hallucination. The boundaries of time are blown up in Harry's mind and mingle with each other. The boundaries between the real and the imaginary dissolve. Harry's images, dreams and memories pour into each other. The scene is one of chaos. The inside and the outside worlds of Harry meet in this Walpurgis-night.

> On either side of him a dividing line ran into the distance—on his left a beach with waves and white foam and on the right a fence of wire. . . .
>
> Harry thought—I have been here before. The head made the ground liquid. . . .

> The grains of sand were numberless. Each grain was a world, with crystals whirling. The towers crashed and collected themselves. Space was void. . . .
>
> Bones rotted. Like leaves and branches, they went back to earth. The living had to be protected from the dying: the dying make way for unborn children. to propriate the dying, a temple had been built in the desert.
>
> Lying on the boards of the hot room on their honey-moon he had opened one eye and seen the dust in ridges and a white skin. Tribes in Africa put on the masks of animals. He an Melissa were naked. He was tied at his legs and fingers. . . . [409]

However, contrary to the postmodern tradition, at the end of this journey an order—a meaning—emerges. The chaos is not to convey the absurdity and meaninglessness of life, but the possibility of finding a meaning in it; of making an order out of the chaos. Melissa and Harry have seen through their illusions, liberated themselves from their pain and suffering and now choose to accept their responsibilities and go home together to their son, Richard. They do not succumb to the helplessness and self-pity characteristic of Mosley's earlier characters. This is the first novel of Mosley that ends with an optimistic outlook about freewill and the ability of humans having some influence in shaping their lives. The notes of Father Patterson, whose figure had been inspired by Father Raynes, herald the turning point in Mosley's new artistic plans:

> The fall of man into not evil but helplessness.
>
> A world which appears to have no meaning.
>
> The need to know the area within which meaning is experienced.
>
> When there is no meaning it is like a car out of gear: the engine moves but to no effect.
>
> When there is meaning this is experienced as a movement in relation to the thing outside it.
>
> What is the action that puts the car in gear?
>
> The need to know the point at which free will operates.[410]

Like its predecessors, *The Rainbearers* and *Corruption*, *Meeting Place* also drew directly from Mosley's life and was 'an effort to make a pattern from experiences in [his] own life at [that] time';[411] namely the dilemmas concerning his affair, his marriage, his fatherhood, his conversion and now the development of his need to get away from the cocoon of organised religion. However, this novel tried not only to convey the dilemma and its impossibilities, but also to investigate the dilemma and by this the possibilities for going on from there. In the case of *Meeting Place*, the moral dilemma is that of a couple running away from their responsibility for their child and their malfunctioning marriage by doing 'good' work, but paradoxically committing 'evil' by abandoning their child. In search of a way out of his dilemma, Harry embarks on a series of activities both directly and indirectly connected to his situation: tending to his duties as a Samaritan, by trying to save a self-destructive young boy, revisiting his past—his ex-mistress—and spending a weekend with a care-free girl. All these activities both lead to a reconciliation with his past and the culmination of a near-catastrophe (his son, Richard, almost gets seriously hurt while Harry is on his quest) in the present. [412] It is this catastrophe—due both directly and indirectly to Harry's own conduct—that makes him face his situation, accept his responsibility for his marriage and fatherhood and leave the Samaritan work to make amends with his wife, Melissa. The quest leading to the last phantasmagorical section of the book is then resolved through the somewhat open promise of homecoming. In this way, the novel does not only become the recording of the past and present situation of Mosley, but also a means of 'interaction' with the future by way of at least recognising the promises and possibilities hidden in it. But the novel does not fully succeed in showing *how* these possibilities can be exploited and *how* they could help the protagonists get out of their moral dilemmas, as the following novels such as *Accident* and *Impossible Object* do.

II. *Accident*: the necessity of experimentalism for freedom

With *Accident* Mosley successfully departed from his transitional period both in the biographical and the artistic sense. The publication of his theological essay *Experience and Religion* and his novel *Accident* at the same time[413] could be seen as his public sign-off from organised religion and the beginning of a new, 'experimental' artistic career. *Accident* also brought Mosley recognition as an original novelist on the literary and scholarly scene on both sides of the Atlantic[414]—Joseph Losey's highly acclaimed film of the novel in collaboration with Harold Pinter, especially, put Mosley in the rank of 'avant-garde' artists of the time.

Unlike his former novels *Accident* is not autobiographical. The question investigated is: are humans free to determine or influence the outcome of outer events by their inner choice? In order to do this Mosley put his narrator in a clear-cut moral dilemma, which arises due to the accident. Stephen Jervis—and his alter ego the novelist Charlie[415]—are faced with the death of Stephen's student William, which seems to have been caused by the drunk driving of his other student Anna. On one hand, they want to protect Anna and therefore cannot go to the police, on the other hand, they cannot plan to cover up for her as the discovery of this could ruin their reputations and the stability of their families. Furthermore, they cannot leave the situation to hazard, as they, being respectively her teacher and lover, feel responsible for Anna. They seem to be trapped in a morally impossible situation, where every decision for getting out of the dilemma leads to the opposite of this intention. *Accident* succeeds in dramatising what *Meeting Place* half achieves: it illustrates the process of aesthetic vision through which the narrator is enabled to make the right choice and thus leave the moral trap.

Stephen Jervis and his alter ego Charlie overcome their situation by detaching themselves from it through observing it within a different framework—i.e., the framework of art. As discussed earlier in this chapter, a moral dilemma arises when the two-valued logical system puts the individual before a paradoxical situation: the individual is compelled to choose *either* this *or* that, where the only choice for getting out of the situation is the logically impossible *both* this *and* that or *neither* this *nor* that. Within the framework of art, however, such a choice is possible.[416] In *Meeting Place* Mosley achieved the aesthetic treatment of moral dilemmas that had happened in the past. That is, the protagonists freed themselves from their pasts. In *Accident* he found a way of dealing with them as they were *happening in the present*. The protagonists free themselves from their present situation.

> [this is] the style . . . what my characters try to find—by distancing themselves with part of themselves from another part that is experiencing what *is taking place*, they are able to hang on to something aesthetic and thus not get lost—although this does not of course save them from confusion and suffering. They still have . . . some handle, by which to survive confusion and suffering.[417]

It is important to note that the observation of experience in the framework of art is not meant as a means of self-deception: the aim of aesthetic observation is not to beautify ugliness, or surround oneself with beautiful objects which would serve as a blindfold against reality. What the narrator does is assume the role of the 'reader' of a fiction in which he himself lives.[418] The narrator steps outside life—the three-dimensional reality—in order to conceive of it in a different context: i.e., that of a work of art. He 'shapes' his characters by reducing them to their outward shape, using a few words, as if he were summarising a photography, or a painting. The character becomes thus a work of art that the reader—just as the narrator—can observe. Anna is 'a big girl in a long green dress. Her hair done up. Looking Dutch, with pink cheeks and round cheek bones . . .' or 'a marvellous blond girl with her back to [Stephen]: long hair, from the waist down, no stockings.'[419] The narrator makes no efforts to analyse these characters—in other words, he does not describe the inner feelings, the thoughts of these characters, but just watches them.

In order to do this Mosley employed what he had learned from the *nouveaux romanciers*. In his characterisation, especially, we can see both the implication of the *nouveau roman* techniques, and a rejection of them. Whereas they insisted on the flatness and 'meaninglessness' of their 'texts,' Mosley used and also added his own transcendental voice to their technique. In accordance with his contemporary French novelists, Mosley's narrator does not give the reader any access to the emotions and thoughts of the other characters. In other words, these are not described by an omniscient narrator who analyses their psychology or behaviour. Instead, the characters and their actions are reduced and limited to their outward shapes. These, in turn, are further removed from 'reality' by being frozen into images and metaphors. They are, thus, shown as works of art—as aesthetic objects. However, their dialogues—their communications—constantly remind the reader of their being human and alive.

> I held her. Her eyes on the edge of the precipice. Horses. The wind in fir trees.[420]

The character Rosalind—the narrator's wife—whom the narrator is observing is alienated from human-like description, but precisely because of this the reader can feel her 'liveliness': the empathy of the narrator is expressed strongly through the image he uses to describe her: it is one of movement—an undercurrent teeming, which is best described by yet another image: 'life coursing along underground. A river through caverns and gorges.'[421]

Mosley's narration also differs from Robbe-Grillet's or Simon's in that the reader is given access to the narrator's mind. We witness his thoughts and his reflections and self-reflections. We can *identify* with Stephen. This does not mean that he gives the reader access to his mind by analysing his 'inner world.' He observes himself in the same vein as he observes the other characters from the outside.

> As I lean on the window-ledge of my room I see this image of myself—a man in a gown with rather long hair flowing caught against the wall of crumbling building.[422]

Yet, he is aware of his ability to conceive of himself as such—the ability to observe himself as part of an aesthetic pattern. He, in the same breath, sees himself as a 'mask' with nothing behind it[423] and also as one who 'would run to the hospital past the ashes, the lava, the skeletons with their knees drawn up. I would say—I am alive! . . . I felt myself still in a cage of narrow walls. I would say—I am feeling, I have got to go now. This was what I was so often thinking.'[424] He can, therefore, detach himself from his own experienced impossibility and observe himself as if observing another person. This movement—i.e., the continuous switch between experiencing his life and observing it from outside—creates a tension in which life can be depicted as something 'teeming, burgeoning.'[425] By seeing himself as a motionless and distanced but lively work of art he can free himself from the structures of the situation he finds himself in.

Jervis's conception of his own identity is an especially effective device for achieving this. The narrator—who introduces himself as Stephen Jervis[426]—occasionally changes his identity to become his novelist-friend Charlie.[427] Stephen and Charlie both merge[428] into one protagonist—the 'writer'—and still are separate characters. The narrator switches between being Stephen and Charlie. By detaching himself from his own identity—i.e., by becoming Charlie—he actually takes on responsibility for Anna's state. He can look at himself as having had an affair with Anna—i.e., as Charlie—and as one who has been the witness of another man's affair with Anna—i.e., as Stephen. In other words, he can both see himself as responsible and not responsible for her. By observing himself in the context of fiction this impossible situation is realised and can be embraced. That is to say, he neither succumbs to guilt, nor does he deny responsibility. In either way he would make the wrong choice: he would either be moral and self-destructive (punishing himself for his sin) or he would refrain from doing anything and thus give in to hazard—to fate. In an aesthetic framework, as opposed to an ethical one, he can grasp his situation and try to undertake action: while he is being interrogated about the accident he simultaneously answers the questions and detaches himself from what is happening to him through his thoughts. The inconsistency between his thoughts and the events enable him—and the reader—to view his situation aesthetically:

> I was in a pew like a miniature chapel. Questions came out sideways not wanting to be considered. There was a solicitor from Williams family, a doctor, the police with papers under their arms. A man whispered 'You represent his college?' Everyone whispered. I thought—I no longer know truth nor bravery. A man on a tumbril, watching the face of the crowd. Holding up one of the condemned; a collapsed thing. They drag him out with his feet behind him. Go through the motions. . . .
> . . . 'And what was the position of the deceased?' I could answer this. At the bottom, at the left hand side, on the window. 'Where he appeared to have fallen?' 'Yes.' . . . He was asking something else. 'And what was his condition?' Condition? 'He was dead.' 'How do you know?' How do I know? 'I felt him.'[429]

His thoughts are at odds with what is happening. What he is thinking is in fact not taking place at all, instead his thoughts put that what is happening into a different framework—a framework where out of chaos pattern (meaning) can emerge. His use of clichés make the scene that he is experiencing fictional: a film, a play, a work of art, which the narrator—and the reader—can watch.

Through this aesthetic observation he frees himself from the 'logic' of the story: he 'wrenches' the plot into a different direction.[430] What is important now is no longer the course of the trial but his awareness—i.e., his aesthetic observation of the predicament. This aesthetic observation is in turn put into the framework of experienced reality by his taking part in it as reality. His answers to the questions at the trial are reasonable and causally justifiable. He is constantly moving to and fro between experienced reality and aesthetic observation: he switches between being the participant in the story and the reader of it. In this way he gains some hold over his life (by way of seeing and facing his impossibility), like that of the reader over the novel.

Another means by which Mosley conveys the possibility of getting out of the determinism of the story, is by further evolving the phantasmagorial plot already initiated in *Meeting Place*. By juxtaposing thoughts, dialogues, and actions in a logically inconsistent way, causality is done away with. The narrator frees himself from the logic- and time-bound framework of his experience. Various thoughts, dialogues and actions take place at the same time and place without any reference to each other. To some extent they even contradict each other directly. This mode of narration produces a logical discrepancy within the story, which brings forth the notion of life as, on the one hand, experienced impossibilities and, on the other, aesthetic observation, in which impossibilities are possible. Things that can impossibly happen simultaneously in a logical framework, now can be observed as happening at the same time. For example, he comes across the crashed car to rescue Anna and William ('I came across the car on its side across the road'[431]) and be in the car at the same time ('I opened the front door upwards lying on my back and pushing with a hand and a foot.'[432]) He can even see himself as being in the problematic situation of having to cover up for Anna, who could have caused the accident and consequently William's death—

> There would be an inquest. We had already done too much. We had tried to protect Anna. We had made ourselves responsible for her. Might make it worse. If anything could be.[433]

and as being directly responsible for the accident himself—

> It might have been I who had been all night at the party; had driven off with a girl in a car; had crashed.[434]

Overcoming this predicament by detaching himself from it and observing it in a framework other than that of experienced reality, where such illogicalities can happen, does not mean avoiding responsibility by living in a 'make-believe' world. What he does is actually see the impossibility clearly as it is *happening* and, thus, make it possible within the framework of his observation—i.e., fictionality, life as art-work —in order not to succumb to its causality—i.e., its inevitable tragedy. He must first experience life as rationally conceivable reality; only then could he conceive of this reality as fictionality—within an aesthetic framework—in order to overcome it.

In this way the conventional conception of a story unfolding[435] is done away with; instead, the plot becomes an open one. In *Meeting Place* Mosley aimed at this, but as it was discussed earlier, did not succeed—except for the last hallucinatory section—in doing away with the linearity and causality of the plot. In *Accident* (and also *Impossible Object*) the logical causality is done away with and the question of 'what happens next?' becomes unimportant. The reader is not lured to go on reading the story by the device of 'withholding' information only to be revealed in the end—as was the case in his earlier novels.[436] The information given in this novel (and also the following ones) is of little importance for the development of the 'story' in sense of its dramatisation and revelation. As there is no logical consistency in the plot, there is no predictability in the conventional sense. Like the protagonist, the reader himself must try to find an 'aesthetic' hold of the plot—i.e., to see a pattern—in order to answer the question 'what is happening now?' In this sense, the question 'what is happening now?' replaces the conventional question of 'what happens next?' Therefore, the plot loses its relevance as a closed story and, instead, becomes an open pattern: it is left to the reader to make the connections; to make his own pattern. In this sense, the reader—like the protagonist—is actively engaged in looking at the given impossibilities in an aesthetic way, and by this can make them possible. The narrator's constant juxtaposition of different levels of time, space and logic does away with the logical consistency of the plot. As a result there is no predictability in the novel in the conventional sense: there is no answer to the impossibility introduced in the novel in the form of unriddling a mystery by means of unveiling the logic or rationality behind the story. What looks like a 'detective story, . . . seeded with clues'[437] is told in a manner, where a rational and causal solution to the problem—i.e., the accident and its consequences—seems not only impossible,[438] but futile. The reader cannot—nor can the narrator—pin down the causes for this event.

The resolution of the phantasmal chaos and the return of order happens through the *choice* of the protagonists to face the impossibility—the moral dilemma. This is most poignantly shown towards the end of the novel where Charlie and Stephen talk and impossibly not talk about the accident. The conversation has a Faulknerian quality (bearing in mind that Faulkner was Mosley's favourite writer) as the characters do not directly talk about what is to be done. They seem to talk at cross purposes, but in end effect an impression does arise that they know the underlying purpose of the communication (Mosley calls this sort of communication 'noncommunication'[439]).

> Charlie said 'How are you feeling?'
> I stretched.
> Charlie said 'You must be jolly tired.'
> I said 'Hullo Anna.'
> Anna said 'Hullo.'
> I said 'Did you have a bit of sleep?'
> 'Yes thank you.'
> . . .
> I began waving my fingers to attract Charlie's attention.
> Charlie came and leaned on the arm of my chair and put his cheek close to mine. A threadbare carpet.
> I shook my head.
> Charlie went back and stood beside Anna.
> I felt in my pocket for a piece of paper, found my diary, tore a page out, and wrote on it *there'll be an inquest*. I waited for Charlie.
> Charlie took the piece of paper.
> I said 'You're going home, Anna?'
> Anna said 'Yes.' . . .
> Charlie made his face with all muscles of his neck standing out. . . .[440]

This conversation between Charlie and Stephen, is vital for getting out of their predicament. The omission of this communication/noncommunication in the Pinter/Losey film, to Mosley's deep dissatisfaction,[441] did indeed result in the opposite of what Mosley intended to show in his novel: namely, the idea that the choice of human beings can influence the outcome of events through aesthetic observation and thus help them escape from helplessness. The Pinter script kept to the 'games and the noncommunications in the novel,'[442] but did away with

> the underlying 'communication' of Stephen thinking to himself . . . and this almost final scene with Charlie when there is something practical to be *done*. That is, they have to decide what to do about Anna after the accident. . . . About this impossibility they have to communicate; and see that there is not much of an answer except, simply—to see it clearly. Then things take their course. . . . the way I saw it, there was this *vital* 'communication' at the end—or rather discussion—which was

a verbal expression of the sort of thing Stephen had been 'thinking.' Pinter wouldn't really do any of this—his speciality being 'noncommunication.'[443]

What Charlie and Stephen do is detach themselves from themselves to see themselves as aesthetic figures, as actors, who are part of a fiction; of a play—which is what life is. In this way they free themselves from the impossibility that they are presently in by facing it. They do not discuss the matter, nor do they plan what action to take in 'face' of the moral dilemma. They just observe without taking action: only then could they truly see the pattern of what is happening. It is only through their 'non-action'—i.e., observing the situation in a framework, in which they can grasp it—that they can gain some freedom to undertake action and try to protect Anna at the trial. At the trial itself Stephen can only grasp the impossible situation he is in—protecting Anna and being truthful—by distancing himself from the impossibility by juxtaposing the levels of time and space: he is thus both aware of the relevance and irrelevance of the things as they happen. By moving between the levels of reality and fiction he gains some freedom to make decisions—in other words, he is not in a helpless situation. He can be *at once* amidst events and outside of them by detaching himself from them to observe them.

> When it was my turn, my turn, had been waiting. I stepped up, that quiet thing, so polite, merciful. On a rostrum. . . .
> A long way away. I am doing this two years after. Looking back on it. . . . It happened. What else? The great distance of the sky, the universe. Things are important at the time. Life hangs on them. Then they are over.
> 'And when you came across the car—' I could answer this. A man with grey hair and spectacles. The car had over turned and one wheel was up the bank. . . .[444]

The reader should bear in mind that Stephen can come successfully out of his interrogation because he does not—contrary to Pinter's script—sleep with his pupil Anna. Apart from the omission of the conversation between Charlie and Stephen at the end of the novel, the inclusion of the sexual relationship between Stephen and Anna was a second point of disappointment to Mosley.[445] Mosley, as discussed earlier, came to see moral rules not as absolute codes of conduct, but as structures, which help decision making in *given* situations. In this situation it would have been counter-productive, if Stephen had an affair with Anna[446] because it would have made it even more difficult for Stephen to detach himself from the situation and observe it clearly. The interrogation would have thus degenerated into some sort of a self-defence instead of the demonstration of aesthetic observation. The reader and the protagonist would have been faced with a further moral dilemma—a professor exploiting his position, ignoring instead of facing his responsibilities, and victimising or patronising his student—in place of an aesthetic solution to the initial one. The situation would have unnecessarily been further complicated and would have ended in yet another muddled story of helplessness and emptiness—as it indeed did in the Pinter/Losey film.

It must again be stressed that the narrator's aesthetic observation is not a means to evade responsibility by 'beautifying' or 'romanticising' the dilemma. What he does is, to use a Christian terminology, *trust* the chaos to make a pattern—a sense—which can be observed if he puts himself in the position to observe it. In other words, he can trust whatever happens to make sense in the pattern (i.e., be part of the pattern), if he observes the pattern from 'outside'—from an aesthetic point of view. Therefore, he is both the observer and the maker of the pattern, since the pattern—the work of art—would be non-existent if he did not put himself in a framework where he can conceive of it. In such a framework the narrator can free himself from the logical constraints of deciding about what is experienced reality. However, he does not succumb to irrationality and the constraints of a 'make-believe' world either.[447] The narrator conceives of and conveys the reality that surrounds him as something that will work itself out as a work of art, but simultaneously lives it and is part of it, and thus makes it into experienced reality. In other words he switches between the two sides of life—i.e., life as reality and life as aesthetic observation. In this way he can make the impossibility that he experiences in reality possible in an aesthetic context—in the context of seeing it as art. One could say, that Mosley subverts the conventional form of the novel: instead of merely having the reader of the novel identify with the protagonists, the protagonists identify with the reader. The success of this narrative device is shown through the continuation of life despite the pain and tragedy caused by the accident. The survival of Rosalind's baby at the end of the novel[448] symbolises this.

III. *Assassins*: relapse into conventional writing

After the publication of *Accident* Mosley embarked on writing a 'so-called thriller,'[449] which was 'aimed at being popular, and perhaps being made into a film.'[450] Mosley justifiably does not like to think of *Assassins* (1966) as part of the his experimental novels written in the Sixties.[451] Considering both the form and content of *Assassins* the novel is a regression rather than a development of Mosley's new treatment of freewill. In retrospect Mosley believes that the novel was perhaps an effort to understand something about his childhood amidst the political/personal events—especially in light of his view of his father:

> While the politicians are functioning it is assumed that they are powerful and rational and self-determining beings: then suddenly they are history and they appear all the time to have been helpless and half-witted (Nixon). Whereas in fact, although they are always largely helpless and goodness knows often enough half-witted, there is somewhere a sense in which politics does work—events are influenced, that is, by the decisions people make—but not in the way that is mythically imagined.[452]

Mosley tried to show the influence of political decision-making on outer events by centring the story around an assassination attempt, which by chance goes wrong and results in the abduction of the British Foreign Secretary's fourteen-year old daughter. The abductor and the girl come to some sort of an agreement, by which the abductor pretends to be the rescuer of the girl and thus put an end to the assassination plan. However, the trick runs into a muddle, as the abductor is brought in front of T.V. camera into the presence of the Foreign Secretary and the Eastern European leader (who was to be assassinate) to be thanked. In this moment the questions arise: is the abductor going to keep his promise and refrain from the assassination or had all this been a trick to assassinate the Eastern European leader in front of the cameras? The muddle is then resolved with the killing of the abductor by the bodyguard of the politician.

The novel is in so far a regression from Mosley's experimental novels that the muddle or the dilemma is resolved in death. Like the protagonists of his early novels, the protagonists of *Assassins* do not seem to have any way out of despair other than death (as in the case of the abductor[453]) or a relapse into it (as in the case of the fourteen-year-old abducted girl).

Having witnessed the killing, the fourteen-year-old girl seems to be completely out of control and on the verge of succumbing to madness and confusion: the 'madwoman' portrayal of her, especially at the end of the novel, depict this.[454] The words with which her father Sir Simon tries to 'console' her could have almost been written by Pinter, whose interpretation of *Accident* was criticised by Mosley:

> You have got to forget about all this. We may never know what really happened. People don't, you know. We imagine we know what's at the back of things, what makes things happen, but we don't. Often, when we look too closely, there's just darkness and confusion.[455]

The necessity of facing helplessness and darkness—or 'evil'—is central to all of Mosley's novels. But whereas in his novels after his conversion, the recognition and observation of darkness—conveyed in shape of moral dilemmas—leads the protagonists to see the light behind it by realising the real possibilities for getting out of it, *Assassins* does not offer the possibility of getting out of this darkness. As in *Accident* in this novel too, Mosley had set out to examine the effect of people's choices on the outer events. But the structure and the style of this novel exclude an outcome as positive as in *Accident*. In *Accident* the whole story concentrated on the efforts of Stephen to get a clear picture of the central moral dilemma and thus get himself and everyone else out of it. In *Assassins*, there is not a single dilemma holding the novel as a red thread, but muddles leading to muddles, without anyone having the vision—as Stephen in *Accident* would have had—for putting them in an aesthetic context and thus handling them. Furthermore, the novel is not written in a self-conscious style and form to allow for the realisation of seeing the events in an aesthetic framework. As was discussed earlier, in *Accident*—and as we shall see in *Impossible Object* and *Natalie Natalia*—the narrator of the novel becomes the reader of his own fiction at the same time as living his 'real' life. The reader has access to the mind of the narrator as a 'living' and suffering being and one that can distance himself from his 'living' and suffering in order to see himself and his life within an aesthetic framework. In *Assassins*, however, the characters seem helplessly caught in their dilemma because they are in no way self-consciously detached from the situation that they are in. They are not conveyed as observers—as Stephen Jervis was—but are observed by an absent but omniscient narrator from a point of view, which is a mixture of Mosley's early tragic/romantic voice and the *nouveau roman* style. In this novel we have more or less a distanced, 'objective' camera-eye, which records the behaviour and appearance of the protagonists and alienates them further by putting them into artificial contexts:

> [Mary] looked back at him. He had taken the lid down from his eye. His face seemed in different pieces, patches of red and brown on an oval . . .
> She put her cheek down on the table. There were breadcrumbs like boulders.
> He was pushing at the top of the table as if driving splinters underneath his nails . . .
> His face was both ugly and beautiful, like a dog's.[456]

Or:

> [Colonel Wedderburn] moved his hand down. Connie watched where it brushed like clouds across a landscape. . . .
> . . . Colonel Wedderburn pressed [Connie's] waist with his thumbs and fingers. There was a faint pale line between his lips. Her body did not move. She swallowed: stretching like a fish against a hook.[457]

This narrative device and characterisation does indeed remind the reader of *Accident*. However, in *Accident* this is done from Stephen's point of view, as means of moving between the frame work of art and life simultaneously in order to free himself from his predicament by way of seeing a pattern in his situation while it was happening. Jervis's freewill lay in his being the creator of his pattern—the reader/writer of his novel: he had the ability to create a relation between his inner choice and outer events aesthetically, so that the outcome of events was positive. In *Assassins* we have the feeling that the omniscient narrator—Mosley—is the sole creating observer, or at best, the protagonists can only see what is outside them—for example, the other protagonists—in aesthetic contexts. But what the narrative device and the form of the novel do not enable them to do is being conscious of themselves as both part of the artwork and the artist: in other words, as both the created and the creator. *Assassins* is in this way closer to *Meeting Place*: the 'objective' external descriptions and the linear plot, whose cinematic cuts do not really do away with the causality and the 'what happened next?' concept of the novel are present here too. However, the last phantasmagorial section of *Meeting

Place does to some extent succeed in breaking the boundaries between time and space, the imaginary and the real, the logical and the arbitrary as a way of breaking out of determinism and helplessness. In *Meeting Place* the hallucination helped Harry to reshuffle or recreate what had happened, what was happening and what would happen and in a way be able to look optimistically into future. He could choose to act by being aware of choices hidden in future. It is true that we are not shown—as we are in *Accident*—how this happens or what Harry does later, but we see his awareness of the possibilities for getting out. In *Assassins*, though, the chaos at the end is not liberating and only further enhances the protagonists' helplessness in face of chaos and darkness.

IV. *Impossible Object*: impossibility of the riddle, aesthetic vision and freedom

> Oh indeed, most stories were about people like helpless pebbles on a beach being pushed around by the sea; and so people are; but people might see this; and so they might see the connection between themselves as observers and themselves as pebbles, and thus come alive; and so might readers see such connections within and between my stories and thus come alive.[458]

Assassins, as was discussed above, can therefore not be seen as a successor to either *Meeting Place* or *Accident*. It is *Impossible Object* (1968), the novel written after *Assassins* that fulfils the development of Mosley's idea about liberating oneself from the moral and logical dilemmas of life by standing back from them in the frame work of art. *Impossible Object* differs from Mosley's other novels of this era, as it actually takes on the form of Mosley's idea instead of mainly talk about it. Its highly original form marks the culmination of Mosley's experimental novels in the Sixties and will therefore be discussed in greater detail in the following.

Impossible Object confirms Mosley's importance as a contemporary British novelist. Scholars of English literature such as Steiner and Scholes praised its originality. Scholes compared the 'vigor and control' of the 'brilliant prose construction, combining images and perspectives' to the 'later work of Picasso' and Steiner remarked:

> What Virginia Woolf's pointillist fables were to Bennet's solid carpenting, the art of Mosley is to Snow's workmanship. *Impossible Object* is all witchfire and mercury.[459]

Impossible Object was also short-listed for the first Booker Prize in 1969, but 'caused most trouble and took most time' and finally did not succeed in winning the prize because 'in some ways and places everyone thought it strained, miscalculated, even absurdly pretentious; but . . . everyone found too that the author's method could produce resonances so strange and fine that the novel was not to be set aside.'[460] The judges' mixture of awe and repulsion only justifies the praise that *Impossible Object* received for its originality.

Like *Accident*, the novel *Impossible Object* is concerned with overcoming the experienced impossibilities of life by putting them into an aesthetic framework. While the moral dilemma in *Accident* was an imaginary one, the impossibilities dealt with in *Impossible Object* were directly experienced by Nicholas Mosley. Similar to his previous moral dilemma—his first affair—here, too, he is confronted with an extra-marital affair. However, whereas the first affair was dealt with in a conventionally ethical way—i.e., by confrontation, repentance and abstinence—his second extra-marital affair, which took place after he had signed off from organised, conventional Christianity, was dealt with 'aesthetically.' That is not to say, that the second affair is beautified or embarked upon dispassionately. What is meant by the term aesthetic or aesthetic vision as opposed to ethical vision is seeing the paradoxicalities and polarities simultaneously: in other words, aesthetic vision is a double-vision or a multiple-vision, whereas the ethical is a single-vision.[461] The ethical only offered the possibility of seeing the first affair as a passionate tragedy, in which any choice could only end in some sort of self-sacrifice and suffering and ultimately the bedevilment of the choice-maker (although, it must be noted that in *Corruption* there is a feeling that the protagonist sees a possibility of getting out of the illusion of self-sacrifice. However, here too, he sees a retreat into abstinence as his only choice). The aesthetic was a view where many, more often than not *contradicting*, possibilities for seeing a moral dilemma could simultaneously co-exist: what the choice-maker in face of a moral dilemma had to do was to become aware of the possibilities in his situation and then the 'right' choice would be *available* in order to be met.

As was shown earlier, this is what Mosley set out to do in *Accident*. The main difference between the style of *Accident* and *Impossible Object* is that *Accident* treats this idea in the form of a more or less straight forward narrative, in which the protagonists try to deal with the impossibilities of life by means of switching between life as experienced reality and as aesthetic observation. *Impossible Object*, though, supersedes *Accident* by taking on the shape of this idea. The novel itself is an impossible object: its structure is logically impossible in as far as that the connections between the parts cannot be worked out in a logically consistent way.

Impossible Object consists of 'eight stories, each of which has connections with the others, plus italicised inner-chapters that serve, in some oblique way, as introductions to stories, though they too are connected with the stories and other inner-chapters.'[462] However, such a description is limited only to the "surface"—the visual structure—of the novel.[463] Yet, it is important to take note of the visual structure, as it contributes to an understanding of the continuous switches between life as experienced reality and life, as aesthetic observation that take place in the novel. The stories and the inner-chapters resemble a series of "interlocking circles, each of which intersects at some point with all the others";[464] the impossible shape which these create is described by the narrator—in so far as one can identify a narrator—as *'something impossible, like a staircase climbing a spiral to come out where it started or a cube with a vertical line at the back overlapping a horizontal one in front. These cannot exist in three dimensions but can be drawn in two; by cutting out one dimension a fourth is created.* **The object is that life is impossible;** *one cuts out fabrication and creates reality.*'[465]

In this novel, perhaps more than any other novel in his long career, Mosley conveyed his concern with the paradoxical ability of art—itself being fabrications—to overcome illusions and thus achieve freedom. *Impossible Object* is therefore the most self-conscious, the most experimental novel of Mosley, in which the novel 'de-constructs' itself not in order to overcome the paradox that the post-structuralists set for themselves (i.e., the paradox of writing a novel that claims it has no meaning or nothing to say), but to break the reader's old habit of taking 'the finger for the moon.' In this novel Mosley—being a modern writer—set to cut out the 'fabrications' that had dulled the truth-telling ability of the novel: namely, the conventional conceptions of the features of the novel. Narrative devices, setting, characterisation and plot are used in a way, in which they break the reader's 'conventional' associations with them by redefining their defining boundaries. That is why it is almost impossible to write a short summary about the content of the novel, as it has radically done away with the plot and story line. The focus is mainly on the form. On grounds of this, the following discussion of *Impossible Object* will concentrate much more closely on Mosley's technique than the discussions of the previous novels. It will be shown how these features make up an impossible shape—the novel itself—which can be realised through the reader's switching between experienced reality—i.e., realising the logical inconsistency of the connections and the clues in the novel—and aesthetic observation—i. e. grasping the impossible shape for what it is: an art-work.

Impossible Object, as mentioned earlier, supersedes *Accident* in that it deals with the moral impossibilities—here again a married father having an extra-marital affair—introduced in it by taking on the shape of an impossibility itself, and is thus more open to both the protagonists and the reader to make out an aesthetic pattern. It makes the reader see the necessity of making an aesthetic pattern, in order to conceive of the impossible shape of the moral dilemma. However, it leaves it to the reader to see his own pattern in the novel. Through the juxtaposition of thoughts, dialogues and actions the consistency and logic of the story is done away with in a way that the narrator can move inside and outside of his experience as it is happening and thus make the impossibilities as they are happening possible in a framework of aesthetic observation. For example, in the story 'Humming Bird' the narrator deals with the dilemma of his wife's confessions about her encounter with the policeman on the beach by seeing the situation both as real and as an art-work—i.e., fictional drama:

> 'He assaulted you?'
> 'In a way.'
> 'What way?'
> She said, 'I mean, it wasn't like that.'
> I jumped off the bed and stood with my teeth clenched. I thought—
> *This is real. Isn't it?*
> She said 'Oh I knew I shouldn't have told you!'
> I said 'Of course you should have told me!'
> I thought—I do feel jealousy: am I gratified?
> . . .
> I was pacing up and down *as if action had been decided on.*
> Then I thought—*This will make an extraordinary story.*[466]

The narrator can simultaneously experience life as reality and detach himself from it in order to see it as a drama; as fiction. He, hence, switches between the two sides of life—i.e., life as experienced reality and as aesthetic observation—in order to make his impossible situation possible: by putting it into an aesthetic framework, he can have some hold over it. So far, *Impossible Object* shares the same narrative devices with *Accident*.

However, this similarity only applies, if one looks at each short story in *Impossible Object* separately. The narrative technique of *Impossible Object* as a unity—as a coherent whole—supersedes that of *Accident*.

Whereas in *Accident* and in the single short stories of *Impossible Object* the switches takes place on a micro-level, i.e., between and within sentences, in *Impossible Object*, as a whole, the switching process is further enhanced on a macro-level, i.e., between the short stories and the inner-chapters. The short stories can be conceived of as the reality which the protagonists experience. They are related to each other as they happen to the same protagonists. However, these stories, at the same time, contradict each other. That is to say, the novel becomes an impossible whole that cannot be experienced in three-dimensional reality. The impossibility of the inter-connections between the different short stories is shown on the level of characterisation, plot and setting, which will be discussed later in the essay.

The italicised inner-chapters are clearly differentiated from the short stories both visually and in their style: on the one hand they are written in italics—as if in hand writing—and on the other, they are in 'surrealistic' prose. They can be seen as the narrator's fictional conception of the short stories: whereas the short stories are written in a style which makes them seem like experienced reality, the surrealistic pieces do not pretend to be the reality, but images. In this sense they can be seen as the aesthetic observation of the short stories. They are not an exact reflection of the short stories, but rather an alienated, aesthetic interpretation of the impossibilities introduced in the short stories. It seems as if the protagonist steps out of his experienced reality altogether and reflects upon it to write it down in the form of a surrealistic prose—surrealistic work of art; like a writer whose works can help him to come to terms with his own experiences. One is reminded of Mosley himself, who says: 'I think I write to explain, aesthetically, the world to myself; . . .'[467] It is by means of this detached, aesthetic observation that the impossibilities within and between the short stories are made possible. In this way, the protagonist—and the reader—can come to terms with the impossibility by putting it in a different framework, in which he can 'explain' his 'impossible' situation (trying to be a good husband and having an affair) to himself—aesthetically—and thus see the possibility for further actions. In other words, he switches between experienced reality and aesthetic observation. The whole novel, therefore, can be seen as a 'unity' of switches between short stories—i.e., experienced reality—and the italicised inner-chapters—i.e., the detached, aesthetic reflection on the experienced reality. The novel literally alternates between short stories and italicised inner-chapters.

The impossibility experienced in the short stories—i.e., reality—is the (morally) 'impossible' co-existence of a good marriage and a love affair. This impossibility can be grasped in an aesthetic observation as the surrealistic italicised prose pieces. In one of the inner-chapters God, the incarnation of the good and the absolute in conventional Christianity, is subverted into a human criminal. In this way the 'good' and the 'evil' are made to co-exist.

> *So now God sat among the millionaires in shark skin uniforms and the old ladies like commercialised Christmas and he took the girls on his knees and gave them diamonds. And sometimes he read in the papers that one or another of his subordinates had been captured; was serving on an aerodrome or in a committee. He watched the roulette tables which were like green fields and beyond them the sea with the washed-up bodies. This was all that was left of his empire now: the experiment had succeeded and anyone was free. They could come to the Argentine. It was only sometimes dull never to be treated like a criminal.*[468]

This passage, like all other inner passages, does not correspond separately with a particular short story, in which the 'impossibility' of the co-existence of a good marriage and a love affair is conveyed. That is to say, this passage is not a separate aesthetic observation of a particular short story. It just a framework in which the co-existence of—a (moral) contradiction—'go(o)d' and 'bad'—can be seen as possible. All of the italicised passages are rather a means to see patterns—independent from time and locale—that run through the novel. In this sense, the italicised inner chapters pick up elements from all over the novel in a seeming arbitrary way. It is as if the narrator, like any author, picks elements and events from all over his life—depicted in the short stories—to put them together in a surrealistic prose; an art-work—the italicised inner chapters—in order to present an interpretation of his experiences in form of an aesthetic pattern. For example, the visit to Nietzsche's asylum in Turin in 'Journey into the Mind' on page 127 is taken up in a surrealistic prose some seventy pages earlier. By taking up elements from the different short stories and putting them in an aesthetic pattern the italicised chapters can be seen as holding the short stories and the novel as a whole together.

The settings of the different parts of *Impossible Object* convey the narrator's switches between experienced reality and aesthetic observation particularly well. They are realistic like those of *Accident*: all the short stories take place in real places, such as a pub in London, a villa in Rome or a beach in Morocco. As in *Accident* the setting is at the same time also removed from reality through the observation of the narrator. The narrator conveys its fictionality by putting it into an aesthetic observation; that is to say the setting is also portrayed as an image. In 'Journey into the Mind,' for example, one reads: 'The road ran over the hills like a rollercoaster. The landscape was made of plywood. It was painted with flowers and dark green trees,'[469] or 'The outskirts of Pisa were an industrial town with painted pipes like modern sculptures';[470] very poignantly also: 'The street was hot. We sat in the car and both wore dark glasses like people in a film. A whole city had been built outside Rome exactly like Rome, in order to film it.'[471] Thus, the protagonists can also be seen as being on a stage, they are at the same time in real Rome and in the fictional Rome taking part in a film, in a work of art. In this way, the setting again switches between reality that can be experienced and fictionality that is observed.

On the micro-level, i.e., taking the short stories on their own, the switching process of the setting is therefore comparable to that of *Accident*. On the macro-level, looking at the novel as a whole, the conception of the setting goes a step further than that of *Accident*. The switches do not only take place within or between different sentences but between the different parts of the novel. In this sense, the inner-chapters—i.e., fictionality—reflect on the short stories—i.e., 'reality'—within a different setting. Thus, the realistic settings of the short stories become surrealistic settings in the italicised inner-chapters.

The inner-chapters take place in realistic locale as well—i.e., the Argentine, Turin, etc. However, they gain their surrealistic or 'anecdotal' quality through the placing of the characters in them: God, for example, features throughout these passages—

> *When God arrived in the Argentine he had his forged papers and remodelled nose and just the clothes he stood up in and nothing else . . .*[472]

By integrating God into this 'real' setting—i.e., the Argentine—it is clearly indicated that this passage has to be taken as an alienation from reality and therefore to be understood as aesthetic observation. It is a further fictionalisation—work of art—within the novel itself. The juxtaposition of the realistic settings of the short stories and the clearly fictional settings of the inner passages—like that of the passage mentioned above—contributes further to the switches between reality and fictionality through which the protagonists seek to grasp the impossibilities of their life.

Regarding the characterisation techniques of *Impossible Object*, on the micro-level of the novel—i.e., taking the short stories on their own—the switching process between reality and fictionality is conveyed in a similar way as in *Accident*. The characters are only described through their outward shape and the reader is not given any access to their thoughts and feelings (except those of the narrator) through character analysis in the conventional sense. Their human outward shapes are, then, alienated from reality by the narrator's conception of them in an aesthetic framework. On the other hand, as in *Accident*, their liveliness is shown through their communications—i.e., dialogues—and the images that the narrator uses in order to show the movement and the depth beyond their outward shape. The characters, therefore, switch between reality and fictionality. The girl from 'Public House,' for example, is described as one with a 'small dark face surrounded by a fur hat from which her gold eyes looked out.'[473] This realistic description of her is immediately alienated and put into a fictional context by the narrator observing her as 'Anna Karenina at the railway station; her first appearance there and the last, because her end was foreshadowed in the beginning.'[474] The image of the girl as Anna Karenina, then, is yet further alienated from human resemblance by the narrator's conceiving of her eyes as 'a depth like a well; you could drop a stone down and listen for ever.'[475] However, this alienation conveys her liveliness by pointing at a 'depth' behind her appearance. In this sense, an impossibility—i.e., characterisation of the living, without doing away with their liveliness—is made possible as a switching between (three dimensional) reality and (two dimensional) art-work.

However, in *Impossible Object* the characterisation supersedes that of *Accident* by making the characters an impossibility in themselves. That is to say, the characters are realised as such, that their identity seems to shift in every short story just in so far that the reader could impossibly identify them either as wholly new characters or exactly the same characters. In other words not only is the impossibility of characterising 'living people' made possible by means of switching between the realistic and the fictional. The impossibility of 'fixing' their identity without doing away with their 'liveliness' is realised as well. In this sense, the reader is forced to try to identify the protagonists continuously by keeping track of their appearances or the number of their children,[476] only to find further possibilities of identification suggested by this exercise. In this way the characters keep their individuality and 'opacity' because the identification process of them never comes to a close.

It seems as if one could identify two married couples. The couples with three sons from the first story 'Family Game'—A and B—and the couple with two daughters from 'Intelligent People'—X and Y. The man from 'Family Game' seems to be both the narrator of the novel as a whole and the lover of Y. In the first story he is thinking of turning the story that he is writing—i.e., the opening italicised chapter about 'how love only flourishes in time of war'[477]—into a story about a father with his children. This could very well be the story 'Family Game,' thus, about A and B. However, other stories in the novel suggest that 'Family Game,' the 'father-writer' and his plans could be the invention of a different narrator.[478] Half way through the novel in the short story 'Public House,' the impossible becomes possible, that is, the narrator of 'Family Game' seems both to be observed and to be invented by a second narrator and also to be this second narrator himself. In other words, A and his loved one Y are observed by a meta-A, who is both the alter-ego of A and as much different from A as not to be A. The impossibility of A's identity is poignantly conveyed, when meta-A meets A, and, thus, in a way meets himself.

> He said 'What are you doing here?' I said 'I'm writing a book.' He said 'Oh, you write too?' When he was interested it was still as if it were only in himself. I said 'I once wrote a story about you.' He said 'About the pub?' I said 'No, about a journey up through Italy.' I thought this at least would interest him. He said 'I wrote a story about the pub.'[479]

The first person narrator who has been telling 'Public House' now denies being its narrator and the person who has been observed by him now claims to have written 'Public House.' The narrator, thus, becomes an impossibility. However, through his reflection upon the impossibility of his existence, he, again, confirms his existence. This impossibility is only possible in the framework of the novel: in an aesthetic observation that the novel inevitably is. When meta-A and A meet, the narrator becomes aware of this impossibility himself:

> He was standing in front of the plate-glass window of a hotel. . . . In the plate-glass my vision was doubled; as if the man were standing both inside and outside of himself.[480]

> I said 'What was your story about the pub?' He said 'It was told by a man who had seen us that winter.' He banged his head. He said 'But you can't exist! Or you're myself. You see how this is impossible!'[481]

Within the framework of experienced reality this self-invention is logically impossible. But within the (two) dimensions of art the narrator can be his own invention. Such a phenomenon shows that art is only on the 'surface' two-dimensional, and in effect multi-dimensional. The narrator makes use of this characteristic of art to overcome his impossibility: he switches between life as experience and life as aesthetic observation to make his impossible existence possible: like Baron von Münchhausen pulling himself out of the ditch by his own hair.

The plot in this novel treats the impossibility of the co-existence of a love affair and a good marriage by becoming an impossibility itself: the impossible connections between the parts of the novel reflect the impossible relationships between the protagonists. As in *Accident* the plot becomes an open pattern that has to be grasped aesthetically. Its openness is due to the narrator's doing away with logic- and time-bound consistency of the events. As in *Accident*, the plot is not realised by a consistent unfolding of a story. The information given does not contribute to the unveiling of the story by showing a consistent way of finding the connections, which then lead to a revealing of the story.

Whereas *Accident* consists of a single plot—if one can speak of a plot—in which the narrator has to deal with the accident, *Impossible Object* is constructed out of several sub-plots—again, in so far as one can speak of plots—which, apart from dealing with the underlying theme, treat different impossibilities. What makes the overall plot an impossibility itself is the connection between these sub-plots. Through their impossible connections they make up a riddle to which there is no key—a labyrinth, from which there is no way out—except by seeing it aesthetically. That is to say, the plot of the novel is highly complex and can not be worked out. It is only by reflecting on it as a work of art, that one can grasp this riddle: within a work of art one can make the logical and causal inconsistency of such an impossibility—such a riddle—possible. This is done, on the one hand, in the italicised inner-chapters which, as was argued above, can be interpreted as the narrator's efforts to understand his experiences (in the short stories) aesthetically. On the other hand, the plot is open to the reader to make a pattern out of it in order to understand the impossible connections between the different sub-plots.

Within every single short story the protagonist experiences an impossibility, which he has difficulties to come to terms with. As in *Accident* the impossibilities introduced in the single short stories are not unriddled by means of first withholding and then unveiling information in the end. Thus there is no key given to solve the riddle—i.e., the impossibility. The protagonists do not try to find an answer to the impossibility, but rather look at it aesthetically in order not to succumb to its logic: i.e., to its tragedy. What they do is switch between the experienced reality and aesthetic observation in order to be able to grasp the impossibility and, thus, free themselves from it to go on with life.

In 'Humming Bird,' for instance, the protagonist must deal with his wife possibly having consented to having been assaulted. This leads to a dilemma. The protagonist can neither ignore this assault and go on living with his wife as before, nor can he leave his wife as he loves her, nor can he take revenge on the 'molester' as this could be implicating his wife. Life could, therefore, come to a halt, if the protagonist succumbed to this impossibility. There is not much answer to this impossibility other than facing it in an aesthetic framework, in order to have some hold over it. This is symbolised in the story by the protagonist's facing the possible 'molester.' None of them, neither the husband, nor the wife, nor the molester, speak about the incident; none of them tries either to explain or justify. The only thing that the protagonist can do is to distance himself from the situation he is in by 'alienating' it—by seeing it as part of a pattern. In this sense there is a continuous switch between the experienced situation and the alienated conception of it. He simultaneously talks to the 'molester' and conceives of the situation by removing its experienced reality onto an aesthetic level: the 'molester' becomes a 'humming bird,' the narrator himself 'far above him' with his 'huge head from the bottom of the sea.' His wife sees the two 'like a mother proud of children' and the talk between them becomes 'a polite conversation round a breakfast table.'[482] The story provides the possibility of dealing with this impossibility by leaving open whether the assault happened at all. It is up to the protagonist (and the reader) to do with it what he can. By seeing the connection between his own motives for the trip to the south of Morocco and what happened between his wife and the policeman during this absence he can refrain from putting the 'assault'—or the 'affair'—in an ethical good/evil framework and thus avoid a moral judgement. Early on in the story he admits to having had wanted to travel to the south alone, 'because when travelling in Arab countries there is always an impression of an adventure round some corner, an image of a black-eyed girl with her face half covered in a doorway.'[483] Being aware both of his wife's knowledge of this[484] and her conduct during his absence he can simultaneously see himself as the 'good victim' of a planned scheme, on one hand, and the 'bad villain,' on the other. [485] In this way he can leave the realm of conventional ethics and not only avoid tragedy and nihilistic despair, but also realise the possibility of adding a new dimension to his life: in this case, the possibility that the aesthetic vision provides the husband with seems to be having a similar experience himself! In the following story 'Public House' we encounter him with his beloved in a pub in London and later on in an idyllic scene in Tamanet, the same town where he had stayed with his wife in the previous story 'Humming Bird.' His aesthetic vision thus enables him to overcome his moral dilemma by opening up possibilities other than those within the either-or ethical framework. In so far, the treatment of the plot is similar to that of *Accident*.

On the macro-level, the plot of *Impossible Object* supersedes that of *Accident* by becoming an impossible object itself. All the parts are connected to each other at multiple points: to put it in John O'Brien's words: 'the structure of the novel is like a series of interlocking circles, each one of which intersects at some point with all of the others.'[486] There are clear indications that the different sub-plots have to be conceived of as parts of a whole no matter how impossible this task seems to be. The 'same' characters—whose identities occasionally shift only as much so that the reader can identify them as 'impossibly' the same—appear throughout the different short stories. As it was shown earlier in the essay, one can identify two couples, to whom the stories happen. However, it is impossible to work out a logically consistent structure of the plot as a whole. The short stories are connected to each other and simultaneously their connections are inconsistent. Not only do the indications that the reader has in order to identify the characters constantly shift—e.g. the number of the children of the different couples. It is also impossible to have a logically consistent plot, when the narrator—as it was shown earlier in the section on characterisation—undermines his own existence. '[The] geometry cannot be worked out in terms of a realistic fiction.'[487] In this sense, the plot can be seen as a labyrinth from which the reader can only get out by disposing of a two-valued logical system and oscillating between different mutually exclusive connections.

A most poignant and central example for the inconsistency of the connections between the parts is the tragic death of the baby in the last short story 'The Sea.' There are several hints in the novel that indicate that the baby is not dead, after all; in the last italicised chapter the narrator makes a point of having fabricated the ending for the sake of his loved one, who likes tragic endings.

> You used to dislike happy endings, ... So I have given you an unhappy end like those of your favourite films—the girl shot over and over in the snow like a rabbit, the car drowning in a few inches of water. There is also a happy end though it is less explicit. But you always read books more for form than for content.[488]

Earlier in the novel there is also the encounter between the narrator and his mistress in 'Journey into the Mind,' where the woman asks the narrator why he has written the story with a dead baby in it.[489] One could, however, ignore these hints as the novel also offers the possibility of the baby's death: the narrator of 'The Sea' is supposedly the woman Y and the story 'Journey into the Mind' might (as well as might not) take place earlier than the story 'The Sea,' and it could, therefore, have nothing to do with 'The Sea,' In other words, the novel can hold the baby both in a state of death and life simultaneously. This state is possible within the framework of art.[490] It is up to the observer to create the state of the baby; to see it either as dead or alive.[491] The openness of the novel makes it possible for the reader to make up an aesthetic pattern and to see the baby as he wants to. Furthermore, the novel makes the reader see both possibilities which in a logical framework would negate each other.

The state of the baby symbolises the impossibilities that the protagonists face in the novel. This state is shown through the impossible connections between the short stories, which in turn reflect the impossible connections of the protagonists to each other. The novel, therefore, reflects the situation of the protagonists on a macro-level. The novel becomes a model for the life of the protagonists. The connections between the short stories—i.e., the macro-level—and those between the protagonists—i.e., the micro-level—make up a riddle, out of which there is no logically consistent way. The only way to grasp this riddle is to stand outside of it and observe it. That is to say, this impossibility can only be possible when one switches between reality and fictionality. This is done on two levels within the novel: within the short stories and within the italic passages. In the short stories the narrator switches between experienced reality and art by both living his reality and observing it as an artwork. In the italic passages he only aesthetically observes the reality that he experiences in the short stories. The switch on this level takes place by the constant alteration between the short stories and the italic passages. On a third and higher level—i.e., looking at the novel as a whole—the switch is realised by the reader's switching between the impossible connections of the stories. The reader must experience—i.e., read—the novel in order to find out its impossibility—in order to realise that there is no key to the riddle—and simultaneously step back from it and see it for what it is: namely a riddle, which can only be grasped—made possible—in the framework of what it is—a work of art. Ultimately, the reader is asked to learn to see life itself as a riddle, which can only be grasped by seeing it as what it is—a work of art.

V. *Natalie Natalia*: the limits of aesthetic vision

The investigation of the possibility of freedom is somewhat shifted in the novel following *Impossible Object*. Whereas in the other novels the focus was on the possibility of freedom in regards to the structures outside the individual, the focus of *Natalie Natalia* is more on the structures given in the mind of the individual—to put it in a 'platitude,' the focus of the novel is more on how to free oneself from the 'walls in the mind.' In the other novels the individual had to deal with the moral dilemmas outside himself; that is to say, the emphasis of the novels was more on the effect of his choices and actions in relation to the outer events. In *Natalie Natalia* the emphasis is more on the effect of his choices on himself: how can he liberate himself from the paradoxes that he encounters within himself?

Except for the second and central chapter of the novel, it is written in a more straightforward narrative than its predecessor *Impossible Object*. There are two story-lines running through the novel: one is about the public life of the Anthony Greville, an MP, whose interest in politics has always been a mixture of fascination and contempt for power and who is now tired of politics and wants to get out. And the other strand concerns his private life, consists of his wife and three children, on one hand, and, on the other, his affair with the somewhat angelic, somewhat ravenous Natalia ('I sometimes called Natalia Natalie instead of Natalia, when she was the ravenous rather than the angelic angel'[492]), who is married to an MP herself. Both story-lines depict a moral dilemma and Natalia, being ravenous and angelic at the same time, embodies the unity and co-existence of the logically and morally irreconcilable dualities, which have been central to all Mosley's novels since his conversion and his preoccupation with man's freewill. However, whereas the preceding novels in this phase of his writing emphasised the individual's confrontation with the outer paradoxes, in this novel the emphasis is on the individual's confrontation with his own inner paradoxes.

Greville has been involved in the affairs of a near-independent Central African colony, where one of the apparently revolutionary leaders, Ndoula, is imprisoned. Greville gets the assignment to go on a mission to this colony to find out the facts and will thus have the opportunity to visit the leader in prison. Shortly before he sets on his trip, he is approached by a white priest—the description of whom does remind the reader of Father Raynes[493]—who asks him to pass on a coded message to Ndoula. The message seems to do with a rescue attempt to free the African leader.[494] This puts Greville before a moral dilemma, where he must make a choice: being on an official mission for England, he could not possibly do this (and betray his country), on the other hand, he faces the imperative of putting things to right that are historically not right.[495] And most importantly, smuggling the coded message would be a good opportunity for getting out of politics. The conversation between the priest and Greville[496] reminds the reader of the conversation between Charlie and Stephen in *Accident*. In both cases it is important to speak (somewhat indirectly) about the situation and put things into a perspective (i.e., aesthetic vision), where it is possible to get a clear picture of the dilemma and thus become aware of the possibilities for action. However, whereas in *Accident* the decision primarily concerned exploiting one's freedom of choice in order to get over a moral dilemma *outside* oneself and thus save the lives of others, in *Natalie Natalia* the decision that Greville makes has primarily to do with liberating himself from politics, without having to resign and feel that his years as a politician had been futile. Greville chooses to pass on the message to the African leader[497] but the consequences of the decision for others—the Africans and their fight against the British colonisers or the life of the leader—are not further conveyed. In this way *Natalie Natalia* also differs from *Assassins*, for example, where Mosley tried to investigate the relation of political choice on the outer events. In *Natalie Natalia* this seems to be irrelevant. The emphasis is on *how* the choice helps Greville liberate himself—in other words, the state of mind necessary for making this decision and thus getting out of politics both with a 'clear conscience' and without a feeling of futility.

In order to show this the novel is divided into three parts: the first and third part of the novel are 'straightforward' narratives which convey what is happening to Greville in the outside world. In Chapter I we learn of his affair, of his wife, his career and most importantly his mission to Africa and his intentions about getting out of politics. In this chapter we also learn about his moral dilemma concerning the betrayal that he could get involved in, were he to pass on the message: the ethical unacceptability of betraying his country on one hand, and the, 'good cause' that it offers him for getting out of politics on the other. The betrayal could be 'good,' as it could contribute to the rectification of some of the wrongs that his country had done to Africa in the course of history.[498] The narrative techniques introducing the moral dilemma are similar to the foregoing novels. The flashbacks and cinematic cuts remind the reader of *Meeting Place* and Mosley's admiration for Godard and the 'nouvelle vague': characters are left frozen in the middle of action, which gives an impression of impenetrability and arbitrariness of events.[499] Characters are 'reduced' to two-dimensional descriptions from the view point of the narrator, and yet conveyed as living persons through the dialogues and the interactions of the narrator with them. It is also in this chapter, where the central conversation between the missionary priest and Greville (similar to the one between Jervis and Charlie in *Accident*) takes place.[500] As in *Accident*, what is being discussed involves a moral dilemma, which can only be talked about indirectly (again, in a Faulknerian fashion), where the characters seem to speak at cross-purposes, yet transmit the impression of an underlying communication. Greville's dilemma, however, is different from Stephen Jervis's in that it is primarily a personal one rather than a social one: in other words, the novel is not really concerned with the consequences of the outcome of events for others; the 'others' are not concrete entities such as Anna or the family of Jervis, but are rather abstract such as the British government or the people of the central African country. The dilemma is how can he face betraying his government's mission by doing something 'good' as a means for freeing himself from politics and power machinations with a 'clear' conscience?

The dilemma is resolved in the second and central chapter of the novel. In Chapter II of the novel there is a drastic move from the outer into the inner world of Greville. In an interview with John O'Brien, Mosley explained this move as follows:

> I felt it vital to try to express [this]: we react of course to what happens in the outside world but there is also this archetypal patterning inside

us which is how we interpret what happens: and surely to be free in any way of the patterning, we have to be able to make some sort of model of it to be able to have a look at it.[501]

This is the crux of *Natalie Natalia*: in the foregoing novels the protagonists could exploit their freewill and free themselves from their moral dilemma by making the 'right' choice, only through detaching themselves from themselves and the events that they were in by putting these in an aesthetic framework. Greville uses the same device, but in regards to his own mind—his consciousness and his 'conscience.' In order to be able to make the 'right' choice and get out of his moral dilemma, he must first make a model where he can detach himself from his mind. This makes the novel much more self-conscious that the previous ones, as the paradox of such an observation is much more acute: the question is how can the faculty of observation—i.e., the individual's consciousness—look at itself and its patterns in an aesthetic framework, in order to free itself from itself? In the attempt to answer this question Mosley moves into the realms of Jungian theories of the mind:[502] his protagonist tries to 'make a diagram of his mind—the sort of patterning he was stuck with— . . . in terms of . . . the basic archetypal stuff that was there already; like the stuff, and patterning, that produces dreams.'[503] According to the Jungian theories, myths can especially be seen as diagrams of the mind. The diagram that Greville makes of his mind is also in form of a myth, where there is no sense of time, space, meaning, coherence, reason or morals. Mosley had already done this to an extent from *Meeting Place* onwards. But whereas in *Meeting Place*, for example, the protagonist seems to have entered the realms of dreams—where the boundaries between time and space, fact and fiction break into each other—in *Natalie Natalia* the emphasis is not so much on hallucinations and dreams, but on the patterns of which these are made. In *Meeting Place*, for example, the hallucinatory section ends with the protagonist waking up.[504] But in *Natalie Natalia* the mythical blurb in the first part of Chapter II (pp. 153-171) is not some sort of a to and fro between experienced reality and dreams and memories, past and the present, thoughts and events. It starts abruptly and ends abruptly with Greville arriving in Africa, giving the reader the impression, as if some mistake had taken place in the binding of the novel. The section is rather some sort of a 'science-fiction,' in which a model of an alternative, incomprehensible reality is being constructed. It is the illustration of someone helplessly observing things happen in a 'mythological nether-world':[505]

Arms came through the stone and held her. Putting my hands out, I felt the hands through the walls. Like this, we moved across a landscape. We were hand in hand through the snow. Behind us, I see where we had sat in our chairs. We had been there all summer. Men wore the masks of birds and animals. One, with the beak of a bird, had put his head down against her throat. Blood ran on to the snow. We were walking hand in hand across a landscape. . . .[506]

The mythological illustrations remind the reader of the nether-worlds painted by the surrealists (who were also intensely interested in the human psyche) and their macabre antecedents, such as Bosch and Brueghel paintings, all of which contain the elements of universal myths. Like these paintings, the narrator puts what goes on in his mind—his psyche—into aesthetic models and is consequently able to look at them from a distance and to some extent liberate himself from them. In order to achieve this effect, Mosley says that he was 'almost consciously trying to give something like Robbe-Grillet or Butor about a man in a daze.'[507] Just as Stephen had to put what was happening to him from the outside (most notably during the interrogation) into an aesthetic framework in order to be able to make the right choice, Greville has to put what is happening inside of him into an aesthetic framework in order to achieve the freedom necessary for making the right choice in a moral dilemma. The right choice in his case turns out to be the passing on of the coded message to the African freedom fighter, Ndoula.[508] He realises that the consequence of his choice is the liberation from politics ('I could now retire from public life'[509]). Yet, it immediately puts him before another impossibility: he doubts the propriety of his action, nevertheless he feels its necessity. This puts him in a very difficult position, where he has to both *know* and *not know* what he is doing; he has to feel what he is doing is right and, yet take refuge in some sort of a deception and self-deception in order to protect himself from the embarrassment of his act. Simultaneously, he must be aware of his to-and-froing between knowing and not knowing in order to avoid hypocrisy. Right after giving Ndoula the coded message, he thinks to himself: 'Ndoula is a good man: he will know that the sun has confused me.' This accounts for the ambiguous style of narrative that the reader encounters in this section of the novel (pp. 172-195) between Greville and Ndoula. Greville can only express what is going on in a fine balance—or what Mosley calls: 'the mechanisms by which reality is balanced in the mind'[510]—between secrecy and sincerity.

Greville's 'nervous-breakdown' and his recuperation at a rest home in the hills of Central Africa (pp. 196-231) can both be seen as yet another act of balance necessary for his getting out of politics, and an *interruption* of his balancing act, which induces an important change in his life and outlook. At first glance, the nervous break-down is a smoke-screen (or a balancing act), by which Greville, regarding his 'betrayal,' protects himself from himself and the people around him. It is never clear whether his behaviour at the governor's party is due to a 'real' or a 'fake' nervous break-down (pp. 188-95). This could be interpreted as a dishonest exploitation by which Greville avoids his responsibilities. Being a politician he knows how to use confusions for his own ends: he can now get out of politics on account of ill health, or in case his betrayal came to light it could be related to an 'unbalanced' mind! The ambiguity and self-consciousness of the prose, however, demand a less simple interpretation: Greville can yet again (see his delivering the coded message for Ndoula) put his dilemma in an aesthetic context by switching—or balancing—between knowing and not knowing. Like Jervis and the narrator of *Impossible Object* before him he experiences reality (participates in the party as everyone else) and observes himself in it as part of an artwork. But his aesthetic observation is somehow different from and more complex than the other two, as he is also experiencing his nervous breakdown—the break up of the patterns of his consciousness—and *simultaneously* observing it *consciously*. One could thus say that he gets out of politics by an aesthetic observation of what is happening in his mind rather than in his outside world.

Greville's recuperation in a rest-home at the hills of Central Africa, where human evolution is supposed to have started,[511] gives him the chance to distance himself from his mind's patterns and the break up of these, in order to look at them anew. The understanding of these seems to him to be the only way of getting out of the old patterns and at the same evolve new structures. In this last section of Chapter II (pp. 196-231) Greville writes 'long, somewhat feverish'[512] letters to his wife, Natalia and the priest. In these letters Greville contemplates on the evolution of human consciousness and its role in entrapping the individual, on one hand, and its potential in liberating him, on the other. The following quote is a good summary of what *Natalie Natalia* had been trying to say:

> I am trying to write a story that will describe . . . this—occurrences in function rather than in time—or as if time were spatial, so that one could *move to and fro* in it by looking. This is difficult: we see a moment

or a pattern, not both: one cuts out the other. But if we do not know, perhaps from some third point, the moment and the pattern at once, then each seems meaningless. Because, on its own, each is an abstraction, not an experience. The experience is both. But our minds are not constructed for this: which is why, perhaps, we make myths . . .[513]

This quote both summarises the above study of *Natalie Natalia* and articulates the shift in Mosley's exploration of human freewill in the following phase of his writing (*Catastrophe Practice Series*)—that is, the necessity and achievement of an inner liberation for an external one.

Of course, the inner liberation should also always influence one's external life: the two cannot be separated. And perhaps this is where *Natalie Natalia* does not fully succeed. In the final chapter of the novel, Chapter III, Greville comes back home from Africa, liberated from politics. But it seems as if the change that he went through does not have an effect on the other part of his life—i.e., his gyrations between his mistress and his family. At the end of the novel there is the feeling that his family—his son and his wife—might have been liberated from him, as they go off to Africa to do some good work in a disaster stricken area,[514] but Greville himself seems to be unable to find an alternative to his own situation, except for going back to his 'somewhat farcical, sometimes ecstatic'[515] love-affair/love-game with Natalie Natalia. Mosley himself believes that the ending of the book had something to do with his own feelings at the time.[516] He feels that his protagonist could not make a choice, as he did on the political front, and get out of the treadmill of his affair with Natalia, since both he and Mosley needed to learn a bit more:[517] Mosley and his protagonist had a 'passionate commitment'[518] to the journey through the mind, but did not have 'much of an answer . . . at this time.'[519] *Natalie Natalia*, therefore, raises the question concerning the coercive and liberating potentials of the human mind, and could also be seen as the beginning of Mosley's answer to the question. However, it was not before *Catastrophe Practice Series* (1979-1990) where Mosley started to learn intensively about the mechanism of the human mind and became fully dedicated to examining the individual's freewill in light of the structure of his mind.

Conclusion

Mosley's preoccupation with the possibility of freedom in face of moral dilemmas led to his experimentations with the form of the novel. A moral dilemma is 'a moment of absolute choice' when a choice with possibly damaging consequences must be made: that is when man's only 'good' choice is only neither this nor that or both this and that. In other words, a situation in which his options are logically and mutually exclusive. In this case, his only 'good' choice is an impossibility within the two-valued moral and logical system: i.e., a paradox. Thus, within this system, he is always, despite his efforts and intentions, doomed to choose evil. He is trapped.

Mosley's concern with man's freedom in face of moral dilemmas goes back to his early romantic/tragic novels of the Fifties. However, whereas in his early novels the protagonists did not know any other way than death, despair or a some sort of a retreat from life for getting out of the moral dilemma, in his experimental novels, they find a way of doing the impossible and choose 'good' without having to go through some sort of renunciation.

This turning point in Mosley's novels was mainly due to his conversion to Anglo-Catholicism. In the course of his commitment Mosley learnt that paradoxicality was at the heart of Christianity and that the freedom within the Christian context precisely lay in grasping this. That is to say, Mosley came to see, that aesthetic vision—or double vision—was the message of Christianity as opposed to the ethical vision—or single vision. In an aesthetic framework contradictions can co-exist, whereas in the logical, *either-or* ethical system they lead to impossibilities or moral dilemmas, which entrap the individual. Hence, in his experimental novels Mosley conveyed that man could free himself from moral dilemmas, only if he observed them within the framework of aesthetics. Art, as opposed to experience based on a two-valued logical system, can embrace impossibilities and contradictions. Whereas in logic contradictions cancel each other out, in art they can co-exist. Thus, in these novels life is not only experienced, but also observed in an aesthetic framework as it is happening. In this way, his protagonists do not have to resolve their moral dilemmas by some sort of renunciation of life, but by seeing life as a 'successfully going concern.'

The treatment of the paradox also lay at the heart of experimentalist fiction in the Sixties. The death of reality, truth and reason soon gave way to the death of the author and meaningful literature. Language lost all its truth-telling capacity and came to be seen as a game, where all meaning only resided in arbitrary rules. The dilemma of the writers of this era was the paradoxical task of living their deaths. Their fiction was constantly *saying* that it had *nothing to say*. In order to point this out, fiction had constantly to draw the attention of the reader to its awareness of its emptiness, by constantly questioning itself and emptying itself of meaning. Not reaching anything beyond itself, fiction increasingly was seen as an eternal game played for the sake of the game. Self-conscious fiction or metafiction became the keyword of this era.

This is not to say that meaningless fiction was the only form of fiction that prevailed. In England, especially, very original and *experimental* transcendental fiction emerged. Writers such as Fowles, Lessing and Spark exploited metafictional techniques in order to convey the truths and realities outside the work of art. Mosley's novels of this era share a larger affinity with this group of experimental writers, as he too believed in the truth-telling ability of fiction, and thought it vital that 'ossified' forms had to be discarded and new liberating forms created. However, whereas most transcendental writers were anxious to convey the illusions and absurdities of their readers to them, without really offering them the possibility of freeing themselves from these, Mosley saw the primary task of the novel to be showing the reader real possibilities for exploiting his freewill.

In his experimental novels Mosley uses metafictional narrative in order to convey life as a movement between experienced reality and aesthetic observation. His protagonists both experience their moral dilemma and detach themselves from it to look at it as fiction in order to have some hold over it. This switching is made possible throughout the features of his novels by undermining the logical consistency and causality of the story. As determinism is done away with, the question 'what happens next?' loses its relevance and is substituted by the question 'what is happening now?' The novel becomes an open pattern instead of a closed story, from which the protagonists—and the readers—can stand back to make a pattern. By observing this pattern the protagonists can resolve their moral dilemma and do the impossible: that is, meet the 'right' choice necessary for getting out of it. Therefore, they can see life as a 'going concern,' instead of being doomed to fail.

Up to his last novel of this period, *Natalie Natalia*, Mosley had tried to show how his protagonists liberate themselves from the impossibilities and dilemmas outside of themselves by putting them into an aesthetic framework and seeing a pattern in them. In *Natalie Natalia* Mosley's focus of investigation shifted from the outer world of his protagonist to his inner world. He was now trying to show that many dilemmas and impossibilities that man experienced were not only due to the events in the outer world, but also due to the mechanisms of the human mind. If man could make a pattern of his mind and observe it, he would be able to liberate himself from the dilemmas that he experienced. This objective made the last novel of this period especially self-conscious, as Mosley was now trying to have the faculty of observation—i.e., consciousness—observe itself. *Natalie Natalia* is rather a start of this investigation and does not fully succeed in exploring the task that Mosley had set himself. It indicates the direction that Mosley's writing was to take in the next period of his writing (1979-1990). It is in *Catastrophe Practice Series*, written after an eight-year gap, that Mosley extensively embarked on an exploration of man's possibility of liberation from the impossibilities of his own mind rather than those of his outside world.

CHAPTER III

The paradox of freedom and the science of mind (1970s and 1980s):
Catastrophe Practice Series

Introduction:
'We are not really at the mercy of our genes'[520]

> The young man or woman writing today has forgotten the problems of the human heart in conflict with itself, which alone can make good writing because only that is worth writing about, worth the agony and the sweat.[521]

> I thought—All battles are now in the mind; we must make our own war.[522]

In his *Catastrophe Practice Series* (1979-1990) the focus of Mosley's explorations into the possibilities of achieving freedom shifts from the outer world to the inner world. That is to say, whereas in the previous novels the protagonists tried to liberate themselves from the moral dilemmas that the conventions and dictates of the outer world—such as family, society, duties etc.—provided them with, here they set to free themselves from the restricting structures (patterns) of the mind. Consequently, this phase is not directly concerned with moral dilemmas—which mainly arise due to social conventions—anymore, but concentrates on philosophical and scientific concepts of the mind.[523]

Analogous to his previous novels in which the protagonists had freed themselves from the patterns of their moral dilemmas by way of observing them in an aesthetic framework, Mosley suggested a way of freeing oneself from the restricting structures of the mind by means of observing them.

> It seemed that what I wanted to discover was—in what way might it be possible to look at the patterns, the programming, of our own minds; does not the very fact that we can have this notion mean that it is possible?[524]

> If a man has the power to observe the controlling patterns of his mind it is here, and not in the patterns, that there is his freedom.[525]

There are two major—and interrelated—aspects, which distinguish the investigations about the possibility of freedom in *Catastrophe Practice Series* from the previous phase of Mosley's writing. In the previous phase of his writing Mosley had tried to offer an alternative freedom to the existentialist concept of freedom. In *Catastrophe Practice Series* this quest for freedom transformed itself further into a matter of life and death—not only for the individual but for mankind as a whole. This led to the second distinguishing aspect of this phase of his writing. Whereas in his Sixties-novels, the characters felt on their own in their search, in this series the characters inevitably feel to be part of a greater pattern—a network. In the previous novel the characters mainly watched themselves and tried to save themselves from their entrapping moral dilemmas within an aesthetic framework. That is not to say that they felt only responsible for themselves—on the contrary: their moral dilemmas arose because of their feeling of responsibility for those involved. However, they did not make the impression of being 'in the same boat' with everybody else. They were more or less similar to isolated islands. The characters in *Catastrophe Practice Series* supersede their predecessors in that they not only feel the urgency for saving themselves, but also for saving their fellow human beings. In this sense, they both feel part of a smaller network—one which binds those with a similar vocation—and a greater network—humanity, evolution, creation and life as a whole. In this sense, their quest for freedom is more complex than that of their predecessors.

In his *Catastrophe Practice Series* Mosley, in the same vein as Sartre, came to see that by observing the mind's structures consciousness (i.e., the conscious self) can become aware of the restrictiveness of these structures and on this level *initially* free itself from them. Mosley agreed with Sartre that consciousness, not being a 'thing,' is the pivotal site of man's freedom, for it is 'by virtue of [this] no-thing-ness that a man . . . could move, decide, choose.'[526] However, whereas for Sartre (the faculty of) observation necessarily and immediately became the cause of man's self-destructive entrapment, for Mosley it remained the only means for getting out of the trap that it had got itself into. Mosley understood that in Sartre's views consciousness consisted of a gap, which divided the individual into a 'self that was conscious and the conscious self it was conscious of.'[527] Thus, the self was perpetually locked in a self-destructive battle between the two halves 'trying to occupy the same space at the same time.'[528] Not being a 'thing'—i.e., an 'unconscious' object—the conscious self could never free itself from this condition and be at-one-with itself. Sartre described this feeling as such: 'the dull and inescapable feeling of sickness [that] perpetually reveals my body to my consciousness.'[529] Mosley believed that Sartre's 'inescapable feeling of sickness' necessarily arose due to his misconception of the body/consciousness (i.e., the unconscious object/conscious subject) duality as an unbridgeable split caused by the self's faculty of observation. Mosley, again in the same vein as Sartre, realised that the self could not overcome its own split by regressing into the condition of being an unconscious object[530] and that it could indeed succumb into the threat of violence as a desperate attempt for getting out of its self-entrapment.

> Sartre saw human violence as inevitable not just because of economic scarcity . . . but because of this primary predicament in which a man could not be at peace with others because he could not be at peace with himself. Men did in fact form groups: they transferred their anxieties on to groups: but the cohesion of a group was ensured by the threat of violence to an enemy without and to a potential traitor within. This indeed is a description of much in modern politics.[531]

However, Mosley maintained that violence was only a resort, if one dismissed the ability of consciousness 'to heal or surmount its own split':[532] 'valid freedom and healing and choice'[533] do have a chance to prevail through the consciousness's observation of the *split* between the conscious self and the self it is conscious of as that which *unites* the two halves—or as the *unity of* the division. In other words, through the observation of the observation the divided self could be conceived of as a whole. It was in the realm of science where Mosley found the concepts and theories which seemed to point out the possibilities for the split conscious self to 'heal or surmount' itself and thus achieve 'valid freedom and healing and choice.' It is thus suitable to call this phase of Mosley's writing his 'scientific period.' The following tries to investigate the conception of this, perhaps most accessible, phase of Mosley's writing, which culminated in his award-wining novel, *Hopeful Monsters*.

Biographical Background

> 'Free' traditionally does not by any means imply 'disordered' or random. It was only in the desperation measures of the existentialists, faced with the logical positivist universe of their

> time that freedom came to be identified with 'gratuitous acts' or motiveless whims. Freedom implies discoverable meaning in an act. . . . A free act is one that may be unpredictable but that, after it has occurred, is retrodictable in that it 'makes sense.' Predictable events . . . are in certain senses symmetrical with respect to past and future: that is, there is no difference between knowing that they will happen and knowing that they have happened. Free . . . acts are of a different class, asymmetrical with respect to past and future. What can be known about them before they happen is fundamentally different from what can be known about them afterward. What the new science has shown us is simply that there are such acts . . . [534]

It is in spirit of Mosley's *Weltanschauung* that his new novels should be triggered by an accident. First and foremost, the accident can be understood in the same vein as his idea of aesthetic activity being a form of *forward memory*; that is, the idea that aesthetic activity influences and helps construct the pattern of what is to come.[535] Regarding his 'private life,' Mosley had become involved in the complicated and painful divorce process of his mistress 'Natalie,' which eventually led to a break-up of his relationship with the latter instead of securing its continuity. The games and the to-and-froes governing their relationship exasperated him so much that he wished he could set an end to the whole thing. Having almost finished the final draft of *Natalie Natalia*, he was commissioned to write a film-script about a pop concert on the way to which he longed to be able to get out of his and Natalie's 'wire-act' as his protagonist Greville managed to break out of his *cul-de-sac*.

> I was thinking—It will soon be time for me to ride my own damned trick-cycle or indeed car not just like Greville into a swimming pool but over a cliff—just then, on a quiet country road, a car pulled out from the slow-moving line of traffic coming in the opposite direction and like some avenging juggernaut headed fast straight at me, seemed to try to brake, lost control, then rammed the offside of my car hard as I tried to pull off the road. Most of my bones were broken on my right side, and I became unconscious . . .[536]

The other driver's insistence on an 'uncontrollable force' overtaking his steering wheel and thus causing the crash suited Mosley well;[537] it fitted in with his idea that one could take part in shaping the pattern of one's future (fate) and influence its outcome by putting oneself in way of coincidences (chance) through aesthetic observation.[538] After the accident and the period of recovery his love affair, and almost simultaneously his marriage, began to cease and finally came to their ends while Mosley was undergoing psychoanalytical treatment.[539]

Natalie Natalia, in a way, both foreshadowed the absurdity which his love-life had degenerated into and the dead-end that he had reached in his novel-writing. The novel's investigation of the possibilities of freedom from the restrictions of the outside world (i.e., moral dilemmas), inevitably seemed to bring him face to face with the question of the workings of the mind, the inner life being intricately woven into the fibres of the outer-life.[540] The emphasis of his search was now on what role the restricting structures of the mind played in our conception of moral dilemmas—wouldn't moral dilemmas cease to arise if we had a different mind structure? And, consequently, how was the task of freeing oneself from these inner structures possible if the mind depended on them for its operations? These questions were (inescapably) undercurrent in *Accident* and *Impossible Object*, but it was not before *Natalie Natalia* where the necessity of investigating them became explicit. At end of *Natalie Natalia* the paradox of freedom was introduced in form of the paradox of mind—i.e., the (in)ability, and consequently the struggle, of mind to observe itself. But the style to proceed and grapple with it was yet to be acquired.

> In *Impossible Object*, in one of the italic bits,[541] . . . I put this thing about all true battles are now in the mind . . .
> Although I did write that in the italic bit, the story, of course, of *Impossible Object* . . . still [was] talking about the outside world. And then *Natalie Natalia*, as you say, is about the outside world, too—whether it is the personal issue of his mistress or [the public issue of politics].[542]

There was of course the 'stream-of-consciousness.' To Mosley, however, not only was it exhausted already, but it also seemed to portray the battle in the mind as a lost one with the individual being helplessly delivered to overpowering forces. This style did not show the *reality* of the battle and thereby the possibility of getting out of it successfully.

> When I got to *Catastrophe Practice* I wanted to find someway of trying to show that the real battles were in the mind. And I found this awfully

hard to do because I didn't want to write this internal stream-of-consciousness. I thought that would be boring. I think in James Joyce stories it is great fun, but it is not quite the point. I wanted to find a way of *doing* the battle in the mind.[543]

The accident helped Mosley find a way where there seemed to be none and as a result enabled him to pursue his artistic career. Heinrich von Kleist's appearance at this point of Mosley's life and his 'answer' to the problem that Mosley had set himself is again in the spirit of Mosley's notion of aesthetic activity and its influence on one's 'fate.' While recuperating in October and November 1970, he switched on the radio at random and was transfixed by a story, whose author he had never heard of before.[544] The story was Kleist's *Über das Marionettentheater* (*On Puppetshows*), in which the dancer Mr. C. complains about the gracelessness of the dancers caused by their ability to watch themselves—in other words, their self-consciousness. 'Such mistakes,' Mr. C. observes, 'have been unavoidable ever since we ate of the tree of knowledge. But Paradise is locked and bolted, and the cherubs after us. . . .'[545] His view (not dissimilar to that of a trickster) about what must be done—'we must make the journey around the world and see if it may perhaps be open again from the back somewhere'[546]—is an anticipation of his solution at the end of the story to the paradox of the split-self (i.e., *innere Zerrissenheit*). The lost grace—a return to our *Ur*-form—could only be regained, if human beings ate from the Tree of Knowledge of Good and Evil a second time—

> We see that, in the organic world, in proportion as the faculty of reflection grows darker and weaker, physical grace emerges with ever-greater brilliance and authority. Yet just as two lines intersecting on one side of a point, after they have passed through infinity, suddenly do so again on the other, or as the image in a concave mirror, after receding into infinity, suddenly steps right back in front of us: thus also, when cognition has in effect passed through an infinity, grace returns; so that at the same time it seems purest in that human form which has either no consciousness at all, or an infinite one, that is to say, in the lay figure, or also in the god.
>
> Therefore, I said, somewhat perplexed, must we eat of the tree of knowledge again in order to fall back into the state of innocence?

Indeed we must, he answered: that is the last chapter of the history of the world.[547]

The story delivered a major clue for treating the paradoxical problem that Mosley had encountered at the end of *Natalie Natalia*: namely, how to apply the restrictiveness of the mind as a means for achieving freedom. What struck Mosley as important was that Kleist did not render the process of going back to the 'Garden' as a tautology. That is to say, he was not advocating a 'merry-go-round,' where one moves in a circle and will eventually go back to square one. The Kleistian return might bring to mind the spirit of German Romanticism—e.g. Hölderlin's *Hyperion* or Novalis's *The Apprentices of Sais*—where the individual spiralled through a path of knowledge to his origins, but on a higher level. Kleist's approach, however, is drastically different in that it does not try to do away with the paradoxical nature of this task. Going through the path of knowledge—acquiring knowledge—is inevitably a paradoxical activity as it always implies self-reflexivity. Kleist's vision of a return in his short story shows his acute awareness of this. The Kleistian return necessitated the individual's undergoing and *overcoming* the paradoxical activity of acquiring (self)consciousness—in other words, self-observation. The 'concave mirror' as opposed to the Romantic 'spiral' is a very telling metaphor for this. His idea of overcoming this paradox does not so much rest on the traditional idea of spiralling upwards, but on the then newly emerging and revolutionary non-Euclidean mathematics.[548] Here again the parallel with Mosley's activities after the accident cannot be overlooked:[549] Mosley, too, was intensely preoccupied with the newly emerging scientific ideas of his own time as a means to understand the nature of the paradox and consequently to find out ways of overcoming it.[550]

In the course of writing his *Catastrophe Practice Series* Mosley adopted the Kleistian metaphors of return—man's desire to re-enter the locked and bolted Paradise; cherubs being after us; eating of the tree of knowledge again to acquire grace; and finally making the journey around the world to enter the Paradise somewhere at the back—in order to show the process of overcoming the paradox of self-reflexivity and thereby that of freedom.[551] But before that he had to develop an artistic method by which he could *do* the battle going on in the mind. In other words, Mosley was keen to *visualise*—dramatise—this battle and the wave of openness for international and experimental theatre in the late Sixties and early Seventies, proved to be a very fertile ground for this purpose. The staging of Kleist's masterpiece *Penthesilia* in London, which dramatised the Kleistian split-self—i.e., *innere Zerrissenheit*—fascinated Mosley.[552] However, it was not before his acquaintance with Brecht's works that Mosley had a notion of the form necessary for his purpose. That is to say, whereas Kleist pointed out the possibility of an aesthetic framework in which the paradox of the split-self could be overcome, Brecht provided the guidelines for the form to do this.

Mosley's interest in Brecht almost coincided with his interest in Kleist.[553] His first viewing of a Brecht play, *The Good Woman of Setzuan* in London had a great impact on him and incited him to read all Brecht's plays he could find and, most importantly, acquaint himself with Brecht's thoughts on the aesthetics of theatre and acting.[554] Mosley's belated introduction to Brecht in the early Seventies was not necessarily an oddity considering the preceding intellectual climate in England. In the immediate post-war years, except for a small avant-garde circle of dramatists mainly at the Royal Court Theatre and around Kenneth Tynan[555] and Joan Littlewood, Brecht was not at all widely known until 'the fermentation of the late Sixties, [. . .] which left Britain with a much more politically aware young intelligentsia of potential authors and audiences.'[556] Mosley himself—before seeing his first Brecht play, *The Good Woman of Setzuan*—had always 'heard about Brecht as sort of communist—a Marxist theorist.'[557] For Mosley Brecht's paradoxical conception of the split-self (which manifests itself in form of *Entfremdung* or 'alienation') being both the trap and the means for getting out of it was very much in the spirit of Kleist's notion of eating from the tree of knowledge a second time.[558] '[When] I read him,' Mosley recalls, '. . . it was all about this peculiar thing of the actor who observes himself acting and that fascinated me because one can observe one's own ridiculous predicament.'[559] What emerged as a by-product of this self-observation was freedom manifesting itself in shape of 'authenticity': 'Brecht, who was a dedicated Marxist, seemed to be saying "if you can see yourself acting—if you could be an actor on stage and see you were acting—that gives you a sense of authority and authenticity." '[560] This idea was not at all far removed from the Kleistian idea of 'Grace'; however, it also contained some guidelines for doing this.[561] Mosley understood that Brecht saw that the 'predicament of modern "scientific man" was not only (nor even primarily) his alienation from society, but this alienation within himself—'the split between what he knew, especially about himself, and his ability to come to terms with this knowing.'[562] The 'audience of the scientific age,'[563] therefore, necessitated an acting suitable for its needs. 'Actors,' Brecht demanded, 'must be demonstrating their knowledge.'[564] For Mosley Brecht's concrete instructive examples for the kind of acting that he envisaged were especially helpful.[565]

> [The Chinese actor] never acts as thought there were a fourth wall beside the three surrounding him. He expresses his awareness of being watched . . . the artist observes himself: . . . he will occasionally look at the audience and say 'Isn't it just like that?' at the same time he also observes his own legs and arms, adducing them, testing them, finally approving them.[566]

I. Conceiving the problem: role-playing and the trap of man's split nature set by his observation faculties

Mosley's accident could also be seen as an occasion, which provided Mosley with the opportunity to try out what he had learnt from Kleist and Brecht. Film-making made him 'face up to' the question how the battle in the mind could be *done*.[567] Towards the end of his recovery from the accident, Joseph Losey, who in collaboration with Harold Pinter had filmed Mosley's novel *Accident*, asked the latter to write a film script about, perhaps the most controversial figure in the history of Communism, Leon Trotsky. Losey, himself an old Marxist and a victim of the McCarthy witch-hunt of the 1950s US, chose Mosley for this job, as he believed the latter to be able to deliver a script without the 'Marxist jargon which actors found it impossible to make sound not ridiculous.'[568]

> Yet how could one make a film about Trotsky without the jargon? Joe said to me—But you are the most non-political writer that I know; perhaps you could write an actable script about Trotsky?[569]

Mosley did manage to write a script that didn't have much to do with the Marxist jargon, however, it was not an (in the conventional sense) 'actable' one: in Trotsky he seemed to see the perfect candidate for exploring the Kleistian-Brechtian idea of acquiring freedom expressed in form of 'Grace' and 'authority' by making use of the 'split between what he knew, especially about himself, and his ability to come to terms with this knowing.'[570]

For large parts of Trotsky's life he was up to his neck in politics of a kind that was squalid—a dim farrago of deceit and lies and murder and betrayal in which words and commitments could mean anything or nothing and attitudes were histrionic. However, there had always been a part of Trotsky that had recognised this and had not wanted to be totally immersed; in fact he had said as much when had tried to explain why he had not made more effort to succeed Lenin in the 1920s. He had wished, he said, to maintain a certain detachment from the day-to-day tawdriness of politics.[571]

Mosley believed that Trotsky's 'grace' lay in his balancing act above the gap between—or the paradox of—'the realisation, on the one hand, that the revolution could not be maintained without despotism, and the knowledge, on the other, that despotism was just what the revolution had been designed to destroy.'[572] Mosley thought that it was Trotsky's intense struggle with this paradox—as opposed to Stalin's complete suppression of it—that was a handicap for the his political career. Although Trotsky had rejoined Lenin for the cause of the revolution and 'occasionally . . . descended to "degradations of despotism," ruthlessly ordering the death of revolutionaries who were demanding the democratic rights promised by revolution,' after the battle he saw the dangers of despotism (of which he had always been aware) once again.[573] In Mosley's view it was Trotsky's conception of such a struggle, as something out of which beauty could emerge, that revealed him—in spite of his occasional descents to 'degradations of despotism'—as an artist rather than a power-hungry politician. In fact, Mosley saw this as the main reason for Trotsky's inability to be present at key meetings during 1923 (apparently always due to some 'mysterious' illness) and secure his position after Lenin's death, although he was Lenin's 'obvious and natural heir-apparent.'[574] As a frontispiece to his book *The Assassination of Trotsky* (which emerged out of his film-script) Mosley had put a quotation, which expressed the importance that Trotsky attached to irony. Irony, being a paradoxical act, is only possible in the area of detachment, observation and self-reflexivity—in other words, the area of aesthetics:

'There is an irony deep laid in the very relations of life: it is the duty of the historian as of the artist to bring it to the surface.'[575]

Mosley argued that Trotsky himself dedicated a great part of his creative energy to lay bare the 'irony deep laid in the very relations of life.'

He believed that not only did Trotsky undertake this task excellently in his *Autobiography* and *The History of Russian Revolution* ('works of some genius; of a man with a marvellous literary eye and style'[576]), but also fulfilled what Mosley sees to be a necessary outcome of artistic activity: i.e., forward memory.[577] Mosley's mentioning of Trotsky's ruminations on his own death from a 'brain haemorrhage' shortly before he is killed by an ice-pick's blow on the head is a telling example for this.[578]

The book *Assassination of Trotsky* was the fruit of Mosley's disappointment with the inability of Losey and his entourage to bring across this very aesthetic vision of Trotsky, which Mosley believed ennobled Trotsky as opposed to the 'exercise of the brutal and the banal'[579] responsible for the making of Stalin.[580] Losey did eventually, against all his initial intentions, end up being surrounded by various groups of Marxists, Leninist-Stalinists, and Trotskyites ranging from Eastern European to Parisian circles, on the one hand, and New York and Mexico City based groups on the other.[581]

However, what struck Mosley as the main reason for the failure of the filming of his script was the inability of the actors and directors involved to act according to the Brechtian maxim 'actors must be demonstrating their knowledge.' The 'Grace' and 'authority' that Mosley urgently wanted to convey could only be demonstrated if the detachedness of the protagonist from his role—his Brechtian 'knowledge' of his role—could be acted; if the actors could fulfil the paradoxical task of 'acting not acting.' Mosley experienced the same kind of disappointment at the filming of his *Impossible Object* (under the title of *Story of a Love Story*), but had now come to accept it as he realised that film people 'are in the business because they like the business of acting; what is in it for them if they do not?'[582] The actors seemed not to be able to work with his riddles. 'Riddles,' Mosley wrote later, 'can work; but if everyone concerned feels at home with as it were non-answers.'[583] Now suddenly in the midst of his despair he seemed to have bumped into someone who put him on the right track towards the companions, who felt at home with non-answers.

II. Philosophy and science: the theory of the trap of split nature and the possibility of getting out of it

> . . . freedom now recovers its meaning as a word usable by science and philosophy. In a knowably deterministic universe,

> freedom is either a nonsense word or a word mistaken in its usual definition . . .[584]

> [New science has provided] the . . . undeniable evidence of the life and freedom embodied in physical reality.[585]

Towards the end of his preoccupation with film, Mosley's old friend from his 'Church days,' Guy Brenton, reappeared in London: 'Brenton and I met in '58 when we were both trying to make sense of Christianity. He never really succeeded in this and went off on various travels.'[586] Brenton, Mosley recalls, ended up in Hawaii, 'where Bateson was working with dolphins. He sat at Bateson's feet for a time and when he finally came home he put me on to *Steps to an Ecology of Mind* [1972].'[587] Bateson was an eye-opener, in that he provided scientific evidence (in a way he initiated the scientific phase of Mosley's writing)[588] for what Kleist and Brecht had *aesthetically* argued for: that is, achieving freedom by overcoming the paradox of self-observation.[589]

Bateson's three types of Learning[590] examined consciousness as both a splitting and a unifying agent of the self. Bateson, Mosley understood, suggested that what mattered about learning was its pattern.[591] This pattern was not only linear—i.e., logical—but also non-linear. The logical and simpler type of learning always inevitably caused a split—either/or—which it conceived of as a paradox. The 'non-linear'—or what Bateson called 'higher logical type'—learning was the ability of consciousness to overcome the paradox by way of reflecting upon itself and thus act as a unifying agent.[592] Bateson conveyed this by experimenting with dolphins, who were trained to perform simple tricks according to a system of rewards. Then—

> an experiment was attempted in which, each time the dolphin came into the demonstration pool, it was to be rewarded not for doing this or that particular trick, but for doing each time something new. This was a requirement, to do with an abstraction, of a higher logical type . . . what the dolphin had learned was not just a trick, but an attitude to tricks. It had succeeded—with a struggle but in the end joyfully—in an act of learning of a higher logical type.[593]

Once Mosley 'followed the trail,'[594] he came across a host of scientists and philosophers, who seemed to be concerned with the same subject as Bateson. He became acquainted with the evolution theories of the anatomist J. Z. Young, who saw aesthetics as a major contributor to the evolution and survival of human race,[595] and the writings of the biologist Jacques Monod, who seemed to turn Darwinism on its head. Monod wrote an influential book at the time, *Chance and Necessity*,[596] which delivered scientific evidence for what Mosley himself (via Christianity and aesthetics) had seen to be the weakness of Darwinian evolution theory: namely, the role of the human consciousness. Monod, Mosley understood,[597] saw the whole Darwinian determinism in light of mankind's consciousness 'thrown back in our face . . . because we have the power for "unnatural" selection.'[598] What Darwin believed to take place *wholly* in the area outside human range, was brought by Monod—that is, partially—into the range of human power and consequently human choice and responsibility: 'then the whole question becomes how to choose—what criteria does one choose *for* this? . . . Human power in selection could screw things up!'[599] Monod's conjectures appealed to Mosley, as they validated the latter's notion of man's freedom lying in his active *participation* (i.e., exploitation of his freedom of choice) in creation.

Another scientist who interested Mosley at this time was the psychoanalyst R. D. Laing.[600] Laing was more or less the mediator of Bateson's ideas—most famously his double-bind[601] theory. Laing's appropriation of this theory for describing schizophrenia and other neuroses arising in families enjoyed, particularly amongst the specialists, considerable attention. Mosley found his *The Politics of Experience and the Bird of Paradise* ground breaking. However, Mosley believes that what Laing (and Bateson) did not respond to is the fact that the double-bind is 'the stuff of life':

> everyone, in fact, does a double bind, There is no pure, I-love-you-the-whole-time love! Life is a double-bind. . . . Laing said it is awful when mothers do a double-bind. It is a bad thing. It is also what human beings are. . . . and if one wants to get anywhere, one has to face this . . . Beauty is a double-bind.[602]

Mosley thought that Laing had very well conceptualised the paradoxical nature of family life (and thus helped de-mythologise it), but failed to investigate the possibilities that the individual had in order to overcome this.

In Mosley's eyes the philosopher, who (independently from Bateson) conceptualised aesthetics as a way of overcoming the battle—the 'to and fro'—in the mind was Susanne Langer. In a way, what she did was elucidate what Mosley had learnt from Brecht and Kleist:

> Langer wrote a book called *Feeling and Form* . . . [Having read her] all that came together: [i.e.,] the battle being in the mind. I mean, the way one judges rightness isn't really through logic because with logic one can *argue either way* about the person being guilty or being innocent. The person who judges—the jury—actually decides on aesthetic grounds . . .
> [Similarly] the part about scientific theories—that one thinks that what one looks at or discovers is correct—is so because it has an aesthetic value.[603]

Mosley was already acquainted with this idea from his Christian period. Aesthetic vision in that context was understood as 'informed conscience' in face of a moral dilemma—only then could the participant get out of his dilemma without giving into death or despair.[604] Langer to Mosley seemed to apply this concept to the mechanisms of the mind.

Amongst new acquaintances, who shaped Mosley's ideas of this time, were also some old ones, whom Mosley had started to see in new light. There was Arthur Koestler—'one of the first people who argued this sort of holistic idea, that we are not at the mercy of our genes'[605]—and Nietzsche. Mosley's interpretation of Nietzsche, in fact, is very Kleistian. He saw Nietzsche appealing for a style of expression which could hold our knowledge beyond the dichotomy and paradoxicality of good and evil (see Kleist's idea of eating from the Tree of Knowledge of Good and Evil once again) and thereby elevate our position from that of split humans to that of an *Übermensch*.[606] This idea strongly reminds one of Kleist's ideal man who is a graceful god or puppet. The most influential of these old acquaintances, however, was Karl Popper. Next to Bateson, he was perhaps the most important influence on Mosley at the time. Popper, Mosley recalls, had his vogue much earlier on in political science.[607] Mosley had known Popper's important book *The Open Society and its Enemies*, however, it was Popper's new works, which struck Mosley as a groundbreaking philosophical treatise:

> he was rather out of fashion, when he wrote *Conjectures and Refutations* [and *Objective Knowledge*]. Popper's idea was that one got the truth

not by the old verification principle, but by making a conjecture and knocking it down—or falsification principle. . . . You could only say what things were not, not what they *are*; by saying 'it is not that, not that, not that' and gradually it was there. That seemed to have very much to do with everything [I was reading then].[608]

Popper, like Langer, put into philosophical context, what Mosley had seen in art and science. In J. Z. Young's models of the brain, he saw the 'scientific' counterpart to Popper's falsification theory ('Each cell leads to two possible outputs, and learning consists in closing one of these.' This is the physical counterpart of Popper's suggestion that we learn through our mistakes.)[609] And in Brecht's guidelines for role-playing, he saw Popper's artistic counterpart: 'the actor on stage looking at himself said: 'Am I doing this right? No! . . . You find you can talk about what you are doing wrong and then what happens is right.'[610] Most importantly, however, Mosley saw Bateson as the major 'kin' of Popper. He saw the Batesonian three types of Learning parallel to Popper's three worlds. In his *Objective Knowledge* (1972), Popper introduced his three distinct worlds, each superseding the other (as in Bateson's Learnings) culminating in 'the world of objective contents of thought, especially of scientific and poetic thoughts and works of art.'[611] Mosley saw that it was in this world, as in Bateson's Learning III, where man had a chance to overcome the battle—the paradox—in his mind and achieve real freedom.

The extensive preoccupation with the works of these artists, philosophers and scientists was pivotal for the coming phase of Mosley's writing. Not only did it lay the foundations for the ideas upon which Mosley built his *Catastrophe Practice Series*, but in a way it also incited Mosley to 'apply' what he had read to his own mind, as it were, and undergo a more systematic and scientific investigation of his own self.

III. Psychoanalysis: practising the theory

The two years following his accident (October '70 to September '72) saw an intensification of Mosley's problematic relationships with both his wife and his mistress. Only a year after his accident, his wife, Rosemary, suggested separation (eventually leading to divorce) and 'Natalie's' gyrations culminated in suicide threats.[612] In his desperation Mosley contacted Natalie's analyst, who had been treating her for a few years, and told her about the urgency of the situation. The consequence of this conversation was Mosley's acceptance to visit another Jungian psychoanalyst. This decision reflected what he had been reading:

> In the course of my reading I had been struck by how the claims of psychoanalysis were in tune with whatever I thought I was discovering: just by the effort to look at the haunted and haunting patterns of one's past and of one's mind there might be healing; this did not expunge the old patterns, but made them bearable and thus to some extent impotent.[613]

Mosley soon grasped the 'trick' of the psychoanalysis game.[614] Indeed it was not all that different from the process of confessions that he had undergone during his 'Church days'; it very much reminded him of the style of his talks with Father Raynes.[615]

> Indeed there was comfort in the circumstance of finding that the game could be played once more with someone else—not an adversary, but someone who might every now and then as I talked make a remark like an umpire signalling a wide or blowing a whistle. I wondered—Indeed thus one might pick one's way through minefields. To what end? But this was not the point. It was oneself who might change; not the score in the game, but the player.[616]

Mosley was thus testing what he had learnt: the ability of the observation faculty (i.e., the consciousness) to influence and, at best, surmount the split-nature of the individual and thereby lift it onto a higher level.

The examination of the then present destructive patterns in Mosley's life properly took him back to the pattern of his relationships in his formative years. Mosley's imagery of this experience, once again, re-invokes the process of his conversion; he had indeed been here before.

> In analysis whatever journeys there are back to the formative influences of one's past have properly to be done as it were on foot: there are few lifts, few plane-hops, provided by one's analyst; this is the point—there have to be time and space on the journey for processes of learning for oneself. Change happens as a result of the action of the pilgrimage; healing comes almost inadvertently.[617]

Unsurprisingly the three intricately conjoined influences in Mosley's formative years were his mother, his father and his social background.

1. Aristocracy

Mosley had already tried to detach himself from the machinations and games of his aristocratic background earlier on.[618] His marriage to another 'comrade-in-arms,'[619] his serious pursuit of a literary career, his total conversion to Anglo-Catholicism and his deep involvement with anti-Apartheid activities all testify for his attempts at breaking away from his social upbringing. These initial rejections were necessary for spotting the problem. However, they remind one somehow of those of a defiant child, who ironically (and perhaps unsurprisingly) is still the prisoner of his 'adversary.' His new 'psychoanalytical' attempts, on the other hand, seemed to bear more fruit as he was not so much trying to reject his background as to overcome its potency by way of observing and understanding its workings.

Now it seemed as if by the mere action of carefully observing and listening to himself, he was putting himself in way of helpful coincidences. Just after embarking on his analysis, 'by one of those coincidences that seem to crop up when one is perhaps putting oneself in the way of them,'[620] Rosemary's mother died and all the papers belonging to her brother, Julian Grenfell, were handed over to Mosley. His life and death had for long interested Mosley: 'I delved about in these papers. I thought—Indeed there are parallels here with delving about in my own mind.'[621] Once again Mosley's simile of aesthetic observation influencing the pattern of one's fate and forging forward memory lends itself well. Julian Grenfell 'had been a product of his class and culture; he had also rebelled against these. . . . [After leaving school] he began to question every tenet of the society in which he had been brought up . . . When he was twenty-one Julian had written a short book that was his polemic against conventional society—a plea for individuals to be honest with themselves and by this to influence the world. It was an astonishing book for an upper-class young man in 1910 to have written.'[622] Julian's family hated the book and it was never published—after suffering a major nervous breakdown (or what his family called a 'brain-storm') he cheerfully went into WWI and shortly after that got killed: 'There is a sense in which Julian, in 1914, was acting as, according to a Marxist, a good aristocrat should—he was being an energetic member of his class's self-destruction.'[623]

Mosley saw that in this respect there were some parallels between his and Julian's life. The biography was both aided by Mosley's undergoing psychoanalysis and in turn aided his analysis in so far that it clarified the patterns of his childhood. Most importantly, what Julian's case most poignantly illustrated was R. D. Laing's application of Bateson's double-bind theory to psychoanalysis. Julian's battle with the double-standards of his class, the power/self-sacrifice games of his mother and his almost suicidal death painfully conveyed to Mosley that 'the hardest traps to escape from are perhaps those with as it were a double row of teeth—that bite alternately hot and cold.'[624] This pattern was still virulent in his own life in the form of his affair with Natalie and made him re-consider his relationship with his mother, who died very early on in Mosley's childhood.

2. The Mother and the Greedy Baby

Mosley, despite having been nine years old at the time of her death,[625] hardly remembers his mother. It had been said to him that her will to live had suffered severe blows from her husband's infidelities, giving in at last to the latest one with Diana Mitford. This resulted into an image of Mosley's mother being the 'good' wife victimised by her 'evil' husband.[626] However, Mosley's psychoanalytical journey into his past made him see this 'saintly' figure involved in a self-destructive pattern, which had an important influence on the nature of his adult life relationships.

It seemed to him that the absence of his mother from the greatest part of his childhood—almost from the moment of his birth[627]—left him with a 'ravenous need to scrabble for love like cats under dustbin-lids in alleys,'[628] that perpetuated the cycle of his destructive love affairs. He came to see that this 'alley-cat hunger, [the] need to cling to women whose own needs were self-destructive' could be behind the pattern of his 'continuing high-wire act' with Natalie.[629] The recollection of his other mother-figure, his Nanny ('of course I had been dependent on Nanny; she had saved our lives'[630]), reinforced this assumption:

> When she was angry she would refuse to speak to me and I would trail round the house after her as if begging her for—what—a word? a bowl of milk? a dustbin in an alley? And then it suddenly struck me . . . that it was a description of just this sort of scene that I had been giving shortly before when talking about one of the facets of my life with Natalie. . . . And so—You mean, . . . somewhere in my mind, in my heart, my beautiful and apparently oh-so-vulnerable Natalie is indistinguishable from my tight-lipped but oh-so-indispensable Nanny?

And that is why I am hooked? . . . what an exuberant joke! These are the times, I suppose, when there is some liberation.[631]

Mosley's laughter is a sign of liberation—or at least the beginning of such a process—from the relationship patterns in his mind, as laughter necessitates detachment. The termination of his relationship with Natalie, his meeting with Verity and his consent to divorce from Rosemary in order to marry Verity[632] were the realisation of his observation of and eventual liberation from a pattern mainly in his unconscious going back to his relationship with his mother (or the mother-figure Nanny). This immediately raises the question about the (unconscious) patterns of his relationship with the other half—his father.

3. *Surviving the Father*

Considering the controversial, not to say scandalous, political and public life of Oswald Mosley, it was rather surprising how little psychological damage Mosley had suffered from his father's side. Mosley believes it was partly due to, and not in spite of, his father's openly scandalous political and public affairs that he, the son, had been saved from further harm. In his psychoanalytical sessions little uncovering seemed to be required: '[my father] was such an obvious bogey-figure: what on earth had ever been hidden, screened, about my father? He had always been like some lighthouse visible for miles—his eyes flashing on and off to guide sailors or perhaps lure them to their doom.'[633] But mainly, it was Oswald Mosley's handling of his relationship with his son that seemed to have been a success:

> Psychoanalysts explain that the difficulties that children mostly have with their parents are to do with hypocrisy from the parents talking on one way and behaving in another which results in what is called a 'double bind.' This charge, concerning life at home at least, seems impossible to level against my father: he was obviously as it were a single bind.[634]

Nicholas Mosley remembers his father in home life as 'at least one of the few grown-ups who were comparatively sane. He would listen to childish questions and answer them straightforwardly; or if he did not think they merited serious attention, he would respond with a joke that I nearly always found funny. Most other grown-ups seemed rather baffled by children.'[635]

> And what more can be asked of a father? Whatever terrors my father had had for me had been clear: there had hardly been the need for them to be driven into the unconscious. . . . And what struck me now was that my analyst seemed to agree. Psychoanalytically speaking, someone so un-devious as my father seemed not to have been a bad parent.[636]

The trouble for Nicholas Mosley was thus not so much uncovering and observing patterns of relationship in his unconscious (as was the case regarding his mother and Nanny), but coming to terms with his father's evidently self-destructive and morally unacceptable political activities. This could be done in an open battle, upon which Mosley had already embarked in the Fifties by confronting his father, renouncing his politics, falling out with him and getting engaged in anti-Apartheid politics.[637] All this activity had been necessary for the process of liberation to find its course, but was by no means sufficient. Now, in order to liberate himself from his father, Mosley had first to let go of the denunciation, which paradoxically chained him to his father. For this purpose he did not have to delve much into his own unconscious but rather to delve into the mind of the latter.

This process had already—unconsciously—begun with the writing of *The Assassination of Trotsky*. Mosley saw significant similarities between Trotsky and his father. He believed that both men had great opportunities to become very powerful, but had the talent to just 'miss' the right moment and by this prevent the evil entrenched in their ideologies.[638] The little dialogue, cited in Nicholas Mosley's autobiography, between father and son shortly before the former died illustrates this view of Nicholas Mosley's very well:

> [Now my father] would want to talk to me about the past; about my mother, about his infidelities, about the effects of promiscuity on marriage and public life. He said—I sometimes wonder whether, if I had not done so much of that sort of thing when I was young, I might have done better in public life. I said—Dad, it might have been that sort of thing that kept you from doing worse in public life. He laughed.[639]

In the course of his psychoanalysis, what was initiated through the writing of *The Assassination of Trotsky*, took on a fuller form. Mosley was now liberating himself from his protest-position (which after a decade and a half of 'falling out' had in a way locked him to instead of liberated him from his father) by becoming more thoughtful about his father and the self-destructive patterns in the latter's mind. Psychoanalysis's help was two-fold in this matter: he had learned to observe and conceptualise hidden structures in the mind and he had been liberated from two (by now) degenerative relationships and embarked on a fruitful one, with his new wife Verity. This had also—as in a domino effect—freed him from the pattern of his fifteen-year-old hostile position towards his father and gave rise to a new approach.[640] Oswald Mosley's softening due to old age and Parkinson disease contributed to the new understanding that was being forged between father and son: 'it was as if his very frailty made many of the barriers come down which had prevented him from looking at himself and at his past.'[641] At the last meeting with his father ten days before the latter's death (1980), Nicholas told him that he thought

> a biography of him should be written that would include all sides of his life; that it was the relation between his inner energy and outer events that might explain his life. He had aimed very high, he had gambled, and had failed, all right: but could it not be said of him as of Faust, that the very exaggeratedness of his effort gave some redemption? And in fact there had been no severe horrors in his public life: perhaps he had been saved from these by not achieving power: but then perhaps his devil-may-care attitude had saved him from this.[642]

Nicholas Mosley did not *only* intend to 'redeem' his father's public image[643] ('there was a generation now that . . . had an image of him simply as an anti-Semitic thug—even as someone who had been 'on Hitler's side in the war'[644]) by writing the story of his life, but also to observe and *to reflect* on the workings of the pattern of his father's mind, in the hope of learning to cope and overcome whatever of these he might have acquired or inherited himself. Regarding the 'squalid' aspect of his father's private life, Nicholas himself had at moments been accused by each of his wives to be 'behaving towards them in such a way as [his] father had behaved to [his] mother.'[645] He was realising that 'in this respect there might be resonances between [his] father's life and [his] own' and that 'from facing these [he] should not be looking for a diversion.'[646] However, whereas for his father this pattern had, at least in the public aspect, been self-destructive, for Nicholas Mosley it became a restorative agent *not* in the sense of an outlet or excuse for his sexual behaviour, but in the sense of an 'evil' (or, when applying the biblical story of Jacob wrestling an Angel) fighting which became a moral and *aesthetic* imperative. The fight of course presupposed accepting the challenge! It was what Mosley had called the battle in the mind.

> My father had been involved in some form of self-destruction, but had survived. My mother had not.
> I thought—Perhaps I will find here patterns to do with my own self-destruction and survival.[647]

In this sense the child had to detach himself from and overcome what had been *determined* for him through the patterns set by his parents.[648] His psychoanalysis sessions helped him achieve this, but when it came to describing *how* man—or the child—came out of this journey having achieved a feeling of liberation and prevalence over his predicament, psychoanalysis became for the novelist not only redundant, but also inhibiting.

> I would say—I think I am trying to describe what might be the results of analysis: I mean, what it might be like if one is able to look at the patternings in one's own mind—
> My analyst would say—Well, what is it like?
> I would say—I'm trying to find a way of putting it. I can't put it easily into words here, or my being able to write it may stop.
> . . . —you can't talk about the doing of any work of art; you have to let it happen.[649]

This was the end of Mosley's psychoanalytical journey and the start of a new phase of his writing career. Whereas psychoanalysis mainly had to do with undoing the riddles by way of talking, aesthetic had to do with the reverse. In an essay on Bateson, Mosley put it thus—

> Bateson writes . . . of the necessity of an aptitude for beauty, and for the sacred. Beauty is a word to describe that which exists by virtue of relationships and pattern; sacred is a word to describe the fact that this aptitude for beauty is not something that can be encapsulated and passed on in easy words. But it is something that each person can learn for himself, with effort, when necessary.[650]

Literary and Intellectual Background

I. The foreboding Seventies and the thrilling Eighties: the novel at the edge of catastrophe

It is of course difficult to see a pattern in a time so close to the present. One could however identify two main aspects in those decades: firstly, a growing interest in catastrophe and, secondly, the establishment of anti-establishment movements. These developments were reflected in the novels of these decades.

The Seventies, in a way, were the fulfilment of the reverse side of the joyful and climatic Sixties. One often sees the Seventies as the end of social, political and cultural consensus.[651] What was seen as a liberation from the authoritative Establishment was fast realising itself in what many writers of the Sixties had already examined in the realm of fiction: i.e., a paralysing fragmentation.[652] The post-war seeds of mistrust, first sown with the coming of the Cold War, the threat of a nuclear war and the assassination of Kennedy, disseminated rapidly and were full-blown in the following decade. International terrorism, Watergate, Vietnam, hostage drama in Iran, miners' strike, high inflation, oil-crisis, massive unemployment, increasing poverty, racism, break-down of inner cities . . . became the keywords used to describe the mood of this decade.

In Britain, too, these events further exposed the limitations of the balancing and unifying possibilities of economic and political concepts. On the one hand, the crisis of the British national identity, which had already started with the loss of the British Empire, was becoming even more virulent in face of the Troubles and the devolutionary processes in Scotland and Wales. On the other, Keynesian economics seemed unable to bridle the dominance of the stock markets linked with global technologies, which seemed to be eating their way through the certainties of the welfare state. Furthermore, the expansion of technology and industry, which by many utopians of the previous decade had been seen in direct relation to the advancement and prosperity of humanity,[653] was now being seen as the major threat to all life on earth. 'Global warming,' 'Ozone-hole,' 'bio-diversity' and 'ecologically friendly' were starting to enter the vocabulary at the end of this decade and expressed the dawn of ecological awareness and the rise of movements such as *Greenpeace*, *Ecowarriors* and Green parties, which were to become a major factor in shaping the *Zeitgeist* of the following decades.

The crises in the Seventies, culminating in the 'Winter of Discontent' in 1978, paved the way, for Margaret Thatcher in Britain, whose name was to become the label of the Eighties. Thatcher declared that society 'did not exist.' With the death of society, came the death of welfare state—or 'nanny state,' as the New Tories liked to call it—and the rise of individualism. The annihilation of the altruistic Sixties was thus completed in the self-centred, instantaneous and entrepreneurial Eighties. The optimistic Feyerabendian maxim 'anything goes' was now lending itself well to the emerging yuppies. Far from uniting the country, as was promised, Thatcherism divided it in to a 'cosmopolitan,' 'Super Class' and an increasingly growing 'Under Class.'[654] With the ascent of her comrade-in-arms, Ronald Reagan, to presidency in the US, a 'total eclipse' seemed finally to have obliterated from view that vision of a common culture projected by the planners of 1945, the liberal middle classes of the Fifties and the New Left of the Sixties.'[655] In his study of this 'late capitalist age,' Jameson, leaning on Walter Benjamin, showed that commodification and exchangeability of all values, pleasures and human emotions against money were its hallmark.[656] Success was measured by money and had to be visible—this was the age of surface glitter and depthlessness.

Along with the end of social and humanist values came rapid climate changes, unprecedented famines and numerous civil wars. All fears and prediction of the foregoing decade concerning the total annihilation of humanity and civilisation seemed to confirm themselves.

Within such a context the novel became increasingly concerned with the phenomenon of catastrophe. There was, however, a major difference between the novel of the Seventies and the novel of the Eighties: whereas the former generally treated the catastrophe in dark and gloomy prose, the latter tended to greet it with joy and glee. The following briefly contrasts the two.

The Seventies are often regarded as a despairing time for the British novel: at most they are seen as an appendix of the fruitful foregoing decade and a prelude to the advancing boom and excitement of the Eighties.[657] Pondering on the famous 'state of the novel' in *The New Review* (1978), or *Granta* magazine (1980) the critics and cultural doyens saw a meagre present and a bleak future only.[658] Peter Ackroyd envied the 'formal self-criticism and theoretical debate which sustained European modernism' and attacked his British contemporaries on grounds of their out-dated humanism, empiricism and fossilised ideas of Englishness.[659] He claimed that by clinging onto a misconception of subjectivity and realism, they failed to deliver worthwhile British novels: 'It is clear that, now, England is a dispirited nation. . . . The humanism which we take to be our inheritance and our foundation . . . has turned out to be an empty strategy, without philosophical content or definitive form. . . . Our own literature has revealed no formal sense of itself and continues no substantial language.'[660]

The 'loss of faith' in the British novel together with the loss of certainty now spawned apocalyptic novels, that prophesied the end of society, the end of civilisation, and even the end of all life. Doris Lessing's *The Memoirs of a Survivor*,[661] for example, envisaged an outer world in the form of a collapsed society and environment, recovering from a nuclear explosion and an inner world in form of a decaying room in a rundown apartment block. Rescue would only be possible in form of an esoteric trip to the innermost self—'into another order of world altogether.'[662] The apocalyptic contemporary novel of Margaret Drabble, *The Ice Age*,[663] on the contrary, remained *consciously* (which depicted its author's integration of the techniques of the self-conscious fiction) rooted in the tradition of the nineteenth century moral realism and examined the world of the individual within his moral and social surroundings. For her the resolution of the individual was a dangerous enterprise, which could now happen in the coming age of increased materialism and monetarism. She drew a desolate portrait of a Britain, which has fallen low precisely because it has put itself beyond the old moral values, and instead of progressing into a free condition, now found itself trapped in a virulent materialism, resulting in social collapse, scandals and impotence. Somewhere in between these two novels, one could place John Fowles *Daniel Martin*,[664] which in a hybrid of metafiction and realist fiction reminiscent of his style in the Sixties, lamented both the lost times and the advent of a present, which in spite of, or because of the vast areas of materialistic, sexual and sensual pleasures on offer was empty and seemingly futureless. There are, however, a few images in the novel showing the possibility of hope—such as the bitch with her new-born puppies in a barren landscape or the reunion of the narrator with the love of his youth.[665]

In the meantime a newly emerging style of writing was taking the novel to its extreme in order to convey the prevailing sense of void[666] at the brink of catastrophe. J. G. Ballard's menacing vision in *Crash*[667] of a humanity dehumanised in its union with the symbol of Twentieth century, the automobile, is a good example of this.[668] *Crash* is the perversion of the traditional and modernist ideas in the novels mentioned above, which in spite of everything sought to find meaning in the unity of things in one whole. In this novel all human activities and forms are violated to the extreme, fragmented and reduced to mechanical functions serving only one purpose—that is, if one can speak of purpose at all—which is arriving at non-being, or better still, the undoing of the human. Loveless and desireless sex rendered in clinical, mechanical vocabulary offers itself well as an appropriate means to convey this: 'In the chromium ashtray I saw the girl's left breast and erect nipple. In the vinyl window gutter I saw deformed sections of Vaughan's thighs and her abdomen forming a bizarre anatomical junction . . .'[669] Ian McEwan and Martin Amis, both of whom went on to epitomise the young, exciting Eighties novelist explored and exploited this 'brutal realism' or 'dirty realism.' Ian McEwan in his *The Cement Garden*,[670] eerily depicted the life of psychopathic, self-absorbed children, who hide the corpse of their mother and continue to live 'normally.' Martin Amis in his *Dead Babies*,[671] promised, already in choice of the title, not only to shock what both social and fictional 'realities' had long taken for granted, but also to brutally depict the destruction that they were heading for.

In the Eighties the representation of the apocalyptic took on ecstatic, sensual and jovial forms. At its most obvious, the decade offered a very good opportunity for social satire, which has always been a forte of English fiction. Like his father's *Lucky Jim*, which caught the intellectual and literary mood of the Fifties Britain, Martin Amis's *Money*[672] captured the prevailing *Zeitgeist* in moral satire. The narrator, with the telling name John Self, embodies all the narcissism, superficiality, 'diverse' homogeneity and cultureless culture of his era; the era that was given birth to by the optimistic and 'anything-goes' playfulness of the Sixties: 'The Sixties taught us this, that it was hateful to be old. I am the product of the Sixties—an obedient, unsmiling, no-comment product of the Sixties.'[673] The depiction of the characters' fragmentary identity, dispossession of reality and permanent paralysis in a perpetual present without any sense of a past or future rejects traditional realist fiction, however, it also seems to lament the loss of the well-rounded character, with a real sense of identity and conflicts. The sheer boredom and tiredness of the characters can only be momentarily alleviated by drugs, pornography and most important of all by Money. Self's 'tongue-in-cheek' self-reflection betrays his awareness of his state of being, however, (unlike Mosley's characters) it is a paralysing rather than a liberating self-consciousness: 'I am a thing made up of time lag, culture shock, zone shift. . . . Scorched throat, pimpled vision, memory wipes.'[674] Once again (as was the case with the novel in the Sixties) the fictional self-consciousness, cross-references, juxtaposition of slang and high literature, put *Money* firmly in the Modern tradition of Joycean and Faulknerian novels, but unlike its predecessors the novel does not offer any hope of redemption or reconciliation. The underlying apocalyptic prophesy in this novel is characteristic of fiction in this era and manifests itself in various forms. McEwan, whose novels were consistently read in the company of Amis's to mark two of the most important representatives of young English novelists of this era, was an exponent of this apocalyptic vision. His *The Child in Time*[675] offers an eerie glimpse of a near future, near-collapse 'Thatcherised' Britain (the vision is somewhat reminiscent of Burgess's *A Clockwork Orange*) by juxtaposing a brutally realist voice and science-fiction.

The novelists of this era helped themselves to any form that suited the celebration of catastrophe. In fact this 'bastardisation'[676] of the novel was a process that had already started to take place in the Feyerabendian Sixties.[677] Thus the Eighties saw a resurgence of the 'carnivalesque' and Gothic novel. The excitingly vicious and seethingly libidinous and violent air in the novels of Angela Carter (*Nights at the Circus*[678]) and Peter Ackroyd (*Hawksmoor*[679]), for example, depicted 'the sense of an ending' in a voice that testified for a continuation of the fictional portrayal of previous 'endings' throughout European history. Furthermore, under the influence of South-American and Eastern European fiction, the British novel transformed itself into the complicated shape of 'magic realism.' Rushdie's *Midnight's Children*[680] and Winterson's *Passion*[681] are fine examples of this style of writing.

II. Against the 'Western Canon'[682]

Apart from interest in catastrophe, the second distinguishing aspect of these decades was the protest against establishment. It seemed that in the Seventies and Eighties the final postmodern nails in the coffin of history, originality, and grand narratives were secured: 'simplifying to the extreme,' Lyotard defined the postmodern as 'incredulity toward metanarratives.'[683] History, identity and the literary 'canon' itself could now be re-written. This lent an enormously fertile ground to subversive literature. The historical novel enjoyed a massive resurgence thanks to this phenomenon: the past was now a re-cyclable 'text,' ravenously scavenged by novelists. The keyword was 'deconstruction.' John Fowles's *A*

Maggot,[684] A. S. Byatt's *Possession*,[685] and Rushdie's *Midnight Children* are good examples of the self-conscious, deconstructive historical novel. John Fowles adopted the voice of English writing in the eighteenth century only as a means of parody, Baytt revisited the Victorian norms and simultaneously poked fun at the prevailing dominance of literary theory over literature, and Rushdie 'deconstructed' the *Ur*-text *Thousand and One Nights* to re-create the recent history of independent India intertwined with the fabulous myths and past(s) of India.

The re-writing of the past is obviously, inevitably and intricately linked with deconstructing and re-inventing identity. Fowles, Byatt and Rushdie were all re-examining and re-inventing the notion of Englishness. Fowles and Byatt being English had an 'inborn' right to do this and thus were doing this within the establishment. It was Salman Rushdie, Timothy Mo, Kazuo Ishiguro, Ben Okri et al, whose compulsion to *take* this right drastically redefined the notion of Englishness and English fiction.[686] Owing to such writers, who were born and bred in the 'cross-over' territory, the sub-genre 'post-colonial' literature came to dominate the Eighties. It must be noted that non-English novelists—from Wilde to Mansfield to Achebe and Lessing—have continuously contributed to English literature, but it seems that it was only in the late Seventies and Eighties that the term 'post-colonial' literature was conceptualised. Thanks to the Foucauldian theorisations on the relation between power and text, literature increasingly was seen as a tool for (de-)establishing power and status.[687] Foucault famously saw writing, reading and teaching literature as a 'way of maintaining or modifying the appropriation of discourses, along with the knowledges and powers which they carry.'[688] Looking back at the works of 'proto-types' such as Joyce and Mansfield such a statement does not strike one as groundbreaking. However, such statements did help bring to life a widespread and conscious effort amongst writers and readers to subvert the prevailing literary order. And the postmodern meta-fictional pun, parody and pastiche proved appropriate tools for integrating this awareness and forging a new mode of fiction writing.[689]

Almost in relation to the Thatcherite crusade against dissenting voices, the subversion of literary order continued. The oppressed groupings on the margins of society seemed all to have found an arena for disseminating their attitudes and asserting their position in society. New Feminist literature, already emerging in the Sixties and Seventies, along with postcolonial literature displayed this move very well.[690] Contrary to earlier feminist works and thoughts, from George Eliot to Beauvoir and Woolf, postmodern feminism did not so much seek to 'emancipate' women (the word itself, like 'progress' and 'development' in case of ex-colonies, had become problematic), as to affirm their difference and demand their rights not in spite of but because of this.[691] Janet Todd, in a study on post modern feminists such as Kristeva, Toril Moi and Jane Gallop, sees the emergence of a pattern of 'desirable marginality,' where the writers use 'stigmatic exclusions' such as gender, sex life, language, social status and race to simultaneously subvert the ruling order and assert their identity.[692] 'To deconstruct language' according to Elaine Showalter was now 'to deconstruct gender' and 'to subvert symbolic order' was now 'to subvert sexual difference.'[693] Greer, Weldon, Carter and Winterson were some of the key figures in exploiting post-Saussurean theories in order to shape feminist fiction anew. In novels such as *The Life and Loves of a She-Devil*,[694] *The Passion*, and *The Bloody Chamber*[695] Weldon, Winterson and Carter respectively declared war on the literary (mis-) representation of women (which for them was the perpetuator of women's oppression) by challenging the boundaries and rules of fictional realism. Through their flight into the realms of the fantastic, the improbable and the mysterious they opened up new possibilities for the definition of the female and inevitably—in the same vein as their above mentioned fellow novelists—continued the process that had begun with the experimentalism of the Sixties;[696] namely, the process of tilling new grounds for the novel. Perhaps one of the important ways through which these anti-establishment novels opened new grounds for fiction (just as was the case with their predecessors) was the fact that they could not get out of the paradox that was the inevitable fruit of their endeavour.[697] The more they became accepted, the more they became part of the canon and establishment that they were fighting against. The jokes about the secret of literary success depending on being 'black, Jewish, lesbian, single mother living on the dole' in all their tastelessness and crudeness, seemed to reflect the trap that subversive literature in its endeavour for recognition had stumbled into. This paradox in its turn called (and still calls) for new fiction, which could embark on the task of getting out of this trap.

In view of the subversive 'anti-Canonical' movement, Nicholas Mosley could in a sense be seen as being at the same front as his contemporaries. The seed of his first experimental endeavour had been the desire 'to be a freedom fighter!'[698] The short story 'Suicide' in *Impossible Object* [1968] starts with a 'sacrilege' of the 'indisputable' genius of Shakespearean tragedy: 'I had the idea that all great lovers committed suicide—Romeo and

Juliet, Tristan and Isolde, Othello and Desdemona. You put a penny in the slot and first Juliet did it and then Romeo and for your money's worth Juliet again. They gave value in the old days . . .'[699] His disapproval of the inability of the 'Western Canon' to liberate the individual by indicating to him alternative state(s) for his predicament is expressed in an essay, 'The Iliad,' which was triggered by his interest in Harold Bloom's *The Western Canon*.[700]

> critics have agreed that [*Iliad*] sets the tone for much of the literature that came after. The view of human life that it suggests is one in which there is no refuge from war or fate; the course of life is known, thought not determined, by petulant and jealous gods. Destiny itself is arbitrary, beyond the scope of enquiry and questioning. . . . There is certainly no hint that humans might influence their fate.[701]

Mosley's fight against and subversion of the literary Canon was of a different nature than that of the majority of his contemporaries: whereas their subversion increasingly involved the politicisation and moralisation of the novel, Nicholas Mosley's battle took place on a philosophical level. Having collided with the artists, scientists and philosophers mentioned earlier, his quest was not so much for 'social justice' or the betterment of man's socio-political and economic circumstances by way of criticism, but for the changing of man himself by way of 'trying to express what might be the "new human type" that was necessary.'[702] This is how he hoped for a change in man's circumstances—or better still, this was how he hoped to depict the possibility of liberation from catastrophe.

This was the second point where Mosley differed from his contemporaries. Like his contemporaries he was intensely interested in the phenomenon of catastrophe; however, unlike them he neither awaited it in hopeless resignation, nor welcomed it with joyful celebration. Contrary to them he tried to show the way out of catastrophe. Thus, whereas the majority of his contemporaries were either gloomily or joyfully accepted their 'fate,' Mosley tried to outline a 'strategy' for getting out of the trap of fate. To do this a 'new human type' was necessary.

Mosley is of course aware of the dangers of suggesting that a 'new human type' should evolve: the idea was also taken up by the Nazis and the Stalinists only to give rise to the most horrific events in the history of mankind.[703] He believes that Brecht could not have been thinking in the same terms as the Nazis when he called for a 'new human type.'

The Nazi ideal of a 'new human type' was completely blind to his own *self*. In contrast the Brechtian 'new human type' evolved only when the human mind liberated itself from its own observational functions and structures by way of observing these. In this sense, Brecht's idea(l) is akin to Nietzsche's *Dividuum* versus *Individuum*[704]—the divisible self, who through (self)reflection could overcome not only imprisoning morals and values but also his own self in order to become the creator of new values and a new self—in one word in order to become the author of his life.[705] Nevertheless, Mosley realises, that one has to be very careful when using this language. He insists that without an idea of an 'objectivity'—i.e., a pattern outside of and greater than mankind and his doings—this idea could only lead to 'playing God' and eventually great destruction, as it did in case of the atheist Fascists and Stalinists.[706] The following tries to explain this idea as the driving force behind *Catastrophe Practice* and the novels that were born out of it.

Catastrophe Practice Series

I. *Catastrophe Practice*: Gödelian knot and man's liberation from the mind

Catastrophe Practice, in the same vein as *Impossible Object*, has a highly experimental form: it consists of three plays and a novella, which are separated and at the same time interconnected by four essays which illuminate the highly complex pieces. The result is a very difficult, if at all 'understandable' and 'readable,' novel. It would thus be helpful to first look at the essays separately only to integrate our understanding of them into the reading of the fictional parts and in this way re-construct the work as a whole. The essays reveal the plethora from which the author has drawn the ideas upon which this novel and the ones following it have been built. It would thus make sense to regard *Catastrophe Practice* as a 'manifesto' in order to come closer to an understanding of the novels of this series.[707]

In these essays Mosley tried to express the necessity of a risky and dangerous venture: namely, the evolution of a 'new human type' by way of observation: i.e., by way of the mind observing its own observing faculties and structures. The declaration of the author summons this up:

> writers have been quoted by random selection here—Popper, Monod, Bateson, Young, Langer—random in that they were come across by

> this writer at least without plan but selected in that, it seemed, they all were connected by the same authority and liveliness and thus seemed to form, and not just in the writer's mind, their psycho-celestial football team. And this was the sort of occurrence that the writers themselves seemed to describe—the way that out of the activities of randomness there are formed structures as *of a* mind and *by a* mind: that such is life.[708]

This scientific insight is the continuation of what Mosley had recognised as the message at the heart of Christianity—the idea of man's partnership with God in the business of Creation.[709] Now these scientists, philosophers and artists too seemed to suggest that man is not wholly under the tyranny of his determining factors, such as genes. His very faculty of observation testifies for this freedom: 'even the hard-line Darwinist Richard Dawkins remarked in the *Selfish Gene*: "We alone on earth can rebel against the tyranny of the selfish replicators." '[710] Genetic engineering and gene manipulation show this power of man all too clearly and in a way, as Mosley understood Monod to claim, negate the Darwinian evolution theory:

> Now we do have in our hands the power to influence [evolution] and it depends what we do with it. I think that is what [Monod] said. So, the whole Darwinian determinism of natural selection has been thrown back in our face now because we have the power for 'unnatural' selection.[711]

But in the same breath he warns that this rebellion is not enough—and is even dangerous—for the evolution of the Brechtian 'new human type,' if it were conducted on the level of protestation only:

> Then the whole question becomes how to choose—what criteria does one choose for this? And one can't do very much. There are people who say it is much better if one doesn't choose. . . . Human power in selection could screw things up! And I think there is a lot in there. Obviously, if you try to breed a new race of men, that is not going to work . . . that is ridiculous. [That is] again Popper's idea—you can't plan what is right. . . . You have the power to stop things going wrong, but not the power to say *that is* what is right. I think that's terribly important.[712]

The evolution of a 'new human type' could only make sense in the area of man's attitudes towards and his perception of reality. It is thus in the functions and structures of his observation and perception faculties—i.e., the mind—where man could hope to find the possibility for influencing his genetically determined makeup and *become* a higher human type.

Regarding the human 'mind,' Mosley, in view of Bateson's three types of Learning and Popper's three worlds, differentiates between three levels: on the first, or the lowest level, the behavioural patterns of man are identified. These patterns are the pre-given, deterministic characteristics of man. The second level consists of the observation of these patterns—i.e., the conscious self observing the unconscious one. On this level, by looking down on the behavioural patterns, the individual achieves an independence from them. However, he becomes entrapped in another set of powerful patterns: namely, those of his observation. This is the level on which the Sartrean *nausée* and despair arise, as man is helplessly delivered to his own observation and cannot be at one—at 'peace'—with himself. To overcome this predicament Mosley suggests that man has to go beyond this second level and move on to a higher level: the level of observation of observational patterns. On this level the conscious self looks down on its own patterns and thereby achieves independence from them. It is here where one can leave the existentialist despair by transcending the level of observing the consciousness—the split—as a gap (i.e., second level) and instead conceive of it as a connection. By observing the gap (the faculty of observation) between the two halves of the self the observer paradoxically unifies them and consequently liberates himself from the division.

On this level of observation (i.e., third level) the self not only frees itself from the inner division, but also encounters 'the other' outside of itself; namely, the greater pattern beyond itself. In fact, Mosley's conception of freedom from the inner division regards the encounter with 'the other' as both a necessary 'prerequisite' for and a consequence of the observation of observational faculties. Freedom from the idiosyncratic patterns of observation is only achieved because on this level the conscious self enters a unity—a connectedness—with a higher order, from which it can look down on its own observational patterns. Without the conception of a higher pattern beyond those of the conscious self's any attempt at transcendence of the split-self (as many post-war writers have shown[713]) could lead to a *regressus ad infinitum*, into a nothingness and a further feeling of helplessness and imprisonment. Hence, in Mosley's sense, the paradox of the consciousness 'healing and surmounting' itself—or pulling itself up by its boot laces, as it were—does not end up as a tautology. By entering a connectedness with a greater pattern beyond its idiosyncratic observational patterns, the operations of the consciousness are 'guided' by that greater pattern—that is, the consciousness now 'uses' the patterns beyond itself in order to look down on its own patterns from them. In this way, one can say that through the observation of its observational patterns the conscious self influences them, as it is not anymore confined to and operating according to them. In other words, by observing its observational patterns consciousness can change itself. The following aims at conveying the close relation between freedom and change in Mosley's eyes.

To elucidate this conception, Mosley, amongst other scientists and philosophers, draws on Popper and Bateson. He sees Popper's three distinct worlds and Bateson's three types of learning as analogous and complementary to his own understanding of the levels in the human mind. Mosley understands Popper's three worlds as

> 1. the world of physical objects: 2. the world of states of consciousness: and 3. the world of objective contents of thought—'especially of scientific and poetic thoughts and works of art.'[714]

He further elaborates on Popper's idea about the necessity of man's move to 'world 3,' if man were to achieve real freedom and consequently prevail instead of succumbing to self-destruction.

> This 'world 3' as Popper calls it 'is man's special accomplishment': it is the tangible representation of the world of communal subjectivity in which he can move and have a choice: it is man's creation, yet it has its own autonomy: it is a world of man's ideas, yet held objectively in books and records and symbols. This world 3, perhaps, contains the means by which a man can stand back and see himself: *by which he can be in relationship with others without the absurdity of collision.*[715]

Mosley's understanding of Popper's 'world 3' is a continuity of his understanding of the 'aesthetic' by which one can detach oneself from the pattern of a moral dilemma and overcome it. By detaching oneself from it and observing it from a higher point of view, one can see the dilemma as a whole and consequently and necessarily conceive of its 'place' in a wider pattern, instead of seeing it as a sum of meaningless contradictory structures only.[716] In his previous experimental novels, Mosley explored this question: could man detach himself from the limiting patterns of a seemingly inescapable situation by seeing the possibilities for the *operation* of his freedom of choice? Now, drawing on Popper amongst others, he sees the aesthetic world—'the world of scientific and poetic thoughts and works of art'—as one, where the individual could overcome the limiting patterns of his own split self and be at one with himself by connecting onto a greater pattern beyond himself; namely that of a relationship with 'the other.' In this world the self-entrapment and (self-) destructive violence that Sartre so well described would as a matter of course disappear, as

> [by being in relationship with the other] there can be evaluation and elimination of the products of the imagination: there need be a violation of neither knowledge nor ethics. 'It is only science which replaces the elimination of error in the violent struggle for life by non-violent rational criticism and which allows us to replace killing (world 1) and intimidation (world 2) by the impersonal arguments of world 3.'[717]

Mosley, however, realises that the Popperian vision of achieving a sense of wholeness and peace suffers from an important shortcoming: how is the all-embracing and impersonal haven of Popper to be achieved, when it is mostly in worlds 1 and 2 that most people live?[718] In other words, what learning process is man to go through? Gregory Bateson's distinctive Learnings[719] offer guidelines to these questions:

> There is Learning I, which is the sort of learning available to animals as well as to humans and which depends on the responses to stimuli becoming habitual . . . Learning II . . . is an accomplishment of man, and depends on a man's ability to stand back from the processes of Learning I and to see its patterns—and in this at least in some sense to be free of them.[720]

Mosley's understanding of Bateson's Learning I and II is correspondent to his understanding of Popper's worlds 1 and 2. Learning II and world 2 are both initially a liberation from the patterns of the previous habitual behavioural patterns (i.e., world 1 and Learning I) , but need to be superseded, if they were not to lead to a yet more rigid form of entrapment within the observational patterns of consciousness. In the same way that Bateson's Learning II is seen here as the means to achieve Popper's world 2, his Learning III is seen as the essential attitude for accomplishing

Popper's world 3, where 'man can stand back and see himself: [where] he can be in relationship with others without the absurdity of collisions.'[721] Bateson's Learning III and his vision of the state that the individual can reach through this learning correspond—perhaps even more so than that of Popper's—to Mosley's interest in the idea of achieving 'wholeness' and freedom through observing the split (the consciousness) in the conscious self. Bateson's preoccupation with 'personalities' rather than 'societies'[722] appeals to Mosley especially because it conveys 'how a man's lack of coincidence with himself might be a means of not just accepting but being able to grow in consciousness and learning.'[723] In other words, Bateson is preoccupied with the same paradox as Mosley: the possibility of finding the unity in the division—the split—itself.

> Learning III is a standing back from the patterns of Learning II—*in the same way that Learning II is a standing back from Learning I*—it is the chance for a man to see not just the patterns of his behaviour but also the patterns of his ability to see—and by this, not just to be free of patterns, but possibly to *influence* them.[724]

As mentioned earlier, for Mosley the preoccupation with freedom is fast connected to the concept of change. Learning III not only offers a way of achieving freedom from the patterns of one's consciousness, but also a way of influencing and thus changing these. On this level of learning the individual will be in contact with a greater pattern, whose structures will offer him alternative patterns of observation greater than those of his own. In order to convey the greater pattern to which the individual could connect himself, Mosley draws on Bateson's vision of it as

> a network of 'propositions, images, processes, natural pathology and what-have-you' that is like 'some vast ecology or aesthetics of cosmic interaction': not only within the mind, but in connection with the world outside of which the mind is conscious: some *circuitry* going between, and around, these inside and outside worlds . . .[725]

By observing the patterns of consciousness from this higher point of view one can *understand* them in a new light. A different understanding (or different understandings) of these inevitably leads to changes in them, which would consequently lead to changes in one's decisions and actions.

> To get . . . beyond . . . the patterns of Learning I and even II that cause such anguish—to be able to consider some 'circuit of circuits' [instead of cuttings or arcs of the complete circuit]—it is in this effort that there is freedom, fellowship, lack of hate and thus the chance to survive.[726]

At this point, the preoccupation with the necessity of freedom for the survival of mankind is only a small step away from the preoccupation with freedom and survival of the individual: 'Learning III . . . is rarely glimpsed by men, but perhaps is that which may be necessary for survival.'[727] For Mosley it is apparent that the survival of mankind cannot, as in earlier ages, be left to the mechanisms of 'blind' evolution only. Today, in face of our technical means—in the age of the 'Bomb'—it is too dangerous to leave the development of mankind to the processes of 'natural selection' or 'survival of the fittest.'[728] Mosley suggests that once man 'has broken away from religious and political animism' (this being characteristic of 'modern man') it is difficult for him to think of himself as anything other than an individual.[729] Not being able to feel in 'relationship with others' or in connection with a 'circuit of circuits,' he is a potential danger not only to himself, but also to others. Until recently, and even today in many areas of life, such an attitude could result in the death of a part of the human population, whose elimination did not have a major effect on the existence of the rest of the species and in some cases could even be seen as necessary for its survival.

> It is 'a fundamental instruction of every species that from time to time it shall discard nearly the whole organism and start again.' It is by means of death (and birth) that there is kept alive the continuing strain which, in terms of evolution, is what matters rather than the individual.[730]

With the individual having access to technical means, which can destroy the whole species, such evolutionary mechanisms become far too dangerous to contemplate. That is why the individual(s) must try to influence the patterns of consciousness and consequently the patterns of his/their (destructive) actions by means of observation as in the Batesonian Learning III or the Popperian world 3. It is only in this way that the individual(s) 'will be able to see [himself/themselves], scientifically, as representative[s] of a potentially greater strain—it is this, as well as providing comfort in the face of individual death, that might enable [him/

them], since [he/they] would know that part of this potential were inside as well as outside [him/them], to come to terms with [himself/themselves], and thus, of course, with the world.'[731] By observing themselves being connected to a greater whole—'the world'; 'the others'; 'the circuit of circuits'—humans could exercise influence on the course of the patterns of evolution in the same way that they could influence the patterns of their observation by observing them from the third level of observation (or Learning III). In this sense what Mosley means by man 'influencing' the course of evolution is not taking 'control.' The act of controlling implies imposing one's concept of order—i.e., one's patterns of consciousness—on something else. In Mosley's terms, then, exercising 'influence' on evolution runs completely contrary to 'taking control.' Individuals can only exercise influence by *detaching from* (and not imposing) the patterns of their observation. In this sense, Mosley appropriated what he believed to be Nietzsche's much misunderstood conception of real power. It was only by exercising this sort of power that a truly free and 'higher' type of human being could evolve: in other words, what Nietzsche—and not the Nazis—called Superman:

> Nietzsche's 'higher' type of man might be bold, intelligent, imaginative; but even in these qualities he would be out of line with powerful society: his one undeniable 'superiority' would be his freedom from other people's slavery-to-power.[732]

In *Catastrophe Practice* Mosley tried to invoke this idea aesthetically as well. The outcome of what Mosley sets out to do this time is at first sight completely incomprehensible. Apart form the essays, the novel consists of the three plays *Skylight*, *Landfall*, and *Cell* and a novella *Cypher*. All of these pieces are interconnected by sharing the same protagonists, who at times, as we are told by the playwright's guidelines, change their names. The characters are also the link between the four novels that were born out of *Catastrophe Practice* to make up the *Catastrophe Practice Series*. The subtitle of the plays, *Plays for Not Acting*, neatly sums up the forceful resistance of the plays to interpretation. It is almost impossible to analyse the plays by way of interpreting a meaning into the actions and the dialogues. Mosley's juxtapositions and insertion of gaps between what the characters think, say and do as a means of showing their self-reflection[733] is exaggerated to such a degree that it is almost inconceivable to tell what is going on. The breakdown in plot, coherence, linearity, and causality is complete. There is an uncanny feeling of being amidst a darkness or chaos without any guide to lead one out. The plays defy quotation. John Banks insightfully compared the plays to the Gödelian knot.[734] Looking at this impenetrable riddle one could dare say that the plays carry out the postmodern notion of there being no meaning in the text to the full. Mosley thus proved himself an heir to Beckett.[735]

This is where the comparison between Mosley and the other stops.

Whereas Beckett, despite the determination of viewers and critics to see a meaning in his plays, insisted that his plays illustrated meaninglessness, Mosley goes out of his way to state that there was an important meaning underlying—or beyond—the apparent incoherence, chaos and senselessness in the plays. What goes on the stage is not the 'real' reality off-stage, but it is influenced by and in turn *influences* what goes on offstage. In this sense his plays tried to *reflect* life as it is. What he wanted to say was

> That's how one has got to learn to live—without knowing what's going on!
>
> ... this was the point I was extravagantly trying to make with *Catastrophe Practice*—the characters were stuck on stage where what was going on there didn't much matter; they were trying to keep an ear and an eye open for what was important going on off stage or in the audience; but in the meantime they had to keep things going on stage with bits and pieces of scenes and ideas (almost but not quite random?) from which they occasionally learned something of importance! This seemed to me like life. But it was almost impossible to convey that the goings-on on stage both didn't matter and yet did—because the characters were trying to keep their wondering eyes and ears open.[736]

The urgency of this insight becomes especially apparent regarding the critical human condition at the end of twentieth and beginning of this century. The dramas on the world stage have the potential to destroy at least all human form life. The patterns of this sort of drama, Mosley believes, are dominated by the lack of attendance to the connections between the stage and the off-stage. *Catastrophe Practice* tried to pose this problem and at least provide some points of reference for an answer.

> I think that [*Catastrophe Practice*] was an effort to say: 'it doesn't matter what you say. You *can* argue, but what finally matters is what happens.

Either the world blows up or it doesn't. Either there is a new step in evolution or there isn't. . . . You can talk about anything . . . and how much one can influence that one never really knows. One can hope: 'I can influence this.'[737]

The question is thus how could a participant in this drama—even if one didn't know *how much*—influence what happens on the stage and as a result even change the course of what happens off-stage? If one cannot and should not want to, as Mosley has repeatedly insisted, change things by trying to manipulate and predetermine them, then isn't one left at the mercy of coincidences? Mosley uses the simile of 'kicking a ball about on the deck of a ship that goes on to its destination independent of the game—it *does* effect the course of the way!'[738] As was the case with his Sixties novels, Mosley's answer to these questions seems to be that 'coincidences'—or 'luck'—could be made use of, if individuals prepared the grounds for them to operate. Bearing in mind the meaningfulness of coincidences within Mosley's *Weltanschauung*, Mosley's choice of title eloquently points this out

> I came across an article in a scientific magazine which spoke of something called Catastrophe Theory; this was a mathematical theory which explained . . . how sometimes in both biology and physics there were what appeared to be steady states that took a sudden jump—flipped over on to a different level as it were—and this was the 'catastrophe' in the content of which there might be decisive change.
> . . . It does seem that this sort of situation is what humanity is facing now—There will either be some flip-over into a more embracing form of consciousness, or there will be increasing odds on a simple, antagonistic blowing up. A matter of *luck*—all right—but can we not brush up our attitudes so that this piece of *luck* rather than that might be encouraged and even emerge?[739]

'Brushing up our attitudes' and 'flipping over into a more embracing form of consciousness' were matters of 'aesthetic technique.' Mosley in a way was trying to express the Kleistian notion of 'grace' by applying Brechtian dramatic techniques: if the actors could communicate to the audience that they were only acting and so indicate the existence of 'the other' beyond the stage, then all persons involved might move onto a higher level of consciousness:

it might be shown that in a sense of course one is never off-stage, but it might be by becoming aware of one's different roles, of moving between them, that one becomes aware of what is off-stage. By being aware of one's programming, that is, one might also be apart from it. And this might be the miracle; the act of grace.[740]

In this sense, *Catastrophe Practice* is the continuation of his scripts *The Assassination of Trotsky* and *Impossible Object* (filmed as *Story of a Love Story*), both of which aimed at showing that what was being said was just both a guide to and a shroud over the real 'other' off-stage. The plays in *Catastrophe Practice* are also an attempt at finding a form for the aesthetic conundrum that Greville in *Natalie Natalia* had set himself:

> I am trying to write a story that will describe . . . occurrences in function rather than in time—or as if time were spatial, so that one could move to and fro in it by looking. This is difficult: we see a moment or a pattern, not both: one cut out the other. But if we do not know, perhaps from some *third* point, the moment and the pattern at once, then each seems meaningless. Because, on its own, each is an abstraction, not an experience. The experience is both. But our minds are not constructed for this: which is why, perhaps, we make myths.[741]
>
> By recognising the predicament, that is, we might even deal with it. Recognising two forms of recognition at once, there would be a sort of knowledge—of freedom. This would be optimistic.[742]

The *Catastrophe Practice* plays are an attempt to explore the hidden 'third point'—what Greville saw as 'recognising two forms of recognition' and the *Catastrophe Practice* essays tried to define as the 'observer of the observed and the observer.' In this way the book tries to 'undo' and 'reconstruct' the mind in order to free it from its structures, which hinder it to experience life as a meaningful experience. The protagonists in the pieces try to live this out and in this way shed as much light on the essays as the essays shed light on the pieces.

Mosley opens the plays with a definition of the word 'riddle': 'Riddle . . . to separate chaff from corn, ashes from cinders etc. . . . test (evidence, truth).'[743] This is a warning for the reader not to look for a simple solution to a problem posed in the plays, but to remember that a riddle is uninterpretable in that it embodies the paradox of being both the problem and the solution—both the trap and the liberation—at once. The titles of the plays illustrate this all too well: A *Skylight* is both the sky at top of a mountain, and 'a window in the ceiling of the space in which [the] characters seemed trapped.'[744] A *Landfall* is both fallen rocks that shut one in and the first glimpse of dry land when at sea. A *Cell* is a room where one is imprisoned and the primary unit out of which life can burst.

The setting of the plays seems to be where the essays located the paradox of the individual's imprisonment/liberation to take place: namely, the mind. The guidelines for the first play, *Skylight*, especially are telling: the ground upon which the scene is set is 'the rock of the mountain, grey and gnarled like the surface of the brain.'[745] The plays try to take on the 'form' of the perception of reality in our mind—that is, the initial chaos and meaninglessness. As mentioned earlier in the chapter, for doing this Mosley had found the stream-of-consciousness style both exhausted and inadequate. He wanted to make a model of how one is trapped in one's own mind ('I was trying to have some image—a representation of the mind on the stage . . . and that was a way of trying to *do* the way we were stuck in the mind'[746]) as well as how one could free oneself from this trap. In *Landfall*, for example, the characters seem to be trapped in a hopeless chaos. They are completely bewildered and talk at such great cross purposes, as if they were each in a 'wrong' plot and 'given' lines for different plays—or better still, it is as if both the characters and the audience were entrapped in some 'divine' practical joke that the playwright was playing on them. In *Cell* the idea of entrapment/liberation is expressed perhaps more clearly (if one, regarding these plays, could use this word at all) than in the other two plays. The characters are shown to be involved in activities regarding a flight-attempt out of entrapping structures. The actual stage-set of the play, as Mosley notes in his autobiography, was 'structured as if it might represent a brain: there is a lower level which occupies most of the width of the stage; it is a cellar, or junk-room—or what might be the unconscious part of a mind. One a upper level there are two compartments separated by a central back-to-front partition; these could be the left and right hemispheres of a brain.'[747] All three 'chambers' are occupied by characters who are trying to establish contact with the other ones and possibly to break out. They obviously don't have a scheme about how to go about doing this and seem like caricaturised scientists, who know what they want but do not know how to get there. Accordingly they seem preoccupied with some tests and experiments without knowing what they are doing or what the outcome would be. This is exactly how the viewer feels at well. Mosley assures that anybody who perceives of the plays as such has definitely got it right. The only thing that he has got to add on to this incomprehensibility is yet more obscurity by claiming that even he, the playwright, didn't exactly know what was going on:

> People were *supposed* to *not* know what was going on. People asked me: 'but is there something going on? We, the audience, don't understand what is going on. Did you know what was going on?' And I said: 'Well, no! I don't know! There was nothing going on on the stage. The whole point was there was nothing going on. Something was going on off stage!' And then they said: 'Well, what?' And I said: 'Well, [the protagonists] didn't know. And I don't know. And the audience doesn't know. All you know is that something's going on. And then it works out! . . . What the play has taught us is that there is something going on. We don't know, but we must look and listen.[748]

It is crucial to remember that neither the writer, nor the protagonists or the reader know exactly what is going on. Mosley in this way was trying to remind us of our freedom in daily life, which we so take for granted and thus literally forget that we have it. We all initially in our consciousness perceive of reality as mysterious and chaotic and *then* inevitably and invariably use our freedom to form the raw material that we receive according to the way we see things. In this way *all* participants become the writer, protagonist and viewer of the plays. The reader is once again, as in *Accident* and *Impossible Object*, reminded of the individual's responsibility and power in the business of shaping life. In *Cell* the characters free themselves from their given roles and thus move onto a higher level than mere, farcical actors by being aware of their roles as caricaturised characters. In the tradition of Brechtian theatre they show that they are aware of being watched. The guidelines of the play requires them often to look at the audience midway in their dialogue. This technique makes it apparent that they know the lines that they speak are not their own and that they are being watched. In addition to that, their conversation at great cross-purposes almost makes a joke out of their dialogue, at whose dismantling they seem to take great pleasure. They seem both bewildered and bemused at their experiment with themselves and the audience. In one word, their self-reflexive irony is their means for getting out. The following is an attempt at 'quoting' (again, if one, regarding these plays, could use this term) a passage out of this play:

Anderson appears to be listening. After a time he enunciates carefully—

Anderson   Get out at Westminster, cross the road, go to the gates, and you'll find a policeman. You'll wear knee-breeches, black waist coats, and those conical hats, you know, like witches. . . . And when you come to the police man you will say—Excuse me, mate, where's the team? Excuse me, mate, where's the fucking team—

He seems to listen. . . .
Then Anderson speaks with the deadpan voice of someone on an intercom radio—
. . . He stares at the audience.
. . .

Hortense   Who were you talking to—
Anderson   Myself—
Hortense   What did you say—
Anderson   I love you.

Hortense puts an eye to the microscope.
A faint light comes on in the upper room right. In this room there can be seen, dimly, the figure of the man, previously glimpsed hanging from the ceiling, now sitting on a bed; he is straight-backed, facing front. His arms are wrapped round him. He seems to bed in a straitjacket.
Hortense takes her eye from the microscope.
The light in the upper room fades.

Anderson   It has to be in the dark-
Hortense   Why—
Anderson   Or how would we find where to go?
Hortense   I heard your tapping.
Anderson   Wasn't it rats—
Hortense   Wasn't it music?

Hortense moves round the room. She seems to act—
—There were tanks in the street. There were children dying. When they came to the barricades against its soft grey walls they battered—[749]

This dramatic self-reflexivity was (and is) an important feature in the works of other heirs of Beckett such as Pinter and Stoppard, both of whom have artistically collaborated with Mosley.[750] However, Mosley's characters do not, like Stoppard's Rosencrantz and Guildenstern, perish despite all their liberating irony and knowingness. They manage to get out of the dictate of the structures of the play *and* prevail. Mosley's understanding of freedom, as conveyed in the *Catastrophe Practice* essays, makes this possible. His conception of the individual's freedom to change and influence, as has often been stressed in the course of this study, is not meant in the sense that the individual's will and taste *only* are the measurements according to which he can act. These plays insist that being conscious of, in the Batesonian sense, a greater pattern and thus *objectivity* (the word itself implies being watched and watching from the *outside*) is the basis upon which the individual can use his *subjectivity* to change the old entrapping patterns and achieve some form of liberation. If the awareness of an off-stage only enforced the centrifugal self-reflexivity, as was the case with Stoppard's characters, it could only be (self) suffocating. In contrast, the style of Mosley's characters' awareness is such that an interaction between the inside and the outside of the stage initiates the process of a 'flip-over' out of the present entrapping structures.

> By one's being prepared as it were for catastrophe might one not even be an agent in the mechanisms of change? . . .—my stumbling across this title was the sort of coincidence that happened: this was the sort of event for which my characters were practising—some style, some attitude to do with watching and listening, that might be ready for a chance, a flip-over, that might occur in the outside world—or indeed in the brain. And my characters by their alertness, might even encourage this or that occurrence; and thus they themselves land as it were in liveliness rather than in death.[751]

In *Cell* all the activities, experiments and 'accidents' inside the stage-set lead to and culminate in the introduction of 'angelic' figures called Siva and Florence from outside the stage-set, who help the characters dismantle the partitions imprisoning them and get in touch with each other. The play closes with the anticipation of the whole theatre set giving way:

> There is a bang—as if something has given way and the whole theatre is about to pivot on its left-to-right axis at the front of the stage; the stage coming up and the auditorium going down.[752]

Siva and Florence are catalysts: the embodiment of the interaction between the inside and the outside, who can only operate when the individuals' activities coupled with their awareness of the greater pattern beyond is at hand. Regarding Mosley's Christianity, they could also be understood as the liberating agent in Christian tradition, the Holy Ghost. The liberation of the characters—the fruit of their activities—is conveyed by yet another Christian symbol; namely the birth of a child, for whom all the characters seem responsible. Both Siva and the child, in accordance with Christian mythology, literally appear 'out of the blue.' The birth of the child is only implied and never stated directly, but the characters keep handing something around and talking about it as if it were a baby.

Siva	Hold it in your arms—
Hortense	Is it crying?
	. . .
Siva	Look—
Dionysus	Isn't it sweet—
	. . .
The Moor	It can walk—
Dionysus	It can talk—
Florence	It can—
Anderson	—Look!
Hortense	It's smiling![753]

The baby symbolises hope and the successfulness of the protagonists activities. Mosley repeatedly makes use of this symbol in this series, which could be understood in many ways. The baby signifies the success of the protagonists in liberating themselves from the old structures and 'flipping over' onto a higher level of consciousness. In this play, however, the characters (and the playwright) seem almost superstitious in their reluctance to talk about the child directly. It is as if talking about it directly could make it perish. In this way Mosley conveys the fragility and complexity of his characters struggle for liberation. However, this technique also expresses the idea upon which the *Catastrophe Practice* is based. The baby's gestation and birth have been going on off-stage. The sudden appearance of the baby on stage indicates the 'sudden jump' or the 'flip-over' onto the higher level of consciousness. In this way, the baby connects the inside and the outside. It is the incarnation of the border—that what both *divides* and *connects*—between the physical (the stage) and the metaphysical (the off-stage) worlds.

The other possibility for understanding the appearance of the baby is putting it in light of Mosley's own new 'birth' after the accident: the new start in his private life—learning to survive his parents and his past, divorcing and remarrying—as well as in his artistic career, which had come to a long halt after *Natalie Natalia* both indicate this. It could also be seen in a greater context; namely that of humanity's prevalence in face of disasters and catastrophes. Mosley himself observes that

> At the centre of all the books in the *Catastrophe Practice* series there is the question of the survival and the birth of the child. By what series of coincidences (but are they coincidences?) does a potential child—a seed on its journey to and within the womb or the mind—survive?[754]

The *Catastrophe Practice* plays, despite all attempts to interpret them, remain highly unreadable. Mosley himself felt the need for shedding some light onto them strongly:

> It seemed that as a corollary to my plays there should still be some story of who my six characters might be as it were in reality, off-stage: of course this would be just one more story! But still—what is reality except the recognition of a complexity: the structuring, the imagination, of a dimension that you know is there just because you know the boundaries of a stage.[755]

The story was to be the novella, *Cypher*, at the end of *Catastrophe Practice*. Similar to the titles of the plays, this title too suggests both a predicament and the way out of it: a *Cypher* is both a coded form of communication and the key to such a code. In *Cypher* all the characters of the plays—now 'fleshed out' as Eleanor and Max, Jason and Lilia, Judith and Bert—meet in the 'real world.' The scene is a typical Seventies student riot in some London university. The fiasco escalates when a laboratory is set on fire with the possible threat of some radioactivity being released. This seems to be the Catastrophe off-stage, by which the protagonists seem neither scared nor surprised. It wouldn't be farfetched to say that they knowingly and almost religiously greet the Catastrophe. However, this should not be understood in a millenarian, messianic sense, but in the spirit of the plays and the essays. Their awareness of the Catastrophe makes them observe their own histrionics and role-playings as a stage-set, the awareness of which could liberate them from these old patterns and elevate them onto a higher level of consciousness, or, to put it in the professor's, Max Ackerman's, words: 'It is in our heads that we can get out, with one great jump.'[756] Again, the protagonists' self-reflection is made clear in a Brechtian mode. The story opens with an aura of theatre about it. Enter: the Professor, Max Ackerman. Setting: the Old Science Theatre. Here he holds a lecture on new evolution science entitled *Selection: Natural or Unnatural*. In the auditorium Max sees two characters from the previous plays: the pretty dark haired girl, Judith, and the elderly woman with a pudding basin haircut like Cleopatra, Eleanor.[757] Max recognises them as people from his past life—his actor's life in the *Plays for Not Acting*.

> she reminded him, strikingly, of someone at the centre of his past life; in her student's role listening to him so intently; someone who, he thought, should also be in this audience; . . . And then in fact he did find her, this other one, sitting at the back of the auditorium now and smiling down . . . [758]

Furthermore, there is Jason, the playwright, who seems to have written the previous plays played by the present protagonists, who are supposed to act as if they knew that they were acting.[759] The setting of his plays are those of *Skylight*: 'He thought—But if there's that crack in the rocks; the roof or the floor coming down— . . . This is a geological problem; like that of a mountain, or the surface of a brain.'[760] He and Judith, the dark-haired girl from the Old Science Theatre, actually try to rehearse the piece, in which, as Judith recognises, all the characters seem to 'know each other so well!'[761] The level of self-reflexivity—of metafiction—is in this way pitched to the highest.

The message of the plays which Jason has written, as he tells Judith, is that the characters 'want to change: to be changed.'[762] That is, the protagonists are not interested in 'changing' their circumstance, but in using their circumstance as a tool—a mirror—for changing themselves and attitudes. This can only be done if they tried to *save* themselves in contrast to millenarian sects who would welcome the annihilating powers of the Catastrophe off-stage. In other words, change can only occur, if the protagonists undertook the paradoxical task of resisting the Catastrophe and accepting it at the same time. The explosions, the red glow above the rooftops, the to and fros and the running crowds in the novel can be seen as messengers of the threatening nuclear disaster just around the corner, as it were. What the characters are doing at first seems to be a stoical and passive acceptance of this—instead of joining the panicking and running crowds, they muse over theatre and self-reflexive drama! However, this is what the reader is supposed to see as the only activity worthwhile. This is shown by putting the mission for finding the lost child at the centre of the story. The child, who was tentatively introduced in the previous play, is exposed to life-threatening danger and might be injured or even dead. He can only be found at the end due to the characters' observations which should help them get out of their minds 'with one great jump.' In order to do this the characters too must expose themselves to risks. These risks, though, are taken both in the outer and inner world. There is Max Ackerman, for example, who is caught in a lift-shaft, very similar to the stage-set in *Cell*, in which the characters were trying to establish some contact with each other and the outside world in order to get out. He is almost hurled to his death, hadn't he landed on top of the lift-cage. His being hurled can both be understood literally and also in the sense of Christian (Kierkegaardian) 'leap into the darkness.' During all this time he is watching himself and his circumstance, as if he were in a theatre piece.

> The professor, having launched himself into space with a handkerchief round his hands and his hands round the cables at the centre of the lift-shaft, uttered a shout as if of terror as he went down: he thought—I am too old for this: I am dead: I will retire. He landed on top of the lift-cage . . . He thought—Or is it the cells in my body that require rejuvenation: the ache, the longing in my balls, heart, mind. . . .
>
> He groaned; made bumping noises. He thought—Thus are thunderbolts cast down: babies are born. . . . He thought—And so are we made bearable? Unbearable? His hands and clothes were filthy. He picked at the grease, as if it were afterbirth.[763]

As Judith earlier on, the reader too is supposed to puzzle whether through this sort of self-observation the protagonists do really move 'into the influence of some new constellation? . . . Do things really work like this?'[764] The question is answered in the affirmative by the child, signifying hope and continuity, being found. But it is not only the child that is found, but Jason's script, which seems to have been lost, as well. Jason, however, in face of seeing the child jokingly—parodying the Seventies riot slogans—demands from the others to 'throw away the scripts!'[765]

Through irony he can attach *and* detach himself simultaneously from the script. In other words, he can grasp the paradox of the drama's vitality and triviality at the same time. In this way the idea with which Mosley started *The Catastrophe Practice Series* is summarised: the stage doesn't matter, since what matters goes on off-stage; however, it is what is on stage that points out what that 'other' off-stage is. The viewer is the connection between the two. The connection of the three is the Batesonian greater circuit. By realising this man can be liberated and move onto a higher state of consciousness. Max Ackerman's perception of this connectedness at the beginning of the novella expresses this as such: 'And these connections between the three—himself, the old woman, and the young girl in the second row—in his mind, in the lecture theatre—all seemed to be taking place in some system of recognition; not belonging either to one or to the other but in between them, the inside and the outside worlds.'[766] Thus the circle is closed.

Catastrophe Practice, perhaps understandably, was not taken up by publishers for a long time. In a letter to his agent, Michael Sissons, Mosley examined the problem, justified it and offered a solution

> I see *Plays for Not Acting* and *Cypher* as the nucleus of what in the future will be a much larger structure—a series of novels about each of the characters in *Plays* and *Cypher* separately; about their background, who they are, the turning points in their lives, etc. These stories will for the most part be straight narrative stories; much easier for the reader than *Plays* and *Cypher*. I can do this without too much difficulty once the nucleus is there: it is the nucleus that has to be a bit mysterious because after all what I'm trying to do (as in the Essays) is to show the feel of a new way of looking at things, and I can hardly be expected to be doing this if the language of the nucleus is just something expected. But once this is done, the further building-blocks can be more simple. I think the 'need' for some such way of looking at things is there; and people will see what I am trying to do more and more as further novels come out.[767]

II. *Imago Bird*: applying the Brechtian alienation to political and everyday life as a means for liberation

Imago Bird is the first novel that came out of the *Catastrophe Practice*. It is the story of the boy who is called Bert and Anderson in *Cypher* and takes place slightly earlier than the previous novella. Bert is an eighteen-year-old boy who, due to his parents being abroad, lives with his 'caretaker' Prime Minister uncle, uncle Bill, and his wife, Aunt Mavis. He is in the typical, teenagers' rite-of-passage gap—i.e., between having finished school and going to university—where the desire for change and freedom is at its strongest. Bert's desire for freedom is conveyed particularly by granting him with the features of an ideal victim: he is a shy, 'invisible' stammerer residing amongst the most powerful in society, in whose hands the fate of their land and people lies—the similarities with Mosley's childhood and youth cannot be overlooked. It is through his observation faculty that Bert can reverse the situation and put himself on a higher level than his milieu: he becomes the viewer of the drama around him and sees the participants' imprisonment in their role-playing:

> Ever since I can remember I have thought the grown up world to be mad, its way of talking to itself and being outraged at the answers; the bright look in its eyes as it goes off to feed on disaster. Aristotle said that it was self-evident that human beings wanted happiness; but it seemed to me they are more at home in sadness and confusion; that if these are taken away they are exposed to the heat of the sun like snails without shells or dark places.[768]

The image of the Platonic cave is the red thread throughout the novel (and the following books), woven into a Brechtian 'alienation,' in order to convey the idea of observation as a means for liberation from old patterns. Bert sees the 'grown ups' as a troupe of actors, who try to *cover up* what happens off-stage, in order to give comfort to the audience. This is concretised in the scene where a shooting during a typical politician's party takes place. The shooting, as if on cue, sets the characters into a series of motions. Instead of trying to find out about what has happened, all take up certain roles in order to cover up the event:

> it is their [the actors'] job to pretend, to cover up, to put something over. And by this they give comfort. The people in the hall were already not interested in finding out what in fact had happened in the study: they were interested in discovering what sort of parts they should play in order to preserve, what ever had happened, some customary function and identity. Like this they could give comfort: but did not the reality, locked in the study, remain in their unconscious like a hungry lion?[769]

This is the very turning point in Bert's observation: if actors give comfort by covering up the reality, then they must *know* that a reality exists—that there is a sun outside the cave. Their behaviour conveys their knowledge of the existence of something else behind their role playing. It is in this knowledge that hope lies. Bert conceives of the rows between Uncle Bill and Mrs. Washbourne as a Greek tragedy, where murder and self-mutilation take place as noises off-stage.[770] The impersonal tone of Uncle Bill and the knowing smile of Mrs. Washbourne indicate that they recognise each other as actors on the stage. The shouting and screaming represent in the imagination of their audience, Bert, terrible pain, which doesn't really take place on the 'stage.'[771] The pain is conceived of in the imagination of the 'audience' because of the sounds that go on off-stage. So, couldn't it be that the 'actors' half-consciously do this because they are well acquainted with the patterns of the mind?[772] The 'actors' themselves don't admit that they are acting being fearful of losing their 'jobs.' The Brechtian drama is introduced as the solution to the paradox of how to cover up reality in order to uncover it; how to pretend in order to get at truth: 'Might not actors in fact begin to glimpse their audience as if it were their unconsciousness?'[773]

If they started to see their audience as the unconscious, then they will recognise the patterns in which it works consciously. It is the conscious recognition of what goes on in the unconsciousness that could actually free the mind from the its self-destructive patterns—

> But if what happens consciously off-stage really goes on in the mind, then indeed can it not be seen as funny? even murder and self-mutilation? And might not this, the knowledge of it, stop it?[774]

Conceiving of such a framework necessitates detachment. Bert sees jokes as a means of detachment, for they break up the limitations that imprison men in the truest sense of the word. Jokes, in his view, could stop people from doing awful things—like murder and self-mutilation in plays—because their understanding needs an expanded consciousness and awareness. In a political discussion with his Trotskyite 'bedmate,' Sheila, Bert points out that liberation movements are damned to become copies of the oppression they fight, since they lack humour.

> You can't change things just by putting one sort of organisation in place of another. You've got to free things in people's minds . . . Jokes

are serious. Wasn't it Brecht who said— . . . —jokes break up old patterns—[775]

This is not to say, as Bert insists, that he finds the situation of the 'people below subsistence level' funny.[776] Jokes are only liberating if they can show *both* sides of the coin—the advantages and disadvantages of being a 'victim.' He himself has learnt to utilise his weakness for feeling higher than the powerful people around him and in this way use it as a means for freeing himself from them. That is to say, he is playing the same power-game that he sees others to play: the game of covering up reality for acquiring comfort and advantage. Mosley's maxim about means of liberation becoming means of imprisonment applies to Bert and his stammer: like the half-smiles of his Uncle Bill and Mrs. Washbourne, it is a sign of the unconscious knowledge, which has to become *conscious* if he were to be able to leave the Platonic cave. This is where help from outside in form of psychoanalysis comes in.

Mirroring Mosley's own experience, psychoanalysis shows Bert the possibility of liberation from the mind's destructive patterns. Bert's ruminations bring to mind R. D. Laing's theories which had preoccupied Mosley after his accident.

> What analysts do is to get you to play your words back to yourself so it is as if you can hear yourself speaking. Then you begin to question yourself, because you see different patterns and inflexions.[777]

> What analysts do is make you feel you are tied up in knots. Or rather, they watch you while you make yourself feel tied up in knots. They encourage you almost . . . you cannot begin to untie yourself it seems, until you have some sort of model of what your knot is and it is in this that an analyst gives you, almost puts you in, so you can learn to get out.[778]

Bert's analyst—or better still, catalyst—who helps him get out of (the 'trap' of) his mind is Eleanor Anders, who was Florence, the angelic figure, along with Siva, in *Cell* and the almost witch-doctor figure, wife of Max Ackerman, in *Cypher*. Through her Bert realises that his stammer is a double-edged knife:

> I had told her [Dr. Anders] of what the previous therapist had said

about my possibly not wanting to get rid of my stammer; and she had said, cheerfully — But of course you don't want to get rid of your stammer! And I had felt for a moment that I should be outraged again at this; and then I had felt as if I were starting on some journey.[779]

On this journey within himself, he realises that his conception of the imprisoned situation of others applies for him as well: his stammer is both a struggle with lies and a shell of protection against reality. Neuroses are like shells:

> you lose them and you burn up in the sun. If you don't lose them, they grow so heavy you go mad too.[780]

> I had said—why, if it is such hell, do I not want to get rid of my stammer? And she had said — You think people want to get out of hell? And this had been the first time that I felt the light that was like the glow of a fire in a bedroom somewhere beside me: and it was this that was like the beginning of a journey; and also the glimpse of the end of it . . . I had said — But if I do not want to get out of hell because hell is protection, what is it that I am using my stammer as a protection against? . . . she had said — Might you not be using your stammer as a protection against your own high opinion of yourself?
> There was the white light like something fusing: then her bookcase, her frieze, the spire beyond her window . . .[781]

The objective of this sort of self-observation is not so much to cure the stammer—i.e., the symptom—(which could happen as a by-product, anyway), but to show Bert how to leave the hell of his split-self and become whole. In order to start the journey he will first have to see the pattern of his predicament. In order to be able to see it, he'll have to get it out of his mind, so that he can observe and study it—as if it were a maze, a riddle, that has to be looked at carefully, from above.[782] The 'white light' comes down, as in Biblical mythology, as a sign of illumination. He learns that accepting the 'evil' he is trying to hide (i.e., his high opinion of himself) as well as the 'good' he is trying to show (his stammer as a symptom of his mistrust of lying words) can only happen if he watched *both* of them and became aware of his watching them. Freedom thus lies in this knowledge that can transcend both the conscious and the unconscious; the good and the evil.

Bert's success in embarking on this journey is symbolised through saving the unborn child of his sister, Lilia, who is the wife of Jason, the playwright, and the mother of the baby in *Cypher*. Lilia has decided to abort her child, not knowing whether it is from her husband or the Professor, Max Ackerman. On the other hand, Judith, the dark haired girl from *Cypher* who seemed to have an affair with Ackerman, has also been carrying on with Jason. But now by a series of trivial coincidences, Bert meets her—as was mentioned earlier, *Imago Bird* takes place slightly earlier than *Cypher*—and falls in love with her. Lilia, while waiting her turn in the clinic on a knife-edge, gets worried about Bert and calls up Dr. Anders to see how he is. Dr. Anders tell her that she talks about Bert, as if he were her own child.[783] This makes Lilia make a decision and leave the clinic and so the child is saved.

The relationships of the characters with each other epitomise all the ideas upon which these novels are based. They are an 'allegory' for the Batesonian double-bind, the catastrophic knife-edge, the either-and-or. They make up a network which allows for dramas and histrionics good enough for a soap-opera. But this network is also a greater pattern of connections and *relatedness*, being aware of which, makes it possible for 'coincidences' to operate 'positively' for all the participants. Bert's idea about projecting a film on a double-screen, where the characters in each separate film can influence the outcome of the parallel film by accidental inter-screen nudges is an effort to express this interconnectedness aesthetically. The nudges help things work out, since the characters in the separate stories are conscious of each other and in this way participate in each other's stories. Mosley compares such a relationship to that of lovers—the loved ones being those 'with whom [one's] life will be, is, interwoven in a network.'[784] This attendance—or 'love'—is what saves this group, around whom the series evolves, from carrying out their drama acts to destructive ends. They can get over their drama and their acts of jealousy quickly and take care of more important things that are going on off-stage, which *in turn* influence their drama. The title of the story alludes to this operation: 'Imago: 1. Final and perfect stage of an insect after it has undergone its metamorphosis, e. g. butterfly.'[785] In his autobiography Mosley points out that 'imago' is not meant to refer to a 'final' or 'perfect' human:

> No human is 'final' nor 'perfect'; but with 'metamorphosis' you are on the move; and 'bird' is an image of the Holy Spirit—so perhaps after all the process might be one to be called perfect.[786]

III. *Serpent*: the liberated individual as the guarantor for the survival of mankind

Serpent takes place some three or four years after *Imago Bird*. The protagonists are Lilia, Bert's sister, and her playwright husband, Jason, whose child (which had 'miraculously' been saved from being aborted in the previous novel) is now about four years old. The novel is structured around two stories, which encircle one another: there is the story of Jason and Lilia and then there is Jason's 'umfilmable' film-script, about Josephus, the Jewish historian, who chronicled the Masada mass suicide in 70 AD. The stories reflect on each other, in that they are both about individuals, who by liberating themselves from the destructive patterns that govern the mind guarantee the continuity of the group that they are part of. This is less obvious in the case of Josephus, who did not only save himself by betraying the group and manipulating the suicide pact, but also in popular imagination came to be seen as an accomplice of the Romans and in a way a 'murderer' of the Jews.

The script that Jason has written tells the story of the Masada mass suicide from Josephus' point of view. Jason is concerned with the paradox that were it not for Josephus' choosing 'dishonour' over 'honour,' the Zealots would not have survived: thanks to his story of the Zealots' heroism the group prevailed even beyond its death. The ideal that held this society together survived through the one who liberated himself from it.

> It is true, is it not, that any society, if it is to hold together, has to have ideals which members of the society are ready to die for? What other sort of forces can hold a society together? And it is true, is it not, that if in such circumstances an individual chooses to live, then he will naturally be seen as a traitor by those who choose to die? All this is dependent, of course, on the belief that society is the unit that has to hold together. But then, if the members of a society are dead, what is it that holds together? If anything is to live, is it not individuals that do so?[787]

Jason, therefore, believes that it is unlikely for him to be permitted to make a film from Josephus' point of view. Such a film would be 'morally and politically objectionable.'[788] Jason is aware of the danger that people could conceive of such a film as 'fascist or élitist'[789]—the film could be seen as romanticising the suicide of a society for the sake of a few. However, when a society is determined to define its identity in choosing death, then it is better if the death-loving group and their conditions were allowed to break up in order to make 'fertile soil'[790] for life to continue: 'Things have to be broken up in order that something shall live.'[791]

This clearly refers to Mosley's reflections on evolutionary science in *Catastrophe Practice*, especially in the light of J. Z. Young's idea that it is 'a fundamental instruction of every species that from time to time it shall discard nearly the whole organism and start again.'[792] This conjecture both considers the individual as secondary to the organism and in the meantime points out the importance of the individual for the continuity of the organism: those who do not perish along with 'nearly the whole organism' have the key to the survival of the organism. It is important to note that the prevalence of the group depends on those individuals who have learnt to liberate themselves from the self-destructive patterns that had held the group together till now. But today, with the human race possessing the physical means to destroy itself completely, this assumption would be too dangerous, for if society blows itself up, all individuals are taken along with it.[793] Like Josephus, those individuals, then, who have liberated themselves and learnt to survive, can now no longer remain secret, for they are the ones from whom the human race could learn how to get out of the old patterns of thinking and thus survive: 'Something has to change, in the mind, if the world is to stay alive.'[794]

Thus, Jason believes, making such a film would 'in the long run, be politically correct.'[795]

Bearing in mind that Jason was the playwright of the *Plays for Not Acting*, his mistrust of conventional acting comes as no surprise: conventional acting only gives comfort by reproducing the disasters and miseries of people.[796] In the same vein as Bert, he sees that people need to watch miseries and disasters as 'snails need shells: to get out of the heat of the sun; to sit in a cave watching cinema screens showing miseries; and so they get pleasure.'[797] In order for the mind of the individual to free itself from such destructive patterns the play must put the whole thing into a different framework.

> [The Zen] master says to his pupil—if you say I am holding this stick I will hit you with it, if you do not say I am holding this stick I will hit you with it— . . . —And the thing for the pupil to do is to snatch the stick from the Zen master and to put the whole thing into a different context—[798]

And—

> a really grown-up sort of play would be if everyone, actors and audience, knew that what they said was rubbish . . . if everyone knew that what was said and heard was said and heard as actors and audience . . .[799]

Here again Brechtian theatre is seen as the guide for the evolution of a 'new human type.' If everyone—the actors, as well as the audience—were aware of the role-playing, then they could understand that there is something else going on off-stage. This is what Jason makes the protagonists in his scenario do. The actors stand back from themselves and watch themselves acting. They show that they are conscious of the role playing. By doing this they put the whole play into a different framework, where they demonstrate the two levels within which acting takes place: the level of watching and that of being watched.

> SCENE: Jotapata, in Galilee: a cellar.
> Josephus is with a group of Elders. There is an Old Woman in the background.
> Josephus walks up and down as if he were a director on a film set.
> The Elders watch him as if they were actors.
> From outside there comes an occasional shout or scream, as if the town were being pillaged. . . .
> . . . Josephus glances into the camera.
> Then he walks round as if despairingly.
>> JOSEPHUS
>> A little more passion please! You're doing something terrible after all! Killing yourselves! Of your own free will! No one's making you. People have always been doing it—
> He comes back to the First Elder. He acts— . . .
>> JOSEPHUS
>> As a matter of fact, you'll look ridiculous anyway —
>> But no one will mind that if you're dead.
>> It's called heroic.[800]

Through integrating the acting instructions within the play, the actors' consciousness of their role-playing is stressed. They not only stand back and watch themselves acting, but are also conscious of their audience. Showing that they are aware of their pretensions they convey that what they enact is not the reality: the script is the code that gives the message. It becomes both the code and the message, for it both 'initiates the search for and leads to the key for its own decipherment.'[801] It is, thus, the two ends of a circle—like a serpent that bites its tail to make a perfect circle.[802]

The outcome of the success of this enterprise is shown in the outcome of the main plot of the novel. What Jason does artistically influences his real life, or better still, the stage influences the off-stage through the protagonists' observation of it. Jason and his wife Lilia are separated from one another by having to sit in different classes of the aeroplane which is taking them to Israel, where the filming of Jason's script—if it be accepted—will take place. The compartmentalised machine is a simile of man's imprisonment in his own fragmented mind and inability to unite the two halves. When Jason enters the aeroplane to sit in first class with the 'terrible Hollywood people,' he is inevitably reminded of this predicament:

> [In the first-class compartment] the seats were widely spaced and half empty; behind in the tourist compartment, the seats were tightly packed and crowded. He thought—This is an image of the conscious and the unconscious?'[803]

In contrast to the other passengers on the plane, Jason and his wife are aware of this split and try to unite through finding a passage. Their awareness of the presence of the other—their knowledge of the off-stage—hints at their belonging to the 'chosen,' in whose hands the key to man's liberation and survival lies. This awareness is shown especially through the mode of narration: the story is told in third person narration alternating between Jason's and Lilia's points of view. Each is telling his/her own story while being aware of the other one—almost telling the other one a story without being the other one's interlocutor. The other passengers in the aeroplane do not suffer as much as Jason and Lilia do, for they embody the greater part of humanity in the 'cave,' who sit watching the images on the wall without feeling the need to communicate with each other, as if in a cinema. Jason and Lilia do not feel contempt for these people, but observe their situation and even knowingly become involved in their games (as, for example, Lilia's narrowly missed seduction by the boyfriend of the would-be film producer's[804]), while being aware of that which goes on off-stage. One could say that they are applying the Brechtian techniques in the 'Josephus' script to their own situation by trying to 'look at archetypal destructive and self-destructive impulses, situations, and their antidotes.'[805] In this sense they hope to learn to get out of them by uniting with the beloved. This is again symbolised and initiated through the child, who simply leaves the tourist class in search of his Dad and consequently provides Lilia with an excuse to be allowed into the first-class, where all three are reunited. At the end of the novel there is the image of the family on some queerly peaceful, fantastic beach somewhere in Israel—the image is both a reflection and a subversion of the Holy Family's flight out of Palestine—in this case, the flight is into Palestine: the 'lion's den'—where the child finds a coin, which originates from Masada and has a bird with a twig in its beak on one side and a serpent swallowing its tail on the other. The bird reminds the reader of Bert's liberation in the previous novel, and the Serpent eating itself symbolises the survival of the liberated and the chance for the Brechtian 'new human type' to prevail.

> Jason thought — . . .
> . . . —I mean, new life will grow.
> . . . Jason said 'Do you know if the snake eating itself is a symbol of life?'
> The young man said 'Oh yes, I think so.'
> The girl said 'It is making love to itself.'
> The young man said 'it is being born.'[806]

IV. *Judith*: leaving and re-entering the Garden à la Kleist

In *Judith*, Mosley examines the paradox of freedom in the framework of Kleist's *Über das Marionettentheater*. The heroine of the story, Judith, makes the 'journey around the world' in order to see if 'Paradise may perhaps be open again from the back somewhere.'[807] She is a minor West End actress, whose name is borrowed from the heroine of the Apocrypha. In that story Judith prevented the Assyrians from besieging the Jewish Town of Bethulia, by letting herself taken to the tent of the enemy's leader, Holofernes, and cutting the latter's head off shortly before being seduced by him. She then had the head hung on the city's walls, the sight of which led the Assyrians to flee in panic in the morning. As with Josephus, Judith also belongs to the liberated individuals, who have the key to the group's—the organism's—perpetuity in that they can (as the Zen-master would have it) put things out of the framework of patterns which, having had held a society intact for a while, have become destructive. In other words, both protagonists 'betray' the accepted values and succeed in saving themselves and the organism that they are part of. In *Judith*, yet again, it is insisted that such an act could only succeed if the individual is aware of a greater objectivity off-stage, while preoccupied in his or her own actions. The novel opens with an account of the dramatisation of this idea written in a letter to Bert—the novel is a triptych of three letters written by Judith to Bert, Professor Ackerman, and Jason respectively. Judith tells of her minor part in the staging of this story, in which a famous actor-couple due to some blunders, errors and misdemeanours end up playing their parts in such 'quiet, ironic, self-reflective' style (here again, Brechtian theatre is being alluded to), that

> The effect that this produced was curiously like some powerful moments in life: for do not humans for the most part, of course, talk the most fearful rubbish? But then, if they know this, are not the moments when this knowingness breaks through not to do with rubbish? Judith and Holofernes . . . did their whole love scene, seduction scene, passion-and-death scene, in this style—as if this were indeed, yes, the sort of fix that poor humans found themselves in: but what an odd joke it was! And might there not still be something dignified in the fact that humans could see this?[808]

What Judith is witnessing is a glimpse of Bateson's Learning III, 'the chance for a man to see not just the patterns of his behaviour but also the patterns of his ability to see—and by this, not just to be free of patterns, but possibly to *influence* them.'[809] Relating Judith's experience to Bateson's Learning III is especially appropriate, since Judith sees herself as some sort of a drama student understudying the star playing the role of biblical Judith. Everything that will happen to her in the course of the novel should thus be seen in this light. That is to say, the risks and pains that she endures make up an experiment—or a drama—which she undertakes, in order to test the uses of this style—this knowingness—for reaching Popper's world 3, Bateson's Learning III and Kleist's 'either no, or infinite consciousness.'

 1. *Going back to the state of unconscious: Popper's world 1, Bateson's Learning I and Kleist's Puppet*

The burden of the human split-nature is introduced in the first letter written to Bert, in the spirit of Kleist's *Puppet Master*.

> Human beings were never at ease, because they were split between being doers and being observers of what they were doing. Puppets were graceful, all-of-a-piece, because they were hung by a single string from their centre of gravity.[810]

The burden of split-self is the state for which Mosley appropriated Popper's 'world 2. the world of states of consciousness' and Bateson's 'Learning II: an accomplishment of man, [which] depends on a man's ability to stand back from the processes of Learning I and to see its patterns.' Judith thus embarks on the journey to overcome her split by becoming a 'puppet.' As mentioned above, what is central to this journey is Judith's knowingness: her intentional self-experimentation. The fact that Prof. Ackerman indirectly helps Judith choose this dangerous path, foreshadows the good outcome of the experiment. In this novel, too, the protagonists make up a network with their relationships (i.e., an off-stage), by being open to and aware of which they can liberate themselves from the destructive patterns of their observation faculties. One could say that Judith is (in the way as myths and parables) inviting the reader to take her as an example and regard her life as a parable, the observation of which could teach something valuable. The crux of the matter is Judith's own awareness of this. That's how the reader knows from the outset that Judith's experiment will be alright.

At a lecture of the professor's she comes to understand that 'reality' as human beings conceive of it, is a 'function of the experimental condition.'[811] This means that every 'reality construction'—every theory—is true as long as it cannot be falsified. So, Judith embarks on her experiment of erasing her consciousness and going back to the state of the puppet. She delivers her 'strings' into the hands of her flatmate Oliver, who supplies her with drugs and a television in order to do away with her responsibility. In this way she tries to become a beautiful doll with spikes stuck up in it, or a goddess—with no dividing gap within her.[812] She tries to live a pain-free 'reality-construction.'

Nevertheless, no matter how hard she tries to become a puppet with the strings in the hands of her master, she seems not to succeed: 'Humanity, indeed, cannot get out of its cage, can it—that cage of desire, of consciousness, of where-are-we-from-and-where-are-we-going.'[813]

The paradox is that she cannot (fully and permanently) turn her consciousness off, because of the *deliberation* that she has to undergo every time she takes the drugs. She consciously chooses to be tethered; she deliberately delivers herself to Oliver in order to become all-of-a-piece and knowingly upholds her condition. Inevitably, she needs her consciousness in order to 'delete' it. She, hence, hasn't been able to free herself from contradictions; rather, she has tied herself up in inescapable paradoxes. She has now—as the professor had warned her already—reached some sort of a 'rock bottom'[814] or the famous knife-edge: she is at a point where the quest for freedom has become a matter of life and death: she can either cut the rope around her neck[815] or she can cut her head. In order to choose the right option, she'll have to, as the professor tells her of Kleist, go 'right round the world and into the Garden of Eden by the back way.'[816]

Already, having 'come to the end of [her] . . . tether'[817] she feels the sensation of the cold air coming in.[818] She is now the foetus trying to get out.[819] She metaphorically goes through the motions of being born: she crawls along parapets from the bathroom window in the hope of 'entering a new dimension' through another window.[820] Like birth, it is a dangerous and difficult process. She could be hurled down and hit the 'rock bottom' or she could fall into a 'nest'—and hit the 'rock bottom' gently.[821] In the struggle it will either be Judith or the one who wants to stop her. Her fate runs parallel to that of Judith of Bethulia.

> He began to lift me. I said 'just a minute.' Oliver said 'No more minutes.' I said 'I want to pee.' Desmond said 'You needn't go to pee . . .' I said 'There's something I want in the bathroom.' Oliver said 'All right.' When I looked at them I thought—Eeny meeny miney mo, Holofernes. Oliver was that thick-set man like a probe: Desmond was a glove with the hand sweating up inside him.[822]

Like Judith of Bethulia, she deceives her captors into believing that she would be at their disposal. She wants to free herself not knowing how, but knowing that she can only do it at the cost of whoever chooses to be her Holofernes. Whereas she succeeds in cutting the rope of her tether and softly falls into a 'nest,'[823] her pursuer falls to his death. Her entry into the next door flat by the window is a metaphor for her leaving her 'Old Life' and being born into a new life.[824]

2. *Of uses of Gardens of parables for freedom*

The second letter written to Prof. Ackerman gives an account of Judith's time in an Indian ashram, to which she is sent by the professor in order to be able to heal herself. Having thrown away the narcotic means of protection against her consciousness, she is now in a way in the same state as the ideal existentialist individual—she stands naked and alone in the world.[825] More importantly, however, here Judith learns that it is by expanding the 'god-like' part—i.e., the 'all-seeing consciousness'—rather than 'switching it off' that human beings free themselves from (self)destruction. This is also analogous to the movement to Bateson's Learning III and Popper's world 3, where humans can see themselves as both the object and the subject of observation. By standing slightly above themselves they would not conceive of themselves as absurd unconnected parts, but rather as a unity of parts; of parts that are necessary to make a whole. Thus it is by seeing that they are both the creator and the created *at once* that they can achieve freedom from the old patterns of the mind. The importance of the observation faculty—the creative 'god-like' part of us—is pointed out by Judith's recollection of an experiment echoing what she had learnt at Ackerman's lecture before her descend into hell:

> You know that experiment in which you look into a box through a peephole and there is what appears to be a room with a bed and a table and chairs: and then you look over the top of the box and you see that it contains just disconnected lines and planes and it has been yourself, your way of seeing things that has transformed the bits and pieces into the structure of a room.[826]

The question, then, is how to *transform* one's way of seeing things—one's patterns of observation. The reader is again confronted with the paradoxical task of the mind transforming itself or, as Kleist puts it, of 'cognition [having] in effect [to pass] through an infinity.'[827] It is therefore appropriate that this section of the novel is a parable in the form of a retelling of the myth of Garden of Eden along the lines of Kleist's *Über das Marionettentheater*. The form of the parable is useful here as parables—like jokes and metaphors can grasp the paradox in that they 'bring together, illuminate, things which rationally remain separate; which release energy like a spark between poles.'[828] A paradox can be contained within jokes and metaphors as 'the spark' between the poles of proposition and counter-proposition, between the *either* and the *or* that make up the 'rationality' we are accustomed to. So, in order to understand how to survive as an individual and thus as a whole, the Garden and its guru become the metaphor of things that one can't talk about without being misunderstood:

they are jokingly—metaphorically—referred to as the Garden of Eden and God.

> I [Judith] am going to go on calling him God because one of the points of the Garden, as I have said, was to do with jokes— . . . what do you do about this absurdity (yet terrible necessity?) of human beings setting themselves up as gods: for do you not . . . if you think you know, have to tell others what to do? You can make a joke of it, perhaps: you can let yourself be called God: but then laugh at yourself and tell others to laugh when the world, as it does, goes its own way.[829]

Like Bert before her, Judith realises that laughing at jokes necessitates attachment and detachment simultaneously—seeing something both as it *is* and as it *is not*. It also expresses a level of understanding where what one experiences as contradictions become 'reconciled' as the state of the whole.[830] 'God' can only help the people in the Garden free themselves from the patterns of their consciousness by making jokes as freedom is a prerequisite for irony.[831] Laughter signifies detachment from the shackles of polarisation and freedom of movement between these poles. The retelling of the myth of Adam and Eve and the subversion of the 'masculine' God into the Amazonian Lilith are meant to achieve this.[832]

The retelling of the myth of the Garden is also technically crucial for having Judith leave the Garden. Parables, metaphors and jokes, as Judith pointed out, do not only point outwards but also inwards—they also inform the listener about themselves not being the truth. Judith uses the analogy of the Cretan to elaborate this: 'There was the person who said—All people are liars.'[833] So, Judith learns that she must get out of the Garden, as it was only a means for learning to achieve freedom; the finger pointing to the moon. One could say that she leaves the ashram in the spirit of Nietzsche's Zarathustra, who descends from his hermetic abode in the mountains in order to be and struggle at the centre of life and by this protect himself from the dangers of sterile priesthood.[834]

3. Bateson's Learning III, Popper's world 3 and Kleistian grace

Judith is back in London after her seven-year stay in the Indian ashram. Her last letter is written to Jason, the playwright from *Cypher* and *Serpent*, who along with Bert and the Professor has been her mentor as well as her lover. In this part of the book four of the six protagonists of the series—Eleanor, Bert, Lilia and Judith herself—come together at an antinuclear demonstration at an American base in East Anglia. This scene echoes the backdrop of *Cypher* with its phantasmal threat of violence, unexploded bombs, and the release of nuclear material into the atmosphere. Similarly, it conveys the knife-edge state of humanity at the end of twentieth century on the scale of a small stage-set: will humanity wipe itself out or will a 'new human type' evolve? The novel answers the question in the affirmative as Judith and her 'accomplices' could be seen as the 'new human type'—those who have learnt to break out of the destructive patterns of the mind through self-observation and now see their task as liberating and saving humankind.

As in the previous two parts of the novel, Mosley exploits biblical imagery and parables to express the fruitfulness of the task that his protagonists have set themselves. There is the child, who is now about five or six years old, and is (as in *Cypher*) lost in the middle of all this chaos. He has gone into a strictly forbidden no-man's land area—an artificial battle area—which serves as a training ground for soldiers.[835] The signs forbidding access to the place are a mirror image of the angels with flaming swords, forbidding re-entry into the Garden. The child has gone into this place to look for and look after a two-headed sheep, which, being a mutant, is most likely to die.[836] The protagonists, who enter this place to search for the child are Eleanor, Judith and Lilia. Here Mosley uses the imagery of the Three Magi, however, subverts it by having women look for the Child, since they seem to possess more wisdom and vigilance than men who like to from time to time 'get their tanks and guns out of the nursery toy box.'[837] This Garden is a model village, which is (similar to all the settings and titles of the previous novels) a paradox ; a double-sided coin. It is both a dangerous place and a refuge. Which side of it materialises itself is a matter of attitude and activities of the protagonists. Again, 'right' and 'wrong' are subverted as means of restructuring restrictive patterns in a Zen-like fashion. The Garden is revealed as a place of refuge: the protagonists are in fact saved from the violence outside, where the demonstrators, in order to show the dangers of nuclear weapons release some radioactive material into the air. And it is the place that has offered shelter to the child and the sheep. The biblical imagery is obvious. The fierce Old Testament parables of punishment and banishment lead to, or better still, unveil themselves as the New Testament imagery of hope and deliverance.

The sheep is a symbol for the attitude—the expanded consciousness— necessary for the evolution of the Brechtian new human type. Here the term 'hopeful monsters' (which was to become the title of Mosley's most famous novel) is used for the first time in order to define the new human type, on which hope for the continuance of the whole species depends. The term was first used in the 1940s by the long neglected and ridiculed German-American biologist, Richard Goldschmidt, who argued that the appearance of totally new characteristics was possible through mutation in a relatively short period of time.[838] Judith describes it thus: 'it's when something is born which things outside are not quite ready for.'[839]

> As I approached, the sheep did not move. I thought—Poor old humanity! of course we are on some tightrope: if I move straight enough, you may be still . . . . although one side of each head had a perfectly formed ear and eye and even a nose, in between—and it was this that was stretched like a tightrope-was a third eye. I suppose it was some conjunction of what might have been the other eyes of the two heads: . . . This is the eye that looks inward, isn't it? Perhaps it was just the strain of this attempt that made the third eye, in what was other wise so still, seem always to be moving . . . I thought—you mean, within the eye, there is that which we could discover: which is watching: which is also in the outside world all the time.[840]

The third eye of the sheep is a metaphor for the expanded observation faculty which can unite and thus deliver the split-self—the observer and the observed—into a whole by undertaking the paradoxical task of observing both of them. The success of this task is shown both in the imagery of the three Magi and the young man, Bert, nourishing Lilia's child and the birth of Judith's own daughter at the very end of the novel. The baby-girl, who could be either from the Professor, Jason or Bert, symbolises the fruitfulness of the interactivity of this group, who throughout the series make up a network for the evolution and survival of the new human type.

V. *Hopeful Monsters*: the condition of mankind in the twentieth century and the evolution of a 'new human type'

> Franz said as if quoting '—We are to be actors in this drama—'
> I said 'We are actors anyway—'
> Franz said '—In what Nietzsche called "The great hundred-act play reserved for the next two centuries in Europe"—'

I finished the quotation '—"the most terrible, the most questionable, the most hopeful of all plays"—'[841]

Hopeful Monsters is the last novel of the *Catastrophe Practice Series*. It became the most accessible and famous (winning the Whitbread Book of the Year Award) novel of the series—not to say of Mosley's career. It is a huge venture spanning the first decades of the twentieth century and ending in the present time, where the other novels of the series take place. Mosley saw the novel itself as a 'hopeful monster,'

> an enormous book—the sort of book that sends publishers' hearts into their boots. But how otherwise could the novel itself be a hopeful monster? . . . —And there it was, winging its way like some great whale over rooftops. And I was thinking—perhaps after all it will have some small walk-on part in what Nietzsche called 'the great hundred-act play reserved for the next two centuries in Europe . . .[842]

Having finished *Judith* with the scene in the 'forbidden zone,' where hope for a new life—and a new human type—is generously allowed for, Mosley felt the necessity for writing a story 'about the origins of the attitudes and way of thinking of these people: how much was application; how much was "chance." '[843] It is the story of Max Ackerman, an English boy from Cambridge, and Eleanor Anders, a half Jewish German girl from Berlin, who had been the old couple in the previous novels; the mentors and the guides of the younger protagonists.

Hopeful Monsters examines the Brechtian Maxim—'What matters most is that a new human type should be evolving, and the entire interest of the world should be concentrated on his development'[844]—against the historical, socio-political, philosophical and scientific developments of the first half of the twentieth century; particularly those in Europe between the two Wars. Whereas in *Catastrophe Practice* the theatre stage was the place where the protagonists tried to liberate themselves onto a higher state of consciousness by following Brecht's acting guidelines, now the world is a stage, where Max Ackerman and Eleanor Anders are the Brechtian 'actors' trying to evolve into a higher human type by expanding their consciousness. The title was chosen precisely to depict this process. As mentioned earlier, 'hopeful monsters' was a term used by the German-American biologist Goldschmidt, in order to define the appearance of a new species through mutations in a relatively short period of time. Goldschmidt, in other words, postulated an evolutionary process, which happened in big jumps as opposed to the Darwinian gradualism.[845] Mosley appropriated this idea in order to define his protagonists: 'mutants,' who were the new hopefully viable strand and the possibility for the evolution of their old threatened species. The mutation in case of human species, as Mosley prepared the reader throughout the series, is a 'willed' one in so far only that it takes place in the conscious mind. The 'will' is the conscious individual's ability to free itself from its own observational structures by way of observing these. In other words, the conscious mind has to observe both the observed and the observer halves of itself and in this way liberate itself—and the individual—from its own destructive, splitting patterns of observation. As Mosley puts it 'human nature does not change by effort of will. What a person can do . . . is to stand back and see what the situation is to which they are largely attached but from which part of them might become detached; to see if by this there might be liberated some natural process of change.'[846]

1. *Eleanor and Max: the two halves making a whole*

Testing to see whether by way of observation 'there might be liberated some natural process of change' is what Max Ackerman and Eleanor Anders try to do. The novel is an epistolary novel in that they both narrate the story by alternately writing to each other. Critics have complained that this narrative style leaves little—or no—room for differentiating the characters from each other.[847] However, the structure and the style serve the purpose of the idea upon which this novel—and for that matter, all the novels of the series—was based very well: the idea of two halves—of the mind; of the individual; of humanity—becoming one whole by way of (self-)observation. In the course of the novel the reader has the experience of what Max explains as 'two people coming face to face on a tightrope; they have to keep moving or they will fall; they would like to pass into, through, one another; at moments this is possible!'[848] Or to put it in the scientific imagery that Mosley uses throughout the novel as a means to give an image of their relationship, Max and Eleanor are like those two particles, which having once been together, will remain together even if separated on different ends of the universe.[849]

Apart from being epistolary, the novel is also both a historical novel and a novel of ideas.[850] Eleanor and Max grow up in the turbulent Twenties and Thirties in Europe, where

> Old orders . . . indeed seemed to be cracking up—old systems of society, of science, of states of mind. Human beings had found themselves trapped in a world war; . . . In the 1930s there were the huge experiments to try to deal socially with the danger and the debacle: Communism and Fascism were efforts to reconstitute societies by ideology and efforts of will. But in fact these seemed only to make the processes of destruction and self-destruction more organised and virulent.[851]

They take part in major events that gave the 'Twentieth Century' its 'doomsday' reputation—from witnessing the Spartakus Uprising and the *Kapp Putsch* to watching Hitler's rise to power and Stalin's show trials; from participating in the Spanish Civil War to having a hand at the development of the Bomb. Coming from academic and intellectual households in Berlin and Cambridge, they see influential political figures of the age, such as Rosa Luxemburg and her *confidants*, high-profile Soviet spies, and high-profile Spanish Republican and Trotskyite Generals.

In the meantime they are participants in what gave their century the reputation of being the most progressive and promising era of all—the age where new scientific, artistic and philosophical ideas seemed to offer the possibilities for liberating humans from the shackles of the very old patterns of thought, which were proving so destructive and leading to an almost operatic end of mankind. It is at the lectures given by Einstein and Heidegger, Kapitsa, Wittgenstein and Dirac, at the experiments of Rutherford and Kammerer, and at Brecht's plays where they find hope amidst darkest Europe. In this sense they are 'hopeful monsters,' who help the emergence and sustenance of other 'hopeful monsters'—i.e., the other protagonists of the series.

2. *Modern man's possibility of freedom within his entrapment*

In *Hopeful Monsters* Mosley examines the source (i.e., observational faculty), from which modern man's predicament *and* his empowerment spring by centring the novel around the most important epistemological theory of this century; namely Einstein's General Theory of Relativity. By proving all states of being to be a matter of observation, this theory, on one level, was liberating by breaking up old patterns of 'absolutist' thinking, but, on the other, was entrapping by showing humans that they were trapped within their own visions and constructions of reality. They not only had no access to the ontological reality, but were also 'chained' so as not to have any access to the reality of other individuals. Thus, they saw that they were all trapped in their own minds. Throughout the series this has been introduced as the predicament of the twentieth century mankind.

The 'newly' discovered paradoxical state of light is a metaphor throughout the novel for this predicament. Shortly after World War I, it is shown that light could be bent, which meant that it consisted of particles. On the other hand, its velocity as a radiation could be measured and therefore it was also a beam. Eleanor learns that the velocity and the location of light cannot be measured simultaneously, but separately. This meant that light, depending on the experiment, i.e., the way of observation, that it undergoes, changes its 'state' of being. Eleanor—like Judith—thus learns that all 'state of being is a function of experimental condition.'[852] In physics what one observes is dependent on the fact that one observes:

> You shine a light on an object and you alter it by the fact that you shine a light on it: you don't shine a light and then you cannot observe it. . . . In some experiments light appears to be waves: in other experiments it appears to be particles. You can tell a particle's exact velocity, or location, but you can't tell both at the same time. . . . There is no way of saying what anything is, apart from the way in which you are observing it.[853]

Therefore, the physics of the first half of century was liberating in that it invalidated values and certainty principles, but imprisoning in that it could not offer a way out of the bigger despair that it caused through its findings. Eleanor writes to Max about the famous conference of Physicists in Brussels in 1928, where Einstein himself tried to prove that 'God does not play dice' by setting out to 'falsify' his relativity theory and proving the existence of an 'objectivity'—to his despair Heisenberg and Bohr would 'defeat' him every time, by vindicating his old theories and proving that 'reality remained . . . "a function of the experimental condition." '[854]

Max, too, feels that the new physicists were not really interested in learning what their new findings meant for the liberation of mankind from destructive patterns. Like their 'determinist' colleagues, they too seemed to see man totally delivered to uncontrollable forces. Whereas the former talked about 'laws,' the newcomers talked about 'chance'—in both equations humans remained helpless puppets. It is in the 'heretical' developments in biology and evolution science, where he finds the interest in finding out about such possibilities.[855] Living with a Freudian psychoanalyst mother and a Darwinian biologist father, he comes to learn a lot about both the patterns that determine the individual and his reality conception:

> all life evolved by means of chance mutations in genes, the products of which are put to the test by the environment; most mutations die, because of course what is established is suited to the environment. But occasionally there is a change in the environment coincident with a genetic mutation, the result of which is suited to the change—suited in the sense that it is more likely to survive in the new condition than the established stock from which it comes.[856]

The mutations, it is further explained, are latent and potentially available in the gene pool.[857] The Darwinists, like the majority of new physicists, seemed also to suggest that chance was the origin of survival. In their worldview there seemed to be no space for a 'conscious' or 'willed' effort by way of which an organism could *learn* to change itself: i.e., free itself from its old—in the new environment destructive—adaptive patterns and develop new ones, which would increase its chances of survival in the new environment. As Bateson and Popper put it, in the Darwinists' view all learning seemed to go no further than Learning I or World 1. For Max the Darwinist theory of biological inheritance is not a satisfactory explanation for the great jumps and developments in the process of evolution. The Darwinists believed that *genetically* the parents could only pass on features they had *inherited* themselves—and not *acquired* faults and features. It was the environment only that put the species to test, and not vice versa.[858] Politically this explanation of evolution and its stress on the 'survival of the fittest' could lead to the doctrine of the dictatorship of the environment and have, as depicted in the novel's imagery of Nazi Germany, catastrophic and destructive consequences. Furthermore, Max believes that in their effort to enlighten mankind by doing away with 'religiosity,' these biologists achieved the exact opposite. By denying all possibility of a being beyond chance and a will within organisms they bordered on superstitious behaviour: in their concept coincidental irregularities of hereditary mechanisms passed onto the next generation and suited to the new given environment could only be accounted for as 'miracles'![859] To put it in Eleanor's words: 'But coincidences are not miracles: miracles are when you do not see—.'[860] What concerns Max is why such irregularities are passed on by the parent generation to the offspring. He wants to find out, whether we are really at the mercy of our genes.

Meeting the Austrian Lamarckian biologist, Dr. Kammerer, who is considered an arch enemy by Max's father, Max embarks on an experiment with salamanders in order to find out an alternative to the Darwinian biology. The Lamarckians believed that the possibility of genetically transmitted acquired characteristics, which have proven advantageous for the parent generation existed.[861] Max tries to prove this theory by changing the environment of a pair of lowland salamanders—whose offspring are usually born in water—and getting them to reproduce in the manner of the alpine salamanders by giving birth not to larvae but to two fully formed offspring.[862] Bearing in mind Mosley's warning that a 'willed effort' for making change possible should not be understood as a will to take control, it may be wrong to say Max 'tries to prove' the Lamarckian theory. This phrasing makes it sound as if he wanted to manipulate an experiment by fixing it with a prepared result. What he actually wants to see, or hopes to see, is the relation between self-reflection and evolution or freedom and survival. He wants to see whether an organism's ability to observe itself in a given situation and *learn* to do away with patterns that were once useful, but in the given new environment prove deathly, can help it 'pull out' the 'right' mutation out of the sea of mutations it has access to in order to fit itself to the new environment. The fact that he calls his salamanders 'hopeful monsters'[863] is all too appropriate. In a way his salamanders are like those Berliners, who learned to survive the 1923 inflation by knowing that 'it was important never to have thrown away from a bottom drawer or attic any trinket, bedspread, pair of boots, ancestral ornament—anything saved and hidden might suddenly become life-giving (was this like your so-called "gene-pool"?).'[864]

In his experiment, Max consciously sets a frame for the viability of the salamanders to learn and survive: he virtually makes a fertile ground for the latent mutations to grow on. By this experiment he does not 'isolate' certain mutations to grow, but makes the ground for 'some seeds [of mutations] . . . rather than others'[865] to grow. This means that he is aware that his relation to his Salamanders is like that of God, who set his Adam and Eve in beautiful scenery. To his salamanders he is thus that entity beyond chance that God was to his Holy Couple. The part of the Salamanders/Holy Couple is to rely on their consciousness—their observation and learning faculty—and pull out the right mutation in relation to their setting and that entity beyond. Max is thus testing that what exists beyond determinism and chance. Like Judith's conscious use of her life as a parable, the awareness of the experimenter, Max, of his being part of the experiment is the crux of this experiment. By observing that he is the conscious will—or 'God'—making a setting in which some seeds rather than others might grow, his empowerment through his consciousness is illustrated to him. The experiment grants him with a setting within which his consciousness can observe itself and go beyond its own observational structures. The birth of the salamanders' fully formed offspring symbolises the success of this venture.

3. Consciousness: the Liberator and the Creator

Max and his relation to this experiment is a small-scale model for his and his companion Eleanor's relation to the great socio-historical experiments in Europe and the Western world in the Twenties and Thirties. By being observant and vigilant to the events they can take part in liberating Europe—if not the world—from the clutches of the great destructive patterns woven around it. That is to say, they can 'unmake' the destructive patterns by using them as a means of liberation; in the same paradoxical way that consciousness by way of observation could 'use' its own limiting destructive observational structures as a means to free itself from them. The political events and the War show them the enormous destruction and self-destruction potentialities of human beings. Now these potentialities could actually realise themselves to destroy if not the whole, at least a great part of humanity. The Bomb is on the verge of being created. It is vital that the Nazis, who in some 'Wagnerian' madness would destroy themselves along with the world, do not get the Bomb first. Max thus becomes one of the physicists who works on the development of the Bomb, not only with view of stopping the Nazis on military terms, but also because he believes that the destructive patterns of human mind, knowledge and abilities have become so dangerous, that it is necessary to have before their eyes the *possibility* of the realisation of such force, so that its application could be stopped. The paradoxical makeup of man's mind—its split nature—necessitates

> the existence of the Bomb, *without* the use of the Bomb, if [the human race] was to survive or evolve; human nature having evidently such a propensity for evil that with all the technological advances it was

only the existence of something so shocking as the Bomb that would prevent the evil from going into runaway, out of control.[866]

Having helped develop the Bomb, he resigns from the project, thinking the necessary work had been done. When the Bomb is indeed used on a small scale in Japan ('personally and from a military point of view he felt relieved that the Bombs had been dropped on Japan since it was likely that this had shortened the war by months if not years, also it would serve as a ghastly warning for the future'[867]), he feels responsible as a scientist to make some public protest about this—his activities with the CND are a continuation of his public protest.[868] When told that there is no sense 'in suggesting that there should be different moralities for different individuals or groups or indeed within the same person,'[869] he retorts that such an attitude is not an 'elitist' or even a dangerous contradiction, but on the contrary, a necessary one, if society were to work properly: 'Courses of action could only be said to be right if there had been a genuine interplay of what indeed might be conflicting moral inclinations,'[870] and this 'genuine interplay' could only take place if

> each person practised what he or she thought was right and recognised the obligations of others to do this, then ends could be left to themselves. In fact this was just the sort of attitude that might be required for, and indeed exemplify, a proper change in human nature.[871]

The making of the Bomb and protesting against it, then, could only be understood as hypocritical, if Max did not observe both sides of the coin: that is, if he did not see the creative as well as the destructive patterns of the Bomb—or for that matter the destructive and creative forces of a pacifist movement, since refusing war (as was the case with Chamberlaine's reluctance to declare war on the Germans, when these annexed Austria and Czechoslovakia) could also have horrible consequences. And by being aware of his ability to observe both contradictory sides of the situation—i.e., by observing his observation—he can move onto Bateson's Learning III and free himself from the tyranny of a fixed way of observation, which had once—in a given situation—proved to be liberating. This is in line with what Mosley had understood about Trotsky and his idea of permanent revolution. Trotsky was not talking about a mass movement but a state of consciousness—an attitude; that is, the idea that the means of liberation, could become the means of entrapment, if one did not continuously observe oneself in relation to them, and in this way stopped them from becoming hard and restrictive.[872]

Furthermore, this echoes what Mosley, some thirty years before writing *Hopeful Monsters*, had learnt and committed himself to when converting to Christianity: namely, the idea of an 'informed conscience.' An 'informed conscience,' he had learnt, was an entity—or an effort—that contained all the contradictory and paradoxical possibilities that one encountered in face of a 'moral dilemma'; a 'moral dilemma' being a paralysis of choice-making, where all choices seemed to be both right *and* wrong or neither right *nor* wrong.[873] The right choice was met automatically—or, to put it in a religious imagery, 'itself came one's way'— only when the conscience (or consciousness) was observant to all the possibilities and paradoxicalities that cropped up due to the *situation* that one found oneself in.[874] This is what Max means by saying 'ends could be left to themselves.' By genuinely observing the situation one both attaches and *detaches* oneself fully from the situation and can *overcome* it. In other words, one can influence it, so that it would work out to one's advantage rather than disadvantage. What is being done here, then, takes the observer a step further than being the liberator—he becomes the *creator*. He not only 'unmakes' the patterns by observing them, but also creates new patterns: the act of liberation becomes the act of creation. This is the heart of *Hopeful Monsters* (and the novels following it) which links Mosley's scientific investigations to his understanding of Christian spirituality; namely the idea that human beings are God's equal partners in creation (and destruction) and that it is by the *awareness* of this partnership —or what Mosley calls 'walking hand in hand with God'[875]—that man has the *freedom* to change himself and his environment in order to secure the continuity of life on earth: 'Max and Eleanor were confronted by *possibilities* and not *necessities*. They were aware of choice—though not knowing what to choose.'[876]

The right choice—i.e., what man should do in order to secure the continuity of life on earth—could be made by this very awareness. In other words, such an awareness ensues

> A feeling of not being determined; of finding oneself in a position of being on a pinpoint and seeing that there are possibilities. The right possibility is then not [chosen] by *choosing* but by knowing that one is on a pinpoint.

... By this feeling Max and Eleanor had the feeling of going hand in hand with 'Destiny'; with 'God.' When you feel you are in contact with possibilities then you do have a feeling about 'it'; about God.[877]

Max depicts this feeling of freewill and humans' partnership in creation as such—

> It is a fact that this is a universe that has produced consciousness. But do we not also say, we physicists, that it is consciousness that in some way produces the universe: I mean produces what we see of the universe—this or that—and of what else indeed can we say is the universe? ...
> ... I wrote down—
> The universe is such that it produces us who observe:
> We are such that we produce the universe by observing:
> It is thus that what is, is—
> We and the universe are a mutually creating organism.[878]

With this observation Max, from a scientific-philosophical level, moves onto a religious and spiritual level—the novel itself continues and ends in this spirit.[879] When Max (sometime slightly later than the ending of *Judith*) at the end of the novel is dying with all the protagonists of the series gathering around his deathbed, it is the angelic/magical/godly appearance of Eleanor, which mysteriously prevents Max from giving into cancer. There is the imagery of Eleanor as Death ('Before she had appeared, it had seemed that it might be Death waiting outside') a Guardian Angel ('Now, with her cloak like plumage and her movement on crutches that made her seem to float above the ground, it was as if she might be an angel that had won a brief contest with Death in the corridor') and the all creative/all destructive, Shiva.[880] Bearing in mind the importance of jokes as a means of simultaneous attachment and detachment necessary for observing both sides, Eleanor of course also cuts a very funny figure, laughing out loud in her scarf, woollen hat and carrying two paper bags.

Regarding what Mosley had set out to do more than ten years earlier in his *Catastrophe Practice Series* project, the religious note with which the novel ends makes sense. Having appropriated Bateson's three levels of Learning, the mystical experience of the protagonists is a consequence of trying to observe their inner and outer world from Bateson's level III. Their consciousness could only do this task of observing itself—in other words, pulling itself up by its own bootlaces—without falling into a tautological solipsism by being aware of and thus holding onto a pattern greater than itself, which was both inside as well as outside itself. Bateson himself must have realised this, but as Mosley understands, did not admit it. This is where Mosley (like his friend Brenton, who introduced Mosley to Bateson's ideas) becomes critical of Bateson:

> Bateson was too much of a scientist to admit that his 'level III' suggested a spiritual or mystical dimension—he did use the word 'oceanic' but he wouldn't use 'god.'[881]

By avoiding bringing a spiritual dimension into the equation, the scientific theories of Bateson remained exactly what they were; namely, scientific theories—and thus more of a tool, which showed the problem only without really being able to offer a way out of the problem. Max, who has been modelled on Bateson himself,[882] 'corrects'—if one could use this word—this shortcoming in Bateson's view. He becomes a cyberneticist and uses the Christian symbol of the Trinity to describe the parallels between the sort of observation that cybernetics—or 'the study of systems of communication and control'[883]—offers and the belief that Christianity asks of its followers:

> At the level of God the Father there was a simple cause-and effect view of the world—God made his covenants with humans, which was a way of describing something like the mechanical functioning of a thermostat: if humans got too far above themselves then disasters knocked them down; if they got too far below themselves then they were ready to be boosted by the inspiration of a prophet: on this level humans did not have much say in the style of the to-and-fro. At the level of God the Son humans were given information about how to handle such mechanism: life was indeed a matter of paradoxes—by dying you lived; fulfilment was achieved by sacrifice; . . . and so on: but still, in this style humans seemed to experience a somewhat helpless oscillation between ecstasy and despair. But then there was . . . the domain of the Holy Spirit, in which humans could be led into responsibility for themselves. This was not so much a level as an ability to move between levels, to see a pattern by means of an inbuilt knowledge of truth—such means, if observed and honoured, allowing ends to look after themselves. . . . with this spirit humans could keep an eye on

(take a walk away from every now and then) the mechanisms that to some extent necessarily ran themselves on the other levels; the nature of the world seeming to be such that this watchfulness, alertness, gave a sense of the miracle of control.[884]

Conclusion

Mosley's investigations into the possibilities of achieving freedom in face of moral dilemmas led him onto investigating the possibilities of acquiring freedom from the mind's own restricting structures. That is, in *Catastrophe Practice Series* the focus of his explorations shifted from the outer world into the inner world. Analogous to his previous novels in which the protagonists freed themselves from the patterns of their moral dilemmas by way of observing them in an aesthetic framework, in his *Catastrophe Practice Series* Mosley suggested a way of freeing oneself from the restricting structures of the mind by means of observing them. For this purpose Mosley had to first learn about the structures of the mind and its functioning—that is why, this period of his writing could be seen as the 'scientific' and 'philosophical' phase of his career.

Mosley's point of departure was Sartre's observation about the individual's failure to be at-one-with itself due to possessing the faculty of observation and self-observation; i.e., consciousness. Sartre described this feeling as such: 'the dull and inescapable feeling of sickness [that] perpetually reveals my body to my consciousness.'[885] Thus human beings were perpetually locked in a self-destructive battle between the two halves 'trying to occupy the same space at the same time.'[886] In this way, the battle for freedom, as Mosley does not tire to emphasise throughout his series, becomes a matter of life and death—and not only for the individual(s), but with the help of modern technology, potentially for the human race as a whole.

By appropriating a host of philosophical, scientific and aesthetic ideas Mosley set out to convey the way out of this seemingly inherent predicament of mankind—that is, the 'genetic make up of the mind.' With the help of Bateson's three levels of Learning and Popper's three worlds, along with Brecht's 'alienation' drama; Kleist's vision of going through infinite knowledge as a way of entering the Garden by the backdoor; Nietzsche's idea of a Superman being one who can overcome himself; Monod's demand for a 'new covenant' between scientific knowledge and ethics; and Langer's image of art as 'a vision of thinking itself' Mosley shaped his own aesthetic framework within which the possibility of the paradoxical activity of self-liberation from the observation patterns of the mind could be expressed.

All the above thinkers, scientist and artists seemed to suggest that by observing its own observational faculties the individual could unite the two split halves—the observer and the observed—into a whole and thus free itself from the potentially deathly battle between the two. In short, the consciousness could free itself from itself by expanding itself. However, such an activity was only possible, if consciousness observed itself by being aware of a greater pattern that it was both part of and detached from—i.e., a pattern both inside and outside itself—if it was not to fall into further entanglement into itself leading onto equally self-destructive forms of solipsism or aggression. The above thinkers also seemed to suggest that by such a strife for freedom the nature of humankind would inevitably change and evolve into, to speak with Brecht, a 'new human type.' The evolution and continuation of the human race—and potentially life on earth—would depend on this. This sort of evolution would inevitably run contrary to Darwinian gradualism (where the environment only tests the fitness of the organism) and occur in big jumps. Mosley uses the term introduced by the German-American biologist, Richard Goldschmidt, as an image for this: 'hopeful monsters,' that is, things born perhaps slightly before their time; when it's not known if the environment is quite ready for them.[887]

The 'flaw' that Mosley conceives in the ideas that he had appropriated is the reluctance to see this sort of self-liberating and self-creating self-reflection on a spiritual and mystical level. Bateson, for example, would use the word 'oceanic' for a greater pattern, but not God. This in Mosley's (and Max Ackerman's) view was also what made such scientific conjectures more of an instrument to show the trap of the split-self, with little potential—or courage—to explore ways of getting out of it. These conjectures, to use a religious image, had little potential to 'deliver' mankind. One could thus conclude that Mosley's investigations into the possibilities of achieving freedom on a 'scientific' level inevitably led him onto investigations into the nature of freedom on a mystical level. In this sense, what Mosley set out to do in his ten-year-project, *Catastrophe Practice Series*, was completed in *Hopeful Monsters* and ended with the prospect of his future, present, work.

CHAPTER IV

The paradox of freedom and mysticism (1990s to present):
*Children of Darkness and Light, Journey into the Dark,
The Hesperides Tree, Inventing God*

Introduction:
Mysticism and the mystery of freedom

It is now a commonplace that in the higher reaches of physics the same language and concepts as in traditional mysticism are used.[888]

In modern physics the universe is thus experienced as a dynamic, inseparable whole which always includes the observer in an essential way. In this experience, the traditional concepts of space and time, of isolated objects, and of cause and effect, lose their meaning. Such an experience, however, is very similar to that of the Eastern mystics.[889]

The present and fourth phase of Mosley's writing further develops the note upon which *Hopeful Monsters* ended. Freedom and, consequently, man's survival are necessarily and ultimately achieved beyond the chance/fate plane. That is to say, whereas in his previous novels Mosley saw man's freedom in his ability to choose a possibility rather than another by way of observation, in his present novels he sees man's freedom in choosing one *reality* rather than another. In this sense, the present novels examine man's freedom on a spiritual and mystical level.

As in the *Catastrophe Practice Series*, in this phase science is used as a means for illuminating the possibility, or, *reality* of freedom. However, there is a shift in the emphasis on science. In the *Catastrophe Practice Series* science was the primary area for investigating the nature of freedom; spiritual language only appeared on the periphery—or the horizon—as in the scene of Max's epiphany in war-ridden Spain.[890] In the present novels mysticism moves to the centre and scientific language is used as a 'valid' language—or 'currency'—in our age for depicting the spirituality of freedom. Just as, say, medieval man would understand scientific ideas in 'spiritual' imagery (as Eleanor came to see in her anthropological studies[891]), modern man would grasp the spiritual in scientific language. The problem, however, arises when modern scientists take their scientific language for the ultimate reality instead of seeing it as a tool. At this point science becomes an entrapment instead of a liberation.

This is what Max Ackerman, himself a scientist, came to see in *Hopeful Monsters*. In their denial of a reality beyond science many physicists of the age, like their determinist Newtonian predecessors, saw man totally delivered to uncontrollable forces. Whereas the old ones talked about 'laws,' the newcomers talked about 'chance'—in both equations humans remained helpless puppets. In the present novels Mosley shows how seeing man as the opposite of a helpless puppet beyond the rationale of chance/law duality would inevitably be a mystical activity.

In this sense the notion of freewill is inherently spiritual. In non-spiritual systematic thought choice making is usually *conceptualised* in either deterministic or coincidental terms. However, this attempt to define the *logic* of (free) choice making always leaves out the element of freedom and consequently and inevitably fails to define the phenomenon of choice making. In deterministic terms, choice is determined by (given) preference structures. The element which makes choice what it is—namely the element of freedom—thus is substituted by the assumption of given preference structures. Consequently, 'freedom' does not appear in the explanation of 'free choice.' Moreover, how the preference structures themselves arise can never be answered. Any attempt at answering this question with recourse to 'met-structures' leads to a *regressus ad infinitum*. The approaches for explaining 'free' choice with recourse to 'chance' are faced with the same problems. Here 'freedom' is substituted by 'chance.' It thus does not appear in the explanation of 'free choice.' Neither here is 'chance' explained. Any attempt at its definition and rationalisation inevitably ends up in the indefinable; the 'mysterious.' In this sense freedom ultimately resides outside the boundaries of systematic thinking. Spirituality (and aesthetics) is the territory outside the boundaries of systematic thinking. It is here where Mosley investigates the nature of freedom.

Biographical background

I. Writing autobiography or the mystical 'mechanisms' of looking back forward

> When the past speaks it always speaks as an oracle: only if you are an architect of the future and know the present will you understand it.[892]

Having published *Hopeful Monsters* [1990] Mosley thought that he would not write any more novels.[893] On one hand, *Hopeful Monsters*' vast scope seemed to have exhausted his creativity, and on the other, its form seemed to make it impossible for Mosley to anticipate another novel. The novel was concerned with the same idea as the whole *Catastrophe Practice Series*: namely, the *possibilities* of modern 'scientific' man for achieving freedom, the realisation of which would influence the evolution of a 'new human type' necessary for the continuation of human race—if not Life—on earth. However, it superseded the other novels in the series in that it looked at the species as a whole *through* the eyes of its protagonists, instead of looking at a group of protagonists only. In *Hopeful Monsters* Mosley needed to look at the development of modern scientific man—the stuff which made up 'what Nietzsche called "The great hundred-act play reserved for the next two centuries in Europe . . . the most terrible, the most questionable, the most hopeful of all plays." '[894] For this purpose he had to use the form of a retrospective in order to examine the emergence of our time—our century—which he successfully accomplished in a historical narrative.

> *Hopeful Monsters* became one of the most approachable of my novels . . . because it was written somewhat more in the style of my biographies . . . In *Hopeful Monsters* . . . I was for much of the time looking at the past—at the history and politics that I had been trying to understand in the volumes about my father. And for years in an amateur way I had been trying to get a grasp of the science of this period too; and there had been enough written about it both by popularisers and experts for the diligent enquirer to imagine at least that he could see what was there. So perhaps because of this it was natural for me to write *Hopeful Monsters* somewhat more in the style of my biographies; and because of this it had a wider success than that of my previous novels.[895]

However fruitful and successful this form seemed to be in *Hopeful Monsters*, Mosley felt that he couldn't use it any longer in order to continue his investigations into the nature of freedom and thus the evolution of mankind in our present time. The other half of the Nietzschean drama could not be treated in the form of a historical narrative as

> Biographies deal with the past: a biographer's job is to clarify what is there: in novels I try to portray experience of the present, in which it is so often an open question what is, or what might be, there.[896]

The question was now how could he continue writing about the other half of mankind's drama? In *Hopeful Monsters* Mosley had History to hold onto. This enabled him to embark on the aesthetic activity of *ordering* the patterns of History's tracks in the form of fiction. In the present absence of History Mosley was (and is) in darkness with no maps, with questions upon questions.

> In *Hopeful Monsters* the signposts are there: the events, the people . . . although *Hopeful Monsters* is more packed with ideas than other novels, . . . people can say: 'Oh, yes, I am learning about history.' Would there be any period again, where I could do it again? . . . One could see the change between, say, 1910 and the 1960s. One could even see a pattern. I can't do that again because no one knows what the pattern is really . . .
>
> In 1920s and 1930s history was so open to the eye. Now, things that influence the course of history are so secret that one hardly knows about them. Is it anarchy? Or are things sorting themselves out? Enormous money, information—do they bring things out of control? Or organise them more?[897]

This state of confusion further helped the 'paralysis' of Mosley's creativity. What he now had to do in order to regain his powers was a re-creation—a re-formation—of himself in the same vein as he had set art to recreate the modern individual into a 'higher type' by reflecting on its history in the first half of twentieth century. Now, through reading the '*Orakelspruch*' of his own history, in other words, through the aesthetic activity of self-reflexivity he was to re-write his own history and thus himself. In the Nietzschean sense this reading could only be properly realised in the hands of the artist anyway, who for Nietzsche was the supreme historian. The task of the artist/historian is

> to think of history objectively in this fashion is the silent work of the dramatist; that is to say, to think of all things in relation to all others and to weave the isolated event into the whole: *always with the presupposition that if a unity of plan does not already reside in things it must be implanted into them.* Thus man spins his web over the past and subdues it, thus he gives expression to his artistic drive . . .[898]

The Nietzschean call for conquering and overcoming the past is a call for battle—albeit an aesthetic one.[899] In the same vein as 'organisations, empires'⁹⁰⁰ had earlier 'made' history, the artist, who in Nietzsche's eyes is the *real* fighter and warrior should '*organise the chaos*'⁹⁰¹ of the past. In other words, should *create* order out of the chaos; artwork out of the raw material of the past. This definition of the artist especially fits Mosley's attempt at reflecting on his own life. With the dawn of his experimentalist, or better still *avant-guard*,⁹⁰² writing Mosley started to see himself—necessarily ironically—as a 'freedom fighter!' against the 'vast army of contemporary pessimism!'⁹⁰³ Accordingly, his autobiography could be read in the context of Nietzsche's understanding of a true biography:

> And if you want biographies, do not desire those which bear the legend 'Herr So-and So and his age,' but those upon whose title-page there would stand 'a fighter against his age.'⁹⁰⁴

The title of Mosley's reflection upon his fight 'against the vast army of contemporary pessimism,' *Efforts at Truth*,⁹⁰⁵ indicates a very Nietzschean enterprise. An autobiography in Nietzsche's sense should be a process of thinking 'all things in relation to all others and to weave the isolated event into the whole: always with the presupposition that if a unity of plan does not already reside in things it must be implanted into them.'⁹⁰⁶ For Nietzsche this creative process of self-observation is only possible when individuals are 'honest' with themselves: 'By following the Delphic teaching and thinking back to themselves, that is to their *real* needs, and letting their pseudo-needs die out.'⁹⁰⁷

Nietzsche's emphasis on 'real needs' necessitates an existentialist sincerity—or the Christian idea of honesty being the emptying of a bucket of mud over one's own head. Mosley's autobiography, as the title suggests, was a self-lacerating endeavour to examine his life as truthfully as possible and thereby an attempt to function as an 'architect of the future,'⁹⁰⁸ in order to *liberate* him out of the creative paralysis which he had entered after having finished *Hopeful Monsters*. As the writer of his biography he necessarily watched himself watching his (other) self/selves: he, in other words, created a pattern out of the manifold patterns that he had made in the past; in Nietzshe's words what Mosley did was 'organise the chaos.'

> All creation is an uncovering of what is there—actuality out of potentiality. All those efforts to say these things, even in ordinary life—one is finding what the best action is . . .⁹⁰⁹

But this process of self-observation could only fulfil Nietzsche's categories of weaving 'the isolated event into the whole' and thus be creative instead of destructively solipsistic by being aware of and thus *using* an objectivity—a wholeness—greater than itself.

> When one is in a state of observing oneself observing oneself, then one is in a relationship with the whole. . . . One does not get stuck—one becomes aware of the possibilities.[910]

This liberating experience of self-observation is analogous to Bateson's third level of Learning, which the latter refused to see as mystical and preferred to 'conceptualise' it by using the term 'oceanic.' For Mosley, however, there is no way around the spirituality of this experience, as the awareness of a 'wholeness greater than oneself' inevitably leads to a connection—a unison—with that entity, which necessarily is a spiritual, 'otherworldly' experience. It is what in the Christian vocabulary—and in Kleist's aesthetics—is called the 'state of grace.'

> When you feel you are in contact with possibilities then you do have a feeling about 'it'; 'God.'
> . . . It is a mystical feeling—the ability comes from something larger than oneself. That can be scary! . . . To feel that all possibilities are open can be dangerous, but if one feels in harmony with all the possibilities, one can get things right. I mean, one can't *grab* [this] 'state of grace'—. . .
> When the artist says 'that's right' *it* is there. . . .[911]

The individual, then, as in Nietzsche's and Kleist's terms, is the artist who can use the determining forces of life—i.e., chance/fate—in order to put himself beyond them. The artist does this by setting up experiments in whose framework he can observe the determining forces and their effect on life.

> I am experimenting with life—how do things happen if one keeps one's sanity?
> People get muddled—'is he experimenting just for fun? Why does he ask so many questions?' One's right attitude is to ask questions rather than think one has all the answers . . .
> I experiment with understanding life. I mean, that's an effort to understand life.[912]

'Experimenting with life' is only a meaningful undertaking—as opposed to a fun game—when its objective is understanding life; that is, the effort to see the 'underlying order which brings order into chaos.'[913] Thus the artist, or the experimenter, *creates* his life, which in turn is only possible when he is aware of the underlying order—the wholeness bringing order into the arbitrary fragments. The process of experimenting with and understanding life, hence, becomes a religious undertaking.

II. Science entering mystical grounds

Scientists, too, as was depicted in *Hopeful Monsters*, set up experiments in order to see the

> underlying order, which brings order into chaos. Even 'reductionist' scientists use phrases like 'of course, there is an underlying force that brings order out of chaos.' I don't think anyone except old-fashioned Marxist students can say this is religious [language]—this is scientific.[914]

> The thing about most physicists is that they use this word 'chance'—but explaining 'order' is the opposite of chance. They say: . . . 'how is there "order" in evolution? There is this sort of "structure" and it is so by "chance."' . . . It is an amazing idea that order comes by chance. And so chance is order. But that is all quite mystical.[915]

What 'old-fashioned Marxist students' insisting upon rational systems and 'hard-headed Darwinists' maintaining that all is chance have in common is their refusal to admit any possibility for humans to act beyond these determining forces—i.e., to have a freewill. Ironically, then, where they would be right, is that the scientific language which they themselves use does have a religious note to it, as it speaks about that which lies beyond the structures of irrationality (chance)/rationality (systems). In other words, what their findings lead to is that there is ultimately 'mystery' at the heart of all things. It is important to note that mystery is *not* equal to 'irrationality,' as 'irrationality' is definable within the human rational systems as 'chance' or 'coincidence.' Mystery is the indefinable. For Mosley, it is only in the recognition of this that science could liberate humans from the destructive patterns that they find themselves in today and thus help the evolution and sustenance of a 'new human type.'

> To explain 'order' [by chance]—it is all rather peculiar. I mean if they would accept that it is an extraordinary idea. . . .
>
> [Scientists] say there are certain things that are still puzzles, but that it doesn't mean it is mysticism; it is only a matter of time till they find out the answers to these puzzles. I mean the more they find out, there is a whole lot more puzzles. . . .
>
> [Scientific jargon] is just a way of talking; they make up words for things they don't know what they are. And as long as they know that's what they are doing, I think that's wonderful! They know they are just making up words. One has the power to make up words for puzzles; enigmas; possibilities. And one makes up one's ideas about what things really are. And then you test them—you put them to test; they either work or they don't. If they don't work they aren't any good. That's a sort of evolution.[916]

In the same way as medieval scientists used 'religious' language to explain scientific findings, modern man uses scientific imagery to explain religious ideas. The difference perhaps is that whereas the masters of medieval science knew that the imagery that they were using was *not* what they were depicting, the majority of modern scientists for the past two centuries have been taking their imagery for reality and in this way they have been dangerously incapacitating human beings. Nietzsche, the so-called murderer of 'God,'[917] with foresight into our devastating era, warned against the growing scientism of nineteenth century, although (or perhaps because) he, too, like Mosley was a vigilant reader of sciences. He never 'embraced the metaphysical theory that scientific knowledge is the only true knowledge and that this knowledge alone will give us an authentic interpretation of reality.'[918] For Nietzsche, who 'embraced a dynamic, spiritual interpretation of reality,' 'matter is not the ultimate reality; rather it is a *phenomenon*, a *manifestation* of a spiritual reality the essence of which is a living power.'[919] In this light Nietzsche's perception of reality has, of course, a great affinity with that of world religions—such as Hinduism, for example, where *Maya* is the term for the 'manifestation of a spiritual reality the essence of which is a living power.'[920]

Mosley realises that the 'top scientists'[921] of our era who have liberated humanity from some of its limiting patterns of thought admit that what science does is making up words for 'puzzles; enigmas; possibilities. And [that] one makes up one's ideas about what things really are.'[922] By recognising these enigmas they necessarily recognise man's freewill. The *integration* of this knowledge into their experiments and conjectures is what differentiates new sciences from conventional scientism.

> I think the top ones do know [that they are moving on a mystical level]. I think the ones who stay in the 'lab' . . . they find it very difficult. Bohr and Heisenberg, too, those people in the 1920s and 1930s said all these extraordinary things like: 'anyone who says he understands quantum physics, doesn't understand quantum physics!' . . . And they just went off and watched what worked. [scientists] are becoming much more open. They say they don't understand what they face—what they face is *mystery*. 'Religious people' are becoming much more lost now.[923]

Like conventional scientists, those 'Religious people,' who have stopped experimenting with life and who continue taking their imagery for reality are the lost ones. They are stuck in the pre-given and deterministic answers that the Church has been providing for hundreds of years to the enigma of reality. Mystery in the Church's jargon is just a word. [924] Having lost sight of mystery (organised) religion loses sight of God. Bearing this in mind, Mosley believes that the new scientists

> are quite right to go on saying that their job is to find out what answers are available; what mathematics work. . . . Having made this enormous telescope to find an answer one finds more questions. . . . All the best ones do [recognise] that.[925]

Mosley sees the reluctance of the new scientists to use the word 'God' in the same vein as the Old Testament's warning against taking God's name in one's mouth for fear of unmaking its mystery and indefiniteness. Such an understanding of the 'new sciences' explains Mosley's interest in Gnosticism, Taoism, Christian mysticism and Sufi thought, which have intensely preoccupied him over the years, but especially in the present phase of his writing. In Mosley's eyes the science (and philosophy) of our era—starting with 'Relativity Theory' and 'Quantum Physics'—only confirm what these mystical currents have been postulating for more than two and a half millennia.[926]

> All this stuff is enormously interesting: at the back of *everything* there is just 'randomness'; and 'a random truth has no explanation, it just

is.' What more succinct way is there of putting all we have talked about?[927]

This sort of imagery used by new physicists and scientists conveys reality—even if they were unaware or in denial of it—on a 'spiritual' level: the idea of reality being 'a truth, without explanation which just *is*' reminds the reader of the *Tao*, for example, which is the inexplicable dark force giving birth to all life. Or the scientific idea of our universe being a *multi-verse* (as the molecular biologist, McFadden, puts it, in view of the new biological findings 'life maybe the product, not of a single universe, but a host of parallel universes'[928]), where 'unseen presences' influence our reality when observed,[929] brings to mind the mystical notion of angels, who 'nudge' and influence man's reality, when he is attentive to them. Furthermore, the new discovery that rejects Einstein's conjecture about the universe being curved is likewise a 'proof' for science entering mystical grounds—'we live in a flat universe, . . . but . . . the finding has an odd side-effect: . . . "it also implies that there's a lot of 'dark energy' out there." '[930] The *need* for 'mystery' as a means of defining 'existence' is well expressed by the German cosmologist Gerhard Börner: 'cosmologists need a mysterious dark energy to define the world's fabric . . . in order to tie our model [of the universe] to measurable reality, we have to *invent* a greatness, whose nature we do not know and whose qualities we *rhyme* for ourselves—and that we call dark energy. No cosmologist is happy with that, but none knows a better solution.'[931] It is not farfetched to say that this is the 'scientific proof'—if one could use this phrase at all—for Mosley's conviction about the existence of 'God.' The dark force whom we *have to* 'invent' is analogous to Mosley's idea of God being an incomprehensible, mysterious, ever-present, all-embracing, and life-giving force, which can only be 'grasped' as and in man's *makings*—inventions, artwork.

> I've become more and more convinced that none of the inquiries into 'reality' make any sense without the idea of 'God'—as guarantor of human freedom to choose, which is itself an 'objectivity.' [There is] Voltaire's quip that if God did not exist it would be necessary to invent him. My people are saying—All right, but doesn't a necessary invention necessarily exist? But you come to this realisation (as you say) properly only *after* you've been round the world with science, à la Kleist. This is what top physicists do seem to be recognising?[932]

III. Spirituality, science and the dichotomy freedom/determinism

Regarding the dichotomy of freedom/determinism the cosmologists' discovery supports Mosley's conception of freedom by actually accepting that the 'mysterious dark force' both defines (and thus creates) man and his universe and *at the same time* is invented by man as a means to define his own and his universe's existence. One could again use the images of 'mystical heresy' hidden at heart of conventional religion in order to elaborate on the scientific theory: man is both created by and is the creator of God; God both operates through man and man operates through God; man uses God and is used by God. Like a lover or a dancer man is God's equal—sometimes above and sometimes under; sometimes leading and sometimes being led. Freedom is thus only possible if man had a sense of this 'walking hand in hand with God'; of being, as the ninth-century Irish monk John Scotus Erigena postulated, 'partner of God';[933] of being, as in the imagery of Sufi poetry, 'God's lover and beloved.'[934]

The new developments in life sciences such as quantum evolution and molecular biology point out that man's freewill is only conceivable because of the existence of this greater Will 'out there' beyond the boundaries of Darwinian 'chance.' Moving away from the Darwinian concept of evolution, which sees the origin of all life in chance only, these scientists claim that freewill exists precisely because the world is not large enough for evolving and sustaining life, if it wholly depended on 'chance':

> The astronomer Fred Hoyle described the likelihood of random forces generating life as equivalent to the chances that a tornado sweeping through a junkyard might assemble a Boeing 747.[935]

It is the very fact of a life-generating Will beyond hazard or 'random forces' that testifies for freedom of choice. The scientific 'explanation' for this thesis almost sounds like a fairy tale or a biblical parable or a science-fiction story: from the view point of quantum evolution the beginnings of life could not wholly take place and evolve in our universe. These had to happen simultaneously in the 'quantum multiverse' beyond our world, as well. The responsibility of further evolution was then 'handed over' to the living organisms in our universe. These could now 'choose' the necessary mutations, but only if they were in some sort of a connection with the quantum multiverse beyond our universe : 'any small primordial pond could generate life, if it had access to the quantum multiverse.'[936]

From this point of view life is something that has to be *chosen*, or which *can only* be chosen, in *relation* to that 'other' beyond the random forces of our 'reality.' In this light, one could therefore say that all life is a sign of freedom (of choice) and all freedom is a sign of that 'other' beyond hazard and chance. Thus all life signifies a greater Reality beyond our limited 'reality.'

> So although our bodies inhabit the familiar world dominated by random motion, the microscopic units that drive our cells tread the multiverse. This . . . is what gives life its extraordinary dynamics and its ability to resist the randomising forces that assail it. Those same dynamics, though involving electromagnetic fields within our brain rather than DNA , are also . . . the source of our free will . . .[937]

It is the knowledge—the observation—of this which Mosley believes to be necessary for the evolution of a 'higher human type,' which would sustain the survival of mankind on earth. For the purpose of acquiring this knowledge, Mosley finds Ibn El-Arabi's (a Sufi active in 13th century Cordoba and generally known as 'Doctor Maximus' in the West) three forms of knowledge more effective,[938] than Bateson's three levels of Learning. Bateson's 'scientism' discouraged him from exploring the possibilities of man for going beyond the limits of his own observational faculty—i.e., consciousness: his term 'oceanic' cut down reality to a definite size, which could still be *comprehended* by consciousness instead of superseding consciousness. In this way, his 'oceanic level' was another structure, within which man found himself imprisoned. Ibn El-Arabi's ultimate level shows the importance of the *incomprehensibility* and *mystery* of that reality, by connecting to which consciousness could succeed in fulfilling the paradoxical task of superseding itself through observing itself. Only thus could man be liberated and evolve into a new higher humankind.

> There are three forms of knowledge. The first is intellectual knowledge, which is in fact only information and the collection of facts, and the use of these to arrive at further intellectual concepts. This is intellectualism.
>
> Second comes the knowledge of states, which includes both emotional feeling and strange states of being in which man thinks that he has perceived something supreme but cannot avail himself of it. This is emotionalism.

Third comes real knowledge, which is called the Knowledge of Reality. In this form, man can perceive what is right, what is true, beyond the boundaries of thought and sense. Scholastics and scientists concentrate upon the first form of knowledge. Emotionalists and experientalists use the second form. Others use the two combined, or either one alternatively.

But the people who attain to truth are those who know how to connect themselves with the reality which lies beyond both these forms of knowledge. These are the real Sufis, the Dervishes who have Attained.[939]

Literary background

Crisis sells well. During the last few decades we have witnessed the sale (on newsstands, in bookshops, by subscription, door-to-door) of the crisis of religion, of Marxism, of representation, the sign, philosophy, ethics, Freudianism, presence, the subject (I omit other crises I don't understand professionally even if I endure them, such as that of the Lira, of housing, the family, institutions, oil). Whence the well-known quip: 'God is dead, Marxism is undergoing a crisis, and I don't feel so hot myself.'[940]

Our *fin-de-siècle* seems caught in a paralysing self-reflection, endlessly encircling itself without a sense of an end or a beginning; without a sense of the new or the old. We are the imprisoned in a sense of *déjà vu*; of we-have-been-here-before. Our knowledge has become our plight.

The sense of 'belatedness' and the paradox of living 'after' all sorts of deaths—from that of God and Truth to that of Civilisation and Humanism to that of the Author and Literature—have been extensively explored and referred to in the course of this study as the backdrop of Mosley's artistic career. Mosley's present 'work-in-progress' still seems to be produced against such backdrop. The paradoxes and anti-utopias predicted in novels such as *1984* and *The Brave New World* seem to have fulfilled themselves: the Human Family living happily in a Global village has revealed itself as countless, feuding bloodthirsty tribes living more and more in alienation from each other. The post-cold war End of History and New World Order have ended up being the opposite of what they claim to be: a return to Disorderliness thanks to the Human Family revisiting its historical myths and mythical history. The paradox of falling into an 'identity crisis'—a keyword of our postmodern age—due to countless 'self-identifications' has been the fate of both emancipatory and reactionary groups, ethnicities and nations.

Britain, Britishness and the British novel, as was explored earlier, have not been spared these crises. The novel, declared dead but more self-reproductive than ever, reflects its socio-historical setting. What could be 'deduced' with some certainty (if one could use this word at all) from the course of this research is that the novel has also been caught in the paralysing self-reflexive mood of its time. It seems as if it doesn't know how to continue. On the one hand, the times seem unable to produce visions through which novelists could charter the shapeless and hazy future. On the other hand, what strikes one, however, as a special feature of the novel and the novelist of the end of our millennium is the attempt to get out of this trap by being acutely aware of that which is supposed to have ended with the birth of the New World (Dis)Order: namely, History. Edmund White rightly claims that 'we are living through a great renaissance of historical fiction.'[941] Many writers are now trying to find a pattern into the future by examining the past. Rushdie's *The Ground Beneath her Feet*, Roddy Doyle's *A Star Called Henry* and Jim Crace's *Quarantine* are a few examples of the novel of this time, which exploits the historical framework, in order to embark on an investigation of the past in the hope of finding a way into the future. It is important to note that none of these novels are—or could be—'conventional' historical novels: the 'innocence' of a 'straight-forward' tale has long been lost in the post-war, post-holocaust, post-colonial, post- . . . years and all these novels are by necessity meta-fictions bound in self-reflection.[942]

Another genre which has been enjoying immense popularity in this period is that of biography and autobiography. The rise of this genre could be seen in the same light as that of the historical novel. Emma Tennant's *Girlitude*, Lessing's autobiographies, Mosley's *Efforts at Truth* and Amis's *Experience* are excellent examples of endeavours, where the artist tries to understand life in light of art and art in light of life in the hope of fulfilling the Nietzschean task of building the future through listening to the oracle of the past. The same could be said of many biographies of artists, poets and historical figures—such as Mailer's *Picasso*, Ian Kershaw's Hitler biographies and Linda Wagner-Martin's *Sylvia Plath: a literary life*. However, we must also bear in mind that our era's strong sense of escapism and sensationalism have been the oil in the fire of many biographies, too: 'sensational life stories,' 'unpublished letters' and 'what-you-never-knew tales.' Hence many biographies being fed by this sensationalism throw the reader back into the narcotic prison of the past without offering any way to the future and further development of mankind.

The other impression that the fiction of this era transmits is that the experiments of the previous decades have become the convention of the present. All the 'marginal' fictions have become mainstream. Feminist literature, post colonial fiction, science fiction, gay and lesbian literature make up an important part of British fiction, and have been moulded and woven into other modes of fiction and in this way opened new windows in the house of British fiction. From 'desirable marginality'[943] these 'currents' have poured into our 'normality' and are increasingly changing the 'matter-of-course' fabric of our perception.

Bearing in mind that, contrary to the deconstructivists' claim, an important (and perhaps the central) role of fiction is being a medium of self-reflection through which mankind could observe and (to speak with Mosley) consequently liberate *or entrap* itself, the fictions of the past decades have had some success. They have opened up new possibilities—new windows—in our perception and could be seen as attempts to mould a future which would help the evolution and sustenance of man and Life. At the same time they have also been the product of and produced a virulently destructive solipsism and stagnation by neglecting their central function. The untimely death of Bradbury at the end of the second millennium, the end of the troubled twentieth century, strangely turns his definition of the novel into an oracle for the novelists of our time

> But the novel is never quite sermon, prophecy, philosophy or history; it deals with not fixed but ever-moving truths, and is not a statement but an investigation. It is an imaginative exploration of living history, time and consciousness, a research into reality.[944]

It is for this reason that Mosley broke away from the form of the historical narrative which had proved so successful in *Hopeful Monsters*. An imaginative exploration of reality, needs an imaginative nonconformity as the forms and modes of liberation could, if remained unexamined, become those of entrapment: 'Most British novels that win prizes now are historical. It was when I saw this (and relevant to *Monsters!*) that I thought there must be something different possible.'[945] The publication of Mosley's first novel after his autobiography is very much in the spirit of Mosley's *Weltanschauung*: it embodies Mosley's idea of the intricate relationship between Life and art—the open-end-story, which is created infinitely. One could say that the resumption of his artistic activity is in the spirit of his understanding of Nietzsche: 'Nietzsche saw that whether one liked it or not one was creating life—always realising that one hasn't come to an end.'[946] *Children of Darkness and Light* is a turn away from his paralysing belief of never being able to write again after *Hopeful Monsters*; it is also the realisation of the possibilities that he saw rising at the closing of his autobiography. In this sense, one could also see his present phase of writing in light of his concept of freedom: by sincerely observing one's limiting observation patterns man can influence them and free himself from them, especially when these restricting structures were once means of liberation and have now become means of imprisonment. Mosley thus freed himself from *Hopeful Monsters* by writing his autobiography, which in turn enabled him to open up his consciousness and realise other hidden possibilities.

Novels

> There is perhaps one more story I might write. This would be about children—as it were my children—walking through a wood. They come across an old man sitting collapsed against a tree. They say—I know, Old Godadaddy, you have been eating again of that tree!
>
> And he says—But this isn't the Tree of Knowledge of Good and Evil, this is the Tree of Life.
>
> And they say — But you would call anything life!
>
> And he says — I've been right round the world, and you know what I found when I got back here?
>
> They say — What?
>
> He says—call it death, call it life, children.[947]

I.   *Children of Darkness and Light*: conceiving the mystery

In the present novels Mosley develops his idea that freedom lies in man's ability to choose *realities* rather than possibilities by observing these. In this sense, his plane of investigation extends beyond the 'ordinary' reality (in *Catastrophe Practice Series* these were scientific findings and in the novels preceding the series moral dilemmas) and reaches the 'otherworldly' realms of human life. That is to say, he investigates freedom as the realisation of the mysterious in 'ordinary' reality and as a result depicts the spiritual realms of 'ordinary' reality. One could thus say that he moves from the *scientific* level of *Catastrophe Practice Series* onto a *spiritual* level, however, without 'abandoning' science. Science is now used as a tool to convey the spiritual idea of the existence of other realities all connected in a life-generating 'dark force'—or a greater 'Will'—which is the guarantor of human freewill. One could thus see these novels as both a break away from *Hopeful Monsters* and a 'sequel' to it.

The first novel, *Children of Darkness and Light*, is a good example to show the break away from *Monsters* in terms of style of narration. Harry is a forty-ish journalist seemingly in the middle of a mid-life crisis, who had once covered a story on a group of abandoned children having visions of the Virgin Mary on a desolate hillside in a Yugoslavia gliding uncontrollably towards a disastrous civil war. He is now assigned to report on a similar group of children with the same visions of the Virgin in a Cumbria stricken with radioactivity.[948]

The novel is a break away from *Monsters* in that the realist, historical form and the hexagonal character-configuration (which in fact started in *Catastrophe Practice*) are abandoned. The most obvious break in style from *Monsters* is that *Monsters* had a feel of a 'documentary' predominantly narrated from a realist-historical point of view. *Children*, despite its linear narration moves on a magical, mythical terrain. The reader often feels as if he were inside a medieval painting; or in a science-fiction scenery.

> There were small clouds with gold and pink edges like bits of paper on fire. I thought—Fire and brimstone are ready to come down: but first, have those angels landed? There was one cloud larger and lower than the rest which bulged above a hill like a genie stuck half in and half out of its bottle. I thought—But I know what that is! I drove to the brow of the hill and stopped; there below me, yes, on the narrow plain between the hills and the sea, were the four huge cooling-towers of the power-station by the reprocessing-plant; it was above them that steam hung like a sluggish and overweight spectre. I sat and watched the pink and gold above the mountains turn to silver and grey.[949]

In a way the style of the narrative is also a return to Mosley's 'Sixties' experimentalist style. This return could be seen in light of Mosley's re-visitation of his past life and art in this phase of his writing. The central couple are called after the married couple in *The Meeting Place* Harry and Melissa. The main protagonist, Harry, is a journalist like the former Harry, and like him, as the above passage conveys, he, too, has a phantasmal view of things. This reminds the reader of the narrative techniques that became Mosley's hallmark, in his novels, such as *Impossible Object* and *Natalie Natalia*. As was the case with his predecessors in the 'Sixties,' the present Harry, too, experiences epiphanies by detaching himself from reality and alienating it into a surrealist if not a magical-mystical artwork.

The novel is simultaneously a sequel to *Monsters* and a continuation of *Catastrophe Practice Series* in its investigation of the possibilities of freedom as a means for the evolution of a 'higher human type' and its survival in our time. As mentioned throughout the study, for Mosley, children are intricately woven into the idea of freedom, the survival of mankind and a new human type. Especially in Mosley's *Catastrophe Practice Series* children were the embodiment of futurity and the continuity of human race. But most important of all they are the incarnation of new beginnings, change and hope. They represent man's *choice* of life and in this way epitomise the connection between freedom and life. In *Children* this is most poignantly shown in the scene where a child who is not 'ethnically correct' is saved from an orphanage in Yugoslavia by an uncanny and absurdly funny collaboration between Harry, the English couple willing to adopt the child, a Taxi driver and the personnel of the orphanage.[950] The scene is an expression of Mosley's idea of man's freedom of choice being both a matter of his active choosing and the choice *being chosen* for him; of

> one's *awareness* of the *possibility* of choice that the makes the 'right' choice likely to occur—(But it is one's *choice* to be aware!) this indeed suggesting some spiritual or mystical mechanism; a link-up with a larger whole.[951]

In *Children*, and the novels following, the 'larger whole' is increasingly referred to as 'God.' So, man can liberate himself from coercive, deterministic structures (whether inner or outer ones) by connecting himself to God through observing—i.e., being aware—of His liberating reality beyond.[952] In order to avoid religious 'smugness' and the limits of 'kitsch,' Mosley, as in *Judith* for example, subverts and inverts parables and myths that recount the helplessness of man in face of death and destruction and in this way de-fuses the 'original' myth in a 'meta-myth,' which in turn *empowers* the protagonist to observe the destructive patterns from a higher point. In this case he does this with the story of 'Herod and the Slaughter of the Innocents.'

> I thought—Ethnically correct? You mean that child, although healthy, has been earmarked to die? Then — Oh yes, there was that massacre of the innocents, was there not! . . . I . . . saw that the wide-eyed child was now standing up as if trying to get out. I thought — So we are going to play God after all, are we, you and I. . . . I thought — Oh come on, can we not defeat King Herod's soldiers?[953]

The saving of the child is depicted in such a way that it could be seen both as the result of 'natural causes' and 'supernatural causes.' The adoptive mother, Mrs Smith says: 'This is a miracle,' to which the taxi driver responds with: 'No miracle. I just told them that they do what you want double quick or their whole fucking place would be blown up.'[954] This is the tone of this novel's investigation of the spiritual. All sublime events and mystical experiences are immediately brought down onto a 'mundane' level. In this way the interplay between the 'supernatural' and 'natural'; the extraordinary and the ordinary; 'God' and 'man' is shown. Miracles are thus shown not to be scientifically 'provable,' but as *real* outcomes of this interplay—of this 'dance'—which could be called 'coincidence,' 'fate' or 'natural causes.'

The 'Child' is the incarnation of the 'miraculous' throughout the novel. Children embody the connectedness of the ordinary and the extraordinary—the outer reality with the inner reality. Here—and in the novels following—they are seen as the necessary 'mutations' chosen from the 'quantum multiverse' to sustain humanity.[955] As in *Monsters*, where the young Max undertook the experiment of observing himself as a 'God' creating the framework—Garden—where his salamanders could choose the 'right' mutation, in *Children* Harry does the same by observing himself half-seriously, half-jokingly as a God who can orchestrate the rescue of the Child by creating the necessary framework out of the chaotic state of war-ridden Yugoslavia, where the rescue-operation could take place: 'one of the good things about a state of chaos or war is that you can sometimes out of it produce some sort of order of your own.'[956] The important factor here, as in *Monsters*, is the self-observation—the simultaneous attachment and detachment from the self and the situation, which is so well depicted in this half-serious/half-joking statement of Harry.[957] This is also the tone of the woman-figure at the end of the novel, who jokes about being the Virgin, but seems to claim it seriously at the same time.

> I said—'I thought you were Sister Bernardine!'
> She laughed: she said 'Oh no I'm the Virgin Mary!'[958]

Making a joke out of a mystical event makes it mundane and hence the joke can be seen as a connection between the two realities; as an integration of the one into the other. It makes the 'ordinary' extraordinary and the extraordinary a matter of every-day-life. Laughter is also the sign of man's sovereignty. It is the sign of man's ability to observe the paradox by detaching himself from the restricting *either-or* system of rationality and move beyond.[959] In this case, it can be seen as a sign of liberation from 'God' the Lord, and a sign of binding with 'God' the equal friend or loved one: 'And, yes, the really powerful saints have 'teased' God (e.g., St Theresa of Avila)—because teasing is a sign of intimacy and love.'[960] Furthermore, jokes are a 'good way' of countering 'the sin of pride' and the risk of 'undoing the miracle.'[961]

> It's very striking how in the New Testament when Jesus has done a 'curing' miracle he tells the recipient 'not to tell anyone'—knowing presumably that news of it will only stir up resentment . . . or when Jesus is *challenged* to do a big miracle he simply refuses—i.e., to get down from the cross.[962]

This idea is the crux of Mary's visitation: the children claim Mary to have instructed them to tell the outer world that they have been lying.[963] The aim of this message seems not only to be warding off 'resentment' or the 'sin of pride,' but also to pull away the ground beneath the feet of the protagonist/reader. The reader and the narrator are immediately put on a journey in uncertain grounds: there is no way of knowing what is reality and what is fiction. Everything seems to be a cover up for something else

> [the children] had set up in some sort of commune on their own in the hills. They were not being prevented from doing this by their families or the local Social Services. There had been the story that the Virgin Mary had instructed them to do this in a vision; then the leader of

the children, a girl called Gaby, had said that she had made this story up. . . .

. . . There were scarcely veiled hints that there might be connections between this story and an earlier story of satanic cults involving children and parents and indeed the Social Services people in the area.

. . . The story about the children stopped, as usual, just when it might have become interesting. It had apparently been the father of Gaby, the leader of the children, who had spread the story about the vision of the Virgin Mary; the hints were that this had been done to cover up dubious relationships between the families and the authorities and the children.[964]

What starts as a sort of detective story soon transforms itself into an espionage and political thriller which in turn takes on the features of science-fiction and myth. The reader/protagonist becomes caught in a seeming sex-cult conspiracy ('Set back from the drive, against the background of a wood, were the ruins of a Gothic abbey: . . . the whole thing was like a skeleton of dinosaur. I thought—Indeed this might be a setting for the Ku-Klux-Klan or indeed the Hellfire Club.'[965]) only to become involved in a political-ecological thriller involving corrupt authorities and eco-warriors trying alternately to manipulate statistics and scientific findings regarding the effects of radioactivity.[966] The reader further moves onto a science-fiction plane where paranormal 'meticulously cut-out shapes in fields of standing corn'[967] appear as if from UFO landings, only to enter a mythical realm ('As we walked up the beach towards the hotel it was as if we might indeed be figures in some mythological representation—a frieze on a temple architrave; a shadow-play on a screen'[968]). On top of all this, the frequent references to new scientific technology, especially revolving around the World Wide Web, make the story even more complex. The characters within this labyrinthine narration seem, on one hand, exactly to know what they are doing and simultaneously not to know at all what they are up to.

Harry and the reader could just as well be travellers in an Italo Calvino novel whose path seems to take endless turns in time and space leading to nowhere. The traveller finds no answer to his questions; no mystery is ever unravelled and every destination reveals itself as mirage. This is the heart of the narrative: the Gödelian knot cannot be untied. However, whereas in postmodern novels this form gives rise to a feeling of loss and suffocation, here it is used to express a sense of liberation. Similar to *Impossible Object* and *Catastrophe Practice*, but with a clearer linearity this novel takes on the shape of a riddle.[969] The protagonist/reader—the traveller in the narrative—is not to untie the riddle, but to use it as a means of liberating himself from the logic of the plot and thus the story itself.[970] He can only do this by detaching himself from it—the detachment being only possible within an aesthetic framework. It is within such a framework that he can observe and *recognise* the riddle/story and thus free himself from it. This view had been the fruit of Mosley's understanding of the spirit of Christianity and accordingly the source of his break with conventional writing. *Children* is in this sense a direct descendant of Mosley's experimental writing career starting with *The Meeting Place*. However, whereas the other novels, although rooted in Mosley's Christianity, hardly ever hinted at his it, *Children* and the novels following it are openly spiritual in that they claim Mystery/God to be at the beginning of all freedom and consequently of all life. The self-reflection which had led to Bateson's 'oceanic' circuit in *Catastrophe Practice* gives way to a self-reflection leading to the (cosmologists,' microbiologists' *and* gnostics') infinite, mysterious, indefinable life-generating dark force.

> There was a path into the wood along the side of the stream; the stream ran so busily! There was all this activity going on—the water fed the trees, the trees were like lungs that breathed, they created and preserved the air—how—by turning carbon dioxide into oxygen? By maintaining the ozone layer without which we should all be burned by the sun? And the air contained clouds by which the trees and the earth might be watered: and the whole apparatus worked, this was the miracle; this was the mechanism that went on as it were off-stage—that one could not exactly see by looking.
> . . . I have no explanation. I think the explanation is that they are bits of information to show that there are some things about which it is not the point to look for an explanation.[971]

The aim of the Calvinesque journey through the maze is not to unravel it, but to *learn* to liberate oneself from the limiting structures of one's observational faculty and consequently of one's 'reality' by *recognising* the 'maze' (i.e., the mystery) as a whole and thus uniting with it. In this way, Bateson's three levels of Learning are substituted by Ibn El-Arabi's three forms of Knowledge, where the highest form of knowledge is 'the Knowledge of Reality. In this form, man can perceive what is right, what is true, beyond the boundaries of thought and sense.'[972] This is ultimately a spiritual undertaking

> It seemed that life depended on some intricate working of a whole; a balancing between what should die and what should not. One reason why this could not be measured was because any effort to do so would itself affect the intricate working of the whole—
> . . . life may be something you have to understand as a matter of faith, because if you try to understand it in any other way then this invalidates what you are trying to find . . .[973]

The traveller—Harry/the reader—is in this sense not travelling futilely in Borgesian 'Chinese boxes' and labyrinths, but going through a spiritual learning process.

> I thought I might say to the local reporter—But you do see, don't you, that all such phantasms themselves might be a cover-up—
> — A cover-up of what—
> — Of learning about any journey, search, that might be being undertaken by the children—or oneself?[974]

II. *Journey into the Dark*: tapping in the dark and glimpses of light

As we have seen for Mosley the journey 'being undertaken by the children—or oneself' mainly takes place in the dark, where light shines through when the individual learns to leave the restricting—and in our time, all-destroying—patterns of his observation by choosing to become aware of and consequently to be united with 'God' or the greater Whole. *Journey into the Dark* picks up and tries to examine this subject. It is difficult to write an analysis of this novel, as *Journey* (excerpted in Mosley's essay collection, *The Uses of Slime Mold*) is more a sketch than a finished work of art. Mosley himself sees it thus:

> *Journey into the Dark*—I wrote it without really planning anything. But no one wants to publish *Journey into the Dark*! Quite rightly, I think! It isn't really a book! It's something I did because I had nothing else to do![975]

For a study of his artistic development it is more fruitful to understand Mosley's self-mockery in a different light. The title of the book indicates

Mosley's own search—his own journey into the dark. *Journey* was written in a time, where he was intensely trying to understand and link up the new developments in science, technology and philosophy in the context of mysticism. In this time he went through a further, yet more complex evolution of the ideas which he had started to address in *Children*. In this sense, *Journey* could be understood as a 'manifesto' in the same vein as *Catastrophe Practice*—in *Journey* Mosley even quotes himself at length out of *Catastrophe Practice*.[976] The major difference is that whereas *Catastrophe Practice* introduced the ideas for future novels, *Journey* stretches both into the past and the future of Mosley's present phase of writing. That is to say, it can also be seen as an introduction to the novel that was; i.e., *Children of Darkness and Light*. Therefore, *Journey* can be seen as the manifesto—and seed—for the present phase of Mosley's career in the same vein as *Catastrophe Practice* was understood for his preceding phase of writing.

Similar to *Catastrophe Practice* this text alternates between essays and pieces of fiction. And similar to those previous essays these too explore the relationship between literature, science, philosophy and life. What distinguishes these essays from the ones in *Catastrophe* is their clearly spiritual tone and their references to God. The novel opens with an essay on the uses and disadvantages of literature for life. Contrasting George Steiner with Harold Bloom, Mosley laments the uselessness of (Canonic) literature for life and can even see its connection to the atrocities in the West, which found their culmination in the Holocaust.[977]

> [Steiner] wondered—'In fact were [humanistic traditions and models of conduct] a barrier, or is it more realistic to perceive in humanistic culture express solicitations of authoritarian rule and cruelty?' . . . Much of the Romantic movement, Steiner argued, was an expression of 'the nostalgia for disaster.'
> . . . Bloom hardly disagrees with Steiner as to the style of [Western literary tradition]. He sees their common characteristic, that which gives them potency, as what he calls *agon*: combat, antagonism, strife. . . . Where Bloom differs from Steiner is in his contention that this style and such attitudes in literature have little effect on human behaviour: 'Reading the very best writers—let us say Homer, Dante, Shakespeare, Tolstoy—is not going to make us better citizens': but neither is it going to make us worse citizens, for—'art is perfectly useless, according to the sublime Oscar Wilde who is always right.' . . . If we read the Western canon in 'order to form our social, political, or personal or

moral values, I firmly believe we will become monsters of selfishness and exploitation.'[978]

Mosley agrees with Bloom in that literature cannot be 'used' for moralistic ends—otherwise it would be propaganda material—but disagrees with him about its 'uselessness' or its being at most a manual for 'the proper use of one's own solitude, that solitude whose final form is one's confrontation with one's own mortality.'[979] As he has done since his break with conventional writing in the Sixties, here, too, Mosley passionately remonstrates against this view by rephrasing Steiner's question: 'what is the worth of love of a literature that has nothing to do with life? . . . About life, in this assessment, there remains little to be learned from literature except perhaps an expertise in games-playing—a style in which people have nothing else to do except to try to come out on top of others.'[980] This immediately reminds the reader of Mosley's disdain for social (with an emphasis on aristocratic), political, artistic and intellectual game-playing, the fight against which has been Mosley's vocation since the early days of his career. As mentioned throughout this study, games for Mosley are only fruitful, when they are used by freedom fighters, such as Brecht: i.e., when they are used to *liberate* rather than imprison the player in their rules and structures. In other words, when they could be used to point out a greater order outside themselves—a different reality off-stage—which can only be taken notice of by the players, if these could be both attached to and alienated from the situation and observe themselves (as in a Brechtian piece) as players. In this respect, his rage is especially reserved for the new fad in philosophy at the end of the twentieth century, deconstructionism—the 'philosophy' which has declared all meaning as dead. Being a novelist, Mosley is especially alarmed by the influence of this school on literature.

> In literature there is no sense in searching for an author's meaning nor indeed for any meaning that might be called authentic; a critic can give to a text whatever interpretation he or she likes. Authors, it was supposed, are at the mercy of their social or psychological predispositions; they cannot, since these are unconscious, be aware of these themselves; critics however can— . . . it might of course be said that critics are at the mercy of their social and psychological predispositions, but such a contention would be part of the game—the lumbering game in which there is no claim to authenticity but just

> the spectacle of academics leaping and cavorting and popping balls through hoops. . . .[981]

> To play the game properly . . . Enmity was naturally required to provide the setting for loyalty; the need for belligerence banished any obligation to examine what was being defended or attacked. . . .[982]

For Mosley these games in a way deliver a model for real life atrocities and wars. In view of September 11th, which took place some four years after Mosley had written *Journey*, this claim obtains horrifying dimensions. In the absence of meaning games can only become more sensationalist and dangerous to hold the attention of their bored audience. Their bored audience, as in Dadaist manifestos, often dreams of and undertakes 'an act of highest virtue,' which is 'to take a machine-gun and fire at random into a crowded street.'[983] 'How is then so surprising that Nazis, with their blinkered and pedantic minds, would have wished to bring organisation to such proceedings?'[984]

Again, Mosley sees that death and imprisonment within the structures of meaningless art are closely related to each other and beseeches the artist to use literature as a means for fighting for freedom and consequently for the survival of mankind. As in his *Catastrophe Practice* essays, he believes that this can only be done if the artist is aware of—*learns* to be aware of—an indefinitely greater network at work, of which he and his work are part of and are thus both inside and outside it. The work of art is only 'authentic' and has a 'use' for life if it points at this greater 'unexplainable,' but 'recognisable' network. Whereas in *Catastrophe Practice* he was reluctant to name this network and preferred to speak of Bateson's 'oceanic circuit,' here, in the spirit of his 'Churchy days,' he identifies it with God. Quoting Steiner, Mosley says—

> I will put forward the argument that the experience of aesthetic meaning in particular, that of literature, of the arts, of musical form, infers the necessary possibility of this 'real presence.' The seeming paradox of 'necessary possibility' is, very precisely, that which the poem, the painting, the musical composition are at liberty to explore and to enact (*Real Presences*, pp. 3-4). . . . The words become tentative: use of the word 'God' is always a matter of choice. But whatever words are risked, if they are too much dissected and analysed, then whatever has been found is likely to die in the light. . . .[985]

In this respect Mosley finds new sciences much more honest and attentive than new literature and art, and most importantly than 'religious' language.[986] 'Religious language' and the scientism of eighteenth and nineteenth century (whose influence we still feel today) necessarily collaborated in killing God: alternately by seeing him as the all-determining Planner or pure Chance.

> It was priests and prelates and theologians who tried to define God, analyse God, pin God down; tell Him what he could and could not do as if He were their acolyte or a butterfly staked out on a table. Or the idea of God might still be put forward as a rival to science by people who wished to harness Him to their own prejudice and prestige: in a mechanistic world why should God not be seen as a Prime Mechanic or Mover . . . But what a role for God! Perhaps it was simply on account of the dismalness of such a role that the idea of Him died. And then had to wait for resurrection at the hands of people who would do what is proper for humans to do in relation to God:—which is—watch and listen, rather than insist on seeing him in terms of their needs and predilections.[987]

It was the new sciences of the twentieth century—starting with Relativity Theory and Quantum Theory—which provided a good chance for the resurrection of God from the dead body of the Newtonian Prime Mechanic. A 'quantum theory' is not logically 'provable,'[988] but it is *the* theory which made the major technological findings of this century—from portable radios to computers to satellites and bombs—possible. It is 'unintelligible,' but it 'works.' It is thus an appropriate model for the 'mysterious.' Mosley mentions how 'maestros of physics such as Bohr, Feynmann and Haldane,' in the same vein as medieval alchemists, not only accepted, but 'guarded this unintelligibility jealously.' From this point on all sciences—from quantum physics to cosmology to microbiology and quantum evolution—have been able to 'work' and make unprecedented discoveries precisely *because* of this 'darkness' that they have accepted:

> Bohr: 'Anyone who is not shocked by quantum physics has not understood it.' Feynmann: 'It is safe to say that no one understands quantum mechanics.' Haldane: 'The universe is not only queerer than we suppose but queerer than we can suppose.' Such pronouncements seem not to provide information so much as to insist that there are limits

to information; yet to recognise that beyond these limits there exists a world of what George Steiner referred to as 'real presences.' A corollary of this indefinability is that it is easy, for anyone who so chooses, to ignore or to mock what it suggests—and what it suggests is indeed that people have this choice.[989]

This statement clearly expresses the heart of this manifesto: new sciences indicate the necessary link between the 'Indefinable'—i.e., God—and man's freedom of choice. And man's freewill is intricately connected with his further evolution and survival at the end of the millennium. As in *Catastrophe Practice* essays, he founds his argument on the new currents in evolution and mind sciences, which divert from Orthodox Darwinism. Mainly based on Lynn Margulis' definition of the theory of symbiosis, Mosley argues that life is a by-product of the organisms' awareness of and connection to each other and a 'larger whole,' rather than that of bloody battles between Selfish Genes.

> Arising contemporaneously but far less noticeably than the idea of the Selfish Gene . . . has been the idea that a process in evolution even more important than the elimination of one form of life by another—than the survival of the few at the cost of enormous waste—is the less spectacular but ultimately more effective process of what is called symbiosis—the alliance with, and assimilation of, one form of life by another—each performing for the other a vital function that it could not perform for itself. . . .[990]

The beginnings of symbiosis—of life—lie in the (coincidental/intentional) invasion of a single-cell bacterium by another, the latter becoming the nucleus of the former 'or at least some semi-autonomous component within it.'[991]

> And by this were made available not only the benefits of intricate symbiotic living, but also eventually the vastly elaborate systems of sexual reproduction by which mutations might occur and proliferate and be available to natural selection; and thus evolution could go bounding on in ever more complex ways . . .[992]

This 'intricate symbiotic living' and, as its result, complex evolution of life could only take place because the cells were made aware of each other and a new whole—an entity greater than the sum of its parts—that was created through their invasion of each other:

> There is that image of that first simple cell just happening to invade, to be accepted by, another such cell: nothing intentional of course; just chance; a by product. Yet something has been superseded; something created: is this not the realisation of some new system: for the recognition by parts, of some new whole?[993]

Mosley applies this imagery to human beings and their observational faculty—i.e., consciousness—in order to show the possibility for humans to get connected with the 'greater whole' and thus liberate themselves from their self-destruction.

> Genes produced human consciousness; memes—human understanding—might produce a symbiosis of consciousness with that which can be conscious of it and become its nucleus: and thus both be, and find itself part of, a larger whole.[994]

In a 'quantum' model of the brain Mosley sees the possibility for doing this as such:

> Recently there have been new efforts to nominate features in the brain by means of which it might be conjectured that consciousness functions. There are bundles of cells called microtubules that in their activities seem to show characteristics more in tune with quantum activity than with orthodox systems of cause-and-effect. They seem to exchange vibrational signals . . . which explore simultaneously any number of possible or potential patterns of activity rather than carry messages. . . .
>
> This network of microtubules is by its nature largely insulated from the more straightforward workings of the brain; it would seem to be connected to it at just those points where potentiality (so it might be conjectured) could be transmuted into this or that particular. It is just how such interaction is effected that, some scientists say, may never be able scientifically to be known; but why should it?[995]

The idea that the brain is *scientifically* a representation of 'mysterious' forces and activities is liberating as it transmits the 'impression of the possibility of choice.'[996]

> The virtue of a model of the brain that includes such a quantum mode of activity is that it does seem representative of what is people's common experience—that of consciousness being confronted at most moments by an array of possibilities from which one outcome rather than another can occur—as a result indeed often of external forces, but usually also a result of at least the impression of the possibility of choice.[997]

But—

> what effects a choice between this or that even when such a choice seems obviously available is not likely to appear exactly as a rationally worked out free will—such an idea can indeed rationally be made a nonsense of—but rather as a combination of rationality and *a largely unconscious network* of everything that a person has ever done and experienced and been; indeed some force of *semi-autonomous interconnectedness*.[998]

In other words, freedom of choice is being both determined by a larger network and is autonomous *within* it. It is involved in a dance (of creation) with a larger whole, which leads one and is led by one. It is by awareness of this that the right choice could be met; is met.

As we have seen, for Mosley it is the loss of this mode of observation (in Steiner's eyes, since the Age of Enlightenment[999]) that has led to the loss of God, and consequently that of freedom and increasingly that of life. In other words, in his eyes humanity could only be saved—and he sees the indications of this redemption in new sciences—if it found God again. In the stories in *Journey* he tries to illustrate this idea in an aesthetic framework.

The interconnected pieces of fiction in *Journey* each depict a different set of networks: the first is the story of the young Jewish girl, Lisa, who is trying to make sense of the connection between God, Holocaust, and the present state of the Chosen people by entering an underground labyrinth of tunnels made up of the ancient paths of the Jewish people in Jerusalem.[1000] There is the story of the Moslem Hafiz and the Christian Joshua in Lebanon, who, while trying to understand the religious and nationalist aggressions in their country, become involved in a genetic weapon experiment and end up in its testing site, which is (yet again) an archaeological mound in a secluded millennialist village. Here they become caught in the labyrinth of (homosexual) love.[1001] And finally there is the story of the American and Chinese Cyberneticists, John Davidson and Ling Fo, who are trying to simulate and enquire into the workings of the brain by having their elaborate computer 'assimilate and correlate bits of information that would come to it as if at random—and thus to be more in the situation and condition of an actual brain.'[1002] They end up with print-outs of 'enormously intricate and strangely beautiful shapes,' which seem to be a respond to 'beautifully calligraphed Chinese poems' and acupuncture charts of the circuits in the body. [1003]

> [In Chinese medicine] it was held that there were circuits in the body which could not precisely be mapped or seen but upon the unblocked working of which the health of the body depended: this understanding had been come upon by trial and error, though to Western eyes it was not scientific. . . . Might there not be in some way similar channels of connection in the outside world—not able to be mapped or proven, but nevertheless experienced? . . . These channels blocked in my head—are there not connections between these and the outside world. . . .[1004]

Chinese medicine is another simile for quantum science(s): a way of studying and working with networks and phenomena, whose existence is recognisably experienced, but scientifically 'inexplicable.' These sciences seem to work by having developed a means of observing—i.e., of being attentive to—the interactions and networks of their subjects of study instead of analysing and measuring these. They work precisely due to their awareness of something beyond the duality of rationality/irrationality. Mosley's characters wonder whether they can apply such an awareness to the workings of man and the world: whether just by attending to a greater network the blockages—the seeming paradoxes—could be 'unblocked' and the individual could be liberated. Like Max Ackerman and his salamanders, the characters are undertaking an experiment, of which they know they are part of—they are being both God and his creatures. They are testing whether by way of observation they can uses their freedom of choice and change the outcome of things, freedom of choice being 'a *combination* of rationality and *a largely unconscious network* of everything that a person has ever done and experienced and been; indeed some force of *semi-autonomous interconnectedness*.'[1005] In everyday parlance we call this 'combination' chance; coincidences. This way of observation has been at the heart of Mosley's artistic career: i.e., the idea of liberation through (self)reflection. As mentioned throughout the study there is, however, a paradox—an impossibility—at heart of this kind of observation: it must be largely unconscious, but is by virtue of observation a conscious act. The paradox is only overcome if the observer can attach himself to the larger 'other' by being aware of it and thus observe both the conscious and unconscious parts from a higher objectivity—i.e., from the locale of his attachment with the larger 'other.' The symbolic liberation of Lisa, the Jewish girl, from the rubble—from the 'knots'; the 'riddles'—of the network of tunnels is a good example for showing this. In one story there is John Davidson wondering about these outer and inner networks (p. 70)—and by virtue of this being observant of them—and randomly pressing buttons on his internet. He comes across a picture of Lisa in a news bulletin, and catches—i.e., *observes*—himself thinking and even fantasising about her (p. 65-66). Lisa herself imagines herself being watched by someone—God? John Davidson? (p. 22). In a following story Lisa is found and freed from her predicament (p. 95-97).

It must be noted that this sort of awareness is not meant as a 'parapsychological' or telepathic activity between the protagonists. They cannot *will* to 'send' messages to each other through the channels of the network that they are part of. They can only *choose*—i.e., use their freedom of choice—to trust and observe that such a network exists and it is by this awareness that one thing rather than another takes place. Whereas a 'parapsychological' or telepathic activity is a rationalisation of the workings of this network (and thus a superstition meant not to function) the attentiveness to and observation of the greater network is a mystical activity—something like a meditation or a prayer.

Coincidences of this kind happen throughout the stories only to culminate in the meeting of all the characters in the last story in a settlement in the West Bank, where humans are on a knife-edge—a knife-edge being Mosley's favourite image for a state of hope—and might (or might not) find a way out of the spiral of hatred. In this way, the stories make up a network themselves, which makes it possible for the characters to meet depending on what the reader makes of them. In other words, the network comes into being depending on whether the reader is aware of these coincidences, which are realised because of the characters' semi-conscious observation of a greater network to which they belong. This is also reminiscent of the way the characters' met in *Catastrophe Practice* and could make the right choices because of their observation of a greater network.

A network—there is a network of ideas and one meets someone here and there. It's all going on. But one thing one doesn't do is form a group, a church, an organisation. As soon as you do that it becomes dead. But having trust in this—trusting the network, trusting life—is quite a brave thing to do; a hard thing to do. One has got no rules or regulations. One learns how to trust it.[1006]

It must however be said that in *Journey* this idea is aesthetically not as well worked out as in the novels of *Catastrophe Practice Series* or for that matter as in the following novel *Hesperides Tree* and *Inventing God*. In *Journey* there are too many loose threads. The coincidental meetings at the end are not as persuasive as in the other novels. This may be due to the setting that the author has chosen: in the chaos of the Israeli-Palestinian conflict, one could hardly hold onto anything to make some order—some aesthetic order. One, on the other hand, must also bear in mind that *Journey*, as Mosley himself points out, is not a finished novel. It leaves an impression of being itself a tapping in the dark, which occasionally comes across glimpses of light.

III. *The Hesperides Tree*: the creation and self-creation of the 'higher human type'

This novel is a successful aesthetic depiction of the idea at heart of this phase of Mosley's writing: the idea that man has a freewill because of the existence of an all-embracing Will and that the evolution (i.e., Life) is a manifestation—a pattern—of the co-operation between man's will and this all-embracing Will. Whereas in his former phase the right choice for the unfolding and sustenance of life could be met through an observation of a network of possibilities connected in a 'larger whole,' in this phase—and most obviously in this novel—he is calling for an awareness of a network of *realities* connected in the Ultimate Reality of God. The realities—alternatives—to choose from are what we normally call 'mutations'; or, as Mosley would rather have it, '"possible mutations" because "mutations" are a *fait accompli*,'[1007] whereas 'possible mutations' are open to choice and as a result to change. Thus man could choose the right 'mutations' for the evolution and survival of a 'higher human type' by being aware of the indefinable ultimate Reality and his partnership with it.

In order to convey this idea Mosley 'subverts' the disciplines of those areas of modern man's knowledge, which are preoccupied with defining the role and place of 'conscious' human beings in the process of life's—creation's—unfolding. As pointed out throughout the study, Mosley believes that all these disciplines seem to acknowledge that humans due to their consciousness are set apart from and more empowered than other creatures, yet they simultaneously tend to see man as powerless either because of his consciousness (as in case of Sartre, for example) or in spite of his consciousness (as in case of Darwin, for example). These disciplines are both the *fruit of* man's self-reflection and the *mirror for* man's self-reflection. Thus the more man reflects upon himself, the more he observes himself in these 'mirrors' and the more hopeless (and helpless) an image he see of himself, the murkier these mirrors become. In Mosley's eyes this circular process of self-reflection is becoming increasingly a vicious circle of virulent destruction and self-destruction. One could say that in *The Hesperides Tree* Mosley continues to do what he was doing throughout his *Catastrophe Practice Series*; namely to look for possible 'mutations' in these disciplines—or mirrors—and in this way depict the possibilities of their survival. As a 'freedom fighter'[1008] he hopes to liberate man from the destructive patterns of his self-observation by offering him different mirrors—different myths or meta-myths for self-definition. For help he looks to the 'heretics' in these disciplines. In this way, he hopes to contribute to man's further evolution and survival.

1. *The science of evolution: God's and man's joint-venture*

The story is about a nameless eighteen-year-old boy whom—regarding the novel as a further development of the themes in *Catastrophe Practice*—it would make sense to see as the grown-up (nameless) Child in *Catastrophe Practice*.[1009] With his parents he sets off for the west coast of Ireland, where his father, a maker of documentaries, wants to make a film about variations amongst birds, who live on an off-shore island, which has once been a refuge for hermits in the Dark Ages. The habits and physical feature of some of these birds had been changing with a rapidity that seems to go 'against the orthodox Darwinian view that genetic mutation results in adaptation only slowly.'[1010] Mosley is, yet again, relating to the heretic Goldschmidt, whose anti-Darwinist idea of 'hopeful monsters,' suggested that small changes in the environment—in this case, pollution, food, changes in the climate—can 'lead quite quickly to new varieties of organism or even conceivably eventually a new species.'[1011]

> Stress caused by a changing environment speeds up the occurrence of random mutations so that amongst [a species] there are quite naturally one or two fitted to dealing with the changing environment. And so these instead of being wiped out would flourish and proliferate. And so it might seem that organisms not only adapt to circumstances but pass on their adaptability . . .[1012]

This brings to mind Max Ackerman's experiment with his salamanders. Max overtook the role of a 'god' in partnership with his creatures in an experiment: in other words, he made a small-scale model of God's experiment. The narrator of this novel goes further by directly suggesting that God in all his reality is conceivably involved in an experiment for making and *saving* life. During his illness he has an especially acute awareness of this:

> When my fever was high I had the experience of being experimented on by a ruthless but still not necessarily malignant God—how had the idea ever arisen that God should be kind? I had once visited with my father a biology laboratory where mice were experimented upon with the aim of finding out whether characteristics of a species could be altered or enhanced; the animals seemed to be in pain and sometimes not: I had thought—if humans can do this to animals why should we, who say we are made in God's image, be surprised if God does it to us?[1013]

The 'mutations'—or 'possible mutations'—that arise and live on in this experiment in order to sustain a species, do so through God making 'things possible.'[1014] What they have to do is to be 'in a state of readiness to take advantage of what turns up'[1015]—in the form of pollution or climate change, perhaps. The readiness for 'what turns up' is a rewording for being attentive to other 'alternatives'—other 'realities':

> sea creatures struggling to get on to earth. Millions would die before one or two got through; but then would these be the start of a new species? The stars were like peepholes through which the gods looked down: but for experiment; not just amusement?[1016]

The reality of God(s) is not only arrived at through aesthetic observation, but also by way of scientific observation.[1017] As he expounded in *Journey* the acceptance of the existence of such a reality is not the consequence of its scientific verifiability, but exactly its opposite: i.e., its 'unverifiability.' The protagonist in *Hesperides Tree* sees it thus:

> In biology we were taught that living organisms should be considered like machines: . . . the machinery was programmed to replicate itself until some chance mistake in copying caused a variation; but nothing more could be said about 'chance'; this was by definition beyond the bounds of science. . . . My father suggested that this showed there was some organising activity beyond that of the mechanism of DNA . . .
>
> I said to my father 'But if it's just chance that might allow one cell to live while enormous numbers of others die—'
>
> My father said 'Yes?'
>
> 'Shouldn't we be finding out more about this chance, if it's that by which we live or die?'
>
> 'It's only science that says we can't find out anything about it.'[1018]

In 'mainstream' science chance, on the one hand, is a 'will-less' force, and on the other, all life is a 'will-less' plaything in its hands, which suggests that 'chance' has some sort of a 'will.' Sciences grudgingly realise the inconsistency of their argument; of this 'random . . . that ordered the universe,'[1019] but not being able to make any 'sense' about it—i.e., not being able to understand it within the duality of rationality/irrationality—leave it at that. This is not a recognition of and a working with the paradox, but an avoidance—a censorship—of the paradox for the sake of keeping the 'scientific argument' intact.

The protagonist does not only come to see this shortcoming of mainstream sciences as the result of his observation of the changes in the birds on the off-shore island, but, more importantly, as due to his *experience* of being human. Humans, as has been repeatedly suggested both in *Catastrophe Practice Series* and the novels of this phase, have a special place in the experiment of evolution/creation due to their consciousness, which, on one hand, sets them apart as observers and thus grants them a feeling of autonomy, and on the other, makes them see themselves as *objects* in the experiment of creation.

> Humans were in the business of creation—of themselves, of the outside world—and this was of a more exciting if risky nature than that of obedience to laws and 'truths' that had been accepted at once time as

useful. But with this sort of understanding there did nevertheless seem to exist an 'out there'—*not unalterable, but one to be worked upon, searched within*—and this could be experienced, because otherwise humans would be flailing in a vacuum, which they did not always feel themselves to be. However one could not talk about this much or one would be pinning down as a captive what one should be in relationship with as it were as a friend. There could be a *partnership, that is, between oneself and a world 'out there'*; and if the experience of this could be accepted, then in time it might come to be trusted. This might be appreciated in the form of a moral or religious understanding: it was just the attempt to *set this fast in words* that made it so often ridiculous.[1020]

2. *The disciplines of words: religion, philosophy and literature*

The other disciplines, such as philosophy and literature, whose task it is normally to articulate—or set fast in words—this creative relationship between man and the 'reality'—the life-generating force—'out there' either end up ridiculing or rejecting it, due to the nature of language: 'words were good at saying what things are *not*, not for saying what things are. A telling legend for humans was, yes, the story of the Tower of Babel.'[1021] At university the narrator learns 'what little weight philosophers and literary people gave to the chance of getting hold of any objective "meaning" as this referred to a "truth" or an "authenticity" to be *discovered* "out there." '[1022] The idea of 'discovering' empowers humans as *active*, autonomous beings able to work with this 'chance' or 'life-generating force' or God as a way of setting 'themselves or the world to rights.'[1023] Literature, as the protagonist observes in his tutorials, is mainly interested in portraying 'humans as characters, types, who are stuck in . . . what they are and have no autonomy except to be clowns, comic or tragic.'[1024]

With Canonic literature and mainstream philosophy failing to articulate man's role in the process of creation, one is left with theology and religion. Mosley admits that religion does celebrate the existence of God as the 'Will'; as the reality 'out there.' But as an *institution* it emasculates man in that it tends to see God as a fixed reality which wholly determines man and in front of which man is wholly powerless: 'the Church . . . having hijacked the whole thing, says we know what reality is. Reality is this: A, B, C, D, which is all wrong.'[1025] By fixing 'Reality' the church not only incapacitates man, but also 'God.' In fact what it does is to empower itself as the only definer of God and man. This, Mosley believes, is an inevitable consequence of organisations and institutions:

> one of the things that Christians . . . refuse to think about [is] when Jesus founded his Church upon St. Peter . . . He said: 'you are Peter and on this rock I will found my church.' And almost in the same verse he is saying: 'but Peter, you know you will—when I have been taken off—deny me.' And Peter does.
>
> . . . Jesus knew Peter was going to deny him, but he founded his Church on the disciple he knew would deny him. That is the most extraordinary thing to do. . . . That's the whole point! Jesus knew the Church is going to deny him. Why did Jesus do it? It is a *reasonable* question. But this is how the world works. Everyone has to learn for themselves. There are no straightforward answers. . . . What the real Jesus is, the church can't show. . . . People have got to recognise it for themselves. If the Church got everything right, there wouldn't be any life! Everyone would know the Church is right and that's that. The Church gets it wrong the whole time and you have to work it out for yourself.[1026]

Institutions by virtue of their being institutions—i.e., fixed structures—can only say what God isn't and not what God is. This reminds the reader of Mosley's earlier 'discovery' in the Sixties about 'organised' religion. He learned from the Church what God was *not* and went on his own journey to find out what he was. This is also what his protagonist in *Hesperides Tree* is trying to do. He finds the guides throughout his journey in the subversives: i.e., the heretics. Not only the birds on the island seem to go against orthodoxy, but also the monks, who tried to free themselves for hundreds of years from the atrocities and 'pollutions' of the world by secluding themselves on these islands. Like the birds, they too were 'mutations'—dissenters in the eyes of the religion of Roman Empire, i.e., the establishment of Christianity. These heretics 'peregrinated (this was their own word) in their cockleshell boats to wherever the wind would take them—to some edge of the known world where they might either live in peaceful communion with God or topple over as it were into His presence.'[1027] The teachings of one of these 'heretics,' John Scotus Erigena, who might have been living on this island for a while in the ninth century, conveys to the narrator the idea of the partnership between God and man in the business of creation:

> He said that it was in this life that one could if one chose have an experience of God; of God and humans going hand in hand, creating what happened hand in hand. In this world God was dependent on humans for what He and they did; to them He had handed over freedom: He remained that by which their freedom could operate, so of course they were dependent on Him too.[1028]

The monks, coming to this island, however, seemed neither to have been able to change the savage reality to which they turned their backs, nor to have produced—like the birds—a new 'species.' There were, as the narrator's mother points out, the undercurrent influences, such as their art and the seeds of their thought.[1029] These, however, did not seem to transfer society and remained largely seeds to be discovered. In the meantime what seems to have been happening since the appearance of these monks is that the idea of God has been suffering the worse blows.

> And what about those monks, hermits, who had turned their backs on worldly pollution and had hoped not to prevent it nor even to transfigure it but rather to gaze out from their rock towards another world that would be free from it, that would be pure and holy. But then it had been this hope that had seemed to fail; because pollution, even for hermits, was in the mind that they carried with them; and anyway had they not been told before they gazed out to see that whatever there might be of another world, their entry into it would be through this one.[1030]

What the monks were doing is, in a way, quite similar to what the narrator sees the people surfing the Net do; namely living in a virtual reality, which to the narrator seems to be an 'extension of an inner world of desires, hardly to represent an outside world at all.'[1031] Instead of trying to change reality by being attentive to and observant of the *operations* of a greater network in this world, these monks—like the Net-surfers—ended up being attentive to the patterns and models in their own minds only. Such an observation, as investigated in *Catastrophe Practice Series*, is only initially liberating. In Bateson's Learning II, for example, one could observe the patterns of one's observation as being fabrications of the observation faculty—i.e., consciousness—and in this way liberate himself from them. However, this level of observation could be virulently destructive, if one did not go further beyond it by being aware of the greater network, which

Bateson tried to 'rationalise' by calling it the 'oceanic.' In absence of the 'greater network' there is only madness or death: either the fabricated patterns of observation faculty are only fortified, or one has to choose the existentialist annihilation of the conscious self in order to get out of its patterns of observation. The monks, like the surfers, were hoping to break through into a different dimension or another reality, but ended up fortifying the patterns and taboos in their minds, which regulated the outside reality for them.

> [the monks] knew the world was rotten so they went there to find something new. They failed, of course, because one thing is that monks can't have babies! They don't have children. The point of that island from a scientific point of view is that the birds keep on having a new generation and the birds hope to learn how to deal with pollution.[1032]

In other words, whereas the mutations in the birds could survive in order to give rise to a new organism if not species, the monks as possible mutations of human species did not succeed in giving rise to a new human type and consequently a new reality. On this island, the protagonist—himself a hopeful monster—wants to learn how a human mutant could avoid the fate of the monks; in other words, how could he become a cross between the monks and the birds. The image of him and his pregnant girl-friend flying off in an aeroplane in the end is a good depiction of this. As a bird he could have the instinct to change and adapt to the reality outside and as a conscious human—or a 'monk'—he could have the consciousness, or the *conscience*, to see the atrocious reality outside and try to change it. In Quantum physics he finds an almost mystical imagery—complementary to that of John Scotus Erigena—for man's freedom of choice. The physics professor, whom the narrator's father interviews for a documentary, uses the two-slit experiment in order to explain how one can effect reality by way of choosing what to observe in an experimental condition:

> Light is composed neither of particles nor of waves but of both, or of one or the other according to the nature of experiment. . . .
> To me, there is only one *rational* explanation for the ramifications that follow from the two-slit experiment. The wave-state is a superimposition, an amalgam, of photons and shadow photons from actual

parallel universes. When the wave-state collapses as a result of a particular observation or experiment, then both the observer and what he observes branch into one particular universe rather than another, though evidence for the others exists through the existence of the wave-length.[1033]

What turns this scientific conjecture into a mystical imagery is the idea that through a certain mode of observation man enters another 'reality' which in turn influences the state of that what he observes. So, the collapse of the wave-function is not an actualisation of different available potentialities, since

> Potentialities are hypotheses. Hypotheses cannot have a physical effect. . . . I don't see any explanation for the interference phenomena, or for the collapse of the wave function, unless it is accepted that they are affected by unseen presences.[1034]

For the protagonist the scientific idea of 'real presences' through whose observation one can enter a different reality, and from which one can effect one's own reality is not something that could be *rationally* 'fixed' and understood—'As the great Niels Bohr said, anyone who thinks he has understood quantum physics hasn't understood quantum physics'[1035]—but something that could only be experienced and accepted.

The attentiveness to this network, as was mentioned in *Journey*, could only effect and change reality, if the conscious individual did not try to manipulate and fix it. An attentive individual knows that he has the power to influence reality, but what this power exactly is or what outcome it exactly has is beyond the reaches of his knowledge.

> My father said 'there's a scientific theory now that this is in fact how things work. Individuals are like grains of sand in a pile. The movement, or addition, of just one grain—one grain being dropped on a hitherto stable pile—can cause an avalanche. You can't tell just what grain will cause the avalanche or when; nor just how events will fall out and resettle; there are too many millions of grains in the pile in their own critical state or equilibrium. But there it is—it's all worked out on computers—one grain dropped here or there can alter the structure, the nature, of a whole system. This seems to be the big scientific theory at the end of the twentieth century—The individual

has power: though he doesn't know what power, nor what the effect will be.'[1036]

This is actually the crux of the individual's ability to meet the right choice: if he exactly knew what to do, he would be fixing the 'reality out there' and thus manipulate it according to his knowledge. In this way he would automatically obliterate all other 'presences' and states. This would be the end of the 'dance' between man and God—or the greater reality 'out there.' Schrödinger's cat is another scientific image for this sort of observation: it can only be both dead and alive as long as one doesn't look directly.

For the protagonist Love corresponds to the idea of this paradoxical observation, where one both knows and knows not that one is looking.

> It might be possible to go hand in hand—if one were attentive enough, respectful enough—with whatever just beyond consciousness might be 'there': somewhat like being with a loved one whom one might long to possess, but if one simply grabbed or willed this love would disappear; love has to have its own autonomy.[1037]

Love is thus an attentiveness—a 'linking up' with the greater reality—through which the individual can free himself from the destructive, limiting patterns of his reality and meet the choice necessary for influencing and changing his reality.

> Humans of course should have to select, but they should do it with some sort of attentiveness to nature.[1038]

> We humans had to go—this was our liberation or curse—we had to go over deserts and plains, in cockleshell boats over rough seas; we had to set things to rights; we had to die in order that things could come alive.[1039]

Having accomplished the right attitude—i.e., love—The right reality (or alternative; or possible mutation) would be chosen by 'coincidence'—or through the operation of the inexplicable greater whole. In religious language one would express this as 'men have to take care of the means; the ends will take care of themselves.' In scientific imagery one could see this process 'like those bits of machinery that fall together in a junk yard and just happen to form a jumbo jet.'[1040]

3. Genesis: retelling the creation

Hesperides Tree could also be seen as a subversive re-telling of the story of creation. On their Garden on the off-shore island, the narrator and the girl can mutate into human-birds—both conscious and instinctive beings. Unlike Adam and Eve they are not helpless playthings in the hands of temptations and taboos—as Massie puts it, 'Mosley's characters never seem to be living pre-determined lives.'[1041] Ruminating on and thus being conscious of *partaking* in the experiment of creation, they can free themselves from the patterns of temptations and taboos by observing these from a higher point of view—from the locale of their connection with the reality 'out there'—with God. Their meeting depicts the idea of love being an awareness of the greater network of realities, which influence man's reality.

> This was a fancy that it had seemed to me one might take note of like a beautiful stranger passed in the street: but what would it be to possess it, experience it, live with it as if it were normality? One would not presume to dictate to it; much of the time one might not quite even know what was going on; often it would be difficult to maintain belief in something so presumptuous.[1042]

Mosley subverts the biblical imagery in order to show this. The protagonist sees himself, for example, as 'a snake shedding its skin to re-enter that old and polluted garden.'[1043] The girl, Julie, whom the narrator had met a year ago, but could not—for the sake of love; for the sake of the Experiment—make a grab at, is like a naked Eve coming upon Adam.[1044] The very fact of seeing themselves in the context of art and myths—in the context of metaphors; of '*as ifs* . . .' and '*likes* . . .'—makes them a different sort of Adam and Eve. They are a couple which in its self-reflexivity within a greater network can both attach and detach itself from itself and its environment and thus be free. Their dialogue which closes the novel is a good example for this.

> 'How did life begin? The chances against it were billions and billions to one.'
> 'Yes.'
> 'And how does life carry on? It's death that's likely.'
> 'Yes.'

'And we'll have survived because if we hadn't we couldn't have written and illustrated it.'

. . . 'So we can stop talking.'

'Yes. Here. Stop talking.'[1045]

Unlike Adam and Eve, they are a knowing couple—one which has eaten of the Tree of Good and Evil a second time—who are now in the business of helping to evolve a 'new human type.'

> I imagined Julie and myself flying to Jerusalem, on our business of being two of the people for the sake of whom the world might be saved. But if one thought like this the plane might crash.[1046]

Having gone around the world and eaten of the Tree of Knowledge of Good and Evil a second time, they have now in the Kleistian manner entered the garden from the back.[1047] This time they are hoping to 'find that other tree, what was it, the one that no one had paid much attention to because it had not been forbidden.'[1048] The tree

> was never forbidden; only hidden and difficult to find . . .
>
> . . . the Tree of Life . . . according to the myth had been in the Garden of Eden but . . . had remained unnoticed . . . The tree should be underground like roots, so that each person had to search for it for themselves.[1049]

Contrary to Good and Evil, which can be obtained by either breaking or obeying collective rules, regulations and Commandments, the fruits of the Tree of Life can be plucked only beyond dichotomies of rationality/irrationality or intellect/sentiment. In other words, in a 'work of art,' which is realised in a partnership between God and the individuals

> Was [this partnership] equivalent to Julie's idea of being able to make life, living, a form of art—trying out this, trying out that, and then when you get it knowing what is right; but even from the beginning perhaps having an instinct for what to try. And this sort of thing with regard not only to oneself, one's own life, but to the events and experiences of those with whom one is in contact; even (and perhaps as importantly) to people one is in no discernible contact with at all. . . .

> You watch and listen; and then perhaps through your attentiveness there may occur what it is beyond your competence to occasion or even imagine.[1050]

Having plucked the fruit of the Tree of Life, the impregnated mutants, the Hopeful Monsters, fly out of their garden to scatter their seed—of a new type of humanity—through the world, in the hope of impregnating the reader with new realities.

IV. *Inventing God*

> 'If God did not exist it would be necessary to invent him'
> Voltaire

> **Invent/** v.t . . . 1. Find out, discover, esp. by search or endeavour. Now *rare* or *obs*.
> The New Shorter Oxford English Dictionary'[1051]

Inventing God could be seen as the last novel in Mosley's present phase of writing. He himself believes that it is the 'culmination'[1052] to this phase of his writing and in this way 'sums up'[1053] the novels discussed in Chapter IV of this study.

Having finished *The Hesperides Tree* Mosley started writing another novel, which he thought would take 'ages to do,'[1054] but in fact was finished in less than nine months after the publication of *The Hesperides Tree*.

> if I could go on to show more about what one has learnt—what has my boy in *Hesperides Tree* learnt? How do we live? How do the boy and the girl live? What do they do? They can't just always be in the aeroplane. They have to come down to earth and look after their baby. And then one has to compromise—well, not compromise; deal with the world.[1055]

This is reminiscent of what Max Ackerman and Eleanor Anders in *Hopeful Monsters* did. In that novel the Kleistian journey of the preceding protagonists, Bert, Jason, Lilia and Judith, was completed: the focus of the story was how 'mutants'—having entered the Garden a second time from the back—could go out and live in the real world and thus help the liberation and survival of mankind. *Inventing God*, in the same vein as *Hopeful*

Monsters, is the story of the completion of a journey—the journey of the protagonists in this phase of Mosley's writing. Like Bert, Jason, Lilia and Judith these protagonists too entered the Garden a second time from the back in order to fulfil what being human demands from them.

> We humans had to go—this was our liberation or curse—we had to go over deserts and plains, in cockleshell boats over rough seas; we had to set things to rights; we had to die in order that things could come alive.[1056]

However, as discussed earlier, what distinguishes these travellers from those in *The Catastrophe Practice Series* is their acute awareness of God: that greater 'other' outside of them, which becomes part of them and of which they become part of through their observation of it. They have thus attained a higher awareness and are, in this sense, on a more 'advanced' level in their journey than the characters in *The Catastrophe Practice Series*.

1. God, science and man's freedom

Inventing God is a continuation of the idea behind the present phase of Mosley's writing: i.e., the idea of seeing man's freedom in light of the relation between science and spirituality. Here, as in *The Hesperides* Tree, Mosley uses the latest scientific findings in order to render their helplessness in face of explaining what makes man *different* from other creatures? In other words, Mosley reveals the inability of science to *talk* about the 'seat' of man's freedom—his observational faculty—convincingly. As one of the characters, the biologist Prof. Andros, puts it

> While the mapping of the human genome is giving us the chance of much power to treat and eliminate abnormality and disease, the prospect of planning to alter or enhance human nature remains something of a fantasy. Scientists cannot tell the result of their experiments until they have been tested; and phenomena in the brain and in the outside world are so intricately interconnected that possible effects and side-effects are almost infinite, and cannot be known in advance. So it seems that what might be called enhancement of human nature will continue to remain in the realm of chance and natural selection. However it can be claimed that what scientists call 'chance' might be subject to enquiry outside the realm of science.[1057]

As discussed in chapter IV of this study, for Mosley that inexplicable life-generating force outside the realms of causality and determinism is God. It is that 'other' outside us the observation of which—or, in the vocabulary of (Sufi) mysticism, 'making love' to which—makes the idea of aesthetics and ethics possible. And it is within these domains that we sense our freedom of choice.[1058] It would hence make sense to say that it is that 'other' which guarantees our freedom.[1059] Considering the taboo of speaking about the reality of God in our enlightened time, this novel comes across as an almost 'shameless' work of art.

The protagonists' 'religiousness' or their awareness of God explains the difference between the form of *Hopeful Monsters* and that of *Inventing God*. Both novels, as mentioned earlier, mark the culmination to a phase of Mosley writing. *Hopeful Monsters* only focused on two characters because the series, which *Monsters* was the culmination to, was concerned with showing the process of the development of Bateson's three levels of Learning. In this sense, Max and Eleanor superseded the other characters in the series and thus personified the third and highest level of Batesonian Learning (and the beginning of a knowledge beyond this level of Learning).

In contrast to *Hopeful Monsters*, *Inventing God* does not have a 'hero' and a 'heroine.' It focuses equally on the story of all the characters in the present phase of Mosley's writing. There is no hierarchy of awareness anymore: all characters have reached the highest level of awareness and have now the vocation to 'set things to rights.' The form of the novel strongly reminds the reader of *Journey into the Dark*, in which Mosley tried to depict what he called 'some force of *semi-autonomous interconnectedness*.'[1060] Similar to *Journey*, *Inventing God* consists of stories about a certain group of people, who by a series of 'natural' and 'miraculous' coincidences meet each other and help out one another to make the right choice. The novel shows the greater hidden network, which keeps the protagonists together and *apart* simultaneously (like gravity) and which can operate in the lives of the protagonists through their awareness of it.

Inventing God is a much more successful rendering of this 'semi-autonomous interconnectedness' than *Journey*. The flow of the story is not interrupted by an alternation between essays and pieces of fiction. Furthermore, the relatedness of the protagonists is more convincing than that of the characters in *Journey*. Although the novel is very crowded, the reader can keep track of the characters and their relationships to each other. Mosley has simply added new characters to a hard core of old characters from the previous novels of this phase of his writing. The reader's familiarity with the old characters helps him place the new ones and in this way identify the greater network which these characters make up. There are Julie and the Boy (now called Ben) with his parents Melissa and Harry from *The Hesperides Tree*. Harry was also the name of the journalist in *Children*, who had a son called Ben with his wife Melissa. Joshua and Hafiz, Lisa and her uncle, Nathan, featured in *Journey*; the angelic, seventeen-year old Lisa (who one day appears in Ben and Julie's life and helps them with the birth of their child[1061]) is also referred to as Gaby; Gaby was the name of the fey-like twelve-year old 'gang leader' in *Children* written five years ago. The new characters in turn are introduced through their relationship to the old characters and to each other: Laura is the best friend of Melissa, Prof. Andros is an old friend and admirer of Laura; Maisie, Laura's niece, is the girlfriend of Hafiz, who in turn is the best friend of Joshua. Joshua and Hafiz are both students of Billy Kahn in Beirut, who has an affair with Leila, who in turn is also in love with the policeman Leon and so on and so forth. In this way, whenever these characters 'bump' into each other, they weave yet another thread in the complex tapestry of the network of relationships. Their connectedness and coincidental meetings are therefore more convincing than those in *Journey*.

This relatedness is also enforced by the plot. Whereas *Journey* did not have a strong plot, *Inventing God*, like *Hopeful Monsters* or *Children* has an intriguing plot, which keeps the network of the protagonists together. Like *Children* the story unfolds in form of a detective or a espionage story. Maurice Rotblatt, the Guru figure of the story, has disappeared and all the characters seem to be searching for him either directly or indirectly as the result of 'bumping' into somebody who is looking for Maurice. Their search for him, brings forth with it the coincidental meetings (Hafiz and Maisie's meeting is especially a good example for this[1062]) that weave a network of relationships.

2. Modern saints: re-inventing the prophet and his disciples

In the same vein as Max Ackerman and Eleanor Anders (and in the spirit of a detective story) these protagonists are depicted as agents in hostile territory—or as saints with the vocation of saving humans; humans who in their ignorance can become dangerous for their saviours. Having re-written the story of Genesis in *The Hesperides Tree*, Mosley is now re-inventing (or re-discovering) the story of God's messengers sent to liberate humans from their old deadly shackles—their destructive patterns of thought.

There is the Guru scientist, Maurice Rotblatt. Like Ben and Julie, who made an unconventional *Ur*-Couple, Rotblatt makes an unconventional 'prophet': he is a mixture of a trickster and a scientist; a bit of a womaniser and a bit of a drinker. However, like all of Mosley's protagonists, he seems to be behaving in this way as part of an experiment, through which he hopes to break the old patterns of thought: those patterns which had been liberating once, but are now proving to be deadly. At a conference in war-ridden Beirut he (the parallels with Moses' fury at the gathering of magicians, Jesus' behaviour towards the money-lenders, or Mohammed's conduct at the congregation of idol-worshippers in Kaaba are obvious) insults Jew, Christians and Moslems equally[1063] in order to bring across that 'People should no longer see themselves as Jews or Moslems, or Christians, because to see oneself like that is not properly to have been born.'[1064] Instead of labelling oneself in relation to others, man should see himself 'in relation to God.'[1065] this viewpoint being that which all of Mosley's characters—his hopeful monsters—in this phase of his writing have been trying to adopt: that is, seeing oneself in partnership with the Creator.[1066] In this novel, too, Mosley is interested in showing that this kind of attitude is actually a hidden undercurrent in all established (and by now destructive) organised religions. Therefore, as he saw hope for humanity in the teachings of the monks such as John Scotus Erigena (cf. *The Hesperides Tree*), here he sees hope in the non-conformist beliefs of the Muslim sect, the Alevis, or in the way of life of the most ancient Christians, the Armenians.

Maurice even adopts the methods of a trickster and considers forging a document 'supposedly from the time of King Zedekiah, that might alter things.'[1067] In it he hopes to tell people to grow up and start being 'responsible for everything.'[1068] A biblical document does in fact turn up in Jerusalem, which is kept under wraps since it could both be a forgery—as governmental bodies claim—and *claimed* to be a forgery, as it gives backing 'to views at present inimical to the ruling forces in [Israel]' and other countries.'[1069] This statement of uncertainty—or this 'either/or'—reflects the central idea in Mosley's novels since *The Catastrophe Practice Series*: the idea that hope for a 'higher human type' at the end of the twentieth century can only operate on a knife-edge; where all possibilities are open: 'The experience is that in spite of, or *because of*, wild uncertainty, everything is all right.'[1070]

Mosley is concerned with the uncertainty in our Nietzschean 'Hundred-act play,' however he makes it clear that catastrophes and disasters have always been an integral part of human history. God's messengers had always been sent to teach humans 'how to learn through failure; even disaster.'[1071] The book of Jonah is a leitmotif in this novel for illustrating this idea. No matter how hard Jonah tried to hide from God and avoid the responsibility of preaching to the people of Nineveh, he did not succeed. He finally had to yield to God's will and could successfully convert the people of Nineveh.[1072] Mosley modern prophet and his disciples too have to fulfil the same task as biblical prophets.

For this purpose they have to revisit the same sites as their predecessors: 'Oh Jerusalem. Nineveh. What is the difference.'[1073] As *Journey*, this novel too takes place in the Middle East, where from ancient times humanity seems to have so obviously been on the edge of Catastrophe. The Arab-Israeli conflict and the Civil war in Lebanon offer a good example for the seemingly eternal trap that humanity has brought itself into by way of sticking to labels and destructive patterns of mind. It is here where the protagonists meet and carry out the teachings of Maurice, who by now, in the manner of prophets, has disappeared. What now matters is his message 'that everything is all right.'[1074] The birth of Ben and Julie's baby at the foot of Mount Ararat is yet another re-writing of the Bible and symbolises the hope for the birth of a new human species, which can see itself in 'relation to God' and thus grow out of the destructive rivalries that had befallen its ancestors.

One might say that the optimistic view of Maurice/Mosley proves itself as rather 'naive' considering the catastrophe of September 11th. The crash happened just a few days after the completion of the typescript.[1075] For Mosley, however, the crash was exactly in the spirit of the novel's message—it was in a way in the spirit of the message of all of his novels since *The Catastrophe Practice Series*. He had often expressed this message through an image out of Thomas Mann's *Magic Mountain*: the image of the beautiful couple walking hand in hand on a beach while hags were dismembering a child in a temple. Appropriating Mann, Mosley believes that the state of Grace could only be achieved if man observed himself as the beautiful couple, the hags and the child simultaneously.[1076] At the end of this novel the 'holy' family is on holiday at the red sea and learns about the crash via an almost coded telephone call from a friend in England. Once again, Thomas Mann's metaphor would apply here very well: the setting is that of a beautiful Byzantine or a medieval painting; its backdrop is the awful news from America. For the protagonists the awareness of this 'oxymoron' is something that 'might change the way people see things.'

The novel ends with a re-cognisance scene as if out of a 'Miracle Play': Lisa, who is travelling with Ben's family and the new born baby, meets Hafiz, who had once saved her life. The party witnesses their embrace and reunion with solemn joy.[1077] There is also a feeling of a 'Nietzschean' *déjà-vu*: 'the great hundred-act play reserved for the next two centuries in Europe; the most terrible, the most questionable, the most hopeful of all plays.'[1078] The crash seems to have marked the end of Part I—the twentieth century—and the opening of Part II of this drama. The hope that this part—the twenty-first century—carries in its awful bosom is the dawn of the knowledge about the real and secret dramas in human life—the dramas that have always been going on.

> Not just the war between the Jews and the Arabs, because that has never been secret: nor the war between capitalists and anti-capitalists, because that will go on for ever. But the drama about evil not being localised but pervasive and people being trapped in their minds. . . . The hope being that there can be a learning, a healing, going to and fro between the inside and the outside worlds; *the terror is that this is an illusion.*[1079]

This knowledge would enable all humans to stop seeing themselves as victims of outer and inner forces—be it in form of neurosis, natural disasters or warring parties—against which they could only bang their heads or give up in resignation. In this sense, for the protagonists, the positive side of this catastrophe is that it could bring people—like the people of Nineveh—to start to observe themselves in relation to a force— a network—much greater than themselves and much greater than good and evil, within which everything has its proper place and, consequently, within which everything will be all right.

Conclusion

> Wissenschaft, Kunst und Philosophie wachsen jetzt so sehr in mir zusammen, dass ich jedenfalls einmal Centauren gebären werde.[1080]

Mosley is now bringing together all of the view-points, which he had been examining in his long writing career as a means for overcoming the paradox of freedom: he has now come to the point of seeing that all liberation is ultimately possible on a spiritual level. Whereas in his former experimental novels Mosley spoke of man's choice making being possible through the individual's self-reflection within a network of infinite possibilities, now he sees man's freedom being dependent on his self-reflection within a network of realities, which are all connected in an Ultimate Reality. Hence, man could free himself by being aware of the presence of a greater Whole—of God—who is part of man and of whom man is part of. Leaning on John Scotus Erigena, Mosley tries to show that the paradox of freedom could be dissolved if man were conscious of being in a partnership with God in the business of creation. In this phase of his writing he is particularly interested in depicting this idea in the images of the findings of new sciences; especially those that are concerned with defining reality through quantum theory.

That is not to say that Mosley wants to *prove* the reality of God through science. He is interested in 'unorthodox' new sciences for exactly the opposite reason: that is, their awareness of a rationally unprovable reality—a so-called 'dark force'—which has to be taken into account for these findings to make sense and to operate. Like Nietzsche, who intensely 'worried over the burgeoning culture of science,'[1081] Mosley too seeks 'to develop an aesthetically imbued philosophical interpretation of reality that would acknowledge the value and power of scientific knowledge, but not surrender to its domination of culture.'[1082] In this way, he tries to fulfil the task of a truly religious writer. To put it in the words of the Catholic philosopher Jacques Maritain, Mosley tries to

> create human life itself; to mould, scrutinise and govern humanity . . . only a Christian, nay a mystic, because he has some idea of what there is in man, can be a complete novelist.[1083]

Maritain's words are an eloquent rewording of Mosley central thesis; namely that man's freedom lies in his *knowledge* of his being God's partner and equal in the business of creation. A true aesthetic vision is the effort to render this.

In this sense, Mosley sees his novels—and beseeches other writers to do the same for the sake of humanity; for the sake of life—as the continuation of the Christian myth:

> The Christian myth ends, as so many stories do, just at the point when something more interesting than usual might have been said—but then

it is just this, of course, that is largely unsayable. The point had been reached at which it might reasonably have been asked—But what happens then?—once there had been got over, that is, scares and excitements about the end of the world and second comings. But indeed, after these, what does happen then? This was reasonably unsayable in that no one knows the future; but could not more have been said about the style and possibilities of choice? Myths suggest to people what they have been and what they are; from such patterns are pointers to what they might make of the future. Christians were indeed given hints about not what would be chosen but how to choose—and about what might be expected to be the effects of this or that style of choice. Quite specifically they were told to observe, to listen, to be attentive to whatever was going on, and by this they would be led into all truth.[1084]

Christians and non-Christians, he believes, find this outlook difficult to accept and are still clinging to the Greek and Old Testament myths of helpless humans in the hands of irrationally playful gods, or rationally just ones. For the survival of the human race, and sustenance of life, Mosley finds it to be the duty of the true artist—the novelist—to provide the reader with new myths and parables; myths which subvert the old ones and in this way liberate man from the destructive patterns of his old myths and empower him by reminding him of his partnership with God in the business of creation.

* * *

It was the twentieth century, which was foreseen by Nietzsche as Part I of the greatest of all human-dramas. In a way, the four phases of Mosley's writing were the four acts in which the idea of this Nietzschean drama was rendered. The second part of this drama would take place in the present century—the century the beginning of which in Mosley's eyes has been marked by Sept. 11th: 'I came to the end only just before the mayhem in America—and it struck me that this has been the fitting symbolic end to the second half of the 20th century.'[1085] In the spirit of a Shakespearean play one could thus expect a fifth phase in Mosley's writing career.

And I feel encouraged to imagine it might *just* be possible that there might be an Act V![1086]

NOTES

[1] Massie (1990b), Bradbury (1981), Steiner (1969).
[2] Cunningham (1986), Waugh (1971), Naughton (1979).
[3] Steiner (1969).
[4] Scholes (1971).
[5] Lister (1971).
[6] Bradbury (1981).
[7] Stanford (2001).
[8] Waugh (1971).
[9] Winegarden (1968).
[10] Marin (1991). Marin characterises the reader of Mosley's works as follows: 'You would have to be a very serious reader even to know of his fiction: his previous ones [in the '60s and '70s] were considered difficult, intellectual and even un-English.'
[11] Marin (1991). In this interview Mosley says: 'the English literary tradition . . . was given over to character, the oddity, the quirkiness of people. It all seemed completely stupid to me, this emphasis on character, as though everyone were trapped by character, as though we were nothing else.'
[12] The MLA lists only ten articles on Mosley, out of which nine have been published between 1981 and 1982 in the American *Review of Contemporary Fiction*. This journal was founded by the founder of the Dalkey Archive Press, which also publishes the novels of Nicholas Mosley in the United States.
[13] Mosley (1996), 261.
[14] Mosley (1996), 294.
[15] Shah (1968), 197-99.
[16] Nietzsche (1998), 70: 161.
[17] O'Brien, (1982a), 76-77.
[18] Mosley, (CP), 83.
[19] Mosley (CP), 83.
[20] Wilson (1971); my emphasis. In this interview Mosley tells Wilson the manner in which things happen to him in real life, after he has written about them in his novels.
[21] This will be shown in greater detail in Chapter II of this thesis.
[22] Cf. Brook (1997), Adonis and Pollard (1997), and Marshall et al (1997).
[23] Mosley (1992a), p. 55.

[24] Cf. Sampson (1992) and Hennessy (1986).
Also cf. Hall and Jacques (1983) and Christopher Lasch (1995).
[25] Ringen (1997b). For a study of the class-myth in modern Britain cf. Bauer (1978) and Stein Ringen (1997a).
[26] Mosley's mother Cynthia (1898-1933) was Lord Curzon's daughter, cf. Mosley (1992a), 12.
[27] Interview, 16.06.1997. Also cf. Mosley (1992a), 93.
[28] Mosley (1996), 21.
[29] 'Upper-class London "society" at this time consisted of about six-hundred people (Tom [Oswald Mosley] used to say) who all knew each other and knew much of what was going on between each other but who kept this secret from the outside world: the *rules of the game* were like those which require *honour amongst gangsters*, that one should not talk'; my emphasis (Mosley, 1992a, 93).
[30] Mosley (1994); my emphasis.
[31] Mosley (1992a), 34-44.
[32] Mosley (1992a), 97.
[33] Interview, 21.11.1997.
[34] Mosley (1996), 73.
[35] Mosley (1992a), 131.
[36] Mosley (1976), 87.
[37] Mosley (1992a), 446.
[38] Mosley (1992a), 452.
[39] Mosley (1992a), 450.
[40] Mosley (1992a), 445.
[41] 'I would hope [for my children] for somewhere more steady than the tightrope between rebelliousness and charm.' (Mosley, 1992a, 452).
[42] Mosley (1976), 93.
[43] Mosley (1976), 93.
[44] 'This again was typical of the best of Eton—both to uphold tradition and to laugh at it; to have the confidence to stand back from, while feeling part of , the society in which one found oneself. This was an achievement, probably, of no other public school.' (Mosley, 1976, 92).
[45] This is analogous to Mosley's criticism of the existentialist idea of absolute freedom being possible in a world empty of meaning and values (interview, 16.06.1997 and O'Brien, 1982a, 65). This will be discussed in detail in chapter II.
[46] Mosley (1992a), 452.
[47] Mosley (1992a), 452.
[48] Mosley (1992a), 480.
[49] In December 1941 Oswald Mosley was transferred from Brixton to Holloway. This was arranged by Diana's brother Tom Mitford: '[Tom] had told Diana that he was having dinner that night in Downing Street with their cousin-by-marriage

Winston Churchill.... That night Tom Mitford managed to get Churchill into a corner: this ... resulted in what had previously been called "an administrative impossibility" being put into effect almost immediately.... My father could now make jokes about being the patriarch of a women's prison ...' (Mosley, 1992a, 468).

[50] Mosley (1992a), 480-91.
[51] Mosley (1992a), 484-91.
[52] Mosley (1992a), 483.
[53] Cf. chapters II, III and IV of this thesis.
[54] Interview, 12.12.2000.
[55] Mosley (1992a), 487.
[56] Mosley (1992a), 484.
[57] Mosley (1992a), 489.
[58] Mosley (1992a), 486.
[59] Letter, 18.05.1998.
[60] Letter, 18.05.1998.
[61] Letter, 18.05.1998.
[62] Mosley (1992b).
[63] Mosley (1992b).
[64] Mosley (1992b).
[65] Forster, it seems, had a great effect on him because he showed Mosley that the difference between 'good' and 'evil' people is not their being *morally* good or evil, but rather the way they view life '[Forster's] idea [is that] there [are] two sorts of people: ... the philistines and ... the sensitive people.... The philistines [are] no good (as in *Howard's End* or *The Longest Journey*), since they can only see life in a stereotype form. The other people who are not philistines are [the ones] who are open-minded. I think that had an enormous effect on me. That's what I ... grew up to think.' (interview, 21.11.1997)
[66] Interview, 21.11.1997.
[67] The closeness of aesthetics and morality is very important for Mosley's later writings, especially in his experimental period. .' .. the exercise of one's imaginative faculty becomes a moral imperative: the writing of a serious novel becomes an aid-to-life.' (O'Brien, 1982a, 67).
[68] Nicholas Mosley (1996), 79.
[69] Mosley (1996), 79.
[70] O'Brien (1982a), 63.
[71] [*The Sound and the Fury*] had opened my eyes to what truth-to-life in a novel might be!' (Mosley, 1996, 79).
[72] O'Brien (1982a), 63.
[73] Interview, 21.11.1997.
[74] Interview, 21.11.1997.
[75] Mosley (1992a), 540.

[76] Magee (1997), 43. Here Magee points out how the very tool—i.e., science—which the logical positivists used to refute the metaphysical worldview, refuted their own philosophy: .' . . . relativity and quantum physics revealed to us that our immediate physical surroundings are bizarre beyond anything imaginable by human beings.'
[77] Naughton (1979).
[78] Marin (1991).
[79] Cf. Mosley (1976).
[80] Mosley (1976), 15.
[81] He, in light of Virginia Woolf's letters, sees her both as a perpetuator and a victim of this mechanism. Cf. Mosley (1978).
[82] Bryan Magee (1997). The book was recommended by Mosley to the present author.
[83] Magee (1997), 34-35.
[84] Magee (1997), 37-38.
[85] Magee (1997), 35.
[86] Magee (1997), 35. While studying PPE at Oxford, Mosley expressed his interest for Hegel to his tutor. The latter informed Mosley that one did not talk about Hegel anymore at Oxford, as he was out of fashion (Interview, 22.02.1998).
[87] Cf. Magee (1997), 39.
[88] Magee (1997), 40.
[89] Magee (1997), 40. Mosley himself remembers that as a philosophy student at Oxford one mainly 'did' Descartes and the 'regular English philosophers': Hume, Locke and Berkeley (cf. interview, 22.02.1998).
[90] Magee (1997), 40.
[91] Magee (1997), 60.
[92] Magee (1997), 61.
[93] Magee (1997), 65.
[94] To get an image of this era compare Sinfield (1983) and (1989). Also cf. Ford (1992) and Lessing (1997).
[95] Lessing (1997), 89-90.
[96] Lessing (1997), 280; my emphasis.
[97] Lessing (1997), 286.
[98] Cf. Connor (1996), 44-82 and Waugh (1995).
[99] Cf. Ratcliffe (1968), 8-18, and Bradbury (1994), 264-34.
[100] Anthony Powell (1956). In this article Powell sees Mosley and Hugo Charteris as representatives of 'New Romanticism,' which stands against the 'New Anti-Romanticism' represented by Amis and his fellow-novelists. However, it must be said that Mosley did not belong to a 'movement' as such.
[101] Lodge (1992), viii-ix. Lodge says that these movements were two distinct but overlapping categories. Whereas the former was a school of poetry, to which Amis and other academic writers belonged, the latter was a journalistic term, first

used in a leading article in the *Spectator* to characterise the works of a number of emerging authors in the Fifties, who expressed avid discontent with life in contemporary Britain.
For a picture of the realistic, social and anti-modernist literary mood in Britain in the Fifties see:
Karl (1972), Gindin (1962), Rabinowitz (1967) and Bergonzi (1970).

[102] Lessing (1997), 207-08.
[103] Lessing (1997), 204.
[104] Lessing (1997),204.
[105] Lessing (1997), 207.
[106] ' Jimmy Porter, with whom so many young men identified, I thought was infantile and as self-pitying as the youths who killed themselves because of *Werther.*' (Lessing, 1997, 207).
[107] Lessing (1997), 207.
[108] Bradbury (1994), 316.
[109] Cf. Spender (1958).
[110] Salwak (1978), x.
[111] Cited in Salwak (1992), 26. The 'emotional hoo-ha' is very apparent in Mosley's novels of the Fifties.
[112] Bradbury (1994), 315.
[113] Bradbury (1994), 315.
[114] Amis (1959), 161.
[115] Amis (1961), 93-96.
[116] .' . . so strong was the general air of collapse that, when the task of the novel resumed in post-war conditions, it resembled the task of beginning all over again.' (Bradbury, 1994, 221).
[117] Cf. Cooper (1959). Tom Maschler's edition of a collection of essays by various writers (1957), gives a good picture of the literary 'rebellion' of the Fifties against the pre-war modernist era.
[118] Compare Bradbury (1994), 264-393. Also cf. Rabinovitz (1967) and Mosley (1996), 82.
[119] Bradbury (1994), 333.
[120] In her autobiography Doris Lessing criticises the media's invention of 'Angry Young Men' as unimaginative and simplistic and gives an account of how she herself became an 'angry young man' for the public by the media. (cf. Lessing, 1997, 207-08 and 247).
[121] Powell (1956).
[122] The mystery of freedom becomes especially central in the present phase of Mosley's writing. Cf. chapter IV of this thesis.
[123] Mosley (1996), 12-13, 82.
[124] Peter Green, for example, praised Mosley's *Rainbearers* as a successful fusion between Virginia Woolf and Ernest Hemingway in Green (1955) and Anne

Duchene found Mosley's *Corruption* 'Eliotic,' (Duchene ,1957).

[125] Green foresaw how the *New Realists* will hate Mosley's *Rainbearers*, cf. Green (1955) and Cranston found that Mosley had nothing 'chic' about his work and that the virtues of his novels were the 'traditional' virtues. The review goes on to say that 'his writing has at the same time a delicacy, which many people now despise.' (Cranston , 1958).

[126] Lewis (1981).

[127] Mosley opened the novel (SD) with these lines from Eliot:
> And through the spaces of the dark
> Midnight shakes the memory
> As a madman shakes a dead geranium.

[128] Powell (1956) could not see anything new about this 'New-Romanticism.' He feels it is as much like the old Romanticism, as the 'New Anti-Romanticism' of Amis is like the old one.

[129] Mosley (SD), 296.

[130] Anon. (1951a), for example, finds the novel is 'an alive and intelligent portrayal' of a warrior turning back finding a mad world. 'Anything,' it continues, 'is better than hanging onto the fallacy that all is for the best in the best of all possible worlds—youth knows better.'
Betjeman found the novel in spite of its 'artificial plot' quite convincing as the young generation of the time neither believed in this nor the next world. Betjeman (1951).

[131] Murdoch (1989), 60.

[132] Murdoch (1997b), 224-25 and (1997a), 108-15.
Also compare Murdoch (1989).

[133] Murdoch (1989).

[134] Mosley (1951),131; my emphasis

[135] Mosley (SD), 246.

[136] Mosley (SD), 249.

[137] Cf. Murdoch's (1989).

[138] Raymond (1951).

[139] Green (1955).

[140] Powell (1956).

[141] Mosley (1996), 20 and 42-58

[142] Mosley (1996), 44-45.

[143] Mosley (1996), 44-45.

[144] Mosley (1996), 47.

[145] Mosley (RB), 304.

[146] Mosley (RB), 304.

[147] Mosley (RB), 304.

[148] Anon. (1955).

[149] Green (1957).

[150] Anon. (1957b).
[151] Sullivan (1958).
[152] Mosley (CO), 270. It is also important to notice that the image of the child becomes a recurring image for hope in his succeeding novels.
[153] Mosley (CO), 270.
[154] Mosley (1996), 76.
[155] Mosley (1996), 81.
[156] Mosley (1996), 81-82.
[157] Mosley (1996), 81-82.
[158] Mosley (1996), 230.
[159] 'For a long time I had been obsessed with the idea (or the way of putting the idea) that to have a **good** life [in all senses] was "impossible."' (O'Brien, 1982a, 59). The words in the brackets are not in the original interview with O'Brien, but were added here in accordance with Mosley's revisions during an interview with the present author, Interview, 15.07.1997; my emphasis.
[160] O'Brien (1982a), 76-77.
[161] O'Brien (1982a), 59.
[162] O'Brien (1982a), 63
[163] Kierkegaard (1992).
[164] '[Kierkegaard's] targets had become the Danish clergy: "servants of Christianity" who in the prevailing tendency to "idolize mediocrity," had "shrewdly" exploited "pagan optimism" which made Christianity commensurable with all things finite, and managed to reap the benefits of a "Both/and" which made being Christian just another item on the list.' (Hannay (1992), 1). Mosley's move was obviously in the opposite direction to Kierkegaard's. In a footnote Booth in Booth (1982)mentions this move, too. Mosley himself, however, had never thought about this comparison before having read about it in the present author's dissertation (cf. letter, 24.08.1999).
[165] O'Brien (1982a), 66.
[166] O'Brien (1982a), 67.
[167] O'Brien (1982a), 72.
[168] Interview, 06.04.1999. Also compare chapter I of this thesis, where the inherent cynicism in Mosley's aristocratic background is discussed.
[169] The acquisition of a sense of dismay with rationality as a prerequisite for seeing things in the Christian way is argued for most notably by C. S. Lewis (1943), 27, 49. Also compare Holmer (1977).
[170] Mosley (SD), 130
[171] Mosley (SD), 130
[172] Interview, 06.04.1999.
[173] Interview, 06.04.1999.
[174] Lessing's autobiography gives a very sharp account of the mistrust and political witch-hunts of these years (cf. Lessing 1997). The essential portray of the

mood of these years will, however, remain Orwell's *1984*.

[175] Interview, 06.04.1999.
[176] Mosley (1996), 115.
[177] Mosley (1996), 118.
[178] Mosley (1996), 123.
[179] Mosley (1996), 118, 123.
[180] Mosley (1996), 118.
[181] Mosley (1996), 118; my italics.
[182] Mosley (1996), 125.
[183] Mosley (1996), 125-26.
[184] Interview, 16.06.1997.
[185] Murdoch (1989), 60.
[186] Interview, 06.04.1999.
[187] Interview, 06.04.1999.
[188] Interview, 06.04.1999.
[189] Interview, 06.04.1999.
[190] Mosley (1996), 44.
[191] Interview, 06.04.1999.
[192] Interview, 06.04.1999.
[193] Murdoch (1989), 59-60.
[194] Murdoch (1989), 60.
[195] Mosley (1996), 28.
[196] In his autobiography, (Mosley 1996, 80) Mosley mentions that the following utterance of the hero of *Wild Palms* had become something of a talisman for him and many others: 'Between grief and nothing I will take grief.'
[197] Mosley (1961a), 200.
[198] 'the equivocal psychological facts of his story are drowned in the baroque flourish of his embellishments' (Peterson, 1958)
[199] Interview, 06.04.1999.
[200] Mosley (1961a), 198-204.
[201] Interview, 06.04.1999.
[202] It is interesting to compare Mosley's view of conversion to that of Muriel Spark's in Whittaker (1982), 25. Like Mosley, Spark draws the attention to the fact that true conversion is quite undramatic and unemotional.
[203] Interview, 06.04.1999.
[204] Interview, 06.04.1999.
[205] Mosley (1996), 47.
[206] Interview, 16.06.1997 and interview, 06.04.1999.
[207] Murdoch (1989), 60; my italics.
[208] Mosley (SD).
[209] Mosley (1996), 47.
[210] Mosley's encounter with Christianity and the changes that this causes in his

outlook and artistic career will be discussed later in this chapter.

[211] Mosley (1996), 64.
[212] Mosley (1996), 47.
[213] Mosley (1996), 47.
[214] Mosley (1996), 47-58.
[215] Mosley (RB), 267, 268.
[216] Mosley (CO), 270.
[217] Interview, 23.06.1998.
[218] Interview, 23.06.1998.
[219] Interview, 23.06.1998.
[220] Interview, 23.06.1998.
[221] Mosley (1996), 112-15. And Interview, 06.04.1999.
[222] Interview, 06.04.1999.
[223] Mosley (1996), 132.
[224] Mosley (1996), 118.

[225] In a letter to his father about the latter's campaign in Notting Hill (1959), Nicholas Mosley writes: 'Your intention in general is to have a movement which is 'manly, disciplined, restrained and self-controlled; which never begins trouble and never exults in it, just is prepared to meet it if others insist.' Again, this is unexceptionable. But what in practice happens is that your movement holds a meeting in Notting Hill which is followed by violence.

To say that the speakers never wanted nor intended violence is meaningless. To believe this would be an opinion of such astonishing political naivety that it were better surely better to be hushed up—it must still be better for a politician to be thought something of a villain rather than an idiot. . . . Failure to take [some sort of action against violence] seems only to mean that in spite of your words on paper, your intention is not seriously to eradicate from people's minds the impression of your need for racial hatred.' (Mosley, 1996, 125).

[226] Mosley (1996), 118-31 Also cf. Robert Skidelsky (1981), 15 ff. In this book Skidelsky recalls how he was first fascinated by Oswald Mosley after having witnessed his debating abilities against Jeremy Thorpe, in Oxford Union, in 1961.
[227] Mosley (1996), 126.
[228] Murdoch (1989), 60; my italics.
[229] Mosley (1996), 115 and 117.
[230] Mosley (1996), 132.
[231] Mosley (1996), 136-41.

Doris Lessing, herself an anti-Apartheid activist, remembers the England of the Fifties and early Sixties (even the England of the intelligentsia) as very patriotic, racist and closed-minded, Lessing (1997).

[232] Mosley (1996), 178-79.
[233] Interview, 23.06.1998.
[234] Interview, 23.06.1998.

[235] O'Brien (1982a), 59; my italics.
[236] O'Brien (1982a), 66.
[237] Mosley (1996), 133.
[238] 'The story [of the Bible] seemed so clearly to say — Alright, after a suitable time of commitment and obedience, what you should have learned is to watch and listen on your own. I regretted nothing of the commitment which had lasted some seven years (a traditional Old Testament stretch!); it might only be regretted, surely, if I had learned nothing from it.' (Mosley, 1996, pp. 177-78).
[239] In his latest unpublished novel, *Inventing God* (2001) this idea is investigated extensively.
[240] Interview, 06.04.1999.
[241] Interview, 06.04.1999.
[242] Interview, 06.04.1999.
[243] Mosley (1965), 60.
[244] Mosley (1965), 61.
[245] Mosley (1965), 57.
[246] Mosley (1965), 57.
[247] Mosley (1965), 58.
[248] Interview, 06.04.1999; my italics.
[249] Letter, 24.08.1999.
[250] Letter, 24.08.1999; my emphasis.
[251] Letter, 24.08.1999; my emphasis.
[252] Cf. the examination of the aristocratic notion of games for games' sake in Chapter I of this dissertation.
[253] This idea will be examined in more detail in the following section.
[254] Or which *determines* and is *determined* by the choice.
[255] Mosley (1996), 61.
[256] Mosley (1996), 106; my italics.
[257] In interview, 06.04.1999 Mosley told the present author how he had actually arrived at the same conclusion as the ninth-century Irish theologian and philosopher, John Scotus Erigena (whose philosophy Mosley has just 'discovered'), more or less through his own observation and study of Christianity.
[258] Interview, 23.06.1998.
[259] Mosley (1996), 106.
[260] Interview, 23.06.1998.
[261] Holmer (1977),14-20. Also cf. Lewis (1975b).
[262] Steiner (1966), 15.
[263] Bradbury (1994), 335.
[264] Bradbury (1994) 264-350 and Bradbury (1993), 81-100. Also cf. Butler (1980) and Waugh (1995).
[265] Sarraute (1987).
[266] Federman (1993), 61.

[267] Cf. Steiner, 1989). Also Cf. Fukuyama (1992) and Bradbury (1993), pp. 82-100 and pp. 115-34.
[268] Cf. Wittgenstein (1994), Hallett (1977), Jonathan Culler (1976) and Harris (1988).
[269] For a fuller study of these schools refer to Derrida (1991), Johnson (1980) Culler (1982), Lodge (1988), Newton (1997), Eagleton (1984) and Worthington (1996).
[270] Cf. Helga Schier (1993), 183-84.
[271] Cf. Helga Schier (1993), 183.
[272] Butler (1989), p. 232. Also cf. Butler (1994) and Levine (1994).
[273] Ihab Hassan (1990), 30.
[274] Ziegler and Bigsby, (1982), 3.
[275] Eco (1984), 67.
[276] Sarraute (1987).
[277] Ziegler quotes William Gass in Ziegler and Bigsby (1982), 151.
[278] Federman (1981b), 5.
[279] Bradbury (1994), 346.
[280] Gerald Graff (1982), 241. Graff goes on to point out the self-undermining potential of this remark.
[281] Sukenick puts it thus: 'Rather than serving as a mirror or a redoubling on itself, fictions adds itself to the world, creating a meaningful reality that did not previously exist.' (Federman, 1981b, 5).
[282] And their paramount examples in the works of Balzac and Victor Hugo. According to Federman, the realist Balzac sees fiction as 'mirrors that one drags along the Road of Reality' and the romantic Hugo sees his poems as 'Mirrors of the Soul.' (Federman, 1981c, 292-3).
[283] Hutcheon (1989). Also cf. Butler (1996), 69-86.
[284] Cf. Baudrillard (1994).
[285] Vinson (1972), 572.
[286] Scholes (1979).
[287] Federman (1981a).
[288] Lodge (1990), 105-10.
[289] Kellman (1980).
[290] Cf. Maack (1984).
[291] Lodge (1990), 105.
[292] Cf. Federman (1993), 47-64, Bradbury (1994), 345-50.
[293] Robbe-Grillet's novel *The Erasers*, with its telling title, or Beckett's *Malone Dies* are fine examples of this sort of novel.
[294] John Barth, David Lodge and Milan Kundera amongst others argue that the suspicion towards the notion of a coherent representable reality has always—from the beginning—been accompanying the novel from Cervantes and Sterne via Flaubert and Mallarmé up to the present age. Cf. John Barth (1984), 204 ff.,

Lodge (1990), 104 ff., and Milan Kundera (1990), pp. 3-20.

[295] Federman (1981c).

[296] Hassan (1971).

[297] Schier (1993), 16. Schier is leaning on John Barth's distinction between the Beckettian Silence and the Borgesian intertextual games, cf. Barth (1967): 29-43, And Barth (1980): 65-71.

[298] David Lodge (1990), 87-114.

[299] David Lodge (1990).

[300] Butler (1980), 159 ff.

[301] Beckett, *Malone Dies*, in Beckett (1994), 258.

[302] Schier (1993) and Stark (1974), 1-10.

[303] Hassan (1967), 22.

[304] Birch (1994), 93.

[305] Also cf. Gerz (1981), 279-81.

[306] Butor (1990), 48.

[307] Robbe-Grillet (1963), 13. Also cf. Sarraute, as quoted in Birch (1994), 191.

[308] Robbe-Grillet is quoted in Randall Stevenson (1986), 220 as follows: 'the evolution has continued . . . we certainly do not attempt to blot out this past. In fact, it is in admiration of our predecessors that we are most united . . . our ambition is . . . to follow in their trail, in our own way, in our own time. . . .' And Federman claims that Surfiction is actually a means for getting closer to reality and truth: 'I'm not destroying illusions simply for the sake of destroying illusions. I'm destroying illusions in order that we may face up to reality, and now what passes for reality. . . . Unless we constantly question what passes for reality, challenge it, defy it, we will always exist in falseness, in a system of twisted facts and glorified illusions and we quickly become lobotomised by it.' (Leclair, 1983, p. 42). These statements put the claim of George Steiner about the 'literature of Silence' being a symptom of a crisis and *discontinuity* in Western intellectual life into question. Cf. George Steiner (1989).

[309] Cf. Waugh (1984), where the Meta-fiction is not only seen as the symptom of the crisis of the novel, but also as a means of its replenishment.

[310] '[The *nouveaux romanciers*] came ever as closer to Samuel Beckett's notion of a writing of "nameless things" and "thingless names."' (Bradbury, 1994, 346).

[311] Simon (1963), 48-49.

[312] Simon (1963), 53.

[313] The long and detailed scene of the shooting in the restaurant —Simon (1963), 82-84—is a good example to show this. For a more detailed study of Claude Simon's narrative technique refer to Sturrock (1969), 43-103.

[314] Hassan (1967), 30.

[315] Cf. Stark (1974), 6.

[316] Stark (1974), 22. This is also in accord with the structuralist and post-structuralist notion that language exists prior to consciousness and not vice versa.

[317] Burgin (1969), 129.
[318] Butler (1980), 39.
[319] Barrenechea (1965), 38.
[320] For a discussion of this fable refer to Butler (1980), 38-52 and Stark (1974), 11-61.
[321] Butler (1980), 40-41.
[322] Pynchon (1996) .
[323] For a fuller discussion of Pynchon's narrative techniques refer to Seed (1988), Schraub (1981) and Stonehill (1988).
[324] Barth (1969).
[325] Ziegler (1987), 88. Also refer to Schulz (1990).
[326] Cf. Stark (1974), 6 ff.
[327] Butler (1980), 41.
[328] Butler (1980), 44 and cf. Sturrock (1969).
[329] Robbe-Grillet (1980).
[330] '[The boy] hesitated as long, with each question, before giving his answer, which gave the questioner [i.e., the soldier] no enlightenment. Where did one get that way? A long, silent gaze towards the unseen end of the road, then the calm voice:
"To the boulevard."
"And that way?"
[. . .]
"To the boulevard."
"The same one?"
[. . .]
"Yes," says the boy. Then after a pause: "No!" and finally with sudden violence: "It is the boulevard!"' (Robbe-Grillet, 1980, 30-31).
[331] Robbe-Grillet (1966).
[332] Burroughs (1964).
[333] Burroughs (1965).
[334] Allen and Creeley (1965), 256-57.
[335] Cf. Butler (1980), 103 ff. Oxenhandler (1981), 181-201.
[336] Johnson (1969).
[337] Vinson (1972), 572.
[338] Beckett, *Malone Dies*, in Beckett (1994), 181.
[339] Cf. Butler (1980).
[340] Waugh's describes the role of parody as follows: 'One method of showing the function of literary conventions, of revealing their provisional nature, is to show what happens when they malfunction. Parody and inversion are two strategies which operate in this way as frame-breaks. The alteration of frame and frame-break (or the construction of an illusion through the imperceptibility of the frame) provides the essential deconstructive method of metafiction.' (Waugh,

1984, 31).

[341] Schulz (1990), 13.

[342] Schulz (1990), 15.

[343] Schulz (1990),13. And Ziegler (1987), 88 ff.

[344] According to Calvino, human beings take childish delight in combinatorial play, without aiming at meaning or truth, and sometimes, without intention, one of these combinations produces an 'unforeseen effect that consciousness could not have achieved intentionally.' This leads to the premonition of an unconscious meaning, which could not be talked about directly. It is at this point, *after* the game, that a myth is born. (Calvino,1981, pp. 75-81).

[345] Cf. Butler (1980), Waugh (1984).
Hoffmann (1996b), 115-94 and Barth (1981), 19-33

[346] Hoffmann (1996b), 115-94.

[347] Butler (1980),159 ff.

[348] 'To affirm the notion of the spectacle is the triumph of the aesthete's position: the promulgation of the ludic, the refusal of the tragic. All of Barthes's intellectual moves have the effect of voiding work of its "content," the tragic of its finality. That is the sense in which his work is genuinely subversive, liberating—playful.' (Sontag , 1983, p. xxx).

[349] Butler (1984), 131.

[350] 'Text of pleasure: the text that contends, fills, grants euphoria; the text that comes from culture and does not break with it, is linked to a *comfortable* practice of reading. Text of bliss: the text that imposes a state of loss, the text that discomforts (perhaps to the point of certain boredom), unsettles the reader's historical, cultural, psychological assumptions, the consistency of his taste, values, memories, brings to a crisis his relation with language.' (Barthes, 1975, 14); original emphasis.

[351] Christopher Butler (1984), 131-32.

[352] Bradbury (1994), 349, 378.

[353] Scholes (1967).

[354] Fowles (1990), 150.

[355] Murdoch (1990), 24. Obviously the Barthesian Bliss/Boredom or the *nouveaux romanciers*' notion literature's inability to reveal truths about life are not shared by this group of writers.

[356] Bradbury (1994), 351-93.

[357] Onega Jaén (1989), 74 ff. In her study of the metafiction, with emphasis on John Fowles' *The French Lieutenant's Woman*, Patricia Waugh characterises this sort of writing as 'Frame-breaking.' Cf. Waugh (1984), 32-33. The narrator, for example, shatters the omniscient role that he had maintained up to chapter 12 of the novel by answering the closing question of this chapter ('Who is Sarah? / Out of what shadows does she come?') as follows in the next chapter: 'I don't know. The story I am telling is all imagination. These characters I have created never

existed outside my own mind.' (John Fowles, 1969, 96 [end of Chapter 2]—97 [beginning of Chapter 13]).

[358] Onega Jaén (1989), 75.

[359] Murdoch, (1990), 19.

[360] Murdoch (1990), 18. Murdoch and Mosley come to the same conclusions about the impossibility of the existentialist absolutist notions of freedom by different routes—Murdoch through non-religious transcendentalist philosophy and Mosley through Catholicism.

[361] Byatt (1965), 10.

[362] Murdoch (1990), 22.

[363] Murdoch (1990), 22.

[364] Murdoch (1990), 23. In this respect she is very close to Fowles' (and Mosley's) idea of man's freewill being possible due to the unpredictability and contingency of future. Spark would agree with this view, too, as she sees man—the creature of God—to be unable of unravelling and foreseeing the designs of God.

[365] Murdoch (1990), 23.

[366] For Murdoch literature in the realm of fantasy is either 'crystalline' or 'journalistic': the former portraying human condition in some small, clear self-contained 'quasi-allegorical' object, and the other telling a straight-forward story 'enlivened with empirical facts.' None of these forms, according to Murdoch, does justice to the reality of persons and the reality of their lives. Both of these forms are based on some facile myth imposed on reality, which assumes reality to be a definable, given whole. Thus none can not hope to bring the individual closer to any form of real freedom. (see Murdoch, 1990, 15-24).

[367] Murdoch (1990), 22-23.

[368] Murdoch (1990), 22.

[369] Kermode (1990), 123.

[370] Murdoch (1962b), 218-19. Kane (1988), 11.

[371] Iris Murdoch (1962a), 270 ff. In the darkness of the villa, the maid Maria, for example, seems to be a ghost consisting of a white apron, a large white cap and two black smiling eyes.

[372] Byatt (1965), 104.

[373] 'One day no doubt all this would seem charged with a vast significance, and he would try one more to find out the truth. One day, too, he would experience again, responding with his heart, that indefinitely extended requirement that one human being makes upon another.' (Murdoch, 1962, 309).

[374] Murdoch (1977), 242.

[375] Golding (1995).

[376] Burgess (1983).

[377] Bradbury (1994), 374-75.

[378] Bradbury (1994), 375.

[379] Bradbury (1994), 373.

[380] Spark (1965b).
[381] Spark (1965 a).
[382] Cf. Whittaker (1982), 91 ff.
[383] Greene (1968), p. 181-82.
[384] Spark (1965 a). The flash-forward very early on in the novel (p. 15) forecasting the thoughts of a pupil moments before she dies in the fire, of which the reader had not yet been given any information is a especially good example for Spark's omniscient narrative techniques.
[385] Spark (1963), 175.
[386] Spark (1966), 72 and 108 respectively.
[387] Whittaker (1982), 93-94.
[388] The contradictions of the post-structuralist theory in regards to the liberation of the individual have already been mentioned.
[389] Again David Lodge warns us against this view. The *nouveaux romanciers'* insistence on observation as opposed to interpretation falls under criticism, when one realises that the very fact that observation alters reality (Lodge, 1990, 103).
[390] Interview, 06.04.1999.
[391] Interview, 06.04.1999.
[392] Mosley puts his view of humans as such: 'Humans are in fact not rational and all-of-piece; [. . .] they are ridiculous and wonderful and frightening all at once . . .' (Mosley, 1996, 195).
[393] To put it in other words, 'das literarische Werk verwirklicht was ist, als das, was noch nicht ist: die Wirklichkeit der Möglichkeit der Wirklichkeit.' (Malte Fues, 1987, 144). 'The literary work realises what *is*, rather than, what is *not yet*: the reality of the possibility of the reality'; my translation and italics.
[394] O'Brien (1982a), 72.
[395] O'Brien (1982a), 72.
[396] Mosley (1958a).
[397] Mosley (1996), 90 and 98.
[398] As has already been mentioned Mosley sees his theological essay *Experience and Religion* (1965) as his signing off from organised religion.
[399] Mosley (1996),155.
[400] Mosley (MP), 249.
[401] At the very end of MP (p. 249) Melissa asks Harry: 'How are we going home?' Harry's answer—'By air'—underlines the unknowable quality of the future that awaits them. Now all they know is the means and not the end.
[402] Mosley (1996), 155.
[403] Peter Lewis depicts this turning point as such: 'After a five year gap, Mosley transfigured himself as a novelist in a way that repudiated much of his previous work. In the 1960s, his novels (and sentences) became much shorter, his style simpler and his narrative method more elliptical. . . . An unfashionable yet far from naive optimism replaced the modish gloom; a sense of potentiality replaced

the closed system . . . Mosley's novels of this period, *Accident, Impossible Object* and *Natalie Natalia* are strikingly original . . .' (Lewis, 1981).

[404] The novel was translated into French in 1965 and was indeed compared to the works of Butor, Robbe-Grillet and Sarraute. Cf. Ardagh (1967).

[405] Nicholas Mosley (MP), 11.

[406] Booth (1982), 88.

[407] 'The very unconventionality of Mosley's novels [*Meeting Place, Accident*] recalls French anti-novel and even the "nouvelle-vague."' (Anon, 1965).

[408] Booth (1982), 88.

[409] Mosley (MP), 228 ff. Regarding this section of the novel, parallels with Joyce and Fellini definitely come to mind.

[410] Mosley (MP), 49.

[411] Mosley (1996), 155.

[412] Mosley (MP), 201.

[413] Mosley (1996), 175.

[414] Wardle (65), for example, saw the novel as one that has 'the excitement of an operation conducted on the aesthetic frontier,' Poore (1966) praised Mosley's 'excellence of theme, the quality of his perception and the absolute control of a brilliantly inventive style' and Pryce-Jones (1966) admired his great skill at handling dialogues and evoking an intense sense of the moment

[415] Booth (1982), 92.

[416] Mosley was well aware of the literary tradition of dealing with impossibilities through aesthetic observation. He mentions Proust as one novelist who has a 'specific' idea about life being 'impossible except in terms of art and memory. . . .' However, Proust and other writers treated the 'impossibilities' of life as they happened in the past, and Mosley wanted to find a way of dealing with them in present. (O'Brien, 1982a, 63).

[417] John O'Brien (1982), 67.

[418] O'Brien (1982), 67.

[419] Mosley (AC), 30 and 36.

[420] Mosley (AC), 120.

[421] Mosley (AC), 180.

[422] Mosley (AC), 14.

[423] Mosley (AC), 191.

[424] Mosley (AC), 191.

[425] O'Brien (1982a), 61.

[426] Mosley (AC), 13.

[427] Mosley (AC), 45, 46, 192.

[428] Francis Booth (1982), 92.

[429] Mosley (AC), 185-86.

[430] O'Brien (1982b), 146.

[431] Mosley (AC), 5.

[432] Mosley (AC), 5.
[433] Mosley (AC), 168.
[434] Mosley (AC), 164.
[435] O'Brien (1982b), 146.
[436] O'Brien (1982b), 146.
[437] Booth (1982), 92.
[438] Booth (1982), 92.
[439] O'Brien (1982a), 64.
[440] Mosley (AC), 179-80.
[441] Mosley (1996), 166-67; O'Brien (1982a), 64-65.
[442] O'Brien (1982), 64.
[443] O'Brien (1982), 64; my emphasis.
[444] Mosley (AC), 186.
[445] Mosley (1996), 167.
[446] Interview, 06.04.1999.
[447] Madness and logic in extreme are seen as one and the same. (Mosley, IO, 129).
[448] Mosley (AC), 191.
[449] Mosley (1996), 190.
[450] Mosley (1996), 190.
[451] 'From *Meeting Place* on to *Natalie* the protagonists were trying to make impossibilities possible by some sort of affirmation—if only acceptance. (I think *Assassins* is rather apart from all this).' (O'Brien, 1982a, 77).
[452] O'Brien (1982a), 66.
[453] Mosley (AS), 230.
[454] Mosley (AS), 240 ff.: 'she rolled over and picked up bunches of straw. She tore at them. She took hold of her hair at the back of her neck and held it in a tuft, and began wiping it with the straw violently.'; 'She nodded and made a small noise like a screech.' p. 244.; 'She cried 'Yes!' which came out like a screech again.' p. 245.
[455] Mosley (AS), 224.
[456] Mosley (AS), 48.
[457] Mosley (AS), 126.
[458] Mosley (1996), 199.
[459] Scholes (1969) and Steiner (1969) respectively. For both critics the modern legacy—i.e., the belief in the ability of art to point out truths about the reality outside itself—in the works of Mosley is obvious. In the same review Steiner goes as far as seeing Mosley's work superior to the contemporary *nouveau roman*, prose poems, lyric sketches as 'many of these . . . shed an empty brightness. What they report of man and of his works and days is thinner, more arbitrary than what we already know . . . Mosley doesn't fall under this telling stricture, for [he is] too intelligent, too finely responsive a novelist . . . *Impossible Object* is a beautifully

wrought, exciting novel.'

[460] Mosley quotes from the report of the chairman of the Booker Prize 1969 (Mosley, 1996, 209-10).

[461] Compare my discussion of Mosley's move from the ethical to the aesthetic in light of Kierkegaard's theory earlier in this chapter.

[462] O'Brien (1982b), 142.

[463] O'Brien (1982b), 142.

[464] O'Brien (1982b), 142.

[465] Mosley (IO), 218; original italics; my emphasis.

[466] Mosley (IO), 66-70; my emphasis.

[467] O'Brien (1982a), p.71.

[468] Mosley (IO), 34; original italics.

[469] Mosley (IO), 121.

[470] Mosley (IO), 123

[471] Mosley (IO), 119.

[472] Mosley (IO), 32; original italics.

[473] Mosley (IO), 84.

[474] Mosley (IO), 84.

[475] Mosley (IO), 84.

[476] O'Brien (1982b), 143.

[477] Mosley (IO), 16.

[478] O'Brien (1982b), 142.

[479] Mosley (IO), 104.

[480] Mosley (IO), 102.

[481] Mosley (IO), 104.

[482] Mosley (IO), 76-77.

[483] Mosley (IO), 62.

[484] 'I said "you can't stay here [on your own]" / [. . .] She said "Why not?" / I said "You wouldn't be safe." / She said "You know you want to go on your own."' (Mosley, IO, 62).

[485] His recollection of the Arab girl with 'her hair cut short and a face as if made out of lapis-lazuli; a thin brown body and transparent trousers' betrays his guilt. (Mosley, IO, 70).

[486] O'Brien (1982), 142.

[487] O'Brien (1982), 143.

[488] Mosley (IO), 218.

[489] Mosley (IO), 113.

[490] One is reminded of Schrödinger's Cat in Mosley (HM).

[491] John O'Brien (1982a), 60.

[492] Mosley (NN), 15.

[493] Cf. Mosley (NN), 120-21.

[494] Mosley (NN), 123.

[495] Mosley (NN), 123.
[496] Cf. Mosley (NN), 120-24.
[497] Mosley (NN), 186, 290, 291.
[498] Here one is reminded of Mosley's feeling of responsibility for the South African policies in the early Sixties.
[499] Broyard (1971).
[500] Mosley (NN), 120-24.
[501] O'Brien (1982a), 76.
[502] Mosley's interest in Jungian (and also Freudian) theories of the mind goes back to his preoccupation with freedom in the Christian context. In *Experience and Religion* he compares the Christian idea of man's freedom and his possibilities with those of Freud's and Jung's. Cf. Nicholas Mosley (1965).
[503] O'Brien (1982a), 76.
[504] Mosley (MP), 244. The account of the hallucination ends with the words: 'Then he began to fall towards the earth; awakening.'
[505] Interview, 06.04.1999
[506] Mosley (NN), 158.
[507] Interview, 06.04.1999. This strange section of *Natalie Natalia* also reminds the reader of Brooke-Rose's experimental novels of the Sixties, herself a disciple of the French *nouveau roman* and post-structuralism, such as *Out* (1964) or *Such* (1966), cf. Christine Brook-Rose (1986). In these she manifests a fine capability for drawing images of impossible and impenetrable realities. However when Brooke-Rose's works were mentioned during a meeting with Nicholas Mosley (interview, 21.12.1996), he claimed to have never heard of this novelist.
[508] Mosley (NN), 186.
[509] Mosley (NN), 186.
[510] Mosley (1996), 219.
[511] Mosley (NN), 196.
[512] Mosley (1996), 219.
[513] Mosley (NN), 204; my emphasis.
[514] Mosley (NN), 302-10.
[515] Mosley (1996), 220.
[516] The affair between Natalia and Greville is to a great extent based on Mosley's affair at the time with a woman to whom he refers to by her fictional name, Natalia, in his autobiography—just as in the case of 'Mary' in *The Rainbearers* (Mosley, 1996, 220 ff.).
[517] Interview, 06.04.1999.
[518] Mosley (1996), 219.
[519] Mosley (1996), 219.
[520] Interview, 17.09.1999.
[521] William Faulkner's 1949 Nobel Prize speech quoted in Mosley (1961b).
[522] Mosley (IO), 9.

[523] The idea is if one had the 'right' state or framework of mind, he would inevitably be moral.
[524] Mosley (1996), 252.
[525] Mosley (CP), 12.
[526] Mosley (CP), 77.
[527] Mosley (CP), 77.
[528] Mosley (CP), 77.
[529] Thody (1971), 41.
[530] The controversy of the conscious self's regression into the unconscious state is a central theme in *Judith*, which will be discussed later in this chapter.
[531] Mosley (CP), 77-78.
[532] Mosley (CP), 78.
[533] Mosley (CP), 83.
[534] Turner (1997), XIV-XV.
[535] Cf. introduction of thesis.
[536] Mosley (1996), 225.
[537] 'I liked the idea of this: had it not seemed proper that I might be smashed up by some juggernaut?' (Mosley, 1996, 227).
[538] This is the very activity for which he uses the term being in 'partnership with life.' Mosley felt that this process started with his novel *Meeting Place* (which—as was discussed in chapter II—also marked the transition of his novels from 'conventional' to 'experimental'): '*Meeting Place* does seem to have been an attempt, yes, to see oneself in *partnership with life*; not imposing a pattern on experience (and thus experiencing failure) but trying to look for, and proceed in, a pattern that might be there.' (Mosley 1996, 155; my emphasis).
[539] The impact of psychoanalysis on his life and art will be discussed later in this chapter.
[540] In his—for Mosley groundbreaking—book *Steps to an Ecology of Mind*, Bateson uses the simile of a blind man tapping his way through, and thus puts the strict mind/body duality current in western world view to question: 'Suppose I am a blind man, and I use a stick. I go tap, tap, tap. Where do *I* start?' (Bateson, 1972, 465).
Mosley (cf. Mosley, 1978) is aware that the effervescence of the mind/body boundaries had always been considered in western—and especially modern—art and literature; most poignantly in the works of Woolf. However, he believes that this (aesthetic) issue ultimately gave into the mind/body dichotomy. In the case of Woolf, for example, her attempt at doing away with this division—and in a way uniting the 'two halves'—ended in her increasing withdrawal into one of the two halves, i.e., the mind. This ultimately led to her annihilation of the body by way of suicide.
[541] Mosley (IO), 9.
[542] Interview, 17.09.1999.

[543] Interview, 17.09.1999.
[544] 'I had switched the radio on at random, just after the reading had started, and I was transfixed—I had never heard of Kleist and only just caught the name at the end.' (Letter, 06.10.2000). However, Mosley's attempts at finding an English translation were in vain and it was not before 1978, where he came across a translation in the *TLS*. (Interview, 12.12.2000).
[545] Kleist (1991), 6.
[546] Kleist (1991), 6.
[547] Kleist (1991), 12.
[548] Stern Weiss (1980) argues that Kleist, a 'Liebhaber der Wissenschaften,' was aware of the then newly emerging non-Euclidean mathematics: 'The "Marionettentheater" essay . . . records the impact of late 18th century mathematics on Kleist, a receptive intellectual with a strong affinity for science.' Interestingly Banks (1982a) looks to Gödelian mathematics as a metaphor to elucidate *Catastrophe Practice*.
[549] At the time, Mosley was not aware of the parallel between his scientific preoccupations and those of Kleist. It was only when the present author came across this similarity in the course of her research that Mosley realised this.
[550] Mosley was an avid reader of —what he calls—'pop science' since the days of his wartime correspondence with his father (letter, 06.10.2000).
[551] This will be discussed in detail later in the chapter when analysing the novels.
[552] Cf. Letter, 06.10.2000.
[553] Letter, 06.10.2000.
[554] Letter, 06.10.2000.
[555] Cf. Jacobs and Ohlsen (1977), 35 ff.
[556] Jacobs and Ohlsen (1977), 70.
[557] Interview, 10.10.2000. Mosley goes on to say: 'then I read him and he had nothing to do with Marxism at all.'
It must be noted that Mosley differentiates between early Marx—'before his head seemed to have got jammed down on his shoulders as if by a rationalist hammer' (Mosley 1996, 281)—and late Marx. Marx's theories about labour and its value do not make sense to Mosley at all. 'A very stupid person can put infinite amount of labour into a commodity and it isn't any worth at all, whereas a very clever person can put half an hour into a commodity and it is worth a lot, you see.' It is Marx's early works (his pre 1848 writings), that impress Mosley: '[In those works] he said what mattered was alienation; the curse was to be alienated from one's work. . . . What was the value was to be responsible for one's work. That is marvelous. . . . You see, a sort of rapport between oneself and one's work. If one was happy [with it], that was the true value. That was what made the work worthwhile and oneself worthwhile.' (interview, 10.10.2000).
[558] 'The idea of having to eat of the Tree of Knowledge of Good and Evil a

second time in order to absolve the curse of the first—this was, yes, like Brecht's idea of learning to use 'alienation' rather than to be confound by it.' (letter, 06.10.2000).

[559] Interview, 10.10.2000.
[560] Interview, 10.10.2000.
[561] It should perhaps not come as a surprise that Brecht estimated Kleist's drama highly and saw himself operating in the tradition of the latter. He was especially drawn to the Kleistian *Realismus des Entsetzens und Abscheus*, with which Kleist expressed the individual's *innere Zerrissenheit*—the forefather of Brechtian *Entfremdung*. Another aspect of their art, which related them to each other was their enthusiasm for aesthetic experimentation with help of laws science and music. Cf. Dyck (1982), 133-34, 150.
[562] Mosley (CP), 11.
[563] Brecht (1964), 26.
[564] Brecht (1964), 26.
[565] Mosley (CP), 11.
[566] Cf. Brecht (1964), 92.
[567] Interview, 17.09.1999.
[568] Mosley (1996), 228.
[569] Mosley (1996), 228.
[570] Mosley (CP), 11.
[571] Mosley (1996), 238.
[572] Mosley (1979).
[573] Mosley (1979).
[574] Mosley (1979). Mosley later on sees that Trotsky's inability to acquire real political power was not unlike that of his father's. ('My father was a 'good' fascist; Trotsky was a 'good' communist because [both were] out of power. [Trotsky and my father] unconsciously realised that they didn't want power.' (Interview, 08.12.1996). The sentiments against 'the son of a Fascist' (Mosley 1996, 237) writing a book about Trotsky were considerable. The fact that Mosley wrote a very loving account of Trotsky has not helped—it probably even worked against Mosley. Philip Toynbee's 'half-page hatchet-job' on Nicholas Mosley's book can be viewed as a crystallisation of those sentiments: 'This is the book of a spoiled and protected intellectual child who seems to have quite forgotten the kind of temptations and limitations which this status imposes on him . . .' (Mosley, 1996, 244-5).
[575] Mosley (1972), frontispiece.
[576] Mosley (1972), 110.
[577] Trotsky himself seems to have been aware of the connection between artistic and 'prophetic' activity. Mosley fascinatingly sees how Trotsky in his works and writings 'prophesied the rise of Fascism unless there was a united front of socialists to stop it: he glimpsed the future battleground in Spain.' (Mosley 1972,

110).
[578] Mosley (1972), 138.
[579] Mosley (1979).
[580] Mosley (1996), 236-38.
[581] Mosley (1996), 237.
[582] Mosley (1983).
[583] Mosley (1983).
[584] *Turner (1997), XIV.*
[585] *Turner (1997), XXIV.*
[586] Interview, 10.10.2000. Cf. also letter, 06.10.2000.
[587] Letter, 06.10.2000.
[588] Interview, 17.09.1999.
[589] Kleist, a '*Liebhaber der Wissenschaften*,' and Brecht, who specifically argued for a new form of theatre suitable for the audience of the 'scientific age,' both used scientific theories for their experiments. Cf. Stern Weiss (1980), 122, 124 and Dyck (1982), 134 ff.

Mosley believes that the sense of 'epiphany' that overcame him when he first saw Bateson at a lecture at the ICA, London, owed much to the fact that he was 'totally unheard of' in England before this lecture (interview, 10.10.2000).

[590] These will be explained in detail later in this chapter.
[591] Interview, 10.10.2000.
[592] Mosley (1980a). Cf. also Mosley (CP), 77-89.
[593] Mosley (1980a).
[594] Interview, 17.09.1999.
[595] Mosley (CP), 84.
[596] Interview, 17.09.1999 and 10.10.2000.
[597] After the publication of *Catastrophe Practice*, Mosley's friend and reviewer, John Banks, writes to him, that Monod was a 'strict Darwinian determinist.' To Mosley, however, the contrary seemed to be the case (interview, 10.10.2000).
[598] Interview, 10.10.2000.
[599] Interview, 10.10.2000.
[600] Interview, 10.10.2000.
[601] Double-bind theory conceptualises the identity disturbances (esp. schizophrenia) that arise, when children are given contradictory messages by their parents. A typical example of this would be a parent who constantly beats his child, and yet insists on loving him.
[602] Interview, 10.10.2000.
[603] Interview, 17.09.1999; my emphasis.
[604] This idea was extensively discussed in chapter II of this thesis.
[605] Interview, 17.09.1999.
[606] Mosley (1980b).
[607] Interview, 10.10.2000.

[608] Interview, 10.10.2000; my emphasis.
[609] Mosley (CP), 84.
[610] Interview, 10.10.2000.
[611] Popper (1972), 106.
[612] Mosley (1996), 247-51, 260. Cf. also Interview, 17.09.1999.
[613] Mosley (1996), 260.
[614] Interview, 17.09.1999.
[615] Mosley (1996), 261.
[616] Mosley (1996), 261.
[617] Mosley (1996), 262.
[618] This is discussed in detail in the first chapter of this thesis.
[619] Rosemary was also trying to break away from her aristocratic background and expressed this especially in form of pursuing a career as a painter (Mosley 1997b).
[620] Mosley (1996), 265.
[621] Mosley (1996), 264-65.
[622] Mosley (1996), 265. Julian's brother, Billy, later on claimed that Nietzsche's philosophy was 'just a pirated reprint of the book on Philosophy written by Juju [Julian] when he was temporarily deranged' (Mosley 1976, 158).
[623] Mosley (1976), 232.
[624] Mosley (1996), 266.
[625] Mosley (1996), 7, 298.
[626] Mosley (1996), 298-99.
[627] 'Just after I was born, . . . my mother went off on a summer holiday to Venice and left me with a Nanny and a wet-nurse who was a drunk; . . . I was sick much of the time and nearly died . . .' (Mosley 1996, 262).
[628] Mosley (1996), 262.
[629] Mosley (1996), 263.
[630] Mosley (1996), 264.
[631] Mosley (1996), 264.
[632] Mosley (1996), 266-70.
[633] Mosley (1996), 261.
[634] Mosley (1994).
[635] Mosley (1994).
[636] Mosley (1996), 261-62.
[637] Cf. chapter II.
[638] 'My father was a 'good' fascist; Trotsky was a 'good' communist because [both were] out of power. [Trotsky and my father] unconsciously realised that they didn't want power.' (interview, 08.12.1996).
[639] Mosley (1996), 295.
[640] Mosley (1996), 295ff.
[641] Cf. Mosley (1996), 295.

[642] Cf. Mosley (1996), 295-96.

[643] In his autobiography *Efforts at Truth,* Mosley notes that the biography's first volume *Rules of the Game* was (apart from a few reviews, such as Anthony Storr's, which saw the book as a 'labour of love') greeted with a lot of 'glee,' as it mainly dealt with the loves and promiscuities of Oswald's private life. It was with the publication of the second volume, which dealt with Oswald's ideas and political commitments, that many reviewers started see the connection with the first volume—John Vincent, for example, wrote in *Sunday Times* 'Lucky the father who has such a son to plead his cause.' (Mosley, 1996, 309 and 314 respectively).

[644] Mosley (1996), 297.

[645] Mosley (1996), 315.

[646] Mosley (1996), 315.

[647] Mosley (1996), 294.

[648] The survival of the child in catastrophic circumstances as a sign of hope, liberation and resilience of the human race became a leitmotif in Mosley's *Catastrophe Practice Series.*

[649] Mosley (1996), 269.

[650] Mosley (1980a).

[651] This was lucidly conveyed in the, by now legendary, statement that Mrs. Thatcher made in her 1979 election campaign. According to her, the Old Testament prophets did not say 'Brothers, I want a Consensus.' This also betrayed her vision of herself as a prophet and saviour of the British nation. For an extensive study of the socio-political mood of the time see Kanvanagh (1987), Lasch (1978), Waugh (1995), Young (1989), 93 and (1992), Stuart Hall et al (1978), McLennan et al.(1984), Hall and Jacques (1983) and Sampson (1992).

[652] For a study of these works see chapter II.

[653] Cf. chapter II, footnote 122.

[654] Cf. Brook (1997) and Adonis and Pollard (1997).

[655] Waugh (1995), 14.

[656] Cf. Jameson (1984).

[657] Cf. Bradbury (1994), 379 ff. and Taylor (1989), 2 ff.

[658] Cf. Bradbury (1994), 392.

[659] Ackroyd (1976), 147.

[660] Ackroyd (1976), 146-47.

[661] Lessing (1995).

[662] Lessing (1995), 181-82.

[663] Drabble (1977).

[664] Fowles (1989).

[665] Fowles (1989), 679-80.

[666] Baudrillard (1994), 118-19.

[667] Ballard (1973).

[668] The novel is obviously a direct inheritor of modern movements, such as Futur-

ism led by Marinetti.

[669] Ballard (1973), 143.
[670] McEwan (1978).
[671] Amis (1975).
[672] Amis (1984).
[673] Amis (1984), 66.
[674] Amis (1984), 249.
[675] McEwan (1987).
[676] Bradbury (1993), 412.
[677] Cf. chapter II.
[678] Carter (1984).
[679] Ackroyd (1985).
[680] Rushdie (1981).
[681] Winterson (1987).
[682] Cf. Bloom (1995).
[683] Lyotard (1984), xxiv. For a more detailed study see Baudrillard (1994); Culler (1983), (1997); Connor (1997).
[684] Fowles (1985).
[685] Byatt (1990).
[686] Cf. Cunningham (1992), 229-39 and Kemp (1992), 216-28.
[687] Cf. also Said (1978), Bhabha's (1994) collection of essays from the '70s onwards, Spivak (1987).
[688] Foucault (1987), 64.
[689] Cf. Hutcheon (1980).
[690] Cf. also Waugh (1989).
[691] 'the assertion of identity through difference and specificity is a constant in postmodern thought.' (Hutcheon, 1988, 59).
[692] Todd (1988), 8 ff.
[693] Showalter (1989), 3.
[694] Weldon (1983).
[695] Carter (1981).
[696] Connor (1996) and Waugh (1995).
[697] Cf. chapter II and the discussion about the Barthesian game leading not to freedom from the text, but further imprisonment into it.
[698] Mosley (1996), 170.
[699] Mosley (IO), 135.
[700] 'Bloom says that the whole western culture is based on the *Iliad* . . . European literature is about how awful it is to cut children's throats, but it is written in such a language that makes [this act] beautiful. There is the link to Auschwitz—and reading Schiller afterwards' (interview, 21.12.1996).
[701] Mosley (1997c), 2.
[702] Letter, 19.09.1999. Mosley is quoting Brecht (1964), 18.

[703] Letter, 19.09.1999.
[704] The translation of these terms would (roughly) be *dividual* and *individual*.
[705] Nietzsche (1980b), 76.
[706] 'But as when talking about 'aesthetics' one has to be *so* careful here: for just as the idea of the aesthetic might be hideous without God, so might the idea of a 'new human type': there is no way of ensuring anything ethical without an idea of God.' (letter, 19.09.1999).
[707] Mosley himself had not thought about the novel in these terms, but found this approach to make sense when it was suggested by the present author (Interview, 10.10.2000).
[708] Mosley (CP), 86-87.
[709] Cf. chapter II.
[710] Mosley (1999).
[711] Interview, 10.10.2000.
[712] Interview, 10.10.2000.
[713] Cf. chapter II.
[714] Mosley (CP), 82. Here Mosley refers to and quotes from Popper (1972), 20, 36-37, 70.
[715] Mosley (CP), 82; my emphasis.
[716] Cf. chapter II on Mosley's conception of freedom regarding moral dilemmas.
[717] Mosley (CP), 82. Mosley's quote is from Popper (1972), 84.
[718] Mosley (CP), 82.
[719] Mosley refers to Bateson (1972), 118-19, 277.
[720] Mosley (CP), 83.
[721] Mosley (CP), 82.
[722] Mosley (CP), 82.
[723] Mosley (CP), 82.
[724] Mosley (CP), 83; my emphasis.
[725] Mosley (CP), 83; my emphasis. Mosley's quote is from Bateson (1972), 118-19, 277.
[726] Mosley (CP), 83-4. Mosley quotes from Bateson (1972), 118-19, 277.
[727] Mosley (CP), 83. Mosley in the same vein as his friend Guy Brenton (who introduced him to Bateson's work) is critical of Bateson's denial of any spirituality in Learning III: 'Bateson was too much of a scientist to admit that his "level III" suggested a spiritual or mystical dimension—he did use the word "oceanic," but he wouldn't used "god"' (letter, 06.10.2000).
[728] Mosley also referred to the biologist Jacques Monod, who claimed that evolution through natural selection in case of man is not natural anymore (Mosley, CP, 80).
[729] Mosley (CP), 85.
[730] Mosley (CP), 85. Here Mosley quotes J. Z. Young (1964), 287.
[731] Mosley (CP), 85.

[732] Mosley (CP), 161.
[733] Cf. the analysis of Mosley's '60s novels in chapter II.
[734] Banks (1982a), 124-28.
[735] In one of the essays in *Catastrophe Practice* Mosley mentions Beckett's *Happy Days* as 'one of the most touching of modern plays . . . the heroine—buried at first up to her waist and then up to her neck—can give—oh!—such magnificent performances! Trapped and indomitable, just like ourselves. And so we get comfort. Almost no grown-up plays (or novels for that matter) show anything of life as a successfully going concern: this is reserved for children's books and fantasies.' (Mosley CP, 227).
[736] Letter, 06.10.2000.
[737] Interview, 10.10.2000.
[738] Interview, 08.12.1996.
[739] Mosley (1996), 282; my emphasis.
[740] Mosley (1996), 252.
[741] Mosley (NN), 203-04.
[742] Mosley (NN), 205.
[743] Mosley (CP), 13.
[744] Mosley (1996), 271.
[745] Mosley (CP), 17.
[746] Interview, 17.09.1999; my emphasis.
[747] Mosley (1996), 275.
[748] Interview, 17.09.1999; my emphasis.
[749] Mosley (CP), 171-72, 180-81.
[750] Pinter, as mentioned in the previous chapter, wrote the film-script to *Accident*. Recently, Stoppard has written a number of unpublished scripts for the filming of *Hopeful Monsters*, whose prospects for being filmed are not very good.
[751] Mosley (1996), 282.
[752] Mosley (CP), 226.
[753] Mosley (CP), 224-26.
[754] Mosley (1996), 290.
[755] Mosley (1996), 279.
[756] Mosley (CP), 239.
[757] Mosley (CP), 239-41.
[758] Mosley (CP), 241.
[759] Mosley (CP), 260.
[760] Mosley (CP), 263
[761] Mosley (CP), 263.
[762] Mosley (CP), 263.
[763] Mosley (CP), 303.
[764] Mosley (CP), 302.
[765] Mosley (CP), 331.

[766] Mosley (CP), 241.
[767] Mosley (1996), 286.
[768] Mosley (IB), 1.
[769] Mosley (IB), 7.
[770] Mosley (IB), 3.
[771] Mosley (IB), 3.
[772] Mosley (IB), 3.
[773] Mosley (IB), 4.
[774] Mosley (IB), 7.
[775] Mosley (IB), 41-42.
[776] Mosley (IB), 41.
[777] Mosley (IB), 8.
[778] Mosley (IB), 33.
[779] Mosley (IB), 2.
[780] Mosley (IB), 15.
[781] Mosley (IB), 11-12.
[782] Mosley (IB), 32.
[783] Mosley (IB),109.
[784] Mosley (IB), 289.
[785] Mosley (IB), frontispiece.
[786] Mosley (1996), 289.
[787] Mosley (SP), 23-24.
[788] Mosley (SP), 20.
[789] Mosley (SP), 24.
[790] Mosley (CP), 165 ff. Also compare Booth (1982), 109.
[791] Mosley (SP), 64.
[792] Mosley (CP), 85.
[793] Mosley (SP), 25, 64.
[794] Mosley (SP), 64.
[795] Mosley (SP), 25.
[796] Mosley (CP), 7-8.
[797] Mosley (SP), 72.
[798] Mosley (SP), 121.
[799] Mosley (SP), 18.
[800] Mosley (SP), 105-06.
[801] Banks (1982b), 122.
[802] Mosley (SP), 190.
[803] Mosley (SP), 1.
[804] Mosley (SP), 48-52.
[305] Mosley (1996), 293.
[806] Mosley (SP), 190.
[807] Kleist (1991), 6.

[808] Mosley (JU), 10.
[809] Mosley (CP), 83; my emphasis.
[810] Mosley (JU), 59.
[811] Mosley (JU), 30.
[812] Mosley (JU), 62-65.
[813] Mosley (JU), 82.
[814] Mosley (JU), 32.
[815] Judith compares herself with the girl in a Piero di Cosimo painting hanging in the National Gallery: 'The painting of . . . a girl lying on her side with wounds in her throat and wrists . . . This might be myself?' (Mosley JU, 77).
[816] Mosley (JU), 84.
[817] Mosley (JU), 142.
[818] Mosley (JU), 86.
[819] Mosley (JU), 86.
[820] Mosley (JU), 94.
[821] Mosley (JU), 95.
[822] Mosley (JU), 93.
[823] Mosley (JU), 94, 100.
[824] Mosley (JU), 96-97.
[825] Cf. Murdoch (1997b), 224-25 and (1997a), 108-15. Cf. also Murdoch (1989).
[826] Mosley (JU), 96.
[827] Kleist (1991), 12.
[828] Mosley (JU), 111.
[829] Mosley (JU), 110.
[830] Mosley (JU), 29-30.
[831] Cf. Muecke (1973), 36 ff. And McFadden (1982), 18.
[832] Mosley (JU), 141-44.
[833] Mosley (JU), 204.
[834] Nietzsche (1980a). There is of course, also the analogy to Mosley's own leaving the Garden of conventional Christianity in the hope of being at the centre of religion. Cf. chapter II.
[835] Mosley (JU), 210.
[836] Mosley (JU), 290 ff.
[837] Mosley (JU), 210.
[838] Goldschmidt (1982), 390. Cf. also Bowler (1984), 324. Bowler further mentions that Goldschmidt was taken up in the 1970s by major biologists such as Gould and Allen, who based their theory of 'epigenetic evolution'—i.e., evolution in big jumps rather than gradual Darwinian processes—on his 'hopeful monsters' conjectures.
[839] Mosley (JU), 291.
[840] Mosley (JU), 289-90.
[841] Mosley (HM), 524.

[842] Mosley (1996), 332-33.
[843] Mosley (1996), 328.
[844] Brecht (1964), 18.
[845] Goldschmidt (1982), 390. Cf. also Bowler (1984), 322-27.
[846] Mosley (1996), 330.
[847] 'Eleanor and Max are extraordinarily like each other. Both have had unorthodox sexual experiences . . . the result is that they eventually seem to merge into each other, the male and female halves of a single personality.' (King 1990).
[848] Mosley (HM), 244.
[849] Mosley (HM), 245.
[850] As Massie (1990b) notes: 'the novel is a form of philosophical discourse. . . . Mosley tries to bring the two cultures of literature and science together.'
[851] Mosley (1996), 330.
[852] Mosley (JU), 30.
[853] Mosley (HM), 102.
[854] Mosley (HM), 120.
[855] Mosley (HM), 245.
[856] Mosley (HM), 42-43.
[857] Mosley (HM), 43.
[858] Mosley (HM), 43-45.
[859] Mosley (HM), 43.
[860] Mosley (HM), 457.
[861] Mosley (HM), 49.
[862] Mosley (HM), 70.
[863] Mosley (HM), 71.
[864] Mosley (HM), 82-83.
[865] Mosley (CP), 232.
[866] Mosley (HM), 529; my emphasis.
[867] Mosley (HM), 529.
[868] Mosley (HM), 529, 538.
[869] Mosley (HM), 529.
[870] Mosley (HM), 529.
[871] Mosley (HM), 539.
[872] Cf. the discussion of Trotsky in this chapter.
[873] Cf. also chapter II.
[874] Chapter II elaborated on this idea extensively.
[875] Interview, 31.01.1997. The imagery of 'walking hand in hand with God' was used effectively by the central figure of the Oxford Movement, Cardinal Newman. He saw himself 'substantially [as] the child who walked with God at Ham . . .' (Faber 1954, 35). However whereas Newman saw himself—or mankind—as a child being led on by the father figure God, Mosley, as has often been mentioned before, sees man and God as partners—or to use the imagery of mystical poetry,

as lovers—walking hand in hand and helping each other out, whenever the other is in need. In the same vein as in Eastern (Sufi) poetry, Mosley does away with the conventional vertical order and puts God and man on an equal footing.

[876] Interview, 31.01.1997. This was Mosley's answer to Tom Stoppard's question (who at the time was writing a film-script for *Hopeful Monsters*): 'What does differentiate *Hopeful Monsters* from *unhopeful Monsters*?'

[877] Interview, 31.01.1997.

[878] Mosley (HM), 427, 428.

[879] Rudman (1992) observes: 'Mosley is wonderfully tenacious in the way he interweaves the physical, physics and the metaphysical.' (45).

[880] Mosley (HM), 550-51.

[881] Interview, 10.10.2000.

[882] Interview, 10.10.2000.

[883] Mosley (HM), 542.

[884] Mosley (HM), 543.

[885] Thody (1971), 41.

[886] Mosley (CP), 77.

[887] Mosley (HM), 71.

[888] Lessing (1985), p. 7.

[889] Capra (1982), 93.

[890] Mosley (HM), 227-28.

[891] Cf. her comparison of the mythical language of alchemy to that of modern physics as a way of explaining nuclear energy, in Mosley (HM), 468.

[892] Nietzsche (1983), 94.

[893] This is what the present author was told at her very first meeting with Mosley on 13.06.1994, when interviewing the latter about his *Catastrophe Practice Series*, the series being the subject of her *Magisterarbeit* at Düsseldorf University.

[894] Mosley (HM), 524.

[895] Mosley (1996), 335.

[896] Mosley (1996), 335.

[897] Interview. 31.01.1997.

[898] Nietzsche (1983), 91; my emphasis.

[899] Also cf. chapter III: Mosley's idea of all true battles being in the mind.

[900] 'In the first half [of the twentieth century] you thought you could see everything by organisation, empires, now we don't know what is happening!' (interview, 31.01.1997).

[901] Nietzsche (1983), 122.

[902] The term borrowed from military parlance fits the Nietzschean idea of the artist being a fighter.

[903] Mosley (1996), 170.

[904] Nietzsche (1983), 95.

[905] Mosley (1996).

[906] Nietzsche (1983), 91.
[907] Nietzsche (1983), 122; my emphasis.
[908] Nietzsche (1983), 94.
[909] Interview, 31.01.1997.
[910] Interview, 31.01.1997.
[911] Interview, 31.01.1997.
[912] Interview, 12.02.1997.
[913] Interview, 12.02.1997.
[914] Interview, 12.02.1997.
[915] Interview, 12.12.2000.
[916] Interview, 12.12.2000.
[917] J. W. Dyck argues that the most spectacular resurrection of God, in the same vein as in the Holy Script, is in Nietzsche's *Dionysos-Dithyramben*; namely a resurrection through sacrifice: 'Mein unbekannter Gott? Mein Schmerz, mein letztes Glück!' (Dyck, 1982, 24).
[918] Stack (1992), 15.
[919] Stack (1992), 15; my emphasis. With this reading of Nietzsche, Dyck's argument about Nietzsche's spectacular resurrection of God, seems plausible.
[920] Stack (1992), 15.
[921] Interview, 12.12.2000.
[922] Interview, 12.12.2000.
[923] Interview, 12.12.2000.
[924] 'the Church . . . having hijacked the whole thing [i.e., Christianity], says we know what reality is. Reality is this: A, B, C, D, which is all wrong.' (Interview, 12.12.2000.)
[925] Interview, 12.12.2000.
[926] In this sense Mosley's concern with spirituality could be compared to Kleist's view on the relationship between religion, art and science, who believed that new scientific theories (such as the non-Euclidean mathematics) only re-defined old fundamental values. (see Dyck, 1982, 19).
[927] Letter, 27.02.2000. Mosley is quoting from 'Random Reality,' in *New Scientist*, 26 Feb 2000, p. 26.
[928] McFadden (2000).
[929] Letter, 02.04.2001.
[930] Arthur (2000); Arthur is quoting Andy Fabian of the Institute of Astronomy at Cambridge.
[931] Börner (2001); my translation and emphasis.
[932] Letter, 02.04.2001.
[933] Mosley (HT), 119.
[934] Schimmel (1991), 105-21.
[935] McFadden (2000).
[936] McFadden (2000)

[937] McFadden (2000)
[938] 'When I was reading your stuff last night and my head was so buzzing that I though I would never sleep, I put [your Chapter] down and picked up a Sufi book to calm me down and immediately came across this piece (enclosed) about the three levels of knowledge written in the 13th century! What a business!' (Letter, 25.03.2001).
[939] Shah (1990), 85.
[940] Eco (1983), 126.
[941] White (2000).
[942] This issue was extensively discussed in chapters II and III.
[943] Todd (1988), 8 ff.
[944] Bradbury (1994), 462.
[945] Letter, 02.04.2001.
[946] Interview, 31.01.1997.
[947] This is how Mosley's autobiography ends (Mosley, 1996, 339).
[948] Mosley (CD), 6-14.
[949] Mosley (CD), 24.
[950] Mosley (CD),193-95.
[951] Letter, 28.05.2001. This idea has been extensively explored in chapters II and III.
[952] This has been discussed in detail in chapters II and III, however, whereas here we speak of God, in the previous chapters words such as a 'greater whole' or 'the circuit of the circuits' etc. are used.
[953] Mosley (CD), 194.
[954] Mosley (CD), 194.
[955] McFadden (2000).
[956] Mosley (CD), 192.
[957] For a more detailed discussion of this issue ref. to the discussions of Mosley's Sixties novels and his *Catastrophe Practice Series*, especially that of *Judith*, in chapters II and III, respectively.
[958] Mosley (CD), 240.
[959] Also cf. the discussion of the laughing 'God' in Judith's ashram in Chapter III.
[960] Letter, 28.05.2001.
[961] Letter, 28.05.2001.
[962] Letter, 28.05.2001.
[963] Mosley (CD), 6.
[964] Mosley (CD), 7-8, 10.
[965] Mosley (CD), 112.
[966] 'When I had gone to Russia to do my story on the aftermath of the Chernobyl disaster and had expected to find cover-ups and instead had found almost an exaggeration of its effects, I had seen that there were practical reasons for this

...' (Mosley, CD, 111).
[967] Mosley (CD), 61.
[968] Mosley (CD), 96.
[969] '*Children of Darkness and Light* is effectively constructed as a mystery' (Zohar, 1996).
[970] This idea has been extensively discussed in chapter II.
[971] Mosley (CD), 62.
[972] Shah (1990), 85.
[973] Mosley (CD), 112.
[974] Mosley (CD), 10.
[975] Interview, 12.12.2000.
[976] Mosley (JD), 34-36.
[977] Mosley (JD), 1-12.
[978] Mosley (JD), 2-4. Mosley is quoting from Steiner (1971), 31 and from Bloom (1995), 6, 16.
[979] Mosley (JD), 4. Mosley is quoting Bloom (1995), 30.
[980] Mosley (JD), 4.
[981] Mosley (JD), 25.
[982] Mosley (JD), 26.
[983] Mosley (JD), 2.
[984] Mosley (JD), 2.
[985] Mosley (JD), 11. Mosley is quoting from Steriner (1989), 3-4.
[986] Interview, 12.12.2000.
[987] Mosley (JD), 82.
[988] Mosley (JD), 76.
[989] Mosley (JD), 76.
[990] Mosley (JD), 59.
[991] Mosley (JD), 60.
[992] Mosley (JD), 60.
[993] Mosley (JD), 60.
[994] Mosley (JD), 61.
[995] Mosley (JD), 79-80.
[996] Mosley (JD), 80.
[997] Mosley (JD), 80.
[998] Mosley (JD), 81; my emphasis.
[999] Steiner (1971), 18.
[1000] Mosley (JD), 22ff.
[1001] Mosley (JD), 43ff.
[1002] Mosley (JD), 62 ff.
[1003] Mosley (JD), 69 ff.
[1004] Mosley (JD), 70.
[1005] Mosley (JD), 81; my emphasis.

[1006] Interview, 12.12.2000.
[1007] Letter, 29.07.2001.
[1008] Mosley (1996), 170.
[1009] 'Your working-out of the ages of the children and their connections is good. I haven't been conscious of these at the time of writing, but there they are!' (Letter, 02.04.2001).
[1010] Mosley (HT), 5.
[1011] Mosley (HT), 5.
[1012] Mosley (HT), 5.
[1013] Mosley (HT), 284. There is a very autobiographical note to this passage. During the very early stages of this novel Mosley himself was diagnosed with leukaemia and for the first couple of weeks had strangely high fevers, for which the doctors could not find any explanation.
[1014] Mosley (HT), 9.
[1015] Mosley (HT), 24.
[1016] Mosley (HT), 24.
[1017] One must bear in mind that Mosley—leaning on Susanne Langer and Koestler—sees scientific observation as an observation that makes aesthetic sense. Cf. Chapter III.
[1018] Mosley (HT), 32.
[1019] Mosley (HT), 25.
[1020] Mosley (HT), 112; my emphasis.
[1021] Mosley (HT), 113.
[1022] Mosley (HT), 112; my emphasis.
[1023] Mosley (HT), 45.
[1024] Mosley (HT), 45.
[1025] Interview, 12.12.2000.
[1026] Interview, 12.12.2000; my emphasis.
[1027] Mosley (HT), 218.
[1028] Mosley (HT), 119.
[1029] Mosley (HT), 8.
[1030] Mosley (HT), 194.
[1031] Mosley (HT), 49.
[1032] Interview, 12.12.2000.
[1033] Mosley (HT), 65; my emphasis.
[1034] Mosley (HT), 65.
[1035] Mosley (HT), 65.
[1036] Mosley (HT), 290.
[1037] Mosley (HT), 49.
[1038] Mosley (HT), 59.
[1039] Mosley (HT), 240.
[1040] Mosley (HT), 122. Mosley is referring to how the astronomer Fred Hoyle

described the likelihood of random forces generating life. McFadden (2000).
[1041] Massie (2001).
[1042] Mosley (HT), 283.
[1043] Mosley (HT), 137.
[1044] Mosley (HT), 141.
[1045] Mosley (HT), 312.
[1046] Mosley (HT), 291.
[1047] This is symbolically shown by the narrator having to slither through a back window into the abandoned cottage on the island. Mosley (HT), 137.
[1048] Mosley (HT), 137.
[1049] Mosley (HT), 215, 219.
[1050] Mosley (HT), 230.
[1051] Mosley (IG), frontispiece.
[1052] Letter, 20.10.2001.
[1053] Interview, 29.09.2001.
[1054] Interview, 12.12.2000.
[1055] Interview, 12.12.2000.
[1056] Mosley (HT), 240.
[1057] Mosley, (IG), 303.
[1058] Cf. chapters II.
[1059] Cf. chapter IV.
[1060] Mosley, (JD), 81; my emphasis.
[1061] Mosley (IG), 188 ff.
[1062] Mosley (IG), 206 ff.
[1063] Mosley (IG), 241.
[1064] Mosley (IG), 272.
[1065] Mosley (IG), 272.
[1066] This idea has been extensively discussed in Chapter IV.
[1067] Mosley (IG), 313.
[1068] Mosley (IG), 313.
[1069] Mosley (IG), 323.
[1070] Mosley (IG), 332; my emphasis.
[1071] Mosley (IG), 305.
[1072] Mosley (IG), 272-74.
[1073] Mosley (IG), 274.
[1074] Mosley (IG), 272.
[1075] Interview, 29.09.01.
[1076] Cf. Chapter III of this thesis.
[1077] Mosley (IG), 341.
[1078] Mosley (IG), 340.
[1079] Mosley, (IG), 340; my emphasis.
[1080] Nietzsche (1986), p. 95. 'Science, art and philosophy are growing so much

together inside me, that I will once surely give birth to Centaurs.'; my translation. In the context of Mosley's work Nietzsche's centaurs could fittingly be understood as Hopeful Monsters.

[1081] Stack (1992), 15.
[1082] Stack (1992), 15.
[1083] Maritain (1930), 225-26.
[1084] Mosley (JD), 132.
[1085] Letter, 13.09.2001.
[1086] Letter, 01.10.2001.

Bibliography

Note: novels by Nicholas Mosley are quoted in the footnotes as follows: 'Mosley' and abbreviated title in brackets, e.g., 'Mosley (SD)' refers to Mosley's novel *Spaces of the Dark*. Mosley's letters to and interviews with the present author are quoted in the footnotes as follows: 'Letter' and the date of letter; 'interview' and the date of interview. All other books, articles and reviews are quoted in the footnotes as follows: name of the author followed by the year of publication in brackets.

The present list of the articles written by Mosley only consists of those that have been quoted in this book.

Primary sources

Novels by Nicholas Mosley

Mosley, Nicholas. (SD) Sp*aces of the Dark*. London: Rupert Hart-Davis, 1951.

Mosley, Nicholas. (RB) *Rainbearers*. London: Weidenfeld & Nicolson, 1955.

Mosley, Nicholas. (CO) *Corruption*. London: Weidenfeld & Nicolson, 1957.

Mosley, Nicholas. (MP) *Meeting Place* [1962]. London: Minerva, 1995.

Mosley, Nicholas. (AC) *Accident* [1965]. London: Minerva, 1993; Elmwood Park, IL: Dalkey Archive, 1985.

Mosley, Nicholas. (AS) *Assassins* [1966]. London: Minerva, 1993; Normal, IL: Dalkey Archive, 1997.

Mosley, Nicholas. (IO) *Impossible Object* [1968]. London: Minerva, 1993; Elmwood Park, IL: Dalkey Archive, 1985.

Mosley, Nicholas. (NN) *Natalie Natalia* [1971]. London: Minerva, 1995; Normal, IL: Dalkey Archive, 1996.

Mosley, Nicholas. (CP) *Catastrophe Practice: Plays for Not Acting and Cypher: A Novel* [1979]. London: Minerva, 1992; Normal, IL: Dalkey Archive, 1989.

Mosley, Nicholas. (IB) *Imago Bird* [1980]. London: Minerva, 1991; Elmwood Park, IL: Dalkey Archive, 1989.

Mosley, Nicholas. (SE) *Serpent* [1981]. London: Minerva, 1991; Elmwood Park, IL: Dalkey Archive, 1990.

Mosley, Nicholas. (JU) *Judith* [1986]. London: Minerva, 1992; Elmwood Park, IL: Dalkey Archive, 1991.

Mosley, Nicholas. (HM) *Hopeful Monsters* [1990]. London: Minerva, 1991; Elmwood Park, IL: Dalkey Archive, 1991.

Mosley, Nicholas. (CD) *Children of Darkness and Light*. London: Secker & Warburg, 1996; Normal, IL: Dalkey Archive, 1997.

Mosley, Nicholas. (JD) *Journey into the Dark*, 1997. Excerpted in *The Uses of Slime Mold: Essays of Four Decades*. Normal, IL: Dalkey Archive, 2004.

Mosley, Nicholas. (HT) *Hesperides Tree*. London: Secker & Warburg, 2001; Normal, IL: Dalkey Archive, 2001.

Mosley, Nicholas. (IG) *Inventing God*. London: Secker & Warburg, 2003; Normal, IL: Dalkey Archive, 2003.

Articles and non-fiction by Nicholas Mosley

Mosley, Nicholas. (1958a) *African Switchback*. London: Weidenfeld & Nicolson, 1958.

Mosley, Nicholas. (1958b) 'Memories of Childhood.' Unpublished article, dated 1958.

Mosley, Nicholas. (1959) 'The Church and Art.' *Prism* (February, 1959). Rpt. in *The Uses of Slime Mold: Essays of Four Decades*. Normal, IL: Dalkey Archive, 2004.

Mosley, Nicholas. (1961a) *The Life of Raymond Raynes*. London: The Faith Press, 1961.

Mosley, Nicholas. (1961b) 'William Faulkner's Universe.' *Time and Tide*, 13.01.1961.

Mosley, Nicholas. (1961c) 'Christian Novels.' *Prism*, October 1961.

Mosley, Nicholas. (1965) *Experience and Religion*. London: Hodder & Stoughton, 1965; Normal, IL: Dalkey Archive, 2006.

Mosley, Nicholas. (1972) *The Assassination of Trotsky*. London: Michael Joseph, 1972.

Mosley, Nicholas. (1976) *Julian Grenfell: his life and the times of his death 1885-1915*. London: Weidenfeld & Nicolson, 1976.

Mosley, Nicholas. (1978) 'Walls of Thinnest Air.' Rev. of *A Reflection of the Other Person: The Letters of Virginia Woolf 1929-1931*, edited by Nigel Nicolson and Joanne Trautmann. *The Listener*, 26.10.1978.

Mosley, Nicholas. (1979) 'Cold Feet.' Rev. of *The Tragedy of Leon Trotsky* by Ronald Segal. *The London Review of Books*, 8.11.1979. Rpt. in *The Uses of Slime Mold: Essays of Four Decades*. Normal, IL: Dalkey Archive, 2004.

Mosley, Nicholas. (1980a) 'Runaway mankind.' Rev. of *Mind and Nature* by Gregory Bateson. *The Listener*, 24.07.1980.

Mosley, Nicholas. (1980b) 'Nietzsche and Creation.' Rev. of *Nietzsche: A Critical Life* by Ronald Hayman. *Time and Tide*, 1980. Rpt. in *The Uses of Slime Mold: Essays of Four Decades*. Normal, IL: Dalkey Archive, 2004.

Mosley, Nicholas. (1983) 'Flirting with Films.' *The Times Literary Supplement*, 5.11.1983.

Mosley, Nicholas. (1992a) *Rules of the Game / Beyond the Pale: Memoirs of Sir Oswald Mosley and Family*. London: Secker & Warburg, 1992; Elmwood Park, IL: Dalkey Archive, 1991.

Mosley, Nicholas. (1992b) 'What are Novels For?' *Times Literary Supplement*, 17.1.1992. Rpt. in *The Uses of Slime Mold: Essays of Four Decades*. Normal, IL: Dalkey Archive, 2004.

Mosley, Nicholas. (1994) 'Fathers and Sons: Darkness and Light.' *The Daily Telegraph*, 15.10.1994.

Mosley, Nicholas. (1996) *Efforts at Truth: An Autobiography*. London: Minerva: 1996; Normal, IL: Dalkey Archive, 1995.

Mosley, Nicholas. (1997a) *The Uses of Slime Mould: Essays of Four Decades* [1997]. Normal, IL: Dalkey Archive, 2004.

Mosley, Nicholas. (1997b) 'Rosemary Mosley—A Memoir: An Introduction to an Exhibition of Rosemary Mosley's paintings—1991.' (Unpublished article, 1997.)

Mosley, Nicholas. (1997c) 'The Iliad.' (Unpublished article, 1997).

Mosley, Nicholas. (1997d) 'Books of the Year.' *The Daily Telegraph*, 22.11.1997.

Mosley, Nicholas. (1999) 'The Mind and Body take to the Floor.' *Daily Telegraph*, 28.08.99.

Letters from Nicholas Mosley to the present author

Letter, 18.05.1998.
Letter, 24.08.1999.

Letter, 19.09.1999.
Letter, 27.02.2000.
Letter, 06.10.2000.
Letter, 30.01.2001.
Letter, 25.03.2001.
Letter, 02.04.2001.
Letter, 28.05.2001.
Letter, 13.09.2001.
Letter, 01.10.2001.
Letter, 20.10.2001.

Interviews by the present author with Nicholas Mosley

Interview, 13.06.1994.
Interview, 08.12.1996.
Interview, 21.12.1996.
Interview, 31.01.1997.
Interview, 12.02.1997.
Interview, 16.06.1997.
Interview, 15.07.1997.
Interview, 21.11.1997.
Interview, 22.02.1998.
Interview, 23.06.1998.
Interview, 06.04.1999.
Interview, 17.09.1999.
Interview, 10.10.2000.
Interview, 12.12.2000.
Interview, 29.09.2001.

Secondary sources

Ackroyd, Peter. (1976) *Notes for a New Culture*. London: Vision Press, 1976.
Ackroyd, Peter. (1985) *Hawksmoor*. London: Hamilton, 1985.
Adonis, Andrew and Pollard, Stephen. (1997) *A Class Act: The Myth of Britiain's Classless Society*. London: Hamish Hamilton, 1997.

Alexej Ugrinsky, ed. (1980) *Heinrich von Kleist Studien*. Berlin: Erich Schmidt Verlag, 1980.
Allen, Donald and Creeley, Robert, eds. (1965) *New American Story*. New York: Grove Press, 1965.
Allen, Walter. (1954) 'New Novels.' In *New Statesman and Nation*, 30.1.1954.
Allen, Walter. (1964) *Tradition and Dream: The English and American Novel from the Twenties to Our Time*. London: Phoenix House, 1964.
Amis, Kingsley. (1959) *Lucky Jim*. London: Four Square Books, 1959.
Amis, Kingsley. (1961) *I Like It Here*. London: Four Square Book, 1961.
Amis, Martin. (1975) *Dead Babies*. London: Cape, 1975.
Amis, Martin. (1984) *Money*. London: Cape, 1984.
Amis, Martin. (2000) *Experience*. London: Jonathan Cape, 2000.
Anon. (1951a) Rev. of *Spaces of the Dark*. *Oxford Mail*, 15.3.1951.
Anon. (1951b) Rev. of *Spaces of the Dark*. *Manchester Guardian*, 26.1.1951.
Anon. (1951c) 'Professional backgrounds.' Rev. of *Spaces of the Dark*. *Times Literary Supplement*, 2.2.1951.
Anon. (1955) 'Moments of choice.' Rev. of *Rainbearers*. *Times Literary Supplement*, 7.10.1955.
Anon. (1957a) Rev. of *Corruption*. *Punch*, 24.4.1957.
Anon. (1957b) Rev. of *Corruption*. *Belfast Telegraph*, 20.4.1957.
Anon. (1965) 'Exploiting Anna.' *Times Literary Supplement*, 14.1.1965.
Ardagh, John. (1967). Article on Mosley. *Le Monde*, 29.3.1967.
Arthur, Charles. (2000) 'Universe Is Flat and "Will Be Expanding Forever."' *The Independent*, 27.04.2000.
Ballard, J. G. (1973) *Crash*. New York: Farrar, Straus and Giroux, 1973.
Banks, John. (1982a) 'Contrived Chaos: *Catastrophe Practice* and Gödelian Incompleteness.' In *Review Of Contemporary Fiction* (Summer 1982): 124-28.
Banks, John. (1982b) 'Sleight-of-Language,' in *Review of Contemporary Fiction*, (Summer 1982): 118-23.
Barrenechea, Maria. (1965) *Borges: The Labyrinth Maker*. New York: New York Univ. Press, 1965.
Barth, John. (1967) 'The Literature of Exhaustion,' *Atlantic Monthly* (August 1967). Rpt. In *Surfiction: Fiction Now and Tomorrow* [1975]. Raymond Federman (ed). Chicago: Swallow Press, 1981, pp. 19-33.
Barth, John. (1969) *Lost in the Funhouse*. N. Y.: Bantam Books, 1969.
Barth, John. (1980) 'The Literature of Replenishment.' *Atlantic Monthly* (1980): 65-71.

Barth, John. (1984) *The Friday Book: Essays and other Nonfiction*. New York: G. P. Putnam and Sons, 1984.

Barthes, Roland. (1975) *The Pleasure of the Text* [1973], trans. Richard Miller. New York: Hill & Wang, 1975.

Bateson, Gregory. (1972) *Steps to an Ecology of Mind: Collected Essays in Anthropology, Psychiatry, Evolution, And Epistomology*. London: Intertext Books, 1972.

Baudrillard, Jean. (1994) *Simulacra and Simulation* [1981], trans. Sheila Faria Glaser. Ann Arbour: Univ. of Michigan Press, 1994.

Bauer, Peter T. (1978) *Class on the Brain: The Cost of a British Obsession*. London: Centre for Policy Studies, 1978.

Beckett, Samuel. (1994) *Malone Dies*; *The Beckett Triology: Molloy, Malone Dies, The Unnamable*. London and N. Y.: Calder Publications, 1994.

Bergonzi, Bernard. (1970) *The Situation of the Novel*. London: Macmillan, 1970.

Betjeman, John. (1951) 'Not a nice light book from the library.' *The Daily Telegraph*, 2.2.1951.

Betjeman, John. (1954) 'Amusing Story of Life at a Provincial University.' *Daily Telegraph*, 5.2. 1954.

Bhabha, Homi. (1994) *The Location of Culture*. London: Routledge, 1994.

Birch, Sarah. (1994) *Christine Brooke-Rose and Contemporary Fiction*. Oxford: Clarendon Press, 1994.

Bloom, Harold. (1995) *The Western Canon*. London: MacMillan, 1995.

Booth, Francis. (1982) 'Impossible Accidents: Nicholas Mosley.' *Review of Contemporary Fiction*, (summer 1982): 87-118.

Borges, Jorge Luis. (1971) *Labyrinths*. Harmondsworth: Penguin, 1971.

Börner, Gerhard. (2001) 'Die Quintessenz des Universums.' *Süddeutsche Zeitung*, 8.05.2001.

Bowler, Peter J. (1984) *Evolution: The History of an Idea*. Berkley: Univ. of California Press, 1984.

Bradbury, Malcolm. (1981) Rev. of *Serpent*. *Vogue*, Dec. 1981.

Bradbury, Malcolm, ed. (1982) *The Novel Today* [1977]. London: Fontana, 1982.

Bradbury, Malcolm. (1987) *No, Not Bloomsbury*. London: André Deutsch, 1987.

Bradbury, Malcolm, ed. (1990) *The Novel Today* [1977]. Revised edition. London: Fontana, 1990.

Bradbury, Malcom and Cooke, Judy, eds. (1992) *New Writing*. London: Minerva, 1992.

Bradbury, Malcom. (1993) 'Postmodernism, the Novel, and the TV Medium (1) and (2).' Heide Ziegler (ed.), *The End of Postmodernism: New Directions. Proceedings of the First Stuttgart Seminar in Cultural Studies 04.08-18.08.1991.* Stuttgart: M & P Verl. für Wiss. und Forschung, 1993, pp. 81-100 and pp. 115-34.

Bradbury, Malcolm. (1994) *The Modern British Novel.* London: Penguin, 1994.

Brecht, Bertolt. (1964) *Brecht on Theatre: the Development of an Aesthetic,* trans. and notes John Willett. London: Methuen & Co., 1964.

Brook, Stephen. (1997) *Class: Knowing Your Place in Modern Britain.* London: Gollancz, 1997.

Brooke-Rose, Christine. (1986) *The Christine Brooke-Rose Omnibus: Out, Such, Between, Thru.* Manchester: Carcanet, 1986.

Broyard, Anatole. (1971) 'Comprehending Natalia.' *New York Times,* 23.12.1971.

Bürger, Christa u. Peter, eds. (1987) *Postmoderne: Alltag, Allegorie, Avantgarde.* Frankfurt: Suhrkamp, 1987.

Burgess, Anthony. (1983) *Wanting Seed* [1962]. Feltham: Hamlyn, 1983.

Burgin, Richard. (1969) *Conversations with Jorge Luis Borges.* New York: Holt, Rinehart and Winston, 1969.

Burroughs, William. (1964) *The Naked Lunch* [1959]. London: John Calder, 1964.

Burroughs, William. (1965) *Nova Express.* N. Y.: Grove Press, 1965.

Butler, Christopher. (1980) *After the Wake: An Essay on the Contemporary Avantgarde.* Oxford: Clarendon Press, 1980.

Butler, Christopher. (1984) 'The Pleasure of the Experimental Text.' Jeremy Hawthorn (ed.), *Criticism and Critical Theory.* London: Edward Arnold, 1984, pp. 129-39.

Butler, Christopher. (1989) 'The Future of Theory: Saving the Reader.' Ralph Cohn (ed.), *The Future of Literary Theory.* N. Y. and London: Routledge, 1989, pp. 229-49.

Butler, Christopher. (1994) 'Postmodernism, Radical Theory, And the Fortunes of the Individual.' Gerhard Hoffmann and Alfred Hornung (eds.), *Affirmation and Negation in Contemporary American Culture.* Heidelberg: Universitätsverlag C. Winter, 1994, pp. 195-212.

Butler, Christopher. (1996) 'Postmodernism and Moral Philosophy.' Gerhard Hoffmann and Alfred Hornung (eds.), *Ethics and Aesthetics: The Moral Turn of Postmodernism.* Heidelberg: Universitätsverlag C. Winter, 1996, pp. 69-86.

Butor, Michel. (1990) *The Novel as Research.* Malcolm Bradbury (ed.), *The Novel Today.* London: Fontana Press, 1990, pp. 45-50.
Byatt, A. S. (1965) *Degrees of Freedom: The Novels of Iris Murdoch.* London: Chatto and Windus, 1965.
Byatt, A. S. (1990) *Possession: A Romance.* London: Chatto & Windus, 1990.
Calinescu, M. and Fokkema, D., eds. (1990) *Exploring Postmodernism.* Amsterdam: John Benjamin Publishing Company, 1990.
Calvino, Italo. (1981) 'Myth in the Narrative.' Raymond Federman, ed. *Surfiction: Fiction Now and Tomorrow* [1975]. Chicago: Swallow Press, 1981, pp. 75-81.
Capra, Fritjof. (1982). *The Tao of Physics: An Exploration of the Parallels Between Modern Physics and Eastern Mysticism* [1975]. London: Flamingo, 1982.
Carter, Angela. (1981) *The Bloody Chamber and Other Stories.* London: Penguin, 1981.
Carter, Angela. (1984) *Nights at the Circus.* London: Chatto & Windus, 1984.
Cohn, Ralph, ed. (1989) *The Future of Literary Theory.* N. Y. and London: Routledge, 1989.
Connor, Steven. (1996) *The English novel in History 1950-1995.* London: Routledge, 1996.
Connor, Steven. (1997) *Postmodernist Culture: An Introduction to Theories of the Contemporary* Oxford: Blackwell Publishers, 1997.
Cooper, William. (1959) 'Reflections on Some Aspects of the Experimental Novel.' John Wain, ed. *International Literary Annual, No. 2.* London, 1959.
Crace, Jim. (1997) *Quarantine.* London: Viking, 1997.
Cranston, Maurice. (1958) 'The New Novelists: An Enquiry with Contributions by Anthony Quinton, Lettice Cooper, Frank Kermode, Maurice Cranston.' *London Magazine,* Nov. 1958 vol. 5.
Culler, Jonathan. (1976) *Saussure.* London: Fontana, 1976.
Culler, Jonathan. (1982) *On Deconstruction.* London: Routledge, 1982.
Culler, Jonathan. (1983) *On Deconstruction: Theory and Criticism after Structuralism.* London and Melbourne: Routledge, 1983.
Culler, Jonathan. (1997) *Literary Theory: A Very Short Introduction.* Oxford: OUP, 1997.
Cunningham, Valentine. (1986) Rev. of *Judith. The Observer,* 7.9.1986.
Cunningham, Valentine. (1992) 'Facing the New.' Malcolm Bradbury and Judy Cooke, eds. *New Writing.* London: Minerva, 1992, pp. 229-39.

Derrida, Jacques. (1991) *A Derrida Reader: Between the Blinds*, ed. Peggy Kamuf. London & N.Y.: Wheatsheaf, 1991.
Doyle, Roddy. (1999) *A Star Called Henry*. London: Jonathan Cape, 1999.
Drabble, Margaret. (1977) *The Ice Age*. London: Weidenfeld & Nicholson, 1977.
Duchene, Anne. (1957) Rev. of *Corruption*. *Manchester Guardian*, 24.3.1957.
Dyck, J. W. (1982) *Der Instinkt der Verwandschaft: Heinrich von Kleist und Friedrich Nietzsche, Thomas Mann, Franz Kafka, Bertolt Brecht*. Bern & Frankfurt: Peter Lang, 1982.
Eagleton, Terry. (1984) *The Function of Criticism: From* The Spectator *to Post-Structuralism*. London: Verso, 1984.
Eagleton, Terry. (1988) 'A revolution on the cheap.' Times Literary Supplement, 02.01. 1998.
Eco, Umberto. (1983) *Travels in Hyperreality*. N.Y.: Harcourt, 1983.
Eco, Umberto. (1984) *Postscript to The Name of the Rose*, trans. William Weaver. New York: Harcourt Brace Jovanovich, 1984.
Eve, R., Horsfall, S. and Lee, M., eds. (1997) Chaos, Complexity and Sociology. *Thousand Oaks, Cal. & London: Sage, 1997.*
Faber, Geoffrey. (1954) *Oxford Apostles: A Character Study of the Oxford Movement* [1933]. London: Penguin, 1954.
Federman, Raymond, ed. (1981a) *Surfiction: Fiction Now and Tomorrow* [1975]. Chicago: Swallow Press, 1981.
Federman, Raymond. (1981b) 'Surfiction—Four Propositions in Form of an Introduction.' Raymond Federman, ed. *Surfiction: Fiction Now and Tomorrow* [1975]. Chicago: Swallow Press, 1981, pp. 5-15.
Federman, Raymond. (1981c) 'Fiction Today or the Pursuit of Non-Knowledge.' Raymond Federman, ed. *Surfiction: Fiction Now and Tomorrow* [1975]. Chicago: Swallow Press, 1981, pp. 291-311.
Federman, Raymond. (1993) 'Before Postmodernism and After (Part One) and (Part Two).' Heide Ziegler, ed. *The End of Postmodernism: New Directions. Proceedings of the First Stuttgart Seminar in Cultural Studies 04.08-18.08.1991*. Stuttgart: M & P Verl. für Wiss. und Forschung, 1993, pp. 47-64 and pp. 153-70.
Fletcher, John and Cheryl Bove. (1994) *Iris Murdoch: A Descriptive Primary and Annotated Secondary Bibliography*. New York & London: Garland Publishing, Inc., 1994.
Ford, Boris. (1992) *The Cambridge Cultural History of Britain: Modern Britain, Vol. 9*. Cambridge: Cambridge Univ. Press, 1992.

Foucault, Michel. (1987) 'The Order of Discourse.' Robert Young, ed. *Untying the Text: A Post-Structuralist Reader.* N. Y.: Routledge, 1987.
Fowles, John. (1969) *The French Lieutenant's Woman.* London: Jonathan Cape, 1969.
Fowles, John. (1985) *A Maggot.* London: Cape, 1985.
Fowles, John. (1989) *Daniel Martin* [1977]. London: Picador, 1989.
Fowles, John. (1990) 'Notes on an Unfinished Novel.' Malcolm Bradbury, ed. [1977] *The Novel Today.* London: Fontana, 1990, pp. 147-62.
Fukuyama, Francis. (1992) *The End of History and the Last Man.* London: Hamilton, 1992.
Gasiorek, Andrzej. (1995) *Post-war British Fiction: Realism and After.* London: Edward Arnold, 1995.
Gerz, Jochen. (1981) 'Towards a Language of Doing.' Raymond Federman (ed.). *Surfiction: Fiction Now and Tomorrow* [1975]. Chicago: 1981, pp. 279-81.
Gindin, James. (1959) 'Comedy in Contemporary British Fiction.' *Papers of the Michigan Academy of Science, Arts, and Letters,* vol. 44, (1959).
Gindin, James. (1962) *Post-war British Fiction: New Accents and Attitudes.* Cambridge: Cambridge Univ. Press, 1962.
Golding, William. (1995) *Lord of the Flies* [1954]. London: Faber, 1995.
Goldschmidt, Richard B. (1982) *The Material Basis of Evolution* [1940]. New Haven & London: Yale Univ. Press, 1982.
Graff, Gerald. (1982) 'The Myth of the Postmodernist Breakthrough.' Malcolm Bradbury, ed. *The Novel Today* [1977]. London: Fontana, 1982, pp. 217-249.
Green, Peter. (1955) Rev. of *Rainbearers. The Daily Telegraph,* 24.10.1955.
Green, Peter. (1957) Rev. of *Corruption. The Daily Telegraph,* 5.10.57.
Greene, Graham. (1968) *The End of the Affair* [1951]. Harmondsworth: Penguin, 1968.
Hall, Stuart et al. (1978) *Policing the Crisis: Mugging, the State and Law and Order.* London: Macmillan, 1978.
Hall, Stuart and Jacques, Martin, eds. (1983) *The Politics of Thacherism.* London: Lawrence & Wishart, 1983.
Hallett, Garth. (1977) *A Companion to Wittgenstein's* Philosophical Investigations. Ithaca and London: Cornell Univ. Press, 1977.
Hannay, Alastair. (1992) 'Introduction.' S ren Kierkegaard, *Either/Or: A Fragment of Life.* Victor Eremita, ed., trans. Alastair Hannay. London: Penguin, 1992.

Harris, Roy. (1988) *Language, Saussure and Wittgenstein: How to Play Games with Words.* London: Routldge, 1988.

Hassan, Ihab. (1967) *The Literature of Silence: Henry Miller and Samuel Beckett.* New York: Alfred A. Knopf, 1967.

Hassan, Ihab. (1971) *The Dismemberment of Orpheus: Toward a Postmodern Literature.* N. Y.: Oxford Univ. Press, 1971.

Hassan, Ihab. (1990) 'Pluralism in Postmodern Perspectives.' Matei Calinescu and Douwe Fokkema, eds. *Exploring Postmodernism.* Amsterdam: John Benjamin Publishing Company, 1990.

Hassan, Ihab. (1993) 'Let the Fresh Air In: Critical Perspectives on the Humanities.' Heide Ziegler (ed.). *The End of Postmodernism: New Directions. Proceedings of the First Stuttgart Seminar in Cultural Studies 04.08-18. 08.1991.* Stuttgart: M & P Verl. für Wiss. und Forschung, 1993, pp. 135-52.

Hawthorn, Jeremy, ed. (1984) *Criticism and Critical Theory.* London: Edward Arnold, 1984.

Hennessy, Peter. (1986) *The Great and The Good: An Inquiry into the British Establishment.* Policy Studies Institute, 1986.

Hennessy, Peter. (1992) *Who Governs Britain?* Contemporary Papers, No. 10. London: WH Smith, 1992.

Hoffmann, G. and Hornung, A., eds. (1994) *Affirmation and Negation in Contemporary American Culture.* Heidelberg: Universitätsverlag C. Winter, 1994.

Hoffmann, G. and Hornung, A., eds. (1996a) *Ethics and Aesthetics: The Moral Turn of Postmodernism.* Heidelberg: Universitätsverlag C. Winter, 1996.

Hoffmann, G. (1996b) 'Waste and Meaning: the Labyrinth and the Void in Modern and Postmodern Fiction.' Gerhard Hoffmann and Alfred Hornung, eds. *Ethics and Aesthetics: the moral turn of postmodernism.* Heidelberg: Universitätsverlag C. Winter, 1996, pp. 115-94.

Holmer, Paul. (1977) *C. S. Lewis: the shape of his faith and thought.* London: Sheldon Press, 1977.

Hutcheon, Linda. (1980) *Narcissistic Narrative: The Metafictional Paradox.* Waterloo, Ont.: Wilfrid Laurier Univ. Press, 1980.

Hutcheon, Linda. (1988) *A Poetics of Postmodernism: History, Theory, Fiction.* N. Y. and London: Routledge, 1988.

Hutcheon, Linda. (1989) *The Politics of Postmodernism.* London: Routledge, 1989.

Jacobs, N. and Ohlsen, P., eds. (1977) *Bertolt Brecht in Britain*. London: Irat Services Ltd./TQ Publications, 1977.

Jameson, Fredrick. (1984) 'Postmodernism: The Cultural Logic of Late Capitalism.' *New Left Review* 146, (July-Aug. 1984): 53-92.

Johnson, B. S. (1969) *The Unfortunates*. London: Panther, 1969.

Johnson, Barbara. (1980) *The Critical Difference: Essays in the Contemporary Rhetoric of Reading.* Baltimore & London: John Hopkins Univ. Press, 1980.

Kane, Richard C. (1988) *Iris Murdoch, Muriel Spark, And John Fowles: Didactic Demons in Modern Fiction*. London & Toronto: Ass. University Presses, 1988.

Kanvanagh, Denise. (1987) *Thatcherism and British Politics: The End of Consensus?* Oxford: OUP, 1987.

Karl, Fredrick R. (1972) *A Reader's Guide to the Contemporary English Novel* [1961]. London: Thames & Hudson,1972.

Kellman, Steven. (1980) *The Self-Begetting Novel*. London: MacMillan, 1980.

Kemp, Peter. (1992) 'British Fiction of the 1980s.' Malcolm Bradbury and Judy Cooke, eds. *New Writing.* London: Minerva, 1992, pp. 216-28.

Kermode, Frank. (1990) 'The House of Fiction: Interviews with Seven Novelists.' Malcolm Bradbury, ed. *The Novel Today* [1977]. London: Fontana, 1990, pp. 117-44.

Kershaw, Ian. (1998) *Hitler, 1889-1936: Hubris*. London: Allen Lane, 1998.

Kershaw, Ian. (2000) *Hitler, 1936-1945: Nemesis*. London: Allen Lane, 2000.

Kierkegaard, Søren. (1992) *Either/Or: A Fragment of Life*. Victor Eremita, ed., trans., Alastair Hannay. London: Penguin, 1992.

King, Francis. (1990) 'A Novel about Ideas.' *The Spectator*, 23.06.1990.

Kleist, Heinrich v. (1991) *Über das Marionettentheater*, trans. David Paisey. Hamburg: Otto Rohse Press, 1991.

Kundera, Milan. (1990) *The Art of the Novel*. London: Faber & Faber, 1990.

Lasch, Christopher. (1978) *The Culture of Narcissism: American Life in an Age of Diminishing Expectations*. N.Y.: W. W. Norton, 1978.

Lasch, Christopher. (1995) *The Revolt of the Élites: And the Betrayal of Democracy*. London: W. W. Norton, 1995.

Leclair, Thomas, ed. (1983) *Anything Can Happen: Interviews with Contemporary American Novelists*. Urbana: Univ. of Illinois Press, 1983.

Lee, Robert. (1986) 'Learning What to Expect: Amis's Fiction in the '70s.' Bock and Wertheim, eds. *Essays on the Contemporary British Novel*. München: Max Hueber Verlag, 1986.

Lessing, Doris. (1973) 'Preface.' Doris Lessing. *The Golden Notebook.* London: Granada, 1973.
Lessing, Doris. (1985) 'Introduction.' Idries Shah. *Learning How To Learn: Psychology and Spirituality in the Sufi Way* [1978]. London: Penguin, 1985.
Lessing. (1994) *Under My Skin.* London, HarperCollins, 1994.
Lessing, Doris. (1995) *Memoirs of a Survivor* [1974]. London: Flamingo, 1995.
Lessing, Doris. (1997) *Walking in the Shade: Volume Two of my Autobiography, 1949-1962.* HarperCollins, 1997.
Levine, Paul. (1994) 'Exile and the Kingdom: The Writer After the Cold War.' Hoffmann and Hornung eds. *Affirmation and Negation in Contemporary American Culture.* Heidelberg: Universitätsverlag C. Winter, 1994.
Lewis, C. S. (1943) *The Case for Christianity.* New York: Macmillan, 1943.
Lewis, C. S. (1975a) *Of Other Worlds.* Walter Hooper, ed. New York: Harcourt Brace Janovich, 1975.
Lewis, C. S. (1975b) 'On Stories' [1947]. C. S. Lewis, *Of Other Worlds.* Walter Hooper, ed. New York: Harcourt Brace Janovich, 1975.
Lewis, Peter. (1981) 'The Flight from a Closed System.' *Times Literary Supplement,* 16. 10. 1981.
Lister, Richard. (1971) Rev. of *Natalie Natalia. Evening Standard,* 2. 6. 1971.
Lodge, David. (1984) *Language of Fiction: Essays in Criticism and Verbal Analysis of the English Novel* [1966]. London: Routledge, 1984.
Lodge, David, ed. (1988) *Modern Criticism and Theory.* London: Longman, 1988.
Lodge, David. (1990) 'The Novelist at the Crossroads' [1969]. Macolm Bradbury, ed. *The Novel Today* [1977]. London: Fontana, 1990, pp. 87-114.
Lodge, David. (1992) Introduction to *Lucky Jim.* London: Penguin: 1992.
Lyotard, Jean-Francois. (1984) *The Postmodern Condition: A Report on Knowledge* [1979]. Manchester: Manchester Univ. Press, 1984.
Maack, Annegret. (1984) *Der experimentelle englische Roman der Gegenwart.* Darmstadt: Wissenschaftliche Buchgesellschaft, 1984.
Magee, Bryan. (1997) *Confessions of a Philosopher.* London: Weidenfeld & Nicholson, 1997.
Mailer, Norman. (1997) *Picasso: Portrait of Picasso as a Young Man.* London: Abacus, 1997.
Malte Fues, Wolfram. (1987). 'Kunst und fingierte Gesellschaft.' Christa u. Peter Bürger, eds. *Postmoderne: Alltag, Allegorie, Avantgarde.* Frankfurt: Suhrkamp, 1987.

Marin, Minette. (1991) Interview with Nicholas Mosley. *Daily Telegraph*, 25. 1. 1991

Maritain, Jacques. (1930) *Art and Scholasticism* [1923], trans. J. F. Scanlan. London: Sheed & Ward, 1930.

Marshall, G., Swift, A and Roberts, S. (1997) *Against the Odds? Social Class and Social Justice in Industrial Societies.* Oxford: Clarendon Press, 1997.

Maschler, Tom, ed. (1957) *Declaration.* London: Mac Gibbon & Lee, 1957.

Massie, Allan. (1990a) *The Novel Today: A Critical Guide to the British Novel 1970-1989.* London: Longman, 1990.

Massie, Allan. (1990b) Rev. of *Hopeful Monsters. The Scotsman*, 23. 6. 1990.

Massie, Allan. (2001) 'Free Kick at the Fates.' *The Scotsman*, 20.01.2001.

Maugham, Somerset. (1955) 'Books of the Year.' *The Sunday Times*, 25.12.1955.

McEwan, Ian. (1978) *The Cement Garden.* London: Cape, 1978.

McEwan, Ian. (1987) *Child in Time.* London: Cape, 1987.

McFadden, George. (1982) *Discovering the Comic.* New Jersey: Princeton Univ. Press, 1982.

McFadden, Johnjoe. (2000) 'The Origin of all Life.' *The Guardian* 10.02.2000.

McLennan, G., Held, D. and Hall, S., eds. (1984) *State and Society in Contemporary Britain: a critical introduction.* Cambridge: Polity, 1984.

Muecke, D. C. (1973) *The Critical Idiom: Irony.* London: Methuen & Co., Ltd., 1973.

Murdoch, Iris. (1962a) *The Flight from the Enchanter* [1956] London: Penguin Books, 1962.

Murdoch, Iris. (1962b) *The Bell* [1958]. London: Penguin, 1962.

Murdoch, Iris. (1977) *Bruno's Dream* [1969]. London: Triad/Panther Books, 1977.

Murdoch, Iris. (1989) *Sartre: Romantic Rationalist* [1953]. London: Penguin, 1989.

Murdoch, Iris. (1990) 'Against Dryness' [1961]. Malcolm Bradbury, ed. *The Novel Today.* London: Fontana, 1990, pp. 15-24.

Murdoch, Iris. (1997a) 'Existentialist Hero' [1950]. Iris Murdoch. *Existentialists and Mystics: Writings on Philosophy and Literature.* Peter Conradi, ed. London: Chatto & Windus, 1997, pp. 108-15.

Murdoch, Iris. (1997b) 'Existentialists and Mystics' [1970]. Iris Murdoch. *Existentialists and Mystics: Writings on Philosophy and Literature.* Peter Conradi, ed. London: Chatto & Windus, 1997.

Naughton, John. (1979) Rev. of *Catastrophe Practice. The Listener*, 28. 6. 1979.

Newton, K., ed. (1997) *Twentieth-Century Literary Theory: A Reader*. Basington: Macmillan, 1997.

Nietzsche, Friedrich. (1980a) *Also Sprach Zarathustra*. Friedrich Nietzsche, *Sämtliche Werke: Studienausgabe in 15 Bänden*, vol. IV. Giorgio Colli and Mazzino Montinari, eds. München: dtv-Ausgabe, 1980.

Nietzsche, Friedrich. (1980b) *Menschliches, Allzumenschliches*. Friedrich Nietzsche. *Sämtliche Werke: Studienausgabe in 15 Bänden*. Vol. II. Giorgio Colli and Mazzino Montinari, eds. München: dtv-Ausgabe, 1980.

Nietzsche, Friedrich. (1983) *Untimely meditations*, trans. R. J. Hollingdale. Cambridge: Cambridge Univ. Press, 1983.

Nietzsche, Friedrich. (1998) *Beyond Good and Evil*, trans. Marion Faber. Oxford: OUP, 1998.

Nietzsche, Friedrich. (1986) *Sämtliche Briefe: Kritische Studienausgabe in 8 Bänden*. München: dtv-Ausgabe, 1986.

O'Brien, John. (1982a) 'An Interview with Nicholas Mosley.' *Review of Contemporary Fiction* (summer 1982): 58-79.

O'Brien, John. (1982b) ' "It's Like a Story": Nicholas Mosley's *Impossible Object*.' *Review of Contemporary Fiction* (Summer 1982): 142-48.

Onega Jaén, Susana. (1989) *Form and Meaning in the Novels of John Fowles*. Ann Arbour & London: UMI Press, 1989.

Oxenhandler, Neal. (1981) 'Listening to Burroughs' Voice.' Raymond Federman, ed. *Surfiction: Fiction Now and Tomorrow* [1975]. Chicago: Swallow Press, 1981, pp. 181-201.

Peterson, Virgilia. (1958) Rev. of *Corruption* in *Sunday Herald Tribune* (26.1.58).

Plath, Sylvia. (1996) *The Bell Jar* [1963]. London & Boston: Faber & Faber, 1996.

Poore, Charles. (1966) Rev. of *Accident*. *The New York Times*, 31.3.1966.

Popper, Karl R. (1972) *Objective Knowledge: An Evolutionary Approach*. Oxford: Clarendon Press, 1972.

Powell, Anthony. (1956) 'The Wren Goes to It.' *Punch*, 11.7.1956.

Pryce-Jones, Alan. (1966) 'Well-Built Suspense.' *New York Herald Tribune*, 31.3.1966.

Pynchon, Thomas. (1996) *The Crying of Lot 49* [1965]. London: Vintage, 1996.

Rabinowitz, Rubin. (1967) *The Reaction Against Experiment in the English Novel, 1950-1960*. New York: Columbia Univ. Press, 1967.

Raskin, Jonah. (1970) 'Doris Lessing at Stony Brook.' *New American Review* VIII (Jan. 1970). 166-179.

Ratcliffe, Michael. (1968) *The Novel Today*. London: Longmans, Green & Co, 1968.
Ratcliffe, Michael. (1990) Rev. of *Hopeful Monsters. Observer*, 11.11.1990.
Raymond, Jon. (1951) Rev. of *Corruption. New Statesman and Society*, 17.2.51.
Reynolds, David S., ed. (2000) *A Historical Guide to Walt Whitman*. Oxford: OUP, 2000.
Ringen, Stein. (1997a) *Families, Citizens and Reform*. Oxford: Clarendon Press, 1997.
Ringen, Stein. (1997b) 'The Open Society and the Closed Mind.' *Times Literary Supplement*, Jan 24 1997.
Robbe-Grillet, Alain. (1963) *Pour un nouveau roman*. Paris: Éditions de Minuit, 1963.
Robbe-Grillet, Alain. (1966) *The Erasers* [1953], trans. Richard Howard. London: Calder, 1966.
Robbe-Grillet, Alain. (1980) *In the Labyrinth* [1959], trans. Christine Brook-Rose. London: John Calder, 1980.
Rudman, Mark. (1992) 'Sudden Jumps.' *Pequod: A Journal of Contemporary Literature and Literary Criticism* (1992): 35-46.
Rushdie, Salman. (1981) *Midnight's Children*. London: Cape, 1981.
Rushdie, Salman. (1995) *The Moor's Last Sigh*. London: Cape, 1995.
Rushdie, Salman. (1999) *The Ground Beneath her Feet*. London: Cape, 1999.
Said, Edward. (1978) *Orientalism*. New York: Pantheon Books, 1978.
Salwak, Dale. (1978) *Kingsley Amis: A Referential Guide*. Boston: G. K. Hall & Co., 1978.
Salwak, Dale. (1992) *Kingsley Amis: Modern Novelist*. New York: Harvester Wheatsheaf, 1992.
Sampson, Anthony. (1992) *The Essential Anatomy of Britain: Democracy in Crisis*. London: Hodder & Stoughton, 1992.
Sarraute, Nathalie. (1963) *Tropisms and the Age of Suspicion*, trans. Maria Jolas. N. Y. and London, 1963.
Sarraute, Nathalie. (1987) *L'Ere du Soupçon* [1956]. Paris: Folio-Gallimard, 1987.
Schier, Helga. (1993) *Going Beyond: The Crisis of identity and identity models in contemporary American, English and German Fiction*. Tübingen: Max Niemeyer Verlag, 1993.
Schimmel, Annemarie. (1991) *Rumi: Ich bin Wind und du bist Feuer: Leben und Werk des großen Mystikers*. München: Eugen Diederichs Verlag, 1991.

Scholes, Robert. (1967) *The Fabulators.* N. Y.: Oxford Univ. Press, 1967.
Scholes, Robert. (1969) Rev. of *Impossible Object. The Saturday Review*, 25.1.1969.
Scholes, Robert. (1971) Rev. of *Natalie Natalia. The Saturday Review*, 6. 11. 1971.
Scholes, Robert. (1979) *Fabulation and Metafiction.* Urbana: Chicago & London, 1979.
Schraub, Thomas H. (1981) *Pynchon: the Voice of Ambiguity.* Urbana: Univ. of Illinois Press, 1981.
Schulz, Max F. (1990) *The Muses of John Barth: Tradition and Metafiction from Lost in the Funhouse to* The Tidewater Tales. Baltimore and London: John Hopkins Univ. Press, 1990.
Seed, David. (1988) *The Fictional Labyrinths of Thomas Pynchon.* Basingstoke: Macmillan, 1988.
Seymour-Smith, Martin. (1979) Rev. of *Catastrophe Practice. Financial Times*, 8.9.1979.
Shah, Idries. (1968) *Caravan of Dreams.* London: Octagon Press Ltd, 1968.
Shah, Idries. (1985) *Learning How To Learn: Psychology and Spirituality in the Sufi Way* [1978]. London: Penguin, 1985.
Shah, Idries. (1990) *The Way of the Sufi* [1968]. London: Arkana, 1990.
Showalter, Elaine, ed. (1989) *Speaking of Gender.* N. Y. & London: Routledge, 1989.
Simon, Claude (1963) *The Palace*, trans. Richard Howard. London: Jonathan Cape, 1963.
Sinfield, Alan. (1983) *Society and Literature 1945-1970.* London: Methuen, 1983.
Sinfield, Alan. (1989) *Literature, Politics and Culture in Post-war Britain.* Oxford: Blackwell, 1989.
Skidelsky, Robert. (1981) *Oswald Mosley* [1975]. London: PAPERMAC, 1981.
Sontag, Susan. (1983) 'Writing itself: on Roland Barthes.' Roland Barthes, *Barthes: Selected Writings.* London: Fontana, 1983.
Spark, Muriel. (1963) *The Comforters* [1957]. London: Penguin, 1963.
Spark, Muriel. (1965a) *The Prime of Miss Brodie* [1961]. London: Penguin, 1965.
Spark, Muriel. (1965b) *The Mandelbaum Gate.* London: Macmillan, 1965.
Spark, Muriel. (1966) *The Girls of Slender Means* [1963]. Penguin, 1966.

Spender, Stephen. (1958) 'When the Angry Men Grow Older.' *New York Times Book Review*, 20.7.58.
Spivak, Gayatri. (1987) *In Other Worlds: Essays in Cultural Politics*. London and NY: Methuen, 1987.
Stack, George J. (1992) *Nietzsche and Emerson: An Elective Affinity*. Athens: Ohio Univ. Press, 1992.
Stamirowska, Krystyna. (1992) *Representations of Reality in the Post-war English Novel 1957-1975*. Crocow: Universitas, 1992.
Stanford, Peter. (2001) 'An ambiguous Eden.' *The Independent on Sunday*, 4.02.2001.
Stark, John O. (1974) *The Literature of Exhaustion: Borges, Nabokov and Barth*. Durham: N.C., Duke Univ. Press, 1974.
Steiner, George. (1966) *Language and Silence: Essays 1958-1966*. London: Faber & Faber, 1966.
Steiner, George. (1969) 'Last Stop for Mrs. Brown.' *New Yorker*, 2.7.1969.
Steiner, George. (1971) *In Bluebeard's Castle: Some Notes Towards the Redefinition of Culture*. London: Faber & Faber, 1971.
Steiner, George. (1989) *Real Presences*. London: Faber & Faber, 1989.
Stern Weiss, Sydna. (1980) 'Kleist and Mathematics: the Non-Euclidean Idea in the Conclusion of the *Marionettentheater* Essay.' Alexej Ugrinsky, ed. *Heinrich von Kleist Studien*. Berlin: Erich Schmidt Verlag, 1980.
Stevenson, Randall. (1986) *The British Novel since the Thirties*. London: B. T. Batsford, 1986.
Stonehill, Brian. (1988) *The Self-Conscious Novel: Artifice in Fiction from Joyce to Pynchon*. Philadelphia: Univ. of Pennsylvania Press, 1988.
Sturrock, John. (1969) *The French New Novel: Claude Simon, Michel Butor, Alain Robbe-Grillet*. London: Oxford Univ. Press, 1969.
Sullivan, Richard. (1958) Rev. of *Corruption*. *New York Times*, 26.1.58.
Taylor, D. J. (1989) *A Vain Conceit: British Fiction in the 1980s*. London: Bloomsbury, 1989.
Taylor, D. J. (1991) 'The late success of a lonely experiment.' *The Independent*, 26.01.1991.
Tennant, Emma. *Girlitude*. (1999) London: Jonathan Cape, 1999.
Thody, Philip. (1971) *Sartre*. London: Studio Vista, 1971.
Todd, Janet. (1988) *Feminist Literary History: A Defence*. Cambridge: Polity Press, 1988.
Tucker, Eva. (1979) 'The mathematics of characterisation.' *Hampstead and Highgate Express*, 20. 7. 1979.

Turner, Frederick. (1997) 'Foreword: Chaos and Social Science.' Eve, Horsfall, and Lee, eds. *Chaos, Complexity and Sociology*. Thousand Oaks and London: Sage, 1997.
Vinson, James, ed. (1972) *Contemporary Novelists*. London and Chicago: St. James Press, 1972.
Wagner-Martin, Linda. (1999) *Sylvia Plath: a Literary Life*. Basingstoke: Macmillan, 1999.
Wardle, Irving. (1965) 'After the Accident.' *The Observer*, 10.1.65.
Waugh, Auberon. (1971) 'On Nicholas Mosley's importance.' *Spectator*, 3.7.1971
Waugh, Patricia. (1984) *Metafiction: The Theory and Practice of Self-Conscious Fiction*. London: Methuen, 1984.
Waugh, Patricia. (1989) *Feminist Fictions: Revisiting the Postmodern*. London and N. Y.: Routledge, 1989.
Waugh, Patricia. (1995) *Harvest of the Sixties: English Literature and its Background 1960 to 1990*. Oxford: Oxford Univ. Press, 1995.
Weldon, Fay. (1983) *The Life and Loves of a She-Devil*. London: Hodder & Stoughton, 1983.
Whatley, Rosaleen. (1951) Rev. of *Spaces of the Dark*. *Liverpool Daily Post*, 30.1.1951.
White, Edmund. (2000) 'Books for Christmas.' *Times Literary Supplement*, 1.12.2000.
Whittaker, Ruth. (1982) *The Faith and Fiction of Muriel Spark*. London: MacMillan, 1982.
Wilson, Timothy. (1971) 'Nicholas Mosley.' *Guardian*, 29.06.1971.
Winegarden, Renee. (1968) 'Amorous enigma.' *Sunday Telegraph*, 22.09.1968.
Winterson, Jeanette. (1987) *The Passion*. London: Bloomsbury, 1987.
Wittgenstein, Ludwig. (1994) *The Wittgenstein Reader*. Anthony Kenny, ed. Oxford: Blackwell, 1994.
Worthington, Kim L. (1996) *Self as Narrative: Subjectivity and Community in Contemporary Fiction*. Oxford: Clarendon Press, 1996.
Young, Hugo. (1992) *Thatcherism: Did Society Survive?* London: Catholic Housing Aid Society, 1992.
Young, Hugo. (1993) *One of Us*. London: Pan, 1993.
Young, J. Z. (1964) *A Model of the Brain*. Oxford: Clarendon Press, 1964.
Ziegler, H. and Bigsby, C., eds. (1982) *The Radical Imagination and the Liberal Tradition: Interviews with English and American Novelists*. London: Junction Books, 1982.

Ziegler, Heide. (1987) *John Barth*. London & N. Y.: Methuen, 1987.

Ziegler, Heide, ed. (1993) *The End of Postmodernism: New Directions. Proceedings of the First Stuttgart Seminar in Cultural Studies 04.08-18.08.1991.* Stuttgart: M & P Verl. für Wiss. und Forschung, 1993.

Zohar, Dana. (1996) 'Growing up with Godadaddy.' *Independent*, 25.02.1996.

About the Author

Shiva Rahbaran was born in 1970 in Tehran. She left Iran for Germany in 1984, where she studied literature and political science at the Heinrich-Heine-Universtät Düsseldorf. She continued her studies at Oxford University, where she was granted a Ph.D. in English literature. Her latest publication is *The State of the Word: The Role of the Author in Iran after the Islamic Revolution*, which examines the impact of Iran's revolutionized society on contemporary Persian literature and the potential to open spaces of freedom within that society.

SELECTED DALKEY ARCHIVE PAPERBACKS

PETROS ABATZOGLOU, *What Does Mrs. Freeman Want?*
PIERRE ALBERT-BIROT, *Grabinoulor.*
YUZ ALESHKOVSKY, *Kangaroo.*
FELIPE ALFAU, *Chromos.*
   Locos.
IVAN ÂNGELO, *The Celebration.*
   The Tower of Glass.
DAVID ANTIN, *Talking.*
ALAIN ARIAS-MISSON, *Theatre of Incest.*
DJUNA BARNES, *Ladies Almanack.*
   Ryder.
JOHN BARTH, *LETTERS.*
   Sabbatical.
DONALD BARTHELME, *The King.*
   Paradise.
SVETISLAV BASARA, *Chinese Letter.*
MARK BINELLI, *Sacco and Vanzetti Must Die!*
ANDREI BITOV, *Pushkin House.*
LOUIS PAUL BOON, *Chapel Road.*
   Summer in Termuren.
ROGER BOYLAN, *Killoyle.*
IGNÁCIO DE LOYOLA BRANDÃO, *Teeth under the Sun.*
   Zero.
BONNIE BREMSER, *Troia: Mexican Memoirs.*
CHRISTINE BROOKE-ROSE, *Amalgamemnon.*
BRIGID BROPHY, *In Transit.*
MEREDITH BROSNAN, *Mr. Dynamite.*
GERALD L. BRUNS,
   Modern Poetry and the Idea of Language.
GABRIELLE BURTON, *Heartbreak Hotel.*
MICHEL BUTOR, *Degrees.*
   Mobile.
   Portrait of the Artist as a Young Ape.
EVGENY BUNIMOVICH AND J. KATES, EDS.,
   Contemporary Russian Poetry: An Anthology.
G. CABRERA INFANTE, *Infante's Inferno.*
   Three Trapped Tigers.
JULIETA CAMPOS, *The Fear of Losing Eurydice.*
ANNE CARSON, *Eros the Bittersweet.*
CAMILO JOSÉ CELA, *Christ versus Arizona.*
   The Family of Pascual Duarte.
   The Hive.
LOUIS-FERDINAND CÉLINE, *Castle to Castle.*
   Conversations with Professor Y.
   London Bridge.
   North.
   Rigadoon.
HUGO CHARTERIS, *The Tide Is Right.*
JEROME CHARYN, *The Tar Baby.*
MARC CHOLODENKO, *Mordechai Schamz.*
EMILY HOLMES COLEMAN, *The Shutter of Snow.*
ROBERT COOVER, *A Night at the Movies.*
STANLEY CRAWFORD, *Some Instructions to My Wife.*
ROBERT CREELEY, *Collected Prose.*
RENÉ CREVEL, *Putting My Foot in It.*
RALPH CUSACK, *Cadenza.*
SUSAN DAITCH, *L.C.*
   Storytown.
NIGEL DENNIS, *Cards of Identity.*
PETER DIMOCK,
   A Short Rhetoric for Leaving the Family.
ARIEL DORFMAN, *Konfidenz.*
COLEMAN DOWELL, *The Houses of Children.*
   Island People.
   Too Much Flesh and Jabez.
RIKKI DUCORNET, *The Complete Butcher's Tales.*
   The Fountains of Neptune.
   The Jade Cabinet.
   Phosphor in Dreamland.
   The Stain.
   The Word "Desire."
WILLIAM EASTLAKE, *The Bamboo Bed.*
   Castle Keep.
   Lyric of the Circle Heart.
JEAN ECHENOZ, *Chopin's Move.*
STANLEY ELKIN, *A Bad Man.*
   Boswell: A Modern Comedy.
   Criers and Kibitzers, Kibitzers and Criers.
   The Dick Gibson Show.
   The Franchiser.
   George Mills.
   The Living End.
   The MacGuffin.
   The Magic Kingdom.
   Mrs. Ted Bliss.
   The Rabbi of Lud.
   Van Gogh's Room at Arles.
ANNIE ERNAUX, *Cleaned Out.*

LAUREN FAIRBANKS, *Muzzle Thyself.*
   Sister Carrie.
LESLIE A. FIEDLER,
   Love and Death in the American Novel.
GUSTAVE FLAUBERT, *Bouvard and Pécuchet.*
FORD MADOX FORD, *The March of Literature.*
JON FOSSE, *Melancholy.*
MAX FRISCH, *I'm Not Stiller.*
   Man in the Holocene.
CARLOS FUENTES, *Christopher Unborn.*
   Distant Relations.
   Terra Nostra.
   Where the Air Is Clear.
JANICE GALLOWAY, *Foreign Parts.*
   The Trick Is to Keep Breathing.
WILLIAM H. GASS, *A Temple of Texts.*
   The Tunnel.
   Willie Masters' Lonesome Wife.
ETIENNE GILSON, *The Arts of the Beautiful.*
   Forms and Substances in the Arts.
C. S. GISCOMBE, *Giscome Road.*
   Here.
DOUGLAS GLOVER, *Bad News of the Heart.*
   The Enamoured Knight.
WITOLD GOMBROWICZ, *A Kind of Testament.*
KAREN ELIZABETH GORDON, *The Red Shoes.*
GEORGI GOSPODINOV, *Natural Novel.*
JUAN GOYTISOLO, *Count Julian.*
   Marks of Identity.
PATRICK GRAINVILLE, *The Cave of Heaven.*
HENRY GREEN, *Blindness.*
   Concluding.
   Doting.
   Nothing.
JIŘÍ GRUŠA, *The Questionnaire.*
GABRIEL GUDDING, *Rhode Island Notebook.*
JOHN HAWKES, *Whistlejacket.*
AIDAN HIGGINS, *A Bestiary.*
   Bornholm Night-Ferry.
   Flotsam and Jetsam.
   Langrishe, Go Down.
   Scenes from a Receding Past.
   Windy Arbours.
ALDOUS HUXLEY, *Antic Hay.*
   Crome Yellow.
   Point Counter Point.
   Those Barren Leaves.
   Time Must Have a Stop.
MIKHAIL IOSSEL AND JEFF PARKER, EDS., *Amerika:*
   Contemporary Russians View
   the United States.
GERT JONKE, *Geometric Regional Novel.*
JACQUES JOUET, *Mountain R.*
HUGH KENNER, *The Counterfeiters.*
   Flaubert, Joyce and Beckett:
   The Stoic Comedians.
   Joyce's Voices.
DANILO KIŠ, *Garden, Ashes.*
   A Tomb for Boris Davidovich.
AIKO KITAHARA,
   The Budding Tree: Six Stories of Love in Edo.
ANITA KONKKA, *A Fool's Paradise.*
GEORGE KONRÁD, *The City Builder.*
TADEUSZ KONWICKI, *A Minor Apocalypse.*
   The Polish Complex.
MENIS KOUMANDAREAS, *Koula.*
ELAINE KRAF, *The Princess of 72nd Street.*
JIM KRUSOE, *Iceland.*
EWA KURYLUK, *Century 21.*
VIOLETTE LEDUC, *La Bâtarde.*
DEBORAH LEVY, *Billy and Girl.*
   Pillow Talk in Europe and Other Places.
JOSÉ LEZAMA LIMA, *Paradiso.*
ROSA LIKSOM, *Dark Paradise.*
OSMAN LINS, *Avalovara.*
   The Queen of the Prisons of Greece.
ALF MAC LOCHLAINN, *The Corpus in the Library.*
   Out of Focus.
RON LOEWINSOHN, *Magnetic Field(s).*
D. KEITH MANO, *Take Five.*
BEN MARCUS, *The Age of Wire and String.*
WALLACE MARKFIELD, *Teitlebaum's Window.*
   To an Early Grave.
DAVID MARKSON, *Reader's Block.*
   Springer's Progress.
   Wittgenstein's Mistress.
CAROLE MASO, *AVA.*

FOR A FULL LIST OF PUBLICATIONS, VISIT:
www.dalkeyarchive.com

SELECTED DALKEY ARCHIVE PAPERBACKS

LADISLAV MATEJKA AND KRYSTYNA POMORSKA, EDS.,
Readings in Russian Poetics: Formalist and Structuralist Views.
HARRY MATHEWS,
The Case of the Persevering Maltese: Collected Essays.
Cigarettes.
The Conversions.
The Human Country: New and Collected Stories.
The Journalist.
My Life in CIA.
Singular Pleasures.
The Sinking of the Odradek Stadium.
Tlooth.
20 Lines a Day.
ROBERT L. MCLAUGHLIN, ED.,
Innovations: An Anthology of Modern & Contemporary Fiction.
HERMAN MELVILLE, *The Confidence-Man.*
STEVEN MILLHAUSER, *The Barnum Museum.*
In the Penny Arcade.
RALPH J. MILLS, JR., *Essays on Poetry.*
OLIVE MOORE, *Spleen.*
NICHOLAS MOSLEY, *Accident.*
Assassins.
Catastrophe Practice.
Children of Darkness and Light.
Experience and Religion.
The Hesperides Tree.
Hopeful Monsters.
Imago Bird.
Impossible Object.
Inventing God.
Judith.
Look at the Dark.
Natalie Natalia.
Serpent.
Time at War.
The Uses of Slime Mould: Essays of Four Decades.
WARREN F. MOTTE, JR.,
Fables of the Novel: French Fiction since 1990.
Oulipo: A Primer of Potential Literature.
YVES NAVARRE, *Our Share of Time.*
Sweet Tooth.
DOROTHY NELSON, *In Night's City.*
Tar and Feathers.
WILFRIDO D. NOLLEDO, *But for the Lovers.*
FLANN O'BRIEN, *At Swim-Two-Birds.*
At War.
The Best of Myles.
The Dalkey Archive.
Further Cuttings.
The Hard Life.
The Poor Mouth.
The Third Policeman.
CLAUDE OLLIER, *The Mise-en-Scène.*
PATRIK OUŘEDNÍK, *Europeana.*
FERNANDO DEL PASO, *Palinuro of Mexico.*
ROBERT PINGET, *The Inquisitory.*
Mahu or The Material.
Trio.
RAYMOND QUENEAU, *The Last Days.*
Odile.
Pierrot Mon Ami.
Saint Glinglin.
ANN QUIN, *Berg.*
Passages.
Three.
Tripticks.
SHIVA RAHBARAN, *The Paradox of Freedom.*
ISHMAEL REED, *The Free-Lance Pallbearers.*
The Last Days of Louisiana Red.
Reckless Eyeballing.
The Terrible Threes.
The Terrible Twos.
Yellow Back Radio Broke-Down.
JEAN RICARDOU, *Place Names.*
JULIÁN RÍOS, *Larva: A Midsummer Night's Babel.*
Poundemonium.
AUGUSTO ROA BASTOS, *I the Supreme.*
JACQUES ROUBAUD, *The Great Fire of London.*
Hortense in Exile.
Hortense Is Abducted.
The Plurality of Worlds of Lewis.
The Princess Hoppy.
The Form of a City Changes Faster, Alas, Than the Human Heart.
Some Thing Black.
LEON S. ROUDIEZ, *French Fiction Revisited.*
VEDRANA RUDAN, *Night.*
LYDIE SALVAYRE, *The Company of Ghosts.*
Everyday Life.
The Lecture.
The Power of Flies.
LUIS RAFAEL SÁNCHEZ, *Macho Camacho's Beat.*
SEVERO SARDUY, *Cobra & Maitreya.*
NATHALIE SARRAUTE, *Do You Hear Them?*
Martereau.
The Planetarium.
ARNO SCHMIDT, *Collected Stories.*
Nobodaddy's Children.
CHRISTINE SCHUTT, *Nightwork.*
GAIL SCOTT, *My Paris.*
JUNE AKERS SEESE,
Is This What Other Women Feel Too?
What Waiting Really Means.
AURELIE SHEEHAN, *Jack Kerouac Is Pregnant.*
VIKTOR SHKLOVSKY, *Knight's Move.*
A Sentimental Journey: Memoirs 1917–1922.
Energy of Delusion: A Book on Plot.
Theory of Prose.
Third Factory.
Zoo, or Letters Not about Love.
JOSEF ŠKVORECKÝ,
The Engineer of Human Souls.
CLAUDE SIMON, *The Invitation.*
GILBERT SORRENTINO, *Aberration of Starlight.*
Blue Pastoral.
Crystal Vision.
Imaginative Qualities of Actual Things.
Mulligan Stew.
Pack of Lies.
Red the Fiend.
The Sky Changes.
Something Said.
Splendide-Hôtel.
Steelwork.
Under the Shadow.
W. M. SPACKMAN, *The Complete Fiction.*
GERTRUDE STEIN, *Lucy Church Amiably.*
The Making of Americans.
A Novel of Thank You.
PIOTR SZEWC, *Annihilation.*
STEFAN THEMERSON, *Hobson's Island.*
The Mystery of the Sardine.
Tom Harris.
JEAN-PHILIPPE TOUSSAINT, *Television.*
DUMITRU TSEPENEAG, *Vain Art of the Fugue.*
ESTHER TUSQUETS, *Stranded.*
DUBRAVKA UGRESIC, *Lend Me Your Character.*
Thank You for Not Reading.
MATI UNT, *Things in the Night.*
ELOY URROZ, *The Obstacles.*
LUISA VALENZUELA, *He Who Searches.*
PAUL VERHAEGHEN, *Omega Minor.*
MARJA-LIISA VARTIO, *The Parson's Widow.*
BORIS VIAN, *Heartsnatcher.*
AUSTRYN WAINHOUSE, *Hedyphagetica.*
PAUL WEST, *Words for a Deaf Daughter & Gala.*
CURTIS WHITE, *America's Magic Mountain.*
The Idea of Home.
Memories of My Father Watching TV.
Monstrous Possibility: An Invitation to Literary Politics.
Requiem.
DIANE WILLIAMS, *Excitability: Selected Stories.*
Romancer Erector.
DOUGLAS WOOLF, *Wall to Wall.*
Ya! & John-Juan.
PHILIP WYLIE, *Generation of Vipers.*
MARGUERITE YOUNG, *Angel in the Forest.*
Miss MacIntosh, My Darling.
REYOUNG, *Unbabbling.*
ZORAN ŽIVKOVIĆ, *Hidden Camera.*
LOUIS ZUKOFSKY, *Collected Fiction.*
SCOTT ZWIREN, *God Head.*

FOR A FULL LIST OF PUBLICATIONS, VISIT:

www.dalkeyarchive.com